Fifth Edition

FASHION
FROM CONCEPT
TO CONSUMER

GINI STEPHENS FRINGS

 PRENTICE HALL Upper Saddle River, New Jersey 07458

Library of Congress Cataloging-in-Publication Data

Frings, Gini Stephens.
    Fashion: from concept to consumer/Gini Stephens Frings.—5th
ed.
        p.   cm.
    Includes index.
    ISBN 0-13-370891-8
    1. Fashion.   2. Clothing trade.   3. Fashion merchandsing.
I. Title.
TT518.F74   1996   95–47897
    687—dc20   CIP

Production editor: *Janet M. McGillicuddy*
Acquisition editor: *Elizabeth Sugg*
Marketing manager: *Frank Mortimer, Jr.*
Director of manufacturing and production: *Bruce Johnson*
Manufacturing buyer: *Ed O'Dougherty*
Editorial assistant: *Kahdijah Bell*
Formatting/page make-up: *Janet M. McGillicuddy*
Interior design: *Miguel Ortiz*
Template design: *Janet M. McGillicuddy*
Printer/binder: *Von Hoffman*
Cover design: *Barbara Gold*
Cover sketch: *Courtesy of Gianfranco Ferré*

 © 1996 by Prentice-Hall, Inc.
A Simon & Schuster Company
Upper Saddle River, NJ 07458

Printed in the United States of America

10 9 8 7 6 5 4 3 2 1

ISBN 0-13-370891-8

Prentice-Hall International (UK) Limited, *London*
Prentice-Hall of Australia Pty. Limited, *Sydney*
Prentice-Hall Canada Inc., *Toronto*
Prentice-Hall Hispanoamericana, S.A., *Mexico*
Prentice-Hall of India Private Limited, *New Delhi*
Prentice-Hall of Japan, Inc., *Tokyo*
Simon & Schuster Asia Pte. Ltd., *Singapore*
Editora Prentice-Hall do Brasil, Ltda., *Rio de Janeiro*

Contents

Foreword

Everyone has to wear clothes. Clothes are an important part of our lives. The clothing we buy for special occasions—proms, graduations, weddings, and so on—becomes part of our memories. We remember these occasions by what we were wearing.

This is what makes my business special. I enjoy designing those special dresses that my customers will remember. My customer knows what she wants; she wants to look beautiful. She wants to feel nostalgic about her purchase. I design with my customer in mind. My success comes from my strong focus, my point of view. I developed a special style and stuck to it over the years. I adapt current trends to my own style. Buyers know they can find a consistent look from me and so do my customers. I try every day to make my designs better than yesterday. I am never satisfied with myself. I have always felt that I have a special talent, a special creative force, but, aside from that, I'm my own toughest critic.

Fashion design is not work to me, it is my fun, my life. I'm up at six, to work by eight, break half an hour for lunch—usually at my desk to look at fashion magazines so I can keep my eye on what's happening—then spend the rest of the day in the workroom making sure my designs are going the way I want. I create 150 designs a season, five times a year for our seven lines. But it's not enough to be creative. I have to combine my creative ability with a business sense, too. I love my business. No, it's more than that. What I do for a living is exactly the way I want to live.

I have known the author of this book for over 20 years. In her role as an educator, Gini would bring her students to meet with me to discuss my fashion philosophy and see my current line. Then the students would design and make a sample garment for the next season and bring them back to me for a critique. One of Gini's students later became my assistant.

Because of people like Gini, who has experience in the industry, fashion education is much better today. I am happy to introduce her excellent book, which prepares the student to know how the fashion business operates and what to expect working in it. The book covers the fashion business in logical sequence with complete and realistic information. I hope each student will take advantage of this text and absorb its contents for later use.

As a student, you have to realize that your college education is just the beginning, a time to open your mind to new possibilities. Students want to be successful the minute they graduate and enter the field. But you can't expect to be a success overnight. As a graduate you must be focused and use your first job as a new learning situation and grow in your knowledge day by day.

Best wishes in your fashion career,

Jessica McClintock
San Francisco

Preface

*T*he purpose of this book is to tell the whole story of how the fashion business works, in sequential order from concept to consumer. The fashion business is a series of buying supplies, creating and developing new products, and marketing those products. The fashion business includes all the processes involved with producing raw materials, apparel, and accessories, and the retail stores that sell fashion merchandise to the public. It is important for executives in the fashion industry to know how all the levels interrelate.

Fashion designers and merchandisers who work for manufacturers must work with textile producers to develop fabrics that they need for their apparel and accessories. Manufacturers must also understand the importance of selling on the retail level. Retail fashion buyers should understand how garments and accessories are designed so that they can be creative merchandisers and make wise buying decisions.

Part One concentrates on fashion fundamentals. Chapter 1 traces the development of fashion and the fashion industry as a background to understanding today's business. Chapter 2 shows how consumer demand affects fashion marketing. Chapter 3 explains fashion change and consumer acceptance. Chapter 4 covers market research, fashion analysis, and design resources, information needed by everyone in the fashion business.

Part Two covers the development, production, and marketing of raw materials, including textiles, trimmings, leather, and fur—the supplies needed for fashion manufacturing.

Part Three discusses international fashion centers and traces the fashion manufacturing process from design and merchandising development through production and sales. The first test of a successful fashion product is at the wholesale market, the meeting ground of the manufacturer and retailer.

Part Four covers retailing: types of retail organizations, the buying and selling process, and promotion.

Each chapter contains a career focus, chapter objectives, review questions, terminology, and projects to aid in reviewing the subject matter.

The appendix contains information on career guidelines. A glossary of fashion terminology is also provided.

Just as the fashion industry has changed dramatically over the last 10 years, each edition of *Fashion: From Concept to Consumer* changes with it. As the industry has become more marketing oriented, so has this book. As the industry has seen a tremendous growth in men's wear and accessories, the book has also much more information on men's wear and accessories. As computer technology has changed how fashion is produced and distributed, the book describes applications in every area. The book explains the changes in relationships between levels of the industry—how manufacturers have become retailers and retailers have become manufacturers. *Fashion* describes how these major changes have affected every aspect of the fashion business.

This book completely tells the story of the fashion business and is a valuable tool for any introductory course in fashion: Introduction to

Fashion Design, Introduction to the Fashion Industry or Manufacturing, Introduction to Fashion Merchandising or Retailing, or Introduction to the Fashion Business. There is also important information for textile marketing, apparel manufacturing, accessory design, production and marketing, and advertising and promotion. This is a text for specialists as well as those who are taking only a single course in fashion. In fact, it will interest anyone who wants to know more about fashion and the fashion business.

Acknowledgments

I wish to thank the many friends and business associates who took time to answer questions, make suggestions, review chapters, and donate photographs during the revision of this book. I am particularly indebted to the following persons:

■ *Gianfranco Ferré*, who graciously gave his permission to use his wonderful sketch on the cover

■ *Jessica McClintock*, whose talent, genuine interest, and cooperation in the training of fashion students makes her foreword especially meaningful

■ *Joe Sammartino*, Milliken; *Cathy Cregan-Valent*, Omega; *Van Lowry*, Hoechst Celanese; and *Bill Foster*, DuPont, for sharing their knowledge of textiles

■ *Jessica Mitchell*; *Jay Margolis*; and *Gail Cook*, Dana Buchman, for expert advice on marketing

■ *Jim Nordstrom*, Nordstrom's; *Joan Bergholt*; *Annette Dresser*, Nordstrom's; *Bonnie Pressman*, Barney's; *Sally Frame Kasaks*, Ann Taylor; *Bob Connolly*, Montgomery Ward; *Walter Loeb*, Loeb Associates; *Walter Levy*, Goldman-Sachs; *Linda Greenman*, Williams Sonoma; and *Gae Marino*, Doneger, for generously sharing their superior knowledge of retailing

■ *Stephanie Mulvey*, Ex Officio; *Patricia Bilello*, JH Collectibles; *Jeannette Chai Cantone*, Natori; *Barry Fishman* and *Barbara Colvin* Hoopes, Koret; *Linda Knapp Murdock*, Equiwear; *Michael Alexin*, Levi Strauss; *Mary Ann Parker*, Marker Express; and *Lillian Jang*, Esprit, for advice on design and production

■ *Ian Wright*, Adrienne Vittadini Shoes; *Marcia Sherrill*, Kleinberg-Sherrill; *Carol Hochman*, Liz Claiborne; *Lawrence Green*, Louise Green; *Bernard Grossman*, Betmar; *Bruna Maney*, Fownes; *Rosemary Prock* and *Ray Fox*, Grandoe; *Joe Aulisi*, Gates; *Michael Mayer*, Berkshire; *Walter Imboden*, Sara Lee Hosiery; *Tracy Smith*, Florsheim; and

Stacey Levesque, Macy's, for recommendations on accessories

■ *Erwin Pearl*; *Mary Solkin*, Andin International; and *Scott Erdman*, Macy's for their views on the jewelry business; *Ysabel Trujillo*, the Canadian Fur Association, and *Terry Vourantonis*, Theo, for information on furs.

■ *Rob Corder*, Macy's; *Roland Theile*, Nordstrom's; *Brian Preussker*, Macy's; and *Virginia Meyer*, Cato Corporation, for their expertise in fashion promotion

■ *Jaime Villablanca*; *Norman Karr*, The Fashion Association; *Tony Brown*, Macy's; and *Erin Gaffney*, Hartmarx, for their opinions on men's wear

■ *Laurie Black*, Nordstrom's; *Beth Bonner*, Strawbridge & Clothier; *Roger Case*, Cary Children's Clothing; and *Rosemary Weidman*, Youngsport, for suggestions on children's wear

■ *Carolyn Moss*, Macy's; *Nancy Richards, Eliska Turina, Janice Markham*, and *David Harvey* in London; and *Florence Roussel*, French Trade Commission, for updated information on European fashion

■ *Beth Mesirow*, Levi Strauss; *Giles Brown*, Rochester Buttons; *Stanley Shatz*, Norman Shatz Company, and *Tom Allison*, Talon, for contributions to the trimmings section

■ My grandmother *Ida Martin*, my parents *Ida and Russell Stephens, Elma McCarraher Page, Dolores Quinn, Eleanor Kling Ensign, Hazel Stroth, Krestine Corbin, Debra Smith, Susan Toussaint*, and friends and family for encouragement throughout my education and career

■ Most of all to my husband *Philipp* and my children *Peter* and *Victoria* for their patience.

For Phillip, Peter, and Victoria

WITH LOVE

Part One

THE FUNDAMENTALS OF FASHION

Part One provides students with the fundamental knowledge they need to understand the workings of the fashion industry. Chapter 1 traces the development of fashion and the fashion industry as a background to understanding changes in fashion today. Chapter 2 offers the essentials of fashion marketing, which are the very basis of the fashion business today. Chapter 3 explains the principles of fashion change and theories of consumer acceptance. Chapter 4 covers the market and design research necessary for product development. Without this information, it is impossible to understand how the fashion industry functions.

Three mannequins wearing gowns from the 1830s in a stable scene at the Costume Galleries, Castle Howard, York, England. *(Courtesy of Richard A. Robson, Curator)*

1

FASHION DEVELOPMENT

CAREER FOCUS

Fashion executives at every level of the industry want and need to know how the fashion business developed. Lessons in history help them to make decisions for today and the future. Ideas from the past are often reinterpreted for today's fashion. Some fashion experts work in the area of fashion history, either as a costume curator for a museum or in the archives department of a fashion company.

CHAPTER OBJECTIVES

After reading this chapter you should have attained competence in the following areas:

1. Awareness of the major changes in American life-styles since the Industrial Revolution and how they have influenced fashion
2. Understanding of how fashion has reflected the social, cultural, political, economic, and technological changes since the Industrial Revolution
3. Ability to outline and discuss major changes in the fashion industry
4. Knowledge of the names of major designers of the past 100 years

3

More than just a designer's whim, fashion is a reflection of the social, political, economic, and artistic forces of any given time. The changing styles that evolve from these forces tell of historical events as poignantly as textbooks, journals, or periodicals. Dressing room mirrors throughout the ages have reflected the trends in how people think, live, and love.

We will examine some of the major influences on fashion in history as a background to understanding contemporary fashion and anticipating future change. This chapter traces the development of the fashion industry in Europe and America from the seventeenth century to the present, emphasizing the last 100 years. It briefly discusses how fashion innovators, together with society, technology, economics, and politics, change fashion.

Fashion, as we know it, is relatively new. In ancient and medieval times, clothing styles remained practically unchanged for a century at a time. Fashion change began to accelerate during the Renaissance, as Western civilization discovered different cultures, customs, and costumes. As new fabrics and ideas became available, people craved more new things.

FRANCE, THE CENTER OF FASHION

France's dominance over international fashion began in the early eighteenth century.

Fashion Dictated by Royalty

Until the industrial revolution, people belonged to one of two main classes: the wealthy, mostly landholding aristocrats, and the poor, mostly laborers and farmers. Because wealth was concentrated in the landowning class, these people were the only ones who could afford to wear fashionable clothes. Royalty, at the top of both the social and economic ladders, set fashion trends; other members of the aristocracy followed their example in order to gain approval.

At the turn of the eighteenth century, members of King Louis XIV's court became the arbiters of taste, making Paris the fashion capital of Europe. The textile industry grew in Lyons and other French cities, supplying the court with silk fabrics, ribbons, and laces. Dressmakers and tailors, sponsored by the wealthy, developed their skills to a high level using these beautiful materials.

Hand Sewing by Dressmakers and Tailors

The elaborate detail and intricate seaming of fashion at this time required an enormous amount of painstaking hand labor. All clothes were not only handmade but also *custom made*. Each garment was made to fit the customer's exact measurements. Dresses and suits were individually sewn by dressmakers or tailors to their employers' specifications. The identities of personal dressmakers were secrets guarded by the wealthy. No one wanted to share the talents of clever dressmakers for fear of losing them. Rose Bertin (Ber-tan') was dressmaker to Queen Marie Antoinette, whose name we know because she was made the official court minister of fashion.

Poorer people wore castoff clothing from the rich or trade classes. Country folk made their own clothing. The very elaborate clothing for special occasions was passed from one generation to another and became the traditional *folk costume*, different in every region. The contrast between the plight of the poor and the extravagancies of the court during the eighteenth century was one cause of the French Revolution, which began in 1789. In response to a general revulsion against excess, fashion changed from elaborately decorated costumes to more simpler garments.

Growth of the Couture

France became the center of fashion due to support from the royal court and the development of the silk industry there. In France, the art of dressmaking was known as *couture* (koo-tour'). A male designer was a *couturier* (koo-tu-ree-ay'); his female counterpart was a *couturière* (koo-tu-ree-air').

Charles Worth is considered the father of the couture because he was the first successful independent designer. Born in England, he came to Paris at age 20 in 1846 (the year Elias Howe patented his sewing machine). Worth attracted prominent women as clients, culminating in Empress Eugénie, wife of Emperor Napoleon III.

Some couturiers became business as well as creative forces, directing salons staffed with seamstresses and tailors. Other couture houses followed Worth, including Paquin, Cheruit, Doucet, Redfern, the Callot sisters, and Jeanne Lanvin. The couture became a bridge between the class-structured fashion of the past and the democratized fashion of today.

From these beginnings, an international market for Parisian high fashion grew. In 1868 the couturiers of Paris formed a trade association. Other European capitals followed the leadership of Paris, Vienna becoming the next in importance. Couturiers were the major influence on fashion design for over 100 years, setting style trends for all of Europe as well as the rest of the Western world.

Fashion dolls, dressed in miniature versions of couture gowns, were sent from

Worth gown typical of the Second Empire period in France, 1852–1860. *(Courtesy of the Union Française des Arts du Costume)*

France as a convenient means of publicizing fashion. Orders from wealthy women were mailed back to Paris, where the gowns were made to fit the customers' requirements. Some of these dolls made their way to the United States. Most people could not afford couture clothes, however, but managed to copy them to some degree.

EFFECTS OF THE INDUSTRIAL REVOLUTION ON FASHION

The Industrial Revolution marked the beginning of technological advances in textile and apparel production.

Growth of the Textile Industry

Early America had virtually no textile or fashion industry. Most materials were imported from abroad: silks from Italy, France, India, and China; and woolens, calicoes, and cashmeres from Britain.

The modern textile industry, which enabled more fabrics to be produced in less time, began in England with John Kay's development of the flying shuttle in 1733, James Hargreaves's invention of the spinning jenny in 1764, Richard Arkwright's water frame in 1769, and Edmund Cartwright's power loom in 1785. To protect its industry, England passed strict laws preventing textile machines, parts, blueprints, tools, and even the mechanics and inventors themselves from leaving the country. However, Samuel Slater memorized every detail of Arkwright's water frame and other machinery and secretly left England. Within two years of his arrival in New England, he had a new mill built and in operation. Textile mills began to produce cloth in America, the first evidence of fashion independence. New England became America's first textile center.

In 1814, Francisc Cabot Lowell of Boston developed the power loom. His factory was the first to have a vertical operation: complete textile production from raw cotton fiber to finished cloth by one company. By 1847, more Americans worked in the textile industry than in any other.

After the Civil War, the American textile industry began to relocate to the South, the source of cotton. Southern states continued to offer other incentives, such as cheaper labor costs. Eventually, the South became the center of textile production in the United States.

Growth of the Middle Class

Great economic, social, and fashion changes throughout the Western world accompanied the Industrial Revolution in the late eighteenth century. Burgeoning trade and industry in turn created a middle class with money to spend on the luxuries of life, including better clothing. Money gave the new middle class power, not only in business and society, but also to influence fashion trends. Fashion became a status symbol, a visual means to show off wealth.

Establishment of the Business Suit

Until 1800, men's and women's fashions had equal amounts of decoration. In Louis XIV's time, men's dress was at least as elaborate as women's. As the middle class grew, businessmen wanted to establish an image of respectability and dependability. At that point, "men's garb descended from brilliant finery…into bleak conformity." Men adopted the conservative, dignified business suit with long trousers, jacket, vest, shirt, and necktie—"a permanent noose, you might say."[1] Men's business attire remained basically conservative with very few changes

Men's clothing, as well as women's, was custom made. The finest tailor shops—such as Henry Poole and Company, established in 1843—were on Savile Row in London, which became the international center of men's fashion.

Some ready-made men's clothing was made by hand in France in the late 1700s. In America, some enterprising tailors made the first ready-to-wear suits for sailors so that they would have clothes to wear when they came on land. At first, tailors cut the fabrics, bundled the pieces, and sent them out to homes to be sewn by the *cottage industry* process. The tailors also acted as

Employees outside the Levi Strauss company headquarters in San Francisco about 1870. *(Courtesy of Levi Strauss & Company)*

retailers. Since the clothing was for sailors, these first primitive clothing factory-shops were located in seaport cities, such as New Bedford, Boston, New York, and Philadelphia.

In 1818 in New York, Henry Brooks started the men's clothier business that became Brooks Brothers. Due to his determination to make and deal only in merchandise of the best quality, he helped to advance ready-made clothing. There, Abraham Lincoln bought an overcoat for his second inauguration.[2]

MASS PRODUCTION OF CLOTHING

The mass production of clothing led to accessible fashion for everyone.

Invention of the Sewing Machine

The democratization of fashion began with the sewing machine, which turned a handicraft into an industry. The mass production of clothing would have been impossible without it, and without mass production, fashion would not be available to everyone. In 1829, a French tailor named Thimmonier patented a wooden chain-stitch sewing machine, but all existing models were destroyed by rioting tailors who feared for their jobs. Walter Hunt, an American, developed a sewing machine in 1832 but failed to patent it. Thus, the man who is usually credited with its invention is Elias Howe, who patented his in 1846. All of Howe's machines were run by hand. In 1859, Isaac Singer, whose name has become a household word because of his mass production of the sewing machine, developed the foot treadle, an improvement that left the hands free to guide the fabric. Singer spent $1 million a year on sales promotion and by 1867 was producing a thousand machines per day.[3] Electrically powered models were not available until 1921.

An early use for sewing machines was to make Civil War uniforms. The Union army recorded the chest and height measurements of over a million soldiers to come up with the first standardization of sizes. After the war, sewing machines and uniform sizing promoted the mass production of everyday men's wear. To save time and to keep control over production, entrepreneurs brought workers and machinery together in factories. This caused many people in search of work to move to the cities where the factories were located.

The first Singer sewing machine, 1851.
(Courtesy of the Singer Company)

Work Clothes

In 1849, the Gold Rush attracted thousands of men to California in search of gold. A 20-year-old Bavarian immigrant by the name of Levi Strauss arrived in San Francisco with some canvas he intended to sell to the gold miners for tents and wagon covers. Instead, in answer to a prospector's request for long-wearing pants with pockets for tools, he made pants with metal rivets to hold the pockets securely. These were so popular, that he set up a shop to manufacture them. Soon he began to use a tough cotton fabric loomed in Nimes, France, called *serge de Nimes* (later shortened to *denim*). This was the beginning of clothes specially made for laborers. They are the only item of wearing apparel that has remained basically the same for nearly 150 years!

Women's Fashion Reflects Social Changes

Fashion conveyed the rigid differences between the roles of the sexes. Men wore trousers, which became a symbol of dominance, while women wore constraining garments characteristic of their restricted life-styles and obedience to their husbands and fathers. Women did not have the right to own anything but their wardrobes.[4]

Aside from the small number of wealthy women who bought couture, most women had about three basic garments in their wardrobes. Fashionable one-piece fitted dresses were impossible to mass-produce because each dress had to be custom made to fit at least three sets of measurements. Even after the invention of the sewing machine, only hoop skirts and cloaks could be manufactured for women.

Mass Production of Women's Separates

A young woman dressed in the Gibson Girl style.
(Courtesy of the National Archives, Washington, D.C.)

The introduction of separate blouses and skirts in the 1880s made it possible to manufacture ready-to-wear clothes for women. A blouse could be made to fit the shoulder and bust measurements, the skirt to fit the hips. Waistlines and hemlines were easily adjusted and blouses were simply tucked in. This innovation made it possible for the working- or middle-class woman to add variety to her wardrobe simply by mixing separates. The cost of a new ready-made blouse was a mere fraction of the cost of a custom-tailored dress.

The *Gibson Girl* was the personification of the ideal young middle-class American woman, as sketched by popular illustrator Charles Dana Gibson in the 1890s. The Gibson Girl gave style to the basic high-necked, long-sleeved blouse-and-skirt look. It was practical yet feminine and could be worn anywhere. The Gibson Girl look paved the way for the simplified, functional dress that typifies American fashion. As the quality of store-bought clothes improved, the market expanded enough for companies to specialize in ready-made clothes.

Children's Fashion

The wealthy were the only ones who had money to spend on fashionable children's clothes; members of the middle and working classes made their children's clothes at home. Small children, both girls and boys, wore dresses. As they grew older, children were supposed to act like adults and they were dressed in miniature versions of adult apparel. In fact, many children wore cut-down remakes of their parents' old clothes. Mothers were particularly grateful for the advent of patterns for children's clothes because, previously, home-sewn garments had been cut and fitted by trial and error.

Paper patterns, inspired by French fashions, were made available to American home sewers in 1850 by Ellen and William Demorest.[5] Demorest Patterns, followed by Butterick and McCall's, fostered fashion consciousness at all levels of society. Women on small budgets were especially happy to have patterns to make the clothes that they could never afford to buy.

RETAILING DURING THE NINETEENTH CENTURY

Modern retailing had its roots in the nineteenth century when afforable fashion was first made available to the general public.

Fairs and bazaars were the predecessors of the retail store. The traveling merchant brought clothes to these markets. Expensive goods were shown only to selected wealthy customers. Prices were not marked on the merchandise, so buyer and seller usually bargained.

As large numbers of people settled in towns, the first general stores were established to cater to their desire for wider assortments of merchandise. Also, artisans sold their handmade goods in their own shops. These shops were grouped together by trade and regulated by guilds.

The Industrial Revolution triggered a self-supporting manufacturing and retailing cycle. As more goods were produced, there were more products to sell. This increased business activity gave the growing middle class more money to spend, which created a demand for more products. This growing demand for the variety of goods being produced was the basis for the growth of retailing. Retail stores grew up in the cities, close to production and population centers. As more people clustered in cities to work, stores opened in areas convenient to shoppers.

Two types of stores finally emerged to bring fashion to the public: the specialty store and the department store. Traditional handicraft stores evolved into *specialty stores* and general stores developed into *department stores*, which carried a wide variety of merchandise. Shopping in department stores became a popular activity, like going to an exhibition. For the first time, people of all incomes could at least enjoy browsing and looking at beautiful things.

The First Department Stores

In 1826, Samuel Lord and George Washington Taylor formed a partnership to open the first Lord and Taylor store in New York City. Jordan Marsh

John Wanamaker's Grand Depot store, Philadelphia, 1877, located on the same site as today's downtown store. *(Courtesy of Carter Hawley Hale Stores, Inc.)*

and Company, opening in Boston, claimed they could sell, cut, sew, trim, and furnish a dress in half a day.[6] Edward Filene opened a comparable department store in Boston, John Wanamaker in Philadelphia, Joseph Hudson in Detroit, Morris Rich in Atlanta, and R. H. Macy in New York. Their stores grew to a prominence that has lasted 150 years.

Harrod's of London, established by Henry Harrod in 1849, began as a small grocery store. By 1880 it had 100 employees and it became the largest department store in Europe. Liberty of London opened its retail store in 1875 and produced its own prints as early as 1878. In France, department stores such as the Bon Marché, Samaritaine, and Printemps opened in the nineteenth century.

The nineteenth century also saw the beginning of customer service, a major contribution to American retailing. In Chicago, Marshall Field once admonished a store clerk who was arguing with a customer, "Give the lady what she wants." "The customer is always right" has been a principle of American retailing ever since.

Early Mail-Order Merchandising

In the 1800s, nearly three-quarters of the American population lived in rural areas, usually served by only a few general stores with a limited selection. The extension of the railroads to the West Coast and the inauguration of a free rural mail delivery enabled merchants to start reaching these potential consumers with mail-order services.

While working for a wholesaling firm, traveling to country stores by horse and buggy, Aaron Montgomery Ward conceived the idea of selling directly to country people by mail. He opened his business in 1872 with a one-page list of items that cost one dollar each. People could later order goods through a distributed catalog and the store would ship the merchandise cash on delivery (COD). The idea was slow to catch on because people were suspicious of a strange name. However, in 1875 Ward announced the startling policy of "satisfaction guaranteed or your money back." Contrasting with the former retailing principle of *caveat emptor* (Latin for "buyer beware"), this policy set off a boom in Ward's business.

In 1886 a Chicago jewelry company erroneously shipped some watches to a jeweler in Richard Sears's hometown in Minnesota. Sears offered to resell them for the jeweler, thereby creating his own watch business. Alvah Roebuck answered Sears' ad for a watchmaker and became Sears' business partner. In 1893, the firm name was changed to Sears, Roebuck and Company. From a modest beginning, they expanded by 1895 to a 507-page catalog including clothing and household goods, often referred to as the "dream book" or "wish book." The mail-order business did more to bring a variety of up-to-date merchandise to rural consumers than any other form of retailing.

CHANGES CAUSED BY COMMUNICATIONS, LEISURE, AND INDUSTRY

Communications, leisure activities, labor conditions, and industrial technology have a continuing effect on fashion.

The desire for fashionable clothing was fostered by its increased availability, as well as by new communications media such as the mail service, magazines, newspapers, telephones, automobiles, and later airplane travel, radio, motion pictures, television, and computers.

The First Fashion Magazines

During the 1800s, fashion magazines began to be published in France and England. Eighteen fashion magazines were being published in New York and Philadelphia in the late 1800s.[7] Two American magazines that began in the nineteenth century are still published today: *Harper's Bazaar* commenced publication in both New York and Paris in 1867 and *Vogue* started in 1894 in New York.

These publications spread the latest fashion ideas from Paris by means of sketches and descriptions. Dressmakers in other countries copied the styles as best they could with available fabrics. As more women became aware of fashion styles through magazines and other forms of mass communication, their desire to wear these fashions increased. The faster a style was adopted by the public, the greater was the demand for more new looks.

Growth of Leisure Activities

The popularity of sports such as tennis and bicycling created a need for functional sportswear. As early as 1851, Amelia Jenks Bloomer had tried to introduce pants for women. However, they were not accepted until the bicycling craze of the 1890s. Bloomers, full in the leg and gathered at the ankle, were also worn under bathing dresses. Finally, after 1900, swimwear was pared down enough that people could actually swim.

Pants became an acceptable part of the horse-riding habit for women around the turn of the century, when women discovered that riding sidesaddle in a skirt, "often caused one to dismount before the ride was over."[8] As women became more and more involved in sports, pants gave them the mobility for a more active life. However, it was not until the 1920s that pants became fashionable as well as functional for women.

Conditions in the Garment Industry

New York Becomes the Center of the U.S. Fashion Industry

By the latter part of the century the influx of European immigrants to New York helped to establish that city as the center of the industry. The immigrants, used to hardship and willing to work for low wages, provided the skilled labor the industry needed in order to grow. By 1900 the American women's clothing industry consisted of 2701 establishments.[9] They produced mostly cloaks and suits, with some shirtwaists (blouses) and underwear.

Unionization

As more workers crowded into the industry, working conditions became appalling. Tenement workrooms were known as *sweatshops* because of the excessively long hours required of laborers in unsanitary surroundings for extremely low wages.

In 1900, cloak makers, mostly immigrants living in cities in the northern United States, met to discuss working conditions. The result was the formation of the International Ladies' Garment Workers' Union, which tried to protect its members against unfair employers. At first the union was not very popular, but it did make progress with strikes against the shirtwaist industry in 1909 and the cloak industry in 1910. The men's clothing workers union, which became the Amalgamated Clothing Workers of America in 1914, also had a successful strike in 1910 against Hart, Schaffner & Marx in Chicago. It brought working hours *down* to 54 hours per week!

"On March 25, 1911, the nation was stunned by the horror of the Triangle Shirtwaist Company fire in New York City."[10] The factory's main exit door had been bolted, and the lone fire escape was a death trap that ended in midair. The 146 deaths, mostly of girls, aroused Americans' indignation against the plight of the sweatshop workers. Finally, action was taken on demands for regular hours, minimum wages, paid vacations, sick benefits, and better working conditions. Added labor costs naturally added to the inevitable simplification of fashion.

Women working in a Levi Strauss factory. *(Courtesy of Levi Strauss & Company)*

EFFECTS OF WORLD WAR I ON THE STATUS OF WOMEN AND FASHION

World War I put women in the work force and gave them new rights and practical clothing.

Women in the Work Force

The status of women has hinged firmly on their participation in the working world. Before 1900, very few women worked outside the home. Without a prominent place in business, women had no authority and no rights. At the turn of the century women began to work in factories, offices, and retail stores. The need for the convenience of ready-made clothing made the apparel industry grow and made ready-to-wear even more acceptable.

In 1914, World War I began in Europe and the United States entered in 1917. World War I greatly promoted women's rights, because it enabled European and American women to replace men in previously all-male jobs. The functional working clothes worn by these women had a great impact on fashion. "Now that women work," Vogue reported in 1918, "working clothes have acquired a new social status and a new chic."[11]

A trend toward masculinity in women's fashion emerged: decorative details disappeared in favor of a tailored look that imitated businessmen's suits. Corsets were discarded and the curved hourglass silhouette was replaced by the tube. Hemlines rose and skirts widened to permit freedom of movement. No one wanted or had time for complicated dressing. This change coincided with the need to simplify clothing construction because of rising labor costs and resulted in the democratization of fashion. Fashion reflected women's growing independence and, in 1920, women finally won the right to vote in the United States.

Important Trendsetting Designers

While mass production was growing in the American fashion industry, the French couture still concentrated on fashion leadership among the wealthy. Paris was a cultural meeting ground for designers, artists, and writers. The exchange of their ideas created the exceptional atmosphere needed for fashion innovation.

Often one or a few designers became *trendsetters*; they dominated the field because they were able to capture the spirit of their times and translate it into highly accepted fashion. American retailers bought French fashion for their wealthy customers and often worked with American manufacturers to have them copied or adapted for the American market.

Paul Poiret (Pwah-ray'), whose tubular dresses liberated women from corsets, was the first Paris couturier of this century to become a trendsetter.

Gabrielle Chanel (Sha-nelle'), also known as Coco, was at the forefront of French fashion following World War I. Chanel popularized the *Garçon* (gar-sohn') or boyish style with sweaters and jersey dresses and was the first designer to make high-fashion pants for women.

Jean Patou (Gsahn Pa-Too) created the famous *Flapper* look in 1925 by accentuating the hipline, strengthening a straight silhouette, and making shorter skirts with uneven hemlines. He confirmed that the young, independent woman was the new ideal.

The ready-to-wear apparel industry began to prosper when designers such as Poiret, Vionnet, and Chanel simplified styles and thereby construction. Couture styles were then copied by mass producers for consumers at every price level. Because individual fitting was not so important to their straight silhouettes, the mass production of dresses became practical. As early as the 1920s, designers such as Lucien Lelong in France and Hattie Carnegie in America were adding ready-to-wear lines to their made-to-order collections. Although custom-made clothing remained important, by the 1920s fashionable ready-to-wear was firmly established.

Coco Chanel, wearing one of the suits she made famous.
(Courtesy of Chanel, Paris, photographed by Hatami)

Jean Patou and his American models arriving at Le Havre in 1924.
(Courtesy of the National Archives, Washington, D.C.)

RETAIL EXPANSION IN THE EARLY TWENTIETH CENTURY

The needs of the growing middle class stimulated both apparel manufacturing and retailing.

Specialty Stores for Quality Fashion

In the early twentieth century, specialty stores emerged with new retailing approaches and offered their customers high-fashion merchandise. Bergdorf Goodman and Saks Fifth Avenue in New York City and Neiman Marcus in Dallas concentrated solely on the finest fashion and customer service. By the 1930s the first women presidents of major retail firms had been installed, Dorothy Shaver at Lord and Taylor and Hortense Odlam at Bonwit Teller. Shaver gave American fashion a boost by mentioning American designers in store ads.

The Expansion of Chain Stores

While great retailing establishments were growing in the big cities, chain stores selling lower-priced merchandise were taking hold elsewhere. James Cash Penney was such an industrious employee at a small Wyoming store that the owners offered him a partnership in their new store in 1902. Called the Golden Rule Store in honor of their belief in high business standards, it proved an immediate success, in part because of Penney's door-to-door advertising campaign. In 1907 the original partners sold their shares to

Penney; the store's name was officially changed to J. C. Penney in 1912. When the chain-store concept caught on in the 1920s, Penney opened stores in all parts of the United States. Chain stores became a national phenomenon.

The Advent of Suburban Retail Centers

As more and more people moved to the suburbs and owned cars, personal mobility increased, creating a revolution in retailing. Finding that its mail-order business was dropping off, Sears & Roebuck opened stores not in the city centers but rather near the highways that led to the growing suburbs, where they could offer free parking. It was also the beginning of suburban shopping centers such as The Country Club Plaza in Kansas City, which opened in 1922.

EFFECTS OF THE DEPRESSION ON FASHION

The experience of the Great Depression of the 1930s still causes manufacturers and retailers to worry at the sign of a recession.

Bursting of the Credit Bubble

In the 1920s, so much credit was extended that eventually there was not enough money to back it up. In the stock market a person needed to put up only 10 percent of the price to buy stock; when the price rose, the shares could be sold at a profit. So it went until September 3, 1929, when the stock market started a steep decline. In less than a month the market value of all stocks dropped $30 billion. Unemployment rose from 1.5 million to 12.8 million, and business profits fell from $10.3 billion to a net loss of $2 billion. Nearly half of the nation's banks had to close. Industrial production fell to half of what it had been and many companies went bankrupt. More than a third of the ready-to-wear manufacturers went out of business. The slump set off a chain reaction that soon put the whole world into a depression.

Hollywood's Influence on Fashion

Americans tried to take their minds off the Depression at the movies. Because people in pre-television days commonly visited the local movie theater once or twice a week, American films brought fashion to every woman. Every young woman wanted to look like her favorite film star. Katharine Hepburn and Marlene Dietrich made slacks popular for women; Clark Gable popularized the sport shirt for men. The 1930s were the most glamorous years in film history, a paradoxical contrast with the deprivations of real life.

Gilbert Adrian emerged as the leading Hollywood designer. He was the first American designer to influence fashion throughout the world. Macy's sold half a million copies of one dress he designed for Joan Crawford to wear in *Letty Lynton* in 1932.[12]

Joan Crawford glances admiringly at Adrian, Hollywood's trendsetting designer of the 1930s. *(Courtesy of the Joseph Simms Collection)*

Paris's Influence on International Fashion

The influence of Parisian couture designers on international fashion remained.

Elsa Schiaparelli (Skee-pah-rell'-ee) was the trendsetter of European fashion in the 1930s. Schiaparelli moved the center of interest to the shoulders, which she began to widen, accentuating them by pleats, padding, or braid, a silhouette that remained popular through World War II.

James Mainbocher (Main-bow-shay') was the first American designer to be successful in Europe. When King Edward VIII of England abdicated his throne to marry the divorced American Wallis Simpson, Mainbocher designed the wedding dress, which became the most copied dress of the 1930s. Scandals and fashion remain intertwined to this day!

WORLD WAR II'S EFFECT ON FASHION

The American economy did not entirely recover until World War II escalated production.

America's Isolation from Paris Fashion

During the war the French couture banded together under the leadership of Lucien Lelong, then president of the Paris Couture Syndicale, during the

German occupation. Under great restrictions and privation—practically no fabrics to work with, no trimmings, no press coverage, no heat, and little food—most designers barely managed to stay in business. Some were forced to close. Of course, under these circumstances little was achieved.

Isolated from Paris fashion leadership during the war, Americans had to find their own style direction. The lack of imports from France was actually a boon to the development of American talent. In 1940, *Vogue* reported on the New York collection openings. With Mainbocher as an example of success, other American designers such as Claire McCardell, Hattie Carnegie, and Vera Maxwell gained recognition.

Claire McCardell, considered the top American designer, was credited with originating the *American Look* in practical separates, inspired by the work clothes of farmers, railroad engineers, soldiers, and sportsmen.

American designers became especially skilled at and known for their sportswear, reflecting the more casual American life-style, which would eventually influence the rest of the world. Sportswear, with its simpler construction, also suited mass production.

Fashion remained relatively stable during the war years. The U.S. government's wartime regulations restricted the use of fabric and hardware. Functional clothes became a necessity as women doing war work wore uniforms or work clothes. Women's suits were heavily influenced by miltary uniforms. The result was a masculine silhouette for the women who now shouldered the responsibilities at home.

Gown by Schiaparelli. (*Courtesy of Claudy Stolz and Maison Schiaparelli, Paris*)

REACTIONARY POSTWAR FASHION

The postwar era brought about a suburban life-style and an accent on family life.

In the postwar search for domestic tranquility, American families wanted to escape the deteriorating cities and find a healthy environment in which to raise their children. For many this meant a move to the suburbs. The informal suburban life-style brought about the popularity of casual sportswear by American designers, new wash-and-wear manufactured fabrics such as nylon, and more convenient shopping centers.

French Fashion Direction

Women were so happy to see men home after the war that most reverted completely to stereotypical feminine roles, leaving jobs open for the returning men. Fashion catered to their feminine ideal. Paris recaptured fashion dominance—almost to the point of dictatorship in Dior's case.

Claire McCardell sketching in a museum.
(Courtesy of the National Archives, Washington, D.C.)

Christian Dior (Chris-tee-ahn' Dee-or') showed his first collection in 1947 and was an instant success. In a reaction against the wartime silhouette, women adopted his *New Look*, with longer, fuller skirts; smooth, rounded, sloping shoulders; and tiny fitted waists. Within a few seasons Dior's name became a household word and he was doing as much business as the rest of the couture combined.[13]

Christobal Balenciaga (Bah-lehn'-see-ah'-gah), a Spaniard who worked in Paris, was regarded as the master of tailors. When American stores purchased rights to manufacture *line-for-line* copies, Balenciaga's designs were always the most popular.

American Fashion Innovators

While Parisian designers set international trends, Americans also enjoyed continued success at home due to the exposure given to them during the war. These women's wear designers included Bonnie Cashin, Oleg Cassini, Ann Fogarty, James Galanos, Charles James, Anne Klein, Norman Norell, Mollie Parnis, Fernando Sarmi, Adele Simpson, Jacques Tiffeau, Pauline Trigere, Sydney Wragge, and Ben Zuckerman.

Movie star Audrey Hepburn and Jacqueline Kennedy, wife of the president, set a new ideal of beauty and established an impeccable look predicated on simplicity that was universally imitated. Jackie practically made a uniform of her two-piece jewel-necked A-line dresses and pillbox hats.

Until the 1950s, the average man's wardrobe had only a few dark suits, white shirts, somber neckties, overcoat, raincoat, and hat. For the first time, designers such as Don Loper and John Weitz developed coordinated sportswear for men.

Some American designers custom-made fashion for the wealthy, but most built their reputation on what Americans did best, ready-to-wear. The French may have been the high fashion innovators, but Americans developed and excelled at producing fashion looks for everyone.

The late 1940s and 1950s also saw the the biggest increase of births ever. As these children became teenagers, industry catered to this newly emerging market. Records, cosmetics, magazines, and junior fashions were created.

THE YOUTH-DIRECTED 1960s

The postwar baby boom had an increasing effect on fashion change. Breaking with convention, young designers created fashions for their own age group.

By 1965, 50 percent of the United States population was under the age of 25. Sheer numbers brought increased buying power and encouraged a youth-oriented market. Reminiscent of the 1920s, young people's tastes were to dominate the fashion scene through the 1970s.

London Emerges as a Leader in Youthful Fashion

Mary Quant and other young British designers such as Zandra Rhodes and Jean Muir set international fashion trends. They were influenced by a group called the Mods, who put together odd separates and old clothes from flea markets to create an individual look. Miniskirts, which rose above the knee, tights (panty hose), and unusual fabrications such as vinyl were characteristic of the *Mod* look.

In the United States young designers, such as Betsey Johnson, also created youthful fashions. Even the couture designers in Paris, such as André Courrèges, followed the lead of these young designers. This was the first evidence of a reverse in the traditional fashion-adoption process. The popularity of the youthful look made all women want to look young.

Revival of Men's Fashion

The English Mod look affected men's wear as well as women's. Carnaby Street tailors made an attempt to return color and fashion to men's clothing. The initial impact of Carnaby Street did not last, but the general interest in men's fashion did. Men became more concerned with their roles outside work and with leisure dressing. French and Italian designers also became important in men's wear.

Pierre Cardin (Car-dahn') signed his first contract for men's shirts and ties in 1959 and opened his men's ready-to-wear department in 1961. Dior, St. Laurent, and other women's designers followed his example. The 1960s brought the first designer clothes for men and the first extensive fashion changes since the introduction of the business suit.

Dior's new look.
(Courtesy of the House of Dior)

Fashion Business Evolution

In the 1960s, the nature of the fashion business began to change. Although some designers, such as Pierre Cardin, were able to make new successes, the youthful direction in fashion caused financial setbacks for the French couture designers of France from which they never fully recovered. The 1960s saw the last of elegant fashion for 20 years.

In the United States, the growing population and economy changed the structure of fashion companies. Small family-owned fashion businesses began to disappear. Some merged or were purchased by large, multiproduct corporations. Others, spurred by the flourishing economy, raised money for expansion by selling stocks, to become publicly owned. Public investment gave apparel companies the needed capital to grow and meet rising textile supplier minimums and growing retail distribution.

Boutiques Set Retailing Trends

British boutiques such as Mary Quant's Bazaar set a new trend in retailing. The French term *boutique* was adopted by Western countries as these small shops gained popularity. Traditional retailing in department and large specialty stores had competition from small boutiques. Following the trend, Yves St. Laurent opened his Rive Gauche (Reev Gosh) boutiques around the world. Henri Bendel's in New York introduced an atmosphere of many boutiques within one store. This idea brought freshness and excitement to retailing.

ANTIFASHION OF THE LATE 1960s AND 1970s

Antifashion became the style statement from the late 1960s into the 1970s.

1960s trendsetting designer Mary Quant.
(Courtesy of Mary Quant Limited)

The tumultuous late 1960s—a time of the Vietnamese War, assassinations, riots, and civil strife—made people turn away from showy displays of frivolity. In suburban America the polyester pantsuit became almost a uniform. It even became stylish to look poor. Workmen's Levis became an antifashion statement and the popularity of denim remains today. Some young people, bored with the lack of excitement in retail merchandise, wore vintage clothing purchased at thrift stores.

The Ethnic Look

Society's dropouts, the "hippies," made their antifashion statement in tattered jeans, long hair, beads, and old clothes. In their desire to emulate the simple life, they combined their old clothes to simulate ethnic or native American costume.

Eventually, the *Ethnic* look widened to include traditional folk costumes from practically every country. Black people developed pride in their heritage, sporting Afro hairdos and the dashiki, traditional African garb. The resumption of diplomatic relations with China in 1972 created widespread interest in the Chinese people and their traditional costume. Designers incorporated the ethnic idea of layering and combining separates into their collections.

Yves St. Laurent (Eve Sahn'Law-rahn') of Paris emerged as the fashion star of the 1970s because he was able to interpret ethnic and other street looks into high fashion. St. Laurent's Rive Gauche boutiques featured his prêt-à-porter (ready-to-wear) collection, which signaled the end of couture dominance. At that time, he was best known for his blazers, city pants, and ethnic looks. The epitome of reverse fashion adoption was St. Laurent's Elegant Peasant collection of 1975: ethnic looks done in silks with high price tags.

Physical Fitness as Fashion

In the 1970s, exercise, such as jogging, became a popular interest. Fashion was not lost in the race, and soon everyone had a jogging suit, even if they did not run. By the 1980s, active sportswear was a firmly established fashion category. Designers and manufacturers created clothing for every sport. The elastic fiber spandex was used to give garments the stretch needed for movement.

1970s trendsetting designer Yves Saint Laurent and a gabardine pantsuit from his 1969 collection. *(Courtesy of Yves Saint Laurent)*

The denim look culminated in "designer jeans" by Calvin Klein and Gloria Vanderbilt. The sexy "Me and My Calvins" advertisements were the most noteworthy example of the growing role of advertising in the fashion business. In the late 1970s, there was a wave of conservative leisure dressing, featuring khaki shorts, penny loafers, polo shirts, button-down shirts, and blazers, called the *Preppy* look.

The Women's Movement

The 1970s witnessed women working to find an equal place with men in the business world. Women were trying to make it up the corporate ladder rather than the social one. To fit into a man's world, they adopted the conservative business suit (with skirt) to give themselves a visual businesslike credibility. "Dressing for success" became the byword for those who wanted to get ahead. In a somewhat misguided attempt at quality consciousness, *status dressing* became important. The label of the garment became more important than the design. Calvin Klein, Halston, Geoffrey Beene, Ralph Lauren, and Mary McFadden became important designer names. Rolex watches, Gucci shoes, and Louis Vuitton bags became the status accessories.

THE ACQUISITIVE 1980s

Overspending and overborrowing in the 1980s caused many of the problems that the fashion business faces today.

During the 1980s, a trend toward aquisition was manifested in the workplace as well as in fashion. Large manufacturers and retailers were getting larger by gobbling up small ones. To regain control of decision making, many companies, such as Levi Strauss, bought back corporate stock in order to have private ownership.

Even the general public was primarily interested in climbing the corporate ladder and acquiring money. Many aging baby boomers went back to college to further their careers. More than 60 percent of women ages 18 to 54 worked outside the home, and increasing numbers of them rose to executive-level positions. Their new status was exhibited by the "power suit," a structured but elegant look that dominated fashion.

Globalization

During the 1980s, fashion evolved into a global phenomenon. Both American and European manufacturers and retailers greatly increased imports of textiles, apparel, and accessories.

Giorgio Armani, of Milan, Italy, became the trendsetter of the 1980s because his tailored look so perfectly suited the career woman. His fashion empire included Emporio Armani and many licenses. Italy became a major international fashion capital; Missoni knits, Armani suits, and Krizia sportswear were in great demand worldwide.

Japan emerged briefly as an important fashion center in the early 1980s led by Kenzo Takada and then Issey Miyake. Japanese designers showed

1980s international trendsetting designer Giogio Armani.
(Courtesy of Giorgio Armani SpA)

their collections in Paris and influenced world fashion with their oversized silhouettes, wrapping, and layering. In 1981, the eyes of the world were on England where Prince Charles wed Lady Diana Spencer. Copies of her wedding gown were in London shop windows 8 hours after the wedding! In France, Karl Lagerfeld's elegance and Christian Lacroix's flamboyant silhouettes and colors helped to rejuvenate the French couture. The 1980s also saw the beginning of international recognition of American designers, led by Calvin Klein. This prompted other American fashion companies to consider exporting.

Domestic Industry Trends

Textiles and Apparel

Textile and apparel manufacturers, faced with increased competition from imports, especially from Asia, began using electronic data interchange to foster cooperation between textile and apparel producers and retailers in order to react quickly to trends and cut out wasted time in distribution.

Growth of Designer and Brand Names

In the mood of acquisitions, well-known designers and brands became even more pervasive by diversifying their product lines. This was often accomplished by *licensing*, a royalty paid for the use of the designer or brand name and supported by tremendous amounts of advertising. The growth of Ralph Lauren, Liz Claiborne, Reebok, and Nike brands, for instance, was astounding.

Retailing Trends

Retailing went through an optimistic period, which unfortunately caused overexpansion. The United States became an *overstored* (industry jargon for too many stores) nation besieged with buyouts and takeovers. Mail-order retailing grew, attracting busy career women who preferred to shop by catalog. Nordstrom, a Seattle-based retailer, built a national reputation for customer service that set a standard for other stores to follow.

THE VALUE-ORIENTED 1990s

In the last decade of the century, Americans have had to readjust to a less indulgent way of life.

Recession

The biggest impact of the early 1990s was an international recession beginning in the United States and the United Kingdom and finally reaching Japan and continental Europe. This had far-reaching consequences for the fashion industry.

Retailing

Retail overexpansion in the 1980s resulted in overwhelming competition, forcing bankruptcies and store closures in the 1990s. I. Magnin and Abraham & Straus disappeared, among other retailers. Macy's, faced with bankruptcy, was taken over by Federated Stores. Sears gave up its catalog, a veritable American retail institution.

Manufacturing

Naturally, textile and apparel manufacturers were affected by the recession as there were less stores to sell to and imports continued to climb. Textile and apparel producers joined retailers to debate the pros and cons of the North American Free Trade Agreement. Textile producers hope that manufacturers will be able to use U.S. textiles if garments are produced in Mexico instead of Asia.

Information Age

Due to growing imports, there has been a shift away from manufacturing to focus on marketing and information. Both have been fostered by the great advances made by computer technology in all phases of the fashion industry. As discussed in Chapter 2, the 1990s have introduced us to elec-

1990s international trendsetting designer Karl Lagerfeld.
(Courtesy of Karl Lagerfeld)

tronic industry partnerships, computer-aided design, high-tech manufacturing, cable TV and computer shopping, infomercials, and the Internet.

Value Orientation

Consumers, facing job layoffs due to consolidations and closures, became value oriented. In 1991, more than half of all apparel sold in the United States was bought on sale.[14] Discount and off-price stores such as Wal-Mart enjoyed success in spite of the recession because their low prices appealed to consumers. Retailers are trying to win back customers with various new strategies, including value, customer service, and private label collections.

Fashion Direction

Karl Lagerfeld, dubbed "King of Paris fashion" by the press, increased his influence and became the foremost international trendsetter with five major collections: Chanel, Lagerfeld, Chloe, Fendi, and KL. His designs have an impact on many market segments and price ranges, from elegant coats and suits to junior dresses. "When Karl speaks, the fashion world listens."[15]

In the United States, it is now impossible to pinpoint a single trend or trendsetting designer. Donna Karan, Calvin Klein, and Ralph Lauren remain dominant. However, there are so many segments of the market created by various age, income, and life-style groups that no one designer influences them all.

Men's wear and accessories are the American fashion winners of the 1990s. Relaxed corporate dress codes have allowed men to wear casual clothing to work, and the men's sportswear market, in turn, is thriving. Men's wear designers, such as Tommy Hilfiger, are rising stars. Women's designers have jumped on the bandwagon with their own men's wear and accessories collections.

The continued slump in women's apparel appears to indicate a lack of interest in feminine fashion altogether. The early 1990s recession "Grunge" look appealed only to young women. However, as designers and manufacturers recognize that the population is aging, they realize that fashion trends need to be adapted for each age range. Many designers are also reviving nostalgic looks from the 1940s and 1960s as the century draws to a close.

SUMMARY

This chapter has briefly covered the growth of the fashion industry. Technological advances, especially the invention of the sewing machine, changed clothing production from custom made to ready-to-wear. The Industrial Revolution also nourished the growth of a large middle class, which demanded and could afford fashion at every price level. As a result, fashion became available to everyone instead of just the wealthy few.

Fashion has also been influenced by the changing status of women and by the changing roles of both sexes. Fashion leadership originated with and was maintained by the French, except during World War II and in the 1960s and 1970s. There are currently three major fashion capitals, Paris, New York, and Milan, and there is no longer one fashion direction. After a long period of dictating fashion, the industry now tries to cater to the needs of the consumer by supplying clothes for business and leisure. Today, people demand quality and value in their clothing more than fashion.

CHAPTER REVIEW

Terms and Concepts

Briefly identify and discuss the following terms and concepts:

1. France, the fashion center
2. Royalty as trendsetters
3. Couture
4. Charles Worth
5. Business suit
6. Isaac Singer
7. Levi Strauss
8. The Gibson Girl
9. Department stores
10. Specialty stores
11. Richard Sears
12. Coco Chanel
13. Gilbert Adrian
14. The New Look
15. Claire McCardell
16. The postwar baby boom
17. Mary Quant
18. The Mod Look
19. Antifashion
20. The Ethnic Look
21. Active sportswear
22. Globalization
23. The power suit
24. Giorgio Armani

Questions for Review

1. How did the growth of a middle class affect fashion in the eighteenth and nineteenth centuries?
2. What factors made Paris the center of world fashion?
3. How did the American textile industry get its start?
4. Give two examples of how fashion reflects social or political history.
5. Discuss the growth of mass production in the United States and the technical developments that made it possible.
6. What are the origins of specialty and department stores?
7. How did retail development and expansion in the nineteenth and twentieth centuries reflect social changes?
8. How did the growth of a garment industry encourage the growth of unionism?
9. How did the change in women's status influence fashion in the twentieth century?

Projects for Additional Learning

1. Trace the fashions of one of the designers listed in the Influential Designers Chart by consulting newspapers and magazines from the period in which he or she was best known. Trace the evolution of the designer's styles with sketches or photocopies. Discuss the characteristics that made his or her designs unique. How did the designs reflect life-styles?
2. If possible, visit an historic costume collection at a museum and examine costumes from each decade since the turn of the century in order to compare design details.
3. Start a small costume collection with your class. Canvass your family, friends, and neighbors for attic donations or shop at flea markets and thrift shops. Keep a record of all items as to donor and approximate year made. Examine them for construction methods and design details. These clothes will not only be fun to wear but can be used as inspiration for future design projects.
4. Visit a local sewing machine dealer. Ask the dealer to trace the technical advances in machines as far back as he or she can remember. The dealer may have old catalogs or old machines that you can examine. Discuss the advantages of the old and the new models.

NOTES

[1] Phyllis Feldkamp, "Men's Fashion, 1750–1975," *New York Times Magazine*, September 14, 1975, p. 66.

[2] "Bicentennial of American Textiles," *American Fabrics and Fashions*, no. 106 (Winter–Spring 1976), p. 12.

[3] Ishbel Ross, *Crusades and Crinolines* (New York: Harper & Row, 1963), p. 12.

[4] Ibid., p. 99.

[5] Ibid., p. 20.

[6] Ibid., p. 116.

[7] Ibid., p. 220.

[8] "Women's Pants," *L'Officiel USA*, Spring 1977, p. 109.

[9] Florence S. Richards, *The Ready to Wear Industry 1900–1950* (New York: Fairchild Publications, 1951), p. 8.

[10] *Signature of 450,000* (New York: International Ladies' Garment Workers Union, 1965), p. 24.

[11] Quoted by Helen Brockman, *The Theory of Fashion Design* (New York: Wiley, 1965), p. 69.

[12] Ernestine Carter, *The Changing World of Fashion* (London: Weidenfeld & Nicolson, 1977), p. 70.

[13] Charlotte Calasibetta, *Fairchild's Dictionary of Fashion* (New York: Fairchild Publications, 1975), p. 561.

[14] Ira Schneiderman, "A Look at the Future," *Women's Wear Daily*, August 1992, p. 15.

[15] As quoted by Heidi Lender, "The Latest from Lagerfeld," *Women's Wear Daily*, February 9, 1993, p. 4.

HISTORICAL CHART OF INFLUENTIAL DESIGNERS

Years	Most Influential Designers and International Fashion Directions
1774–93	Rose Bertin: dressmaker to Marie Antoinette
1790–1815	Hippolyte le Roy: dressmaker for the court of Napoleon, creator of the classic revival Empire style
1860s	Charles Worth (b. England): father of modern couture for women; London's Savile Row tailors set standards for men's tailoring
Late 1800s	Redfern, Cheruit, Doucet, Paquin
Early 1900s	Madame Gerber (house of Callot sisters), Jeanne Lanvin
1909–11	Paul Poiret: his tunics freed women from corsets
1912–15	Charlotte Premet
Post-World War I	Madelaine Vionnet: first to do bias cut
1916–21	Coco Chanel: known for the Boyish Look and for using jersey
1922–29	Jean Patou: known for the Flapper Look
1930–35	Elsa Schiaparelli (b. Italy): hard chic and unconventional styling
1936–38	Mainbocher (b. United States) and Molyneux (b. Ireland): understatement and broadening shoulders Gilbert Adrian: Hollywood glamour copied in ready-to-wear
1940–45	Claire McCardle (American): known for American Look of practical sportswear
	The war years made communication with Europe impossible and made Americans begin to appreciate their own designers.
1947–57	Christian Dior: with his New Look, Paris fashion leadership is regained; American sportswear for men appears
1950s–60s	Balenciaga, Givenchy, St. Laurent, Andre Courreges, Pierre Cardin (France), Pucci (Italy)
1960s	Mary Quant: English designers have international influence.
	Beginning of young designers creating for young people
	Mini skirts and Mod Look
	Pierre Cardin builds empire for men and women's fashion
1968–1975	Confusion in fashion direction; Paris influence is waning Ethnic influence; street fashion
	American jeans become international fashion
1970s	International exchange of fashion
	Major influence from French prêt-à-porter: St. Laurent, Kenzo (b. Japan), Rykiel, Lagerfeld (b. Germany)
	Italian designers important: Armani, Missoni, Krizia (Mandelli), Ferragamo shoes, Gucci handbags
	Geoffrey Beene, Halston, Calvin Klein, Mary McFadden important in American fashion
1980s	Global outlook; acquisition
	Japanese have international influence
	Rise of internationally known, popularly priced sportswear manufacturers such as Liz Claiborne, Esprit, and Benetton
	Armani (Italy) sets the fashion tone for professional women
	Lagerfeld and Lacroix rejuvenate the French couture
	American fashion designers begin exporting
1990s	Recession followed by value orientation
	Karl Lagerfeld is major international trendsetter with five collections
	Calvin Klein, Donna Karan among top American designers
	Men's wear enjoys the fashion spotlight; Tommy Hilfiger
	Casual looks for business

Linda Eller, director of personal shopping at Neiman Marcus, shows a chenille jacket to Lynn Farris.
(Photographed by the author)

2

CONSUMER DEMAND AND FASHION MARKETING

CAREER FOCUS

Fashion executives, including product managers, merchandisers, designers, buyers, and all the people involved in sales promotion, continually learn about consumer demand in order to get clues as to what products they might need or want. All product development and marketing decisions are based on this information. Fashion executives in touch with the needs of the consumer will be the ones most likely to succeed in an increasingly competitive marketplace.

CHAPTER OBJECTIVES

After reading this chapter you should have attained competence in the following areas:

1. Understanding fashion marketing and the fashion marketing chain
2. Knowledge of technical, economic, and global influences on fashion marketing
3. Awareness of the importance of the consumer on fashion marketing and how demographic and psychographic studies help the industry to determine target markets
4. Knowledge of clothing size and price ranges, style categories, and clothing classifications in women's wear, men's wear, and children's wear

CONSUMER DEMAND

Consumers, *people who buy and use merchandise, are the primary influence on marketing.*

Fashion marketing begins and ends with the consumer. This chapter discusses the effect of consumer demand on marketing. It begins with a survey of consumer groups, demographic and psychographic trends, and how these help to define target markets. The chapter goes on to discuss economic, global, and technological influences on consumers and marketing and ends with a discussion of the marketing chain and fashion categories.

The history of the fashion industry in America is the story of a growing economy that consumed more than it could produce, giving power to the manufacturers. However, as competition increased and population growth slowed, the power has shifted to the consumer. As a result, consumers' demands have shifted the industry from a production to a marketing orientation.

With the change in marketing philosophy, manufacturers now first research what consumers will want to buy and then develop the product. Fashion industry executives continually read and learn about consumer behavior in order to get clues as to what products consumers might need or want to buy in the future. Designer Bill Blass once commented, "you have to understand people to make clothes for them."[1]

Analysts have developed sophisticated marketing research methods to determine consumer wants and needs and managers have emphasized product development to answer those needs.

Sales Promotion

Fashion firms are spending large amounts of money on increased advertising and other promotional activities to *create* consumer demand. The ultimate achievement of advertising is to establish the identity of a particular brand name or store so solidly that it will be preferred over the competition (see Chapters 6, 12, and 15). However, there is a limit to which sales promotion can win acceptance for a fashion. If the public is not ready for a product or is tired of it, no amount of advertising or publicity can gain or hold its acceptance.

CONSUMER GROUPS

Fashion executives try to satisfy the wants and needs of particular **market segments,** *or consumer groups.*

Traditionally, society was divided by income classes. The wealthiest were the most fashionable, because only they could afford to buy expensive clothes. Today the traditional class systems have broken down. Almost all clothing is mass produced, and almost everyone can enjoy fashion on some price level.

Today, fashion marketers try to satisfy the wants and needs of each particular segment of society. Consumer goods are directed at groups of people who have money to spend. Market research firms do sophisticated demographic and psychographic studies for textile and apparel producers and retailers to determine what segments of the population, based on age or life-style, have the most buying power.

Demographic Trends

Demographics are statistical studies of measurable population characteristics such as birth rate, age distribution, and income. Demographic studies show that the American population is aging.

Gray Market

Americans born before 1945 are the most neglected by the designers, retailers, and the media. Yet this age group is fast becoming the biggest segment of the population with the most money to spend. People 50 and older control 77 percent of all financial assets in the United States and 50 percent of all discretionary income. Ken Dychtwald, president of Age Wave research company, says,"They tend to feel 10 to 15 years younger than their actual age, but they've been marketed to as if they were 10 to 15 years older."[2] Studies show that mature people have money to spend and enjoy new products as much as anyone. The fastest growing age segment is currently the 45- to 54-year-old group, indicating that the future will need to cater to a more conservative value-, function-, and quality-oriented customer.[3] One of the most successful women's apparel companies, St. John Knits, caters to the mature woman.

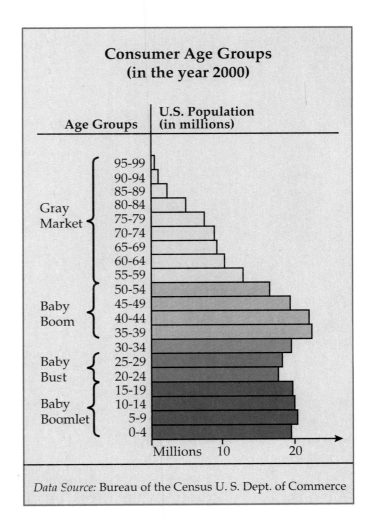

Consumer Age Groups (in the year 2000)

Data Source: Bureau of the Census U. S. Dept. of Commerce

The Postwar Baby Boom

Baby boomers, the age group caused by the increase in the birthrate between 1946 and 1964, are the primary demographic spending group in the United States to influence the apparel market since World War II. In the 1960s this youth-oriented market fostered the growth of junior sportswear, jeans, T-shirts, and other fashions that fit the needs of baby boomers at that time. In the 1970s this generation was responsible for the creation of the upscale "Contemporary" look. By the 1980s this same demographic segment was in

A bridge suit by Linda Allard for Ellen Tracy.
(Courtesy of Ellen Tracy, Inc.)

their thirties and forties and firmly implanted in both career and family building. Their fashion preferences changed along with their life-styles and priorities. Some clever manufacturers changed their images as their customers got older. Ellen Tracy, for example, produced junior sportswear in the 1960s, contemporary in the 1970s, and is now a major "bridge" (one price range lower than designer) resource.

Now the 32 to 50 age bracket is the largest segment of the population. However, the prevalence of too-short skirts and other inappropriate fashion in non-junior categories demonstrates that designers do not consider the aging customer. By the year 2000, half the population will be over 40, and the baby boomers will account for 32 percent of all Americans. Allen Questrom, CEO of Federated Department Stores, points out that "Designers and retailers need to do a better job of merchandising to people over 40."[4]

The Baby Busters

The generation born between 1965 and 1980 is often referred to as Baby Busters because this age bracket is much smaller than the one preceding it. A large amount of media attention is directed at this group, and their fashion tastes are heavily influenced by rock music stars and fashion models. Although this population segment is smaller than its predecessor, these young people are fashion conscious and willing to spend a large percentage of their incomes on fashion. Therefore, designers cater to this group with youthful styles.

The Baby Boomlet

Another potentially powerful consumer group is the Baby Boomlet created by the rise in the birthrate that began in the early 1980s. These are the children of the postwar baby boomers. They have a computer–video orientation that will affect their buying decisions in the future. The impact of this new generation on the fashion market will be evident into the twenty-first century. The growth of the children's wear industry will continue through the 1990s and juniors will again become important before the year 2000. By 2010 the nation will be rather polarized, with the postwar boomers over 50 and the new boomers under 30.

Whatever the age group, market researchers try to pinpoint further delineations of life-styles and resulting fashion preferences.

Ethnic Diversity

Another important demographic trend is the ethnic diversity of the U.S. population. The Immigration and Naturalization Service projects that legal immigration exceeds 700,000 per year. The Census Bureau has determined

Working women have less time to shop and more interest in their families.
(Courtesy of the Santimauro family, photographed by the author.)

that the black, Hispanic, Asian, and Native American segments of the population will all grow much faster than the white majority.[5] People of different cultural backgrounds may look for different things in a fashion purchase. With a multicultural society, retailers and manufacturers cater to various ethnic market segments.

The Working Woman

Today, over 70 percent of the female population aged 20 to 54 works outside the home.[6] It is of great interest to the industry that working women spend about 35 percent more on apparel than nonworking women.[7] For these women, who divide their days between the demands of home and career, time becomes a critical issue. The busy working woman tends to shop less often and favor catalog and convenient, one-stop shopping, which has aided the growth of certain catalogs and super stores.

Large Sizes

Another phenomenon influencing the fashion industry is the increasing number of people wearing larger sizes. As the population has aged, people are getting fatter. In 1980, the average American man, at 5 feet 9 inches tall, weighed 173 pounds; in 1990, he weighed 180 pounds. The average woman, 5 feet 4 inches tall, weighed 144 pounds in 1980 and 153 in 1990. As of 1993, 68 percent of all Americans were overweight. At Haggar, core sizes for its pants used to be sizes 32 to 40; now the core sizes go up to 44.[8]

Psychographic or Life-style Trends

People can share the same demographic characteristics and still be very different from each other. Therefore, manufacturers and retailers often turn to psychographics to further segment and analyze consumer groups and the reasons people use to making buying decisions. *Psychographic* studies use psychological, sociological, and anthropological factors to further separate consumers based on the differences in their life-styles. Observers generally feel that the following are important psychographic or life-style trends:

◆ Concern for the environment: people look for clothing made of natural fibers or with environmentally friendly processes.

◆ Renewed interest in family life: people spend more money on the home and family activities than fashion.

◆ Cocooning: people insulate themselves from crime and world problems by staying home as much as possible, shopping less or shopping by catalog or television.

◆ Value of time: confirming demographic findings, working couples have little free time and prefer to shop by catalog, television shopping channels, or convenient stores.

◆ Decreased materialism: a reaffirmation that people are shopping less.

◆ Emphasis on value: people are looking for their perception of quality at a reasonable price, and value-oriented retailing, such as discount stores, is growing in popularity.

Target Marketing

Manufacturers and retailers try to define their *target market*, the specific market that they want to reach. They use both demographic and psychographic information to find even smaller potential *market niches* within larger markets.

Database Marketing

Fashion merchants are gathering data about consumers in order to strengthen marketing strategies. Through their purchases, consumers unwittingly offer manufacturers and retailers information about their shopping habits, life-styles, and purchases, such as size and color preferences, which is recorded by computer. This information is combined with answers to surveys and other sources, such as sweepstake entries, coupon request forms, and public records, and categorized into *databases*, typical consumer taste profiles for all consumer groups.

Merchants use consumer profiles for their own target group to:

◆ Create new products for this target customer

◆ Find new target markets for existing products

◆ Help find new ways to advertise to these markets
◆ Keep them focused on their customer

Manufacturers and retailers in touch with the needs of their target customer are the ones who succeed in an increasingly competitive marketplace. However, in spite of sophisticated research methods, fashion companies still have a problem understanding changing demographics and creating fashion products that consumers want to buy.

ECONOMIC INFLUENCES ON CONSUMER DEMAND AND MARKETING

Consumer spending, the state of the economy, the international money market, and labor costs have an effect on fashion marketing.

Consumer Spending

The amount of money consumers spend on fashion and other goods depends on their income. Income as it affects spending is measured in three ways: personal income, disposable income, and discretionary income.

Personal income is the gross amount of income from all sources, such as wages, salaries, interest, and dividends.

Disposable income is personal income minus taxes. This amount determines a person's purchasing power.

Discretionary income is income left over after food, lodging, and other necessities have been paid for. This money is available to be spent or saved at will. The increase in discretionary income enjoyed by most people in our society means that more people are able to buy fashion. Young people spend a high portion of their income on fashion. However, apparel expenses become a lower proportion of total personal expenditures for those with mortgages and children to educate.

Purchasing Power

Purchasing power is related to the economic situation. Although incomes in the Western world have risen in recent years, so have prices. Thus, income is meaningful only in relation to the amount of goods and services it can buy, or its *purchasing power*. Inflation, recession, the international value of currency, and productivity affect purchasing power.

Inflation

In an inflationary period such as the United States experienced in the 1980s, people earn more money each year, but higher prices and higher taxes result in little or no real increase in purchasing power. The fashion emphasis of the 1980s was the power suit and luxury accessories, which reflected society's obsession with money and self-interest.

Recession

A recession, such as we experienced in the early 1990s, is a cycle beginning with a decrease in spending. Many companies are forced to cut back production, which results in unemployment and a drop in the gross national product (GNP). Unemployment furthers the cycle of reduced spending.

When the economic situation is unstable, the fashion picture is also unstable. Not only is money in short supply, but people seem to be confused about what they really want. In an economic upswing, colors are basically cheerful and happy, but they have a grayed palette when the economy is in trouble.[9] The "grunge" look during the recession of the early 1990s is a perfect example of this. Also, people are likely to buy conservatively or at least buy fashions that they believe to be of lasting value. The success of discounters such as Wal-Mart during the last recession demonstrated consumers quest for value.

Foreign Exchange Market

When the dollar is strong against other currencies, American consumers are able to buy international merchandise more cheaply. At the same time, American industry is hurt because foreign merchandise competes with domestic goods. Moreover, American exports become too expensive for other countries to buy.

On the other hand, when the dollar is weak (loses value relative to other currencies), then foreign countries can buy American goods more cheaply. This situation encourages American fashion manufacturers to export and is good for business. However, imported goods are more expensive for Americans to buy.

Labor Costs

As people receive higher salaries and live better, the cost of making garments increases. Rising labor costs have made clothing very expensive and caused many manufacturers to search for cheaper sources of labor in the Far East, the Caribbean Basin, Eastern Europe, and elsewhere. This has caused a controversy between American workers, who feel that their jobs are in jeopardy, and proponents of free trade, who feel that consumers should pay the lowest possible price for quality merchandise.

GLOBAL INFLUENCES ON MARKETING

Fierce competition from imports and a saturated domestic market have led to a new global viewpoint in marketing on all levels of the industry.

A major trend in fashion marketing is globalization. Retailers want to give their customers the best quality production at the lowest price. Therefore, ever increasing amounts of textile, apparel, and accessory products are being imported into the United States and the European Economic Community (EEC) because of the availability of cheaper labor abroad. United States and European manufacturers compete with labor rates of as little as 25 cents per hour in China, Thailand, Pakistan, and India and 15 cents an hour in Indonesia.[10]

World trade in apparel and accessories is growing despite high tariffs, an elaborate system of quotas, and drastic currency fluctuations. Many countries may be involved in the production of a single garment. For example, a garment could be designed in New York of Italian fabric, made in Hong Kong, and then distributed all over the world by importers who make the goods available to retail store buyers.

Imports

Fierce competition from imports has caused the American industry to lose over 50 percent of its domestic market and has resulted in consolidations to salvage what is left. *Imports* are goods that are brought in from a foreign country to sell. The people or firms that import goods are called *importers*. Manufacturers and retailers can also be importers. There are three types of imports.

Imported Fashion Merchandise

The first type is the importation of fashion merchandise designed and produced by foreign designers and manufacturers and purchased by retailers at international markets. The United States has long imported fashion from Paris, woolens from the British Isles, sweaters from Scandinavia, and leather goods from Italy. Currently, the European Economic Community, followed by the United States, is the largest importer and consumer of apparel in the world.

Imported Fabrics

Since 1980 textile imports have increased from 4 billion square meters to 12.4 billion.[11] This corresponds to the enormous growth of the textile industries of Japan, China, Taiwan, Korea, and India. Furthermore, manufacturers tend to use fabrics from the region where production is done, thereby taking sales away from U. S. domestic textile producers.

Imported Apparel or Accessory Production

The third type of import occurs when manufacturers become importers and contract production in a foreign country where labor is cheaper (see Chapter 10 for a complete discussion of sourcing). More than 61 percent of the apparel purchased in the United States is made either entirely abroad or of imported fabric.[12] This huge increase in imports in recent years has stimulated a great deal of controversy. The controversy revolves around two key points: the balance of trade and the loss of jobs at home.

Balance of Trade — *creates a "trade deficit"*

The *balance of trade* is the difference in value between a country's exports and its imports. Ideally, the two figures should be about equal. Lately, how-

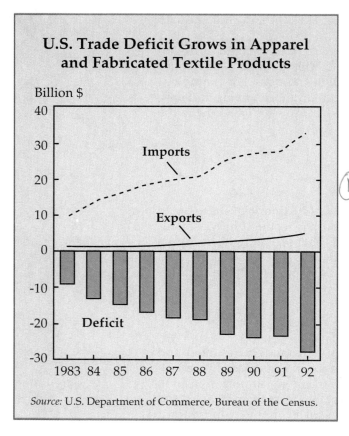

U.S. Trade Deficit Grows in Apparel and Fabricated Textile Products

Billion $

Imports

Exports

Deficit

1983 84 85 86 87 88 89 90 91 92

Source: U.S. Department of Commerce, Bureau of the Census.

ever, the United States has been importing much more than it exports, sending American dollars abroad to pay for these goods and creating a huge *trade deficit*. Many people feel that we should import less goods to balance trade. Others feel that the consumer should be given the best merchandise at the best price regardless of the balance of trade.

Labor Versus Free Trade

Another controversy between labor and proponents of free trade concerns the second type of importing: offshore or overseas production. There has been an enormous increase of imported apparel and accessories, especially from China (which has replaced Hong Kong as the largest foreign apparel supplier to the United States), the Caribbean Basin, India, Indonesia, Malaysia, Thailand, Sri Lanka, Bangladesh, and Macao.[13]

Labor unions complain that overseas production steals thousands of domestic jobs in textile and apparel production. The textile industry has lost at least 350,000 jobs, and 1000 plants have closed since 1980.[14]

Retailers argue that workers overseas produce quality merchandise at lower prices, offering American consumers lower prices. Because both arguments have validity, a solution to the problem is difficult to resolve.

Proponents of *free trade* (trade without restrictions) believe that in the long run it would be best if world trade were based on specialization. That is, each nation would contribute to the world market what it produces best at the most reasonable cost. In this way consumers would obtain the most value for their money, as well as a wide choice of merchandise from around the world.

Import Tariffs or Duties

Duties or *tariffs* are customs charges imposed on imports in an attempt to protect domestic industry. However, even with duties, imported goods are still usually less expensive. Duties vary according to the type of garment, the fiber content, and whether the fabric is woven or knitted. There are no quotas on silk, flax, and ramie because they are not produced in the United States and therefore are not considered to compete with American industry.

Harmonized Tariff Schedule (HTS) The Harmonized Tariff Schedule is an international system of product classification used since 1988 for international customs clearance and the collection of data on imports and exports. Formerly, every country had its own system of naming or numbering imports and exports. Now a system of 6-digit codes allows participating countries to classify traded goods on a common basis.

③ Quota Allocations

Many governments also regulate imports by means of *quotas*, regulations that control the quantity of imported merchandise. Quotas are negotiated agreements between two trading countries and are allocated for a 12-month period. Before considering overseas sourcing, a manufacturer or importer must be sure that there is enough quota to allow the merchandise in question to be produced in that country. Frequently, all the allocations are already held by manufacturers or by governments in a given country. "Capturing quota" is often a determining factor as to where goods are made.

World Trade Organization

The World Trade Organization (WTO), the new trade governing body to replace GATT, is located in Geneva. The organization has members from 124 countries that together account for about 90 percent of world merchandise trade. Its basic objectives are to achieve the expansion of trade and the progressive liberalization of world trade. Additional functions of the WTO are to set rules governing trade behavior, resolve disputes between members, and serve as a forum for trade negotiations. The WTO now governs agreements made under GATT.

The General Agreement on Tariffs and Trade

Created in the United Nations after World War II, the purpose of GATT was to stimulate economic growth in war-torn and developing countries and to reform the global trading system, which was plagued by high tariffs and import quotas.

Members of GATT met at eight negotiating conferences known as *rounds*, which lasted several years. At the Uruguay Round, 1986 to 1994, issues included liberalization of foreign investment, the protection of intellectual

President Clinton signing the GATT agreement on December 8, 1994, with Vice President Al Gore, U.S. Trade Representative Mickey Kantor, Senator Bob Dole, Speaker Thomas Foley, and Secretary of the Treasury Lloyd Bentsen looking on. *(Courtesty of the White House.)*

property, such as computer software, trademarks, and videos, and the fate of the Multifiber Arrangement.

Multifiber Arrangement

Under the jurisdiction of GATT's textile committee, the MFA was negotiated in 1974 as a transitional arrangement to bridge the gap between previous trade restraints and trade liberalization policies. Approval has been reached to phase out the MFA over a 10-year period. American industry does not expect a major impact on trade until 2005, when the phase-out is complete. During this period, the United States will cut tariffs on textiles an average of 11.6 percent and apparel 9.2 percent.[15] Worldwide quotas are to be removed from 51 percent of textile and apparel products. However, despite reduction, textiles and apparel will remain one of the most heavily protected sectors.

The biggest change for importers is the *rule of origin* clause for apparel imports. Effective July 1996, origin for quota purposes will be determined by where a garment is sewn rather than where it is cut. This will end the process known as *outward processing*, which allowed garments sewn in China to come into the United States under liberal Hong Kong quotas. Since most of our imports are sewn in China, it will require importers to find new sources for production.

Exports

The fastest growing economies in the world are the Southeast Asian countries, Eastern Europe, and Latin America. At its current growth rate, China will have the largest economy in the world in 2025.[16] No longer will these countries be simply a place to source goods, but will also be attractive new markets due to their growing middle classes.

To help balance imports, there is a growing trend for American manufacturers to sell their merchandise to foreign retailers either through direct export or by licensing arrangements. Import and export duties and restrictions have kept this business small, but when the U.S. dollar loses value relative to other currencies, exporting becomes especially profitable.

An increasing number of American manufacturers are exhibiting at industry trade shows in France, Switzerland, Germany, Italy, the United Kingdom, and Japan. Some manufacturers that are already exporting are Liz Claiborne, Donna Karan, and Levi Strauss (see Chapter 12). So far the United States has had the most success exporting to Canada, Mexico, and Japan. Latin America is the fastest growing market for U.S. exports.

North American Free Trade Agreement

The North American Free Trade Agreement (NAFTA) creates a free market (devoid of import duties) of 560 million people in Canada, the United States, and Mexico. The agreement hopes to promote economic growth through the expansion of trade and investment opportunities within the free-trade area.

Canada and Mexico are already the largest trading partners of the United States and, in turn, the United States accounts for more than two-thirds of their total trade. Since the Canada–U.S. Free Trade Agreement went into effect in 1989, trade between the two countries has increased.

Mexico stands to profit enormously from NAFTA. Mexico is already a major sourcing spot for the United States and under NAFTA could become even more important to the United States than the Far East. It is hoped that NAFTA will give textile firms the opportunity to ship fabric to Mexico to be made into garments. Importers could monitor production quality and receive shipments within days rather than weeks. In addition, Mexico stands to become a greater consumer country as its standard of living improves. To protect sourcing that has been developed since the Caribbean Basin Initiative (CBI) began in 1987, it is hoped that Caribbean countries will be given the same preferred treatment as Mexico.

Opponents of NAFTA say that it will be devastating to our economy, causing more job losses and plant closings because we cannot compete with their low wages. Proponents anticipate that NAFTA should lead to increased opportunities south of the border and may serve as a model for similar agreements with other Latin American countries.

TECHNOLOGICAL INFLUENCES ON THE CONSUMER AND MARKETING

Changes in technology, such as in communications, computers, and production, have a great effect on the marketing of fashion.

Communications

Modern communications media bring different cultures into contact, making people more aware of other life-styles and modes of dress. In the past it took many months for a magazine showing the latest Paris fashions to be printed and shipped to its readers. Now, computers, fax, and television bring fashion from around the world into our homes instantly.

◆ Fashion industry executives are able to communicate with their office from anywhere in the world on their lap-top computers via satellite.

◆ A facsimile (fax) machine can send a fashion sketch around the world in seconds.

◆ Television has become a vehicle for home shopping (see Chapter 13), infomercials, and direct-response commercials.

◆ The 800 number revolutionized telephone ordering. Now, telephone companies are spending millions of dollars to install fiber-optic cable to carry digital signals to facilitate interactive shopping.

◆ Interactive computers and television will allow manufacturers and retailers to form a new kind of relationship with their customers. However, researchers predict that it will be at least 1998 before regulatory issues and rewiring snafus are sorted out to allow for fully interactive shopping services.

As a result of modern communications, the public is quickly made aware of the existence of new styles. Thus, one of the greatest impacts on fashion is the acceleration of *change* (see Chapter 3). Communication also speeds up the process of copying, so merchandise produced throughout the world tends to look similar.

Computer Technology

Computers have become indispensable to the fashion industry. Fashion business executives work with computer experts to develop software programs based on their needs. If fed the proper information, these programs bring order out of chaos by keeping track of or controlling planning, production, inventory, and distribution.

- ◆ In the planning stages, merchandisers rely on consumer statistics and sales data immediately available to them by computer.
- ◆ In textile production, computers run machines and aid in textile design.
- ◆ In apparel manufacturing, computers can help design apparel and accessories and make, grade, and lay out patterns in marker form.
- ◆ At all levels of the industry, merchandise information systems (MIS) control inventory and distribution, making it easier and faster to fill orders or replenish stock.

Electronic Data Interchange

In an effort to combat imports with faster response to customer needs than imports can provide, textile and computer executives developed a computer strategy called *Quick Response* (QR). This is an attempt to reduce waiting time in ordering and distribution between textile producers, apparel manufacturers, and retailers by forming cooperative alliances between all levels of the industry via *electronic data interchange* (EDI), the exchange of

A computer-automated knitting system.
(Courtesy of Saurer Textile Systems)

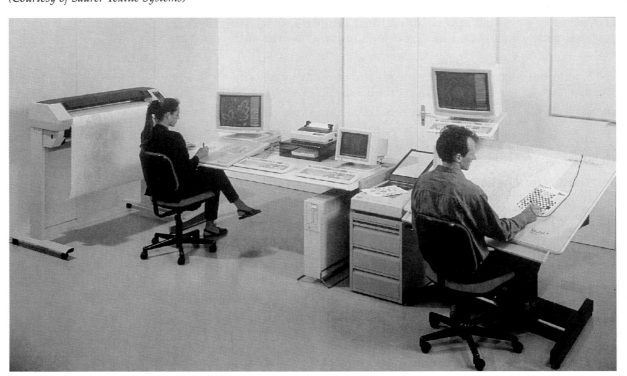

business data between two parties by means of computer. Supporters of Quick Response point out that the greatest dollar loss to industry is time lost in distribution from fiber to final sale.

All goods are given *universal product codes* (UPC) , which identify style, color, size, price, fabrication, and vendor. These bar codes are laser scanned and the information is fed through the EDI pipeline to manufacturers. Standardized codes and linkage systems have been developed throughout the industry.

The goal of the Quick Response strategy is to enable the fabric producer to supply and resupply the manufacturer upon shorter notice and to replenish automatically. Issuing smaller initial cuts until a style is tested helps to prevent markdowns, and quickly replenishing stock with best sellers means higher sales. When a particular style is selling well at retail, coded information on that style (including the best-selling colors, fabrics, and sizes) immediately informs the retail buyer to replenish stock, the apparel manufacturer to issue new cuts, and the fabric producer to send more fabric to the apparel manufacturer.

Of course, Quick Response or automatic replenishment needs the complete cooperation of each level of the industry, a willingness to supply on a reorder basis, and the flexibility to sell smaller quantities of fabric and issue smaller, more frequent cuts. This allows product development to be done closer to the selling season in order to better anticipate consumer preferences. So far, automatic replenishment is primarily suited to basic goods and volume manufacturers.

Information Technology

Computer technology is providing fashion business executives and consumers alike with fashion information and the means to communicate. Commercial networks such as America OnLine, Prodigy, and CompuServe can provide the following:

- Internet access, including services such as World Wide Web (WWW)
- Electronic mail (E-mail) services
- Access to bulletin boards such as alt.fashion
- Interaction with fashion editors
- Databases and directories such as Fashion Group's Fashion Access Network (FAN)
- Communications with suppliers and buyers
- Shopping services (see Chapter 13)

Production Technology

Modern technology makes fashion production more efficient. Computer-aided spinning, design, weaving, knitting, dyeing, and finishing allows our domestic textile industry to compete with imports. Modern agricultural developments have improved the quantity and quality of natural fibers. Technological research has made man-made fibers possible, as well as finishes that change fabric characteristics (see Chapter 5).

The development of modern production machinery, such as power sewing machines and cutting tools, has streamlined the process of manufacturing. Today's power machines can run faster than a car engine, sewing over 5000 stitches per minute. Modern cutting techniques include the use of computers, water jets, and laser beams. Computer technology has again revolutionized manufacturing with computer-aided design, pattern making, grading, cutting, unit and modular production systems, pressing and distribution systems (see Chapter 10).

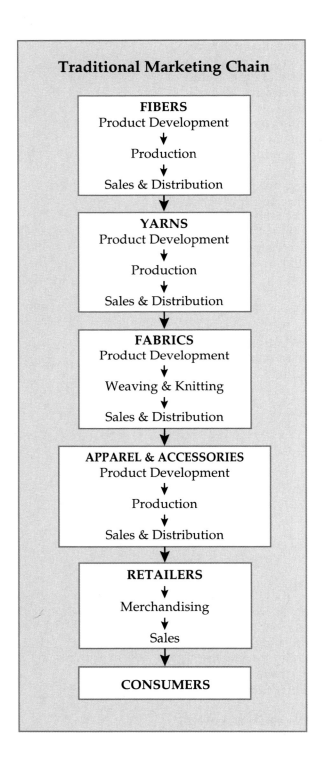

Traditional Marketing Chain

FIBERS
Product Development
↓
Production
↓
Sales & Distribution
↓

YARNS
Product Development
↓
Production
↓
Sales & Distribution
↓

FABRICS
Product Development
↓
Weaving & Knitting
↓
Sales & Distribution
↓

APPAREL & ACCESSORIES
Product Development
↓
Production
↓
Sales & Distribution
↓

RETAILERS
↓
Merchandising
↓
Sales
↓

CONSUMERS

THE MARKETING CHAIN

The **marketing chain** *is the flow of product development, production, and distribution from concept to consumer.*

Fashion marketing is the entire process of research, planning, promoting, and distributing the raw materials, apparel, and accessories that consumers want to buy. It involves everyone in the fashion industry and occurs throughout the entire channel of distribution. Marketing is the power behind the product development, production, and distribution of fibers and fabrics; leathers, furs, and trimmings; the design, merchandising, production, and distribution of apparel and accessories; and the retailing, image building, and promotion of it all.

The traditional *chain* of marketing textiles to apparel manufacturers to retailers to consumers is no longer clearly divided. The old relationships between suppliers and retailers are disappearing.

Manufacturers as Retailers

Many manufacturers are opening their own retail stores. The idea is not new in Europe. Laura Ashley, for example, produces its own fabrics and apparel and sells them both in company stores worldwide. It is a usual practice for couture houses in Paris, such as Chanel or Yves St. Laurent, to have their own shops to sell their ready-to-wear and accessories.

In America, it is also common for men's wear companies, such as Brooks Brothers and Hartmarx (Hastings), or shoe companies, such as Nine West or Johnston & Murphy, to have their own retail stores. However, the idea is rather new for women's wear companies. In an effort to expand market share, in an atmosphere of intense competition, and to be able to merchandise their entire collections directly to consumers, manufacturers are becoming retailers. Firms such as Ralph Lauren, Donna Karan, Adrienne Vittadini, Nicole Miller, Levi Strauss, ABS, Esprit, and Osh Kosh B'Gosh now have their own stores. See Chapter 12 for more information.

Retailers as Manufacturers

It also works in reverse. Retailers have become manufacturers. The Gap and Ann Taylor, for example, now design their own merchandise and have it produced. These stores are considered to be *private label* merchants, those that sell merchandise with the store's name on the label. Multibrand retailers also produce private label merchandise, such as Federated's Charter Club or I.N.C. (see Chapter 14).

FASHION CATEGORIES

In response to consumer demand and changes in consumer life-styles, manufacturers and retailers have developed various size and price ranges, as well as categories for styling and clothing type.

Variety in dress has resulted from manufacturers' responses to changes in our habits and roles and the increase in consumer purchasing power. There is now clothing for all occasions and life-styles. Manufacturers specialize in clothing type (or have a separate label for each), age of target customer, price range, and often gender. There is less specializing today in size ranges. Retailers have separate departments for each category, price range, and size range.

There has been a recent breakdown of some categories, making it difficult for retailers to find a suitable location for merchandise in their stores. In our value-conscious marketplace, consumers seek multipurpose, multiuse clothing. They look for apparel that is wearable in a variety of settings: office, social activities, gym, home, or vacation. As a result, gymwear has become streetwear; underwear is outerwear.

Women's Wear

Clothing Categories

There are many types of women's apparel, including dresses, social apparel, suits, outerwear, sportswear, activewear, and lingerie. There are also specialty categories, such as bridal gowns and maternity clothes, and a huge array of accessories.

Dresses are single garments or two pieces on the same hanger priced as one unit. Styles range from tailored to simple, comfortable dresses for casual wear. Dresses are easy to wear; no thought is required for coordination.

Social apparel includes dress-up attire such as long and short cocktail dresses, dressy pant ensembles, and evening and bridal gowns.

Activewear from Fila's Pro Beach Volleyball Collection. *(Courtesy of Fila Sports, Inc.)*

Suits are jackets and skirts (or pants) sold together as units. Suits range from casual to tailored. There is a trend to casual dressing at the office, but it remains to be seen if professional women will give up their "power" suits.

Outerwear includes coats, capes, and jackets with a primarily protective function. Outerwear can be divided into four categories: traditional wool and wool blends, outdoor–ski anoraks in performance fabrics such as microfibers, leathers, and furs, all available in both classic and fashion styles.

Sportswear is any combination of tops and bottoms, such as jackets, skirts, pants, shorts, blouses, and shirts, that are priced separately so that the customer can combine them as desired. Sportswear lines are organized as separates or as coordinated sportswear (pieces intended to be mixed and matched). Sportswear is popular due to the variety of looks that can be made by combining separates. American designers have excelled in this category that suits informal American life-styles.

Activewear is one of the hottest categories of apparel today, fueled by the popularity of fitness. Activewear is subcategorized into two segments: fitness wear, worn by people who actively participate in sports, and active looks, worn for spectator sports or simply as streetwear. Activewear includes bike shorts, leggings, T-shirts, crop tops, jogging sets, unitards, sweatsuits, and jackets. Activewear is increasingly fashionable as designers put these looks into their collections.

Swimwear makers are beginning to cater to the baby boom market with bulge concealers, push-up bras, extra torso length, and other inner construction. Manufacturers are also adding special sizes and cover ups.

Lingerie, including innerwear, bodywear, sleepwear, and loungewear, is also enjoying increased sales. The popularity of lingerie is partly due to the fashion of wearing corsets to show, as Karl Lagerfeld introduced under suit jackets, and the marketing style of Victoria's Secret. The more fitted look of today's fashion is also influencing the rise in sales of slimming underwear.

Accessories, as discussed in Chapter 11, give consumers an easy way to update their wardrobes with scarves, hats, handbags, footwear, and hosiery. The popularity of particular accessories is cyclical, such as belts with waist interest. Functional accessories, such as backpacks and sun hats, have become fashionable as well.

Size Ranges

Each size range caters to a different figure type. Generally, today's sizing standards are based on more realistic measurements than in the past. However, each manufacturer has its own interpretation of standardized sizing. Designer clothes may deliberately be labeled one size smaller so that the customer who spends a lot of money can feel good about being a size 10 instead of a 12. Some manufacturers such as Liz Claiborne try to accommodate a variety of body types by using a variety of fit models. Women's size ranges include Junior, Missy, Petite, and Large sizes.

Junior customers, sizes 3 to 13, have a less developed figure and a shorter back-waist length (a higher waistline) than missy figures. This figure is usually equated with a slim, young customer.

Missy sizes 6 to 16 (or 4 to 14) are for the mature female figure, usually based on a 5-foot, 7-inch height. In missy separates, some blouses and sweaters are sized 30 to 36 (8 to 14), or small, medium, and large.

Petite sizes are created for the woman under 5 feet, 4 inches. Sizes range from 0 to 16. Most manufacturers limit the size range to 4 to 14.

Large or women's sizes range from 14W to 32W but are usually limited to 16W to 26W. Sometimes these sizes are represented as 1X (16 to 18), 2X (20 to 22), and 3X (24 to 26). Large-sized petites are marked WP.

Fashion for petite and large-sized women was virtually ignored by the fashion industry until 1977. Statistics now show that 54 percent of the total female American population wears either petite or large sizes. Among women over 40, 40 percent wear size 14 or larger.[17] Prestigious manufacturers such as Givenchy, Ellen Tracy, and Anne Klein II are now catering to special sizes. There is tremendous growth opportunity for manufacturers in special sizes because there are no extra costs for styling, only for new patterns.

TYPICAL RELATIONSHIP OF STYLE, SIZE, AND PRICE RANGES IN WOMEN'S WEAR

Style Range	Styling	Age	Size Range	Figure	Price Range
Designer	Unique, top-name designer fashion	25 and up	Missy 4-12	Missy: mature, slim	Designer
Bridge	Designer fashion	25 and up	Missy 4-12	Missy: mature, slim	Bridge
Missy	Adaptations of fashion looks	25 and up	Missy 4-14	Missy: mature, 5'7" block	Better to budget
Petites	Same as missy	25 and up	Petite 0-14	Missy: under 5'4"	Better to budget
Women's or large sizes	Same as missy plus some junior looks	18 and up	16-26W or 16-26WP	Missy: large size + some petite	Better to budget
Contemporary	Trendy	20-40	Missy 4-12	Missy: slim	Better to budget
Junior	Youthful, trendy, figure-conscious	13-25	Juniors 3-15	Not fully developed	Better to budget

Manufacturers still have to deal with a majority of figures that do not fit sizing standards. One reason that sportswear is so popular is that it gives consumers the opportunity to mix sizes to accommodate their less than perfect figures. Women, too, do not have the benefit of free alterations at retail stores as men do.

Styling and Price Ranges

Apparel is also classified by style range. Style ranges grew out of age groups, price, and size ranges.

Couture. This term is reserved for fashion that is made to order to fit an individual client's measurements. These clothes are the most luxurious and the most expensive, between $5000 and $50,000 for a single garment, and reserved for a very small international clientele. Examples of couturiers include Europeans Karl Lagerfeld, Christian Lacroix, Yves St. Laurent, Valentino, and Americans Arnold Scassi and John Anthony.

Designer. This category pertains to ready-to-wear from successful designers who own their own business or have their name on the label. The high prices they charge, $1000 to $5000, allow them to use the best of fabrics and quality mass production. Examples of designer collections include Giorgio Armani, Donna Karan, Ralph Lauren, as well as the ready-to-wear collections of the couturiers and all the designers listed in Chapter 8.

Bridge. This styling and price range was created to give consumers a less expensive alternative to designer fashion. Bridge is simply a step down in price from designer achieved by using a less expensive fabric or different production methods. Some designers have secondary lines such as CK from Calvin Klein, Donna Karan's DKNY, Versus from Versace, or Emporio from Armani. Other collections, such as Ellen Tracy, Dana Buchman, or Adrienne Vittadini, are designed specifically for the bridge market.

Young Bridge. As prices go up, new categories are invented. Young Bridge is a new category between the bridge and better price ranges. Resources include Finity and Episode.

Contemporary. This is a revived category aimed at the style-conscious woman who wants more fashion than Missy but does not want to pay designer prices. Again, price ranges vary from Young Bridge to Budget. Resources include ABS, BCBG, Kenar, Laundry, Max Studio, Parallel, and Ralph by Ralph Lauren.

Missy. This styling category provides more conservative adaptations of proven or accepted designer looks. Missy lines utilize less expensive fabrics and less extreme silhouettes. Missy styling is available in a variety of quality and price ranges: better, moderate, or budget. Vendors include J H Collectibles, Jones New York, Koret, Leslie Fay, and Liz Claiborne. The moderate price ranges are getting more attention in the value-oriented 1990s.

Junior. The style range grew out of Junior sizing; young styling for a young figure. Styling is heavily influenced by the rock music scene and by street fashion in Europe. It also tends to be body conscious. The late 1990s will see a resurgence of growth in this area as the 1980s baby boomlet kids reach their teens. Typical labels include Byer, Esprit, Necessary Objects, and XOXO.

Designers Karen Harman and Dana Buchman check fit on a model at Dana Buchman, a bridge resource.
(Courtesy of Dana Buchman)

Within retail stores, there is sometimes overlapping among these categories. Retailers are free to put lines where they best fit at each particular store. Classification depends in part on the size, location, and clientele of the retail store. Liz Claiborne might be found in the missy department of a large downtown specialty store and in the better department of a suburban branch store. Depending on the store, Anna Sui's collection might be classified as bridge, young designer, or contemporary.

As manufacturers or designer names increase in popularity, they add lines in other categories in order to grow. Claiborne, Vittadini, and Ellen Tracy now make dress lines in addition to sportswear. Claiborne also added men's wear collections. Ralph Lauren, on the other hand, started by designing men's wear and later added women's. Other designers and manufacturers, such as Jessica McClintock and Generra, have added children's wear lines. They also add price ranges, such as the designer's secondary lines at lower prices. However, they trade up as well. Moderate manufacturer Liz Claiborne added the Dana Buchman bridge collection (see Chapter 12).

As women's designers enter the men's wear market and vice versa, and with the popularity of men's sportswear, the production and marketing techniques in men's and women's wear are becoming similar.

Men's sportswear and outerwear from KM by Krizia. *(Courtesy of the Hartmarx Corporation)*

Men's Wear

Men's clothing, too, has changed as a result of changes in their interests and more casual life-styles. Their wardrobes, formerly limited to suits, slacks, and sport shirts, have expanded along with their activities, and increased clothing choices have made them more fashion conscious. They have learned from their fathers to buy quality, fit, and durability, as well as style.

The electronics and marketing fields have paved the way toward casual dress at the office. Many companies have instituted "casual Fridays," and some have found it to be so popular that they have made it an everyday option. There are many theories as to why this is happening. Some authorities feel that members of the baby boom generation, who are now the business executives, are trying to stay young. Others feel that middle-aged men are just more interested in comfort. Also, fewer companies are operating in city center locations and more and more people are working at home.

Due to the easing of corporate dress restrictions, the men's wear industry is in a state of flux. Men's suit sales have decreased, while sportswear is enjoying tremendous growth. Whereas suits represented half of men's wardrobe purchases in the past, men's clothing purchases now are divided equally among suits, furnishings and accessories, and sportswear. As tailored clothing becomes more casual, the category distinctions become blurred. There is an intermixing of business and leisure wardrobes: an Armani suit jacket over jeans or a shirt and tie replaced by a T-shirt.

Casual does not mean cheap or sloppy. By the time a man has purchased all the necessary pieces in a sportswear outfit, it may cost as much as a traditional suit, shirt, and tie. Casual looks are also more confusing for the consumer. Men wonder how to present themselves as successful professionals in casual wear. Some companies, such as Hartmarx, are using hang tags and booklets to tell the customer how to wear the new sportswear looks.

Clothing Categories

There are now as many categories available to men as to women. Many designers and manufacturers, including Ralph Lauren, Tommy Hilfiger, and Hugo Boss, have lines in several men's wear categories. Stores have increased square footage in men's wear areas and use aggressive display and promotional techniques to lure their increasingly fashion-wise male customers. Categories include the following:

Tailored clothing includes suits, tuxedos, overcoats, topcoats, sport coats, and separate trousers for business and evening wear. Tailored clothing requires lengthy, time-consuming, costly production and retailers need to inventory many sizes.

Furnishings include dress shirts, neckwear, underwear, hosiery, robes, pajamas, shoes, and boots.

Sportswear comprises sport jackets, knit or woven related separates, sweaters, and casual trousers that fill the demand for more leisure and casual wear.

Active sportswear includes all garments needed for sports or exercise, such as windbreakers, ski jackets, jogging suits, and tennis shorts.

Work clothes, such as overalls, work shirts, and pants required by laborers, have become popular for leisure wear.

Accessories include small leather goods such as wallets, shoes, boots, belts, jewelry such as cuff links, scarves, gloves, and eyewear.

Styling

The styling creativity and diversity now apparent in men's wear are a result of men's desire to have appropriate clothing for their leisure acitivities. However, so far there are not as many styling categories for men's wear as there are for women.

Designer Styling. Internationally recognized designers often set fashion directions in men's wear. Giorgio Armani has led the way to casual, soft suits that can be worn at the office or for leisure activities. American designers Ralph Lauren and Calvin Klein are also leaders in men's fashion. Most designers have both suit and sportswear collections.

Traditional Styling. Classic suit makers like Gieves & Hawkes, Oxxford, Hickey-Freeman, Hartmarx, and Brooks Brothers (retail brand) or updated collections like Tommy Hilfiger are influenced by traditional tailoring. The styling is somewhat influenced by the less-structured designer looks, but the primary interest is in a wide variety of suiting fabrications. Hilfiger is particulary noted for interesting combinations of patterns.

Traditional sportswear is also classic in styling. Formerly centered around tennis or golf looks, there is now a wide variety of clothing for every activity from brands such as Polo, LaCoste, and Dockers.

A traditional suit from Hart Schaffner & Marx.
(Courtesy of the Hartmarx Corporation)

Contemporary. This styling is usually less expensive than designer, trendier, and aimed at a younger customer. Examples include Perry Ellis, KM by Krizia, and Nautica and Gap (a retail brand) sportswear.

Price Ranges

Custom-tailored suits from Savile-Row in London, for example, cost over $3000. Custom-tailored suits are made with the finest construction and fabrics. Much of the inner, hidden construction is done by hand.

Designer ready-made suits at retail prices run upward from $1000 and sportcoats cost upward from $500. Designer suits and sportswear are also made from fine fabrics, but they are not made to measure and quality varies.

Bridge suits and sportswear, like women's wear, are a step down in price from designer. This can also mean a step down in fabric quality and workmanship.

Moderate suits have a broad range of prices, usually from $325 to $650, sportcoats $200 to $450, and slacks $40 to $90. Many large retailers, such as Macy's and Nordstrom, rely heavily on private label merchandise for this price range in order to be able to control price.

Popular-priced suits are those under $325, the most affordable price range. Many discounters and mass merchants also offer private label merchandise at this price range.

Size Ranges

Men's suits range in size from 36 to 44 (with additional large sizes to 50), originally based on chest measurements. Lengths are designated after the size number: R for regular, S for short, and L for long. European sizes are 46 to 54 (add 10 to each American size). Young men's sizes have a narrower fit in the jacket and hip and a shorter rise in the trouser than regular men's sizes. There has been an attempt to simplify men's sizing because traditional sizing requires a huge inventory of many combinations of chest and length measurements. Men also enjoy free alteration services at most men's stores and departments.

Dress shirts are sized by collar measurement (inches in America and centimeters in Europe) and sleeve length. Sport shirts and sweaters are sized in small, medium, large, and extra large. Trousers are sized by waist and inseam measurements. Dress slacks are left unhemmed to be finished by the store's tailor as a customer service.

Children's Wear

The children's wear business is very complicated because each size range is a separate market. Children's wear is also highly competitive because the consumer is extremely value conscious. Parents do not want to spend much money on clothes their children will quickly outgrow.

Children's wear manufacturers often produce both dresses and sportswear to protect their businesses from shifts in fashion preferences. Some men's and women's wear companies, such as Esprit and Polo, also produce children's lines, but others have tried and found it a difficult business. Children's manufacturers, too, have had stiff competition from Baby Gap and Kids Gap and all private label programs. However, a steady domestic birthrate of around 4 million per year is keeping the children's wear market afloat.[18]

Categories

It is very difficult to categorize children's wear. Categories change with each size and price range. Also, boundaries between categories are becoming increasingly blurred. Some casual dresses fall into sportswear classifications; some dresses fall into tailored clothing classifications. Children's wear, too, has become more casual as today's children lead very active lives.

A group of children's wear from Cary Children's Clothes, Inc. *(Courtesy of Cary Children's Clothes, Inc., photographed by designer Cary Nowell)*

Girls' dresses are available in all size and price ranges. Holiday and spring are the biggest seasons for special-occasion dresses. Some girls' dresses, jumpers, jackets, and skirts are considered tailored clothing.

Boys' traditional clothing groups blazers, other dress jackets, suits, dress pants, and dress shorts.

Sportswear comprises T-shirts, jeans, pants, shorts, overalls, jumpsuits, leggings, girls' skirts, boys' shirts, sweatshirts, sweatpants, and sweatsuits in knits and wovens, particularly denim and fleece. Boys' wear has become very casual and tops outsell bottoms.

Swimwear groups swimwear and beach cover ups.

Outerwear includes dress coats, all-weather coats, raincoats, ski jackets, windbreakers, and snow suits.

Sleepwear includes layette gowns and saques, blanket sleepers, pajamas, nightgowns, nightshirts, and robes. A major issue in this category is the Consumer Product Safety requirement that sleepwear be made out of polyester so that it can have a flame-retardant finish. However, consumers want pure cotton and therefore are buying playclothes to use as sleepwear.

Accessories, such as shoes, hats, gloves, scarves, hair accessories, sunglasses, jewelry, bags, backpacks, hosiery (tights and socks) and underwear; belts, caps, and ties for boys; and infant accessories (bibs, booties) are making an important fashion statement for children, too. Hats have been particularly strong to protect children from the sun and have become a fashion statement. Some manufacturers are including accessories with their apparel, priced as a unit.

Sizing

Children's wear sizing is separated by age groups.

Newborn sizes are Layette (0 to 11 pounds), 3, 6, and 9 months.

Infant sizes are based on age in months, usually 12, 18, and 24 months. In Europe, sizes are based on the length of the baby or the height of the child.

Toddler apparel, for the child who has learned to walk, is sized 2T, 3T, and 4T.

At this point, sizes separate for boys and girls.

Little girls' apparel is sized 4 to 6X; big girls sizes are 7 to 16 (some companies manufacture sizes 2 to 10 or extra-small to extra-large); the developing adolescent girl wears preteen 6 to 14; and the young teen wears young junior 3 to 13.

Boys' sizes are 4 to 7 and 8 to 20.

Styling

The styling of children's wear changes considerably by size range. The only styling differentiation is traditional versus trendy.

Infants, Toddlers, and Young Children. In the case of young children, the consumer is a parent, grandparent, or other adult. Parents want their children's clothes to reflect their own taste. "There are still many parents that want people to look at their child and say 'that is the cutest outfit I've ever seen.'"[19] Many parents are tending to dress their children more as little adults than as babies.

Ease of dressing, washability, durability, and versatility are important design considerations in clothing for young children. For infants and toddlers who have to be dressed, crotch snaps and generous necklines are important. For the toddler, ease of dressing, such as elastic waistlines, is also important because children want to dress themselves.

Novelty, color, and conversational prints are important in infant, toddler, and young children's wear. Apparel printed with licensed cartoon or television characters has also been a phenomenal success.

Older Children. Older children have more definite opinions on what they want to wear, partly because of advertising, television exposure, and peer group pressure. This development has had an effect on styling in that many childrens' wear manufacturers follow junior trends for girls and young men's trends for boys.

Junior resources, such as Eber and Byer, are finding success in the 7 to 14 size range and even 4 to 6X. Some men's wear companies, such as Tommy Hilfiger and Ralph Lauren's Polo, are making boys' wear. In this age range, too, printed apparel with sport teams, celebrities, and brand names, such as Nike or Champion, has been extemely popular.

Price Ranges

In children's wear, price ranges are broader than in women's or men's wear. Also, some manufacturers produce lines in several price ranges and often manufacture for both boys and girls in multiple size ranges. The brand examples are a mixture of all size ranges.

Better resources provide fashion direction, quality fabrics, and workmanship. Vendors include Dorissa, Sylvia Whyte, Monkey Wear, Oilily, Polo, and Tommy Hilfiger.

Moderate includes a wide range of prices and labels at average prices, such as Baby Togs, Eagle's Eye, Esprit, Flap Doodles, Gotcha, Hartstrings, Little Me, Osh Kosh B'Gosh, Quiksilver, Rare Editions, and Youngsport.

Popular-priced merchandise is offered by Byer, Eber, Carter's, Healthtex, and Rampage.

In children's wear, too, retailers often offer private label merchandise in the moderate and popular-priced ranges.

SUMMARY

Consumer demand has caused the fashion industry to convert from a manufacturing to a marketing focus. Manufacturers and retailers study demographic and psychographic trends to learn about consumer groups and identify target markets.

Economics, global trade, and modern technology have a great impact on both consumers and fashion marketing. The fashion industry responds to consumer needs with a variety of size ranges, price ranges, and style ranges in women's, men's, and children's wear.

CHAPTER REVIEW

Terms and Concepts

Briefly identify and discuss the following terms and concepts:

1. Consumer demand
2. Buying power
3. Life-styles
4. Demographics
5. Market segments
6. Disposable income
7. Discretionary income
8. Purchasing power
9. Imports
10. Balance of trade
11. Tariffs
12. Quotas
13. World Trade Organization
14. NAFTA
15. Quick Response
16. Marketing chain
17. Buyer motivation

Questions for Review

1. Why has the fashion industry shifted from a manufacturing to a marketing orientation?
2. What impact do demographics have on fashion marketing?
3. What factors influence consumer spending?
4. What effect do fashion imports have on prices and jobs?
5. How have computers changed the fashion industry?
6. How do you think that television and the Internet will affect retailing of the future?
7. What positive and negative effects have communications had on fashion marketing?
8. What effect has the working woman had on fashion marketing?
9. What are the similarities between style ranges and price ranges?

Projects for Additional Learning

1. Analyze fashion styles today. Is there one that you feel is the result of a social, economic, or technological influence? Briefly explain in writing the reasons for your choice.
2. Interview two executive businesswomen and find out what types of clothes are in their wardrobes. How do their needs affect the fashion industry?
3. In a local specialty or department store, compare two dresses of similar price from different manufacturers. Try them on. Which has the better fit?

Compare fabric choices in terms of quality and suitability to the design. Compare styling: Which is more innovative? Taking all factors into consideration, which dress is the better buy? Discuss your findings in a written report. Describe or sketch the two garments.

4. In a local specialty or department store, compare the missy and junior departments. List the major manufacturers in each department, and explain the general styling differences.

NOTES

[1] Quoted in Barbra Walz, *The Fashion Makers* (New York: Random House, 1978), p. 47.

[2] Ken Dychtwald, president, Age Wave Research Co., as quoted in "Senior Market Ripe for Action," *Women's Wear Daily*, June 15, 1994, p. 18.

[3] "The Consumer Outlook," Special Report Supplement, *Women's Wear Daily*, April 1994, p. 10.

[4] "Senior Market Ripe for Action," p. 18.

[5] "The Consumer Outlook," p. 10.

[6] Ibid.

[7] NPD Special Industry Services, "Career Smart," DuPont brochure, p. 3.

[8] Christie Brown, "Dressing Down," *Forbes*, December 5, 1994, p. 156.

[9] Margaret Walch, associate director, Color Association of the United States, interview, February 3, 1993.

[10] "Textile Report," *Women's Wear Daily*, January 28, 1992, p. 27.

[11] Ibid.

[12] M. L. Cates, Jr., American Textile Manufacturers Institute, "ATMI Calls 92 a Better Year," *Women's Wear Daily*, December 30, 1992, p. 8.

[13] "Apparel and Fabricated Textile Products," *U.S. Industrial Outlook 1994*, Department of Commerce, Washington, D. C., pp. 32–7.

[14] "Textile Report," p. 27.

[15] "The Global Age Begins," *Women's Wear Daily*, December 2, 1994, p. 10.

[16] "Three Revolutions Shape the Future," *Tracking the Trends Supplement, Women's Wear Daily*, April 1994, p. 6.

[17] Amy Feldman, "Hello Oprah, Good-bye Iman," *Forbes*, March 16, 1992, p. 116.

[18] "Infant/Toddler Underwear and Sleepwear," *Earnshaw's*, May 1994, p. 60.

[19] Natalie Mallinckrodt, president, Golden Rainbow, as quoted in "The Infant/Toddler Report," *Earnshaw's*, May 1994, p. 51.

Gianfranco Ferré with models at the showing of his new Dior collection.
(Courtesy of Christian Dior)

3

FASHION CHANGE AND CONSUMER ACCEPTANCE

CAREER FOCUS

Designers, merchandisers, and marketers at every level of the industry must be aware of fashion change, cycles, and consumer acceptance and how these principles will affect product development and marketing.

CHAPTER OBJECTIVES

After reading this chapter you should have attained competence in the following areas:

1. Understanding the dimensions of fashion
2. Identifying the phases and lengths of fashion cycles and relating them to consumer acceptance
3. Comprehending fashion adoption theories in relation to consumer acceptance
4. Understanding buyer motivation

*B*ecause consumers are the end users of fashion, product managers, merchandisers, and designers must consider them in the planning stages in order to make fashions that they will want. Consumers' wants and needs create a cycle of consumer demand, industry catering to that demand, and finally consumer acceptance of merchandise offered in the retail market.

The first part of this chapter discusses fashion acceptance and rejection, a cycle that creates fashion change. The remainder of the chapter covers the consumer's connection to these cycles, how this relates to forms of fashion adoption, and buyer motivation. First, we will discuss terms associated with the acceptance of fashion.

FASHION TERMS

All fashion executives use the following terms daily to discuss the aspects of fashion.

Fashion

Fashion is the style or styles most popular at a given time. The term implies three components: style, change, and acceptance.

Style

Style is any particular characteristic or look in apparel or accessories. Designers interpret fashion ideas into new styles and offer them to the public. The manufacturer assigns a *style number* to each new design in each collection, which is used to identify it throughout production, marketing, and retailing. As the style becomes popular, variations of it are produced by other manufacturers.

A style may come and go in fashion, but that specific style always remains that style, whether it is in fashion or not. For example, the polo shirt style will not always be in fashion, yet it will always have variations on the same styling and details, which make it a polo shirt.

Change

What makes fashion interesting is that it is always changing. Designer Karl Lagerfeld said, "What I like about fashion is change. Change means also that what we do today might be worthless tomorrow, but we have to accept that because we are in fashion. There's nothing safe forever in fashion...fashion is a train that waits for nobody. Get on it, or it's gone."[1]

Many people criticize the fickleness of fashion, saying that fashion changes only to stimulate buying. And it is true that if fashion never changed the public would not buy clothing so frequently. However, fashion is one way for consumers to visually express their relationship to current events and to life itself.

Fashion changes because

◆ It reflects changes in people's life-styles and current events.
◆ People's needs change.
◆ People get bored with what they have.

The speed of change is influenced by modern communication, marketing, advances in mass production, greater discretionary income, and the seasons.

Because fashion is a product of change, a *sense of timing* (the ability to understand the speed of acceptance and change) is an important asset for anyone involved with product development or marketing in the fashion industry. Designers have to decide *when* their customers will be ready to accept a particular style. Italian designer Valentino remarked, "Timing is the key to a successful idea."[2] When top designers show a new look, designers for mainstream manufacturers have to decide when they can include that look in their own lines.

Acceptance

Acceptance implies that consumers must buy and wear a style to make it a fashion. Karl Lagerfeld remarked, "There's no fashion if nobody buys it."[3] However, different market segments adopt different fashions. What appeals to a junior customer would probably not appeal to a missy customer. Designers plan styles to appeal to certain consumer groups—their particular customers. It is then up to the public to decide whether these styles will become fashion.

Advertising stimulates the public's desire for new fashions. However, there is a limit to which sales promotion can win acceptance. If the public is not ready for a product or is tired of it, no amount of advertising can gain or hold its acceptance. Fashion acceptance, however, is greatly influenced by exposure, primarily in the media, and on television in particular.

Acceptance by the public does not prove that a design is necessarily beautiful, only that its timing is right and that it fills a need. Acceptance by a large number of people makes a fashion successful. The degree of acceptance also provides clues to fashion trends for coming seasons.

FASHION EVOLUTION

Generally, fashion changes evolve gradually, giving consumers time to become accustomed to new looks.

Fashion Cycles

Consumers are exposed each season to a multitude of new styles created by designers. Some are rejected immediately by the press or by the buyer on the retail level, but others are accepted for a time, as demonstrated by consumers purchasing and wearing them.

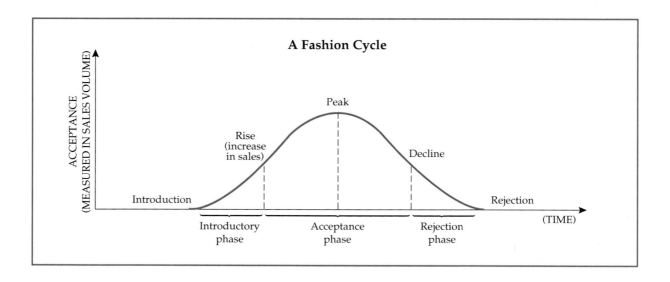

The way in which fashion changes is usually described is as a fashion cycle. It is difficult to categorize or theorize about fashion without oversimplifying. Even so, the fashion cycle is usually depicted as a bell-shaped curve encompassing five stages: introduction, rise in popularity, peak of popularity, decline in popularity, and rejection. The cycle can reflect the acceptance of a single style from one designer or of a general style such as the miniskirt.

Introduction of a Style

Designers interpret their research and creative ideas into apparel or accessories and then offer the new styles to the public. Designers create new designs by changing elements such as line, shape, color, fabric, and details and their relationship to one another. For instance, a change in skirt length might in turn affect the proportion of the skirt to the bodice of a dress. New creations referred to as the "latest fashions" may not yet be accepted by anyone. At this first stage of the cycle, fashion implies only style and newness.

Most new styles are introduced at a high price level. Designers whose names are respected for both their creativity and their sense of timing are often given financial backing and allowed to design with very few limitations on creativity, quality of raw materials, or amount of fine workmanship. Naturally, production costs are high and only a few people can afford the resulting garments. Designers such as Karl Lagerfeld or Donna Karan do not expect to sell their signature collections in huge quantities. Production in small quantities gives a designer more freedom, flexibility, and room for creativity.

Increase in Popularity

As the new fashion is purchased, worn, and seen by more people, it may begin to rise in popularity. In the case of an expensive new style, sales will never be high. Most couture and high-priced designers now have secondary, bridge, and/or diffusion lines at lower prices so that they are able to sell their designs in greater quantities.

The popularity of the style may further increase through copying and adaptation. Some designers or stylists may modify a popular style to suit the needs and price range of their own customers. Some manufacturers may try to copy it with less expensive fabric and less detail in order to sell the style at lower prices.

Peak of Popularity

When a fashion is at the height of its popularity, it may be in such demand that many manufacturers copy it or produce adaptations of it at many price levels. Styles with great appeal are produced in many variations. Donna Karan's "cold shoulder" dress (a black dress with bare shoulders) was worn by Liza Minelli at the 1992 Academy Awards, which was seen around the world. First Lady Hillary Rodham Clinton wore the same style in January 1993 and also received media exposure. By spring of 1993, the look had been copied in many forms of dresses and tops at all price levels and could be found in many stores and catalogs. There is a very fine line between adaptations and knockoffs (see Chapter 9)!

Volume production requires a likelihood of mass acceptance. Therefore, most volume manufacturers follow trends because their customers want clothes that are in the mainstream of fashion.

Decline in Popularity

Eventually, so many copies are mass produced that fashion-conscious people tire of the style and begin to look for something new. Consumers still wear garments in the style, but they are no longer willing to buy them at regular prices. Retail stores put such declining styles on sale racks, hoping to make room for new merchandise.

Rejection of a Style or Obsolescence

In the last phase of the fashion cycle, some consumers have already turned to new looks, thus beginning a new cycle. The rejection or discarding of a style just because it is out of fashion is called *consumer obsolescence*. As early as 1600, Shakespeare wrote that "fashion wears out more apparel than the man."[4]

Length of Cycles

Although all fashions follow the same cyclical pattern, there is no measurable timetable for a fashion cycle. Some fashions take a short time to peak in popularity, others take longer; some decline slowly, others swiftly. Some last a single selling season, others last several seasons. Certain fashions fade quickly, others never completely disappear.

A classic blazer and striped shirt from Hart Schaffner & Marx.
(Courtesy of the Hartmarx Corporation)

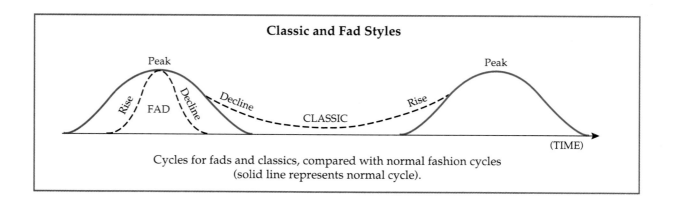

Classic and Fad Styles

Cycles for fads and classics, compared with normal fashion cycles
(solid line represents normal cycle).

Classics

Some styles never become completely obsolete, but instead remain more or less accepted for an extended period. A classic is characterized by simplicity of design, which keeps it from being easily dated. An example is the Chanel suit, which peaked in fashion in the late 1950s and enjoyed popularity again in the 1980s and 1990s. In the interim, the house of Chanel in Paris, as well as other manufacturers, have produced variations of these suits for a small, dedicated clientele. Other examples of classics include blazer jackets, twin sets, polo shirts, ballet flats, and loafers.

Fads

Short-lived fashions, or fads, can come and go in a single season. They lack the design strength to hold consumer attention for very long. Fads usually affect only a narrow consumer group, begin in lower price ranges, are relatively simple and inexpensive to copy, and therefore flood the market in a very short time. Because of market saturation, the public tires of them quickly and they die out. (Fads have included hot pants, baby doll dresses, baggy pants, and unmatched buttons. These looks die quickly because they are not appropriate looks for a wide range of customers).

Cycles within Cycles

Design elements (such as color, texture, silhouette, or detail) may change even though the style itself remains popular. Jeans became a fashion item in the late 1960s and remained classics. Therefore, their fashion cycle was very long. However, various jean silhouettes—including bell and baggy—came and went during that time.

Interrupted Cycles

Consumer buying is often halted prematurely because manufacturers and retailers no longer wish to risk producing or stocking merchandise that will soon decline in popularity. This is obvious to consumers who try to buy summer clothes in August.

Sometimes the normal progress of a fashion cycle is interrupted or prolonged by social upheaval, economic depression, or war. Consider the

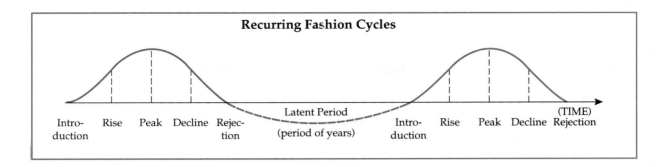

large-shouldered, wedge-shaped silhouette in women's fashion that began in the 1930s. Because people were concerned with things more important than fashion during World War II, the same silhouette continued, without the normally expected decline, for the duration of the war. *The New Look* of 1947, with its sloping shoulders, tiny waists, and longer skirts, was a radical change because the old cycle had been unnaturally prolonged.

Recurring Cycles

After a fashion dies, it may resurface. Designers often borrow ideas from the past. When a style reappears years later, it is reinterpreted for a new time; a silhouette or proportion may recur, but it is interpreted with a change in fabric and detail. Nothing is ever exactly the same—yet nothing is totally new. As the century and the millenium draw to a close, designers are showing many nostalgic looks of the 1940s, 1950s, 1960s, and 1970s. However, the use of different fabrics, colors, and details make the looks unique to the 1990s.

CONSUMER IDENTIFICATION WITH FASHION CYCLES

How the customer relates to the phases of fashion cycles has to do with the consumer group that they belong to.

Consumer Groups

Consumers can be identified with various stages of the fashion cycle. Fashion leaders buy and wear new styles at the beginning of their cycles; others tend to imitate. An individual's preference for one style or another is referred to as *taste*. Good taste in fashion implies sensitivity to what is beautiful and appropriate. Because of differences in taste, what is fashionable for one group is not for another group. Manufacturers and retailers may also be identified as fashion leaders or followers, depending on which consumer groups they target.

Fashion Leaders

The people who look for new fashion and wear it before it becomes generally acceptable are often referred to as fashion leaders. Fashion leaders are confident of their own taste and do not need the approval of others. Individualists, they do not need the security of standardization. They dare to be different, and their acceptance of new designs makes those clothes fashionable. Fashion leaders are a very small percentage of the public. They fall into two categories, fashion innovators and fashion role models.

Fashion Innovators. Some fashion leaders actually create fashion. They may be designers themselves or anyone who dares to express his or her own individual style. These fashion leaders constantly look for inter-

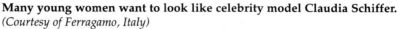

Many young women want to look like celebrity model Claudia Schiffer. *(Courtesy of Ferragamo, Italy)*

esting new styles, colors, fabrics, and ways to accessorize their clothes. They try to find unique fashion in small boutiques or vintage clothing stores or design their own clothes. They are discerning shoppers who would rather have a few beautiful things than many mediocre things. They may give impetus to a certain style by discovering and wearing it. They may be referred to as *avant-garde* (French for "ahead of the pack") or fashion forward.

Fashion Role Models.   Many fashion leaders occupy prominent positions that give them exposure, which, in turn, influences the way other people dress. They usually have enough money to buy expensive clothes. They have a prominent position so that the press reports details of what they wear at public events, in films, or on television. Because of their support, fashion leaders are a stimulant to designers and to the fashion industry as a whole.

Ideally, there are fashion leaders for every market segment. One of the problems with women's fashion today is that there are no outstanding leaders for the large market segment of mature women. Former fashion paragons Audrey Hepburn and Jackie Onassis are gone. Nancy Reagan is out of the spotlight. Even the 1980s international fashion pacesetter Diana, Princess of Wales, has faded from the spotlight. However, young people look to celebrity models, such as Claudia Schiffer and Cindy Crawford, and TV and rock stars for fashion leadership.

Fashion Victims.   There are also those people with too much money to spend who become slaves to signatures. Designer Jean-Paul Gaultier remarked, "Fashion victims are people who blindly and stupidly follow a brand without any discernment and without any analysis. As long as it's the latest rage, they buy it without thinking about adapting it to themselves."[5]

Fashion Followers

Fashion needs followers or there would not be any fashion. Most men and women seek acceptance through conformity and follow world, national, or community fashion leaders in order to feel confident. Fashion followers emulate others only after they are sure of fashion trends. Consumers become fashion followers for one or more of the following reasons:

- They lack the time, money, and interest to devote to fashion leadership.
- They need a period of exposure to new styles before accepting them.
- They are insecure about their tastes and therefore turn to what others have already approved as acceptable and appropriate.
- They want to fit in with their friends or peer group or be accepted by them.
- They tend to imitate people that they admire.

There are various degrees of fashion followers. Some are early adopters, some go with the majority, and some lag behind, primarily because they have no interest in fashion or are cut off from mainstream society.

Because of fashion followers, most members of the fashion industry are copyists or adapters. From a marketing point of view, fashion followers are very important. They make mass production possible, because volume production of fashion can only be profitable when the same merchandise is sold to many consumers.

Fashion Leadership in Manufacturing and Retailing

Manufacturers and retailers respond to fashion leaders and followers in their product development and merchandising. They try to establish a particular merchandising identity with various consumer groups. Designer collections cater to the fashion leaders, while the majority of manufacturers provide merchandise for fashion followers. Joanne Bjork, merchandising director for Koret, explains, "We are followers, not leaders. We wait until the trends get exposure at retail before we get into them."[6]

Retailers, too, cater to fashion leaders or followers. Barneys, for example, is a store that identifies with fashion leaders, while Wal-Mart is able to sell volume to the majority of followers. Retailer identification with fashion cycles is discussed fully at the end of Chapter 13.

ADOPTION OF FASHION

It is important to understand how new fashion ideas are disseminated, or spread, and how they are adapted to the tastes, life-styles, and budgets of various consumers.

Basically, there are three variations of the fashion adoption process: traditional adoption, reverse adoption, and mass dissemination.

Traditional Fashion Adoption (Trickle-down Theory)

The trickle-down theory is based on the traditional process of copying and adapting trendsetting fashion from Paris, Milan, and New York designers. Since this fashion is expensive, it is affordable to only a few people. As the new fashions are worn by publicized fashion leaders or shown in fashion publications, more consumers are exposed to the new look, and some will desire to have it for themselves. To appeal to this broader group of consumers, manufacturers produce less expensive versions or adaptations of high fashion. These are copied again and again at lower prices, until they have been seen often enough to become acceptable to the most conservative buyer. The cheapest versions are seen at discount houses soon after. Consumers then tire of the look and its popularity fades.

The length of this process is influenced by location. If the new look starts in Europe, then people in New York and other large cities will probably be the first to accept it. It may take a year or two for many Americans to fit even a modified version of the look into their life-styles. Fashion implies newness and freshness. Yet as a fashion is copied, modified, and sold at lower and lower prices, it loses its newness, quality, and other essential design elements.

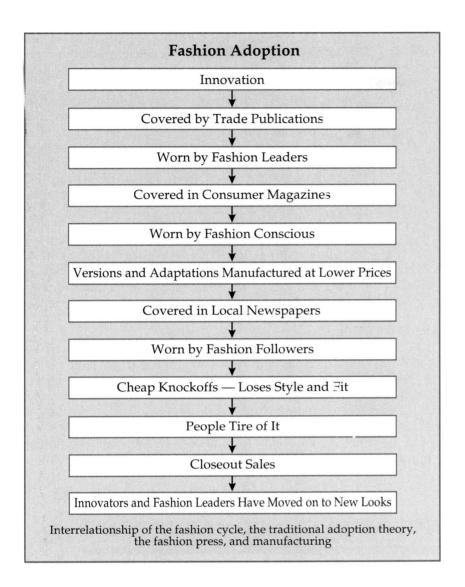

Fashion Adoption

Innovation

↓

Covered by Trade Publications

↓

Worn by Fashion Leaders

↓

Covered in Consumer Magazines

↓

Worn by Fashion Conscious

↓

Versions and Adaptations Manufactured at Lower Prices

↓

Covered in Local Newspapers

↓

Worn by Fashion Followers

↓

Cheap Knockoffs — Loses Style and Fit

↓

People Tire of It

↓

Closeout Sales

↓

Innovators and Fashion Leaders Have Moved on to New Looks

Interrelationship of the fashion cycle, the traditional adoption theory, the fashion press, and manufacturing

Reverse Adoption (Trickle-up or Bottom-up Theories)

Since the 1960s, manufacturers and retailers pay more attention to consumer innovation. They watch people on the streets to find ideas. Some of these ideas eventually reach the designer market. The "Grunge" look of the early 1990s is a good example of a street look that reached the runways. Beginning in Seattle, with the raw-rock music movement, it introduced the idea of mixing loose flowered dresses with hiking boots. Dancewear and activewear, which began as functional needs of the consumer, also have influenced designer collections. The vintage fashion purchased by young people in thrift shops has influenced recent designer collections.

Mass Dissemination (Trickle-across Theory)

Modern communication sometimes seems to make fashion available simultaneously throughout the industry. Such dissemination is evident

A much-copied belted, ribbed mock turtleneck pullover by Prada. *(Courtesy of Prada)*

when manufacturers copy hot new styles almost immediately in order to meet the high demand. Speed of production is of the greatest importance.

Heidi Goldstein, an associate merchandise director at The Doneger Group, commented, "It used to take about six months to a year for a designer trend to go mainstream; this past year it is happening simultaneously. Consumers are being fed fashion from all sources, from TV shows to catalogs. They are seeing the trends, and they want to look as fashionable as anybody else."[7]

Prada's belted, fitted sweater was shown on the runways in October. Within weeks, XOXO's version was shown to buyers in Los Angeles and was on the runway by November. Sometimes it is even difficult to know where the idea began. Did Donna copy Karl? Did Ralph copy Yves? Or vice versa?

There is no longer one channel of fashion dissemination. Many separate markets have developed geared to various age ranges, life-styles, tastes, and pocketbooks. Various designer and manufacturer labels appeal to various groups at different price points. Increased diversity means that many different styles can be acceptable at the same time. There are many more options.

MOTIVES FOR CONSUMER BUYING

To help them make styling and merchandising decisions, designers, buyers, and other industry executives try to understand consumer motivation.

In the past, most people bought new clothes only when a need arose, for a very special occasion, or because their old clothes wore out. The average person simply could not afford to buy more than the basic necessities. In Western society today, discretionary income is larger, and people can buy new clothes rather frequently.

Therefore, buying motives have changed; we are able to buy clothes because we want or like them. Buying motives vary from consumer to consumer and from day to day. There are both rational and emotional motives:

To Be Fashionable. We may buy new clothing to feel that we are trendy or at least in the mainstream of fashion. We discard clothing that is still wearable only because it is out of fashion.

To Be Attractive. We want clothes that are flattering, that make us look our best or show off our physical attributes.

To Impress Others. We may want to project a successful image or establish our identities with fashion. We may want to exhibit our taste level or income level through clothing. Expensive brands have even served as status symbols.

To Be Accepted by Friends, Peer Groups, or Colleagues. Average Americans have conservative tastes; we do not want to differ from our peers. We may want to project a life-style that others will identify with. Buying patterns suggest that we like some direction or guidance as a framework for our choices.

To Fill an Emotional Need. New clothes often help us feel better psychologically. Being secure in the feeling that we are wearing appropriate fashion helps us to feel confident and self-assured. This motive, however, may often lead to impulse buying (buying without careful consideration). Corrin Corbin, director of apparel marketing and merchandising for Initiatives, a DuPont subsidiary, points out that "the apparel chain must work together as a team to fully understand and satisfy the consumer on her deepest emotional levels if the industry is to prosper."[8]

FASHION SELECTION

To determine the acceptability of fashion, both designers and manufacturers find it helpful to consider the criteria consumers use for its selection.

Buying patterns are changing. The value-orientation of the 1990s is a far cry from the conspicuous consumption of the 1980s—a shift to the self-disciplined from the self-indulgent.

- Consumers are looking for their idea of quality at lower prices; often referred to as *perceived value*. They shop more often at discount stores or buy markdowns.
- There is a trend toward more selective buying. They may buy only one important piece, such as a jacket, to update their wardrobes.
- People are spending less on fashion.
- Consumers look for comfortable, functional, multiple-use clothing.
- People are buying closer to need.

Elements of fashion appeal draw the consumer's attention to a particular style. There are also practical considerations, including quality and price, that the consumer usually evaluates before making a purchase.

Elements of Appeal

Appealing elements of fashion are very similar to the elements of design, but are from the purchaser's point of view rather than the creator's (see Chapter 9 for a discussion of design elements).

Appearance

The overall appearance of a garment or accessory is what first attracts a potential buyer. This can depend on hanger or display appeal as well as the following elements.

Color

People relate very personally to color, often selecting a fashion because the color is appealing or flattering.

Texture

The surface interest in the fabric of a garment or accessory is called texture. Texture is sensually appealing.

Style

The elements that define a style include line, silhouette, and details. A consumer's selection is frequently influenced by his or her opinion of what is currently fashionable and what is flattering to the figure.

Practical Considerations

Price

Perceived *value* has become the key to merchandising for the 1990s. Consumers want the best product at the best price. Price is probably the most important practical consideration for the average consumer. The consumer must compare the total perceived worth of the aesthetic aspects of the garment or accessory with the retail price and his or her own budget.

Fit

The try-on is a crucial step in the consumer's selection of a garment because sizing is not a guarantee of fit. The U.S. Department of Commerce has tried to set sizing standards, but each company tends to vary somewhat. It is difficult to set size ranges and grading rules to fit every figure. Each company tries its sample garments on models who are typical of the company's customers, which varies sizing.

The fitting room try-on further enables the customer to test fit and to judge if aesthetic elements enhance his or her figure type and general appearance.

Checking the fit of a suit at Gieves & Hawkes, London. *(Courtesy of Gieves & Hawkes)*

Comfort

Obviously, we need clothes to keep us warm in cold weather or cool in warm weather. As the population ages, as people try to remain physically fit, and as travel increases, we also want clothes that are comfortable to move in, sit in, travel in, and so on.

Appropriateness

It is very important that a particular garment be suitable or acceptable for a specific occasion or for the needs of the consumer's life-style. Consumers consider their clothing needs for job and leisure time activities including specific events. They also consider what is appropriate for their figure type, personality, coloring, and age. Impulse shoppers do not consider appropriateness and therefore purchase many items that do not fit into their wardrobes.

Brand or Designer Label

Brands are a manufacturer's means of product identification. Some consumers buy on the basis of a particular brand's reputation, often as a result of heavy advertising. Designer Giorgio Armani said, "I believe consumers in some markets are becoming less brand conscious. A brand name is important as long as it is combined with a proper relationship of quality and price."[9]

Fabric Performance and Care

The durability of a garment or accessory and the ease or difficulty of caring for it are often factors in selection. Many consumers prefer easy-care, wash-and-wear fabrics because they do not have the time or the interest in ironing or the money to pay for dry cleaning. Consumer concern has spurned textile industry development of easy care fiber characteristics and finishes and the popularity of wash-and-fold cotton garments. To protect the consumer, government regulations now require fiber content and care instruction labels to be sewn into apparel.

Quality

Quality standards fall as labor costs rise and managements favor higher profitability. Unfortunately, many consumers cannot and do not bother to evaluate workmanship. The junior customer cares little about quality; she is likely to throw away a garment before it wears out. The designer or missy customer, on the other hand, generally considers clothing an investment and may not mind spending more for the lasting qualities of fine detailing and workmanship.

Some consumers may look for a particular brand or name on the basis of a reputation for quality. Today, many consumers are demanding higher quality to give them value for the ever higher prices that they are expected to pay.

Convenience

With time and energy in increasingly short supply, consumers are looking for ways to make shopping easier. Consumers are spending less time shopping than before. They want to find what they need easily and quickly. In response to consumer needs, catalog shopping has increased and computer and cable television shopping has been developed. In the stores, consumers are demanding service and in-stock assortments.

SUMMARY

Fashion has three properties: style, acceptance, and timeliness. Change makes the fashion world go round. New styles are introduced, rise to a height of popularity, then decline into obsolescence. Some styles remain fashionable longer than others. Some come back into fashion after a latent period. Because fashion is a product of change, a sense of timing is an important attribute at all levels of the industry.

Consumers can be identified with stages of the fashion cycle. Fashion leaders, a very small percentage of the population, buy and wear new styles at the beginning of the cycle; other consumers imitate. The majority of consumers are followers, which facilitates the mass marketing of fashion.

Fashions may sift down from the original ideas of high-fashion designers to reappear in cheaper fabrics at lower price levels. Other styles are either adapted "up from the streets" or are disseminated quickly through mass marketing. Consumers buy clothes for many reasons, including the desire to be fashionable, attractive, impressive, accepted, or emotionally fulfilled. Considerations in fashion selection include color, texture, style, price, fit, appropriateness, brand, fabric performance, and workmanship. Consumer acceptance is a major influence on styling and merchandising decisions.

CHAPTER REVIEW

Terms and Concepts

Briefly identify and discuss the following terms and concepts:

1. Fashion
2. Style
3. Acceptance
4. Sense of timing
5. Fashion cycles
6. Classics
7. Fads

8. Fashion leaders
9. Fashion followers
10. Fashion victims
11. Mass-market dissemination
12. Buyer motivation
13. Perceived value

Questions for Review

1. Name and define the three components of fashion.
2. How does fashion acceptance affect the timing of design?
3. Describe the phases of a typical fashion acceptance cycle.

4. Discuss the relationship of consumer acceptance to the fashion cycle.
5. What do consumers consider when buying clothes? How do you make buying decisions?

Projects for Additional Learning

1. Is there a well-known movie star or public figure (either male or female) in the news who you feel is a fashion leader? Write a short report documented with examples of how this person influences the way others dress. Clip (or photocopy) illustrations from publications.

2. From current fashion magazines, collect five examples of each of the following types of fashion: (a) high fashion; (b) mass fashion; (c) classic; and (d) fad.

NOTES

[1] As quoted in "King Karl," *Women's Wear Daily*, November 20, 1991, p. 7.

[2] As quoted in "Is the Designer Dead?" *Women's Wear Daily*. April 7, 1992, p. 10.

[3] Quoted in "Fall Fashions: Buying the Line," *Time*, April 23, 1984, p. 77.

[4] *Much Ado About Nothing*, Act III, 1598-1600.

[5] As quoted in "Les Fashion Victims," *Women's Wear Daily*, January 21, 1992, p. 4.

[6] As quoted in "Fashion…in Moderation," *Women's Wear Daily*, November 9, 1994, p. 8.

[7] As quoted in "From Barneys to Bradlees," *Women's Wear Daily*, April 5, 1995, p. 8.

[3] As quoted by Marvin Klapper, "DuPont tells Industry: Learn What Women Want," *Women's Wear Daily*, October 16, 1991, p. 2.

[*] As quoted in "Europe Design Houses Face a New World," *Women's Wear Daily*, June 15, 1992, p. 6.

Designer Jessica McClintock working with the fabrics, trims, magazines, and costume books that inspire her. *(Photographed by the author)*

4

FASHION RESEARCH AND ANALYSIS

CAREER FOCUS

Every designer and merchandiser in the fashion industry is actively involved with fashion research before work on each new line or collection begins. Market research consultants also study and report on demographics and consumer buying habits. Design services and fashion publications also need experts in fashion research and forecasting for every merchandise category.

CHAPTER OBJECTIVES

After reading this chapter you should have attained competence in the following areas:

1. Understanding of the importance of research
2. Comprehension of market studies and fashion forecasting
3. Knowledge of design resources

*I*t would seem a simple matter to make or sell what people want to buy. However, awareness, research, and planning are needed for producers and retailers to make, buy, and sell what consumers will want. Without proper research, or with an unexpected turn of events, merchandise ends up on the sale racks, causing losses for producers, manufacturers, and retailers alike. This chapter discusses fashion forecasting, fashion services and resources, and design sources that executives use for product development at every level of the fashion industry.

It would be impossible to ask all consumers what they will want to wear a year or two in advance—they would not even know themselves. Therefore, designers and merchandisers must anticipate their wants and needs by being *aware* of what is going on in the world and how these events will affect fashion.

Research is done before any other design or merchandising activity, at every level of the industry. It becomes second nature to every decision maker in the field of fashion. Because the very term *fashion* implies a state of flux, textile producers, fashion manufacturers, and retailers all need to absorb a constant flow of information in order to anticipate change and consumer preferences. Designer Karl Lagerfeld has said, "I want to be informed, to know everything, see everything, read everything…You mix all that, then forget about it and do it your way."[1] Ady Gluck-Frankel, owner and designer of Necessary Objects, explained, "It's the times that set the trends. We are all affected by the same issues: politics, ecology, economy, music, etc. We all just interpret them for our own markets."[2] Often what seems to be intuition is actually clever assimilation and analysis of careful research.

Every executive, designer, and merchandiser in the fashion industry must be involved with research and analysis. They *continuously* study the life-styles of consumers, shop the market, and read trend and design reports, fashion magazines, and newspapers in order to understand consumers and what they might want to buy. This research is absolutely necessary to make intelligent planning decisions regarding design, manufacturing, and sales.

FASHION FORECASTING

Designers, merchandisers, and buyers must learn to predict **trends,** *which are new directions in fashion.*

Because retailers want to buy the fashions that their customers will want, and since fashion designers and merchandisers must work so far ahead of the selling season, both must learn to be fashion forecasters. Fashion forecasting involves the following:

◆ Studying market conditions: how the consumer's buying behavior is influenced by society, economics, technology, and the environment
◆ Noting the life-styles of the men, women, or children who are their customers

Trade Publications

Trade publications in the form of newspapers, journals, or magazines offer information not only on fashion trends but on developments in the textile industry, fashion industry, and retailing business as well. Most specialize in a particular branch of the industry. Since busy executives have time to read only a few of these, they need to look for those that provide information relevant to their market. Fashion executives read these publications *daily*. Students should develop that habit. The following are some examples:

Women's wear: *Women's Wear Daily*, the major American fashion newspaper, is published five days a week. Each day features different topics, and there are often special supplements on subjects such as accessories, sportswear, swimwear, or technology. *WWD* also publishes *W*, a monthly magazine. *California Apparel News*, published weekly, concentrates on the California market. *Style* is Canada's trade magazine, *Gap* is published in France, and *Fashion Folio* in England.

Men's wear: *DNR, Daily News Record*, another five-day newspaper (the first one Fairchild published) with color supplements

Children's wear: *Earnshaw's, Children's Business*

Sportswear: *Sportswear International*

Accessories: *Footwear News Magazine* and *Accessories Magazine*

Textiles: *America's Textiles International, Bobbin, Textile World*, and *Textiles Suisse*

Apparel industry: *Apparel Industry Magazine, Apparel Manufacturer*, and *Bobbin*

Advertising and marketing: *Advertising Age, Brandweek, American Demographics, Direct Marketing, Promo, Retail Ad-Week*, and *Sales & Marketing Management*

Retailing: *Stores* (National Retail Merchants Association), *Chain Store Age Executive, Discount Merchandiser, Journal of Retailing, Retail Store Image*, and *Inside Retailing*

Visual presentation: *Artweek, Communication Arts, Display & Design Ideas, Graphis, Inspiration, Lighting Dimensions, Views & Reviews*, and *Visual Merchandising & Store Design*

International Consumer Fashion Magazines

These publications are aimed at the consumer and show fashion that is already available in the retail stores. Therefore, Americans find foreign magazines much more helpful for discovering new trends because European fashion is more avant-garde than American. It is not necessary to read the text of the foreign language magazines; the ideas come from the photographs. Some are published only two or four times a year to report on the collections. Many German and Japanese magazines have patterns included.

Magazines are very important resources for designers, particularly when budget cuts eliminate design services. Designers buy only the magazines that provide suitable ideas for their product. For example, jeanswear designers buy contemporary and junior magazines that have ideas for that specific category. In addition to the following list, many general interest magazines include fashion.

Women's wear: *Collections, L'Officiel de la Couture et de la Mode de Paris, Jardin des Modes, Joyce,* and *Vogue* (France); *Line a Italiana, Donna, Moda, Harper's Bazaar Italia,* and *Vogue* (Italy); *Harper's and Queen,* and *British Vogue* (England); *Burda International, Madam, Fashion Guide,* and *Vogue* (Germany); *Élégance* (Switzerland); *Fashion Yearbook, Hi Fashion, Mode et Mode, Mrs.,* and *Madam* (Japan)

Contemporary and junior; trendy: *Elle, Dépêché Mode, La Mode en Peinture* (France); *Moda In, Moda Viva, Amica* (Italy); *Brigitte, Miss Vogue, Carina* (Germany); *Non-no, 25 ans,* and *McSister* (Japan)

Children's wear: *Vogue Bambini, Donna Bambini,* and *Moda Bimbi* (Italy); *Sesame* and *Baby Fashion* (Japan). (Junior fashions are also a good source of ideas for children's wear.)

Men's wear: *L'Officiel Hommes, Vogue Hommes* (France); *L'Uomo Vogue, Linea Italiana Uomo, Mondo Uomo,* and *Uomo Harper's Bazaar* (Italy); *Männer Vogue* (Germany); *Men's Club, Mr.,* and *Dansen* (Japan)

Bridal: *Mariages* (France) and *Sposa* (Italy)

American Consumer Fashion Magazines

Many established magazines are undergoing extensive facelifts and there is a continuing influx of foreign publishers and editors in the United States. Some magazines have vanished, but there are always new attempts to reach new markets. American magazines as resources are best used for analyzing appropriate fashion for specific target markets, examining American designer collections, and seeing what fashion is currently available in the stores.

Women's: *Ebony, Essence, Harper's Bazaar, Mirabella, Vogue*

Trendy: *Elle (American Edition), Glamour, In Fashion, Mademoiselle, Sassy, Marie Claire*

Junior: *Seventeen, YM (Young and Modern)*

Men's: *Details, GQ (Gentleman's Quarterly), Esquire Gentleman, EM* (*Ebony* men)

Bridal: *Bride's, Modern Bride,* and *Bridal Guide*

Children: *Kids Fashion*

Catalogs

Designers also use catalogs as resources for ideas. Catalogs are essentially free magazines. A leather bomber jacket shown in a sportswear catalog might be the inspiration for a metallic bomber jacket for another fashion or catalog business.

DESIGN SOURCES

There are many sources of inspiration for designers including historic and ethnic costume, the arts, and travel.

Where do ideas come from? Ideas do not simply materialize out of thin air. First the designer does careful research, but what makes a designer's line special is a unique interpretation of design sources.

Historic and Ethnic Costume

Designers often turn to the past (recent or distant) or to folk costume for ideas and themes. Costume falls into two categories: *historic* costume, the fashion of a certain historical period, and *folk* or *ethnic* costume, traditional national or regional dress. Both are inspirational sources of design.

Historic Inspiration

Designers are sensitive to the combinations of colors, motifs, lines, shapes, and spaces of design in each historical period of costume. Some are inspired to use these in their collections. Nostalgic looks are more prevalent as this century draws to a close. John Galliano used ideas from the 1930s and 1950s in a recent collection. Belgian designer Dries Van Noten said that his spring collection is "a mixture of some elements from the Forties, Fifties, and Sixties. In the way it's combined, though, the look changes."[3] A recent Dior collection by Gianfranco Ferré looked like it could have been designed by Dior himself, as it echoed his 1947 New Look.

Folk Influences

Designers find the same inspirational blend of colors, motifs, lines, shapes, and spaces in folk costume. Tommy Hilfiger, for example, used old Austrian folk looks as a basis for his fall sportswear collection.[4] Christian Lacroix said that a recent spring collection "plays with mixes of South America, the Caribbean, and Africa."[5] Donna Karan described one of her resort collections as "a mix, Peru, the Philippines, Mexico, all rolled into one."[6]

Vintage Clothing Shops and Services

In every city, designers shop vintage clothing stores, flea markets, and thrift shops for old garments and fabrics to interpret for today's fashion. There are businesses such as Halloween in New York City that rent vintage clothes on a weekly basis. There are services that shop for old clothes for manufacturers. For example, Stacey Lee, owner of Vintage in New York, shops for manufacturers such as Liz Claiborne.

A designer might use these garments to round out a group theme. For example, a designer might find old ski sweaters in thrift shops and use the knit patterns for sweaters in a "Nordic" theme sportswear group.

A historic costume inspired design by Domenico Dolce & Stefano Gabbana for Complice.
(Courtesy of Genny U.S.A.)

Museums

Museum costume collections offer the unique opportunity of seeing actual preserved garments displayed on mannequins. Designers such as Yves Saint Laurent occasionally sponsor historic costume exhibits. A popular exhibit can influence many designers. The following museums and galleries house important costume collections:

Costume Institute, Metropolitan Museum of Art, 5th Avenue and 82nd Street, New York, New York 10028

Costume Gallery, Brooklyn Museum, 188 Eastern Parkway, Brooklyn, New York 11238

Costume Gallery, Los Angeles County Museum of Art, 5905 Wilshire Boulevard, Los Angeles, California 90036

Costume Institute, McCord Museum, 690 Sherbrooke Street West, Montreal, Canada

Musée du Costume de la Ville de Paris, 14 avenue New York, 75016 Paris, France

Musée de la Mode, Pavillon de Marsan, Louvre, rue de Rivoli, 75001 Paris, France

Victoria and Albert Museum, Brompton Road, London S.W. 7, England (including costumes, old fabrics, and embroideries)

Museum of Costume, Assembly Rooms, Alfred Street, Bath, England

Rijksmuseum, Stadhouderskade 42, 020 Amsterdam, the Netherlands

Kostümforschungs Institut (Costume Research Institute), Kemnatenstrasse 50, 8 Munich 19, Germany

Centro Internazionale Arti e del Costume, 3231 Palazzo Grassi, 30124 Venice, Italy

Many regional museums have fashion collections, and almost every national museum of folklore includes ethnic costumes. Costume can also be studied in paintings in every museum.

Libraries and Bookstores

Costume can also be studied in books. Museum bookstores and libraries are excellent sources of costume references. Many libraries also have collections of old fashion magazines, including *Godey's Lady's Book* (from the 1830s to the 1890s), *Harper's Bazaar* (from 1867), and *Vogue* (from 1894). Many fashion designers have their own libraries of books on historic and ethnic costume, films, sports, artists, designers, and textiles. Some colleges have historical costume and print libraries.

The Arts

Film, video, television, art, architecture, music, and theater are also inspirational sources for fashion design. All designers are influenced by what other designers and artists are creating. Excitement about a new idea acts as a catalyst for more creativity.

Art exhibitions often have an impact on design collections. An exhibition of Eugene Delacroix's paintings was a recent hit in Paris. Gérard Pipart, designer for Nina Ricci, paid homage to Delacroix with multicolored caftans and exotic harem pants like those found in the paintings in his spring collection.[7]

Films (and therefore, their designers) occasionally influence style. Mariuccia Mandelli interpreted the styles of her favorite film stars in her Fall 1995 Krizia collection.[8] Both Adrienne Vittadini and Calvin Klein said that their recent collections were inspired by Audrey Hepburn movies.

Music and the exposure that video gives singers and musicians have made a significant impact on young people.

Television gives broad exposure to fashion as seen on programs. These clothes are either designed specifically for the show or are chosen from ready-to-wear collections. There is a prodigious amount of programs targeted to viewers under 30. The clothes worn by rock stars on MTV and stars of popular TV programs such as *Melrose Place* disseminate youthful fashion trends.

All the arts give designers visual inspiration, be it for color or mood or a certain spirit that seems to capture the times.

Fabrics

Fabrics are the most important inspiration and resource for designers. However, apparel and accessory designers are limited by the fabrics that are currently available to them. Designers shop at international textile markets or fabric showrooms in New York or Los Angeles to see the current fabric lines. The selection of fabrics in the apparel design process is discussed in Chapter 9.

Fabric designers do the same market and trend research as apparel and accessory designers. They also have the same sources of inspiration, especially in fabric and costume collections, old or new interior decoration, or at the fabric market fairs. Fabric design is covered in Chapter 6.

Travel

Travel influences designers' collections. Designers like to visit visually and culturally stimulating places. Designers take working vacations because they are always using their awareness skills to absorb new stimuli. Travel exposes them to new ideas; however, these ideas are not always obvious in their collections. Designer Mary Jane Marcasiano commented, "After going to Egypt, I got back into the earth tones and the practicality of natural fibers, natural colors, and layering."[9]

Form Follows Function

To borrow a phrase from architect Louis Sullivan, apparel designers, too, are inspired by necessity. When consumers became active, the fashion industry created activewear. As activewear became popular, it became fashion. The same was true with the development of spectator sportswear and work clothes. Often the need creates the fashion.

The Street Scene

Designers get ideas just watching people in the streets: people on their way to work, the trendy young girls, or the kids on their skate boards. They look in the shop windows. They take photos or make sketches of clothing that appeals to them. Caroline Parent, a designer at Levi Strauss, made videos of "street fashion" to show to her colleagues for ideas.

The Close of the Century

Some designers look to the future for inspiration as the century and millenium draw to a close. Rifat Ozbek and Geoffrey Beene, for example, have shown futuristic looks in recent collections.

Awareness

Designers surround themselves with photographs of ideas, fabric swatches, and anything else that will stimulate creativity. They leave their studios to shop, visit museums, study nature, attend the theater, or people watch. Designers usually carry sketchbooks to jot down ideas whenever and wherever they find them. They hunger for information, letting ideas mingle and shape themselves into new forms.

Awareness is the key to creativity. Designers must learn most of all to keep their eyes open, to develop their skills of observation, to absorb visual ideas, and to translate them into clothes that their customers will like. Some people are more sensitive to good composition than others, but practice and observation make a person more aware, sensitive, and confident. Exposure to beautiful things helps a designer or buyer distinguish genuine beauty and quality from fads and mediocrity.

Designers and merchandisers must be aware of everything around them that affects the clothing industry, including economics, politics, demographics, and social change (see Chapter 2). It is impossible to predict where an idea will come from or which idea may inspire a whole group or line.

SUMMARY

Research and observation are critically important in the fashion business. By observing and researching consumer buying habits, watching for directions in designer collections, reading the most appropriate fashion publications, observing fashion trends, and being aware of the arts, manufacturers and retailers try to predict what the majority of their customers will want in the foreseeable future. To keep up with the changing world of fashion, fashion awareness should become second nature.

CHAPTER REVIEW

Terms and Concepts

Briefly identify and discuss the following terms and concepts:

1. Fashion editing
2. Fashion forecasting
3. Fashion trends
4. Target market
5. Evaluating collections

6. Fashion services
7. Trade publications
8. Consumer publications
9. Awareness
10. Design sources

Questions for Review

1. Explain what factors are involved in fashion forecasting.
2. How do designers use trend and information services?
3. Why is market research important for textile and apparel manufacturers and retailers?

4. Explain the difference between trade and consumer fashion publications.
5. What role does historic or folk costume play in today's fashion?
6. Give an example of how films have influenced fashion.

Projects for Additional Learning

1. Trend research: Make a survey of fashion resources available to you. Read the latest issues of fashion magazines and compare the contents with fashion looks six months ago and a year ago. From the information that you find, try to analyze the fashion direction for the future. Organize your ideas into a few basic trend forecasts for color, fabrics, silhouette, and line.
2. Fashion magazine evaluation: Examine and compare the content of four different fashion magazines. How many pages are devoted to paid advertisements? How many pages are devoted to editorial fashion reporting? What do these magazines have in common? How would a fashion forecaster use this information?

3. Look through costume books for pictures of ethnic dress. Using these as inspiration, design a garment using the line, shapes, colors, and details from these garments in a new combination for today's life-style.
4. Make up a consumer survey. Type up questions you would like to ask. Be as specific as possible, such as "What length skirt do you prefer to wear?" Go to a local shopping mall and ask customers to answer your survey (explain that you are working on a student project). Tabulate your findings in a brief written report.

NOTES

[1] As quoted in "King Karl," *Women's Wear Daily*, November 20, 1991, p. 7.

[2] As quoted in "Juniors, a Trend Ahead," *Women's Wear Daily*, December 1, 1994, p. 6.

[3] "The Paris Retro," *Women's Wear Daily*, October 11, 1994, p. 6.

[4] Tommy Hilfiger, interview, September 23, 1994.

[5] "The Paris Scoop," *Women's Wear Daily*, October 14, 1992, p. 11.

[6] As quoted in "Resort," *Women's Wear Daily*, June 4, 1992, page 1.

[7] Godfrey Deeny, "Ricci's Pipart: Staying Power," *Women's Wear Daily*, January 26, 1995, p. 10.

[8] Trish Donnally, "Silver Screen Classics for Fall," *San Francisco Chronicle*, March 7, 1995, p. E1.

[9] As quoted by Sara Fiedelholtz, "Sportswear Makers: Boosting Figures the Natural Way," *Women's Wear Daily Sportswear Trends Supplement*, February 1993, p. 2.

Part Two

THE RAW MATERIALS OF FASHION

Before we can even begin to think of fashion apparel or accessories, we must consider the raw materials from which they are made. Collectively, the producers of these raw materials, fibers, fabrics, leathers, furs, and trimmings, are the suppliers to the apparel and accessories industries and the first level of the fashion industry. Chapter 5 covers the production of fibers and fabrics for those students who do not have a background in textiles. Since most garments are made from fabrics, the textile industry is our major concern. Chapter 6 describes the marketing and distribution of these fibers and fabrics, basic knowledge needed by anyone working in textiles or manufacturing. Chapter 7 surveys both leathers and furs, also raw materials for clothing and trimmings, the necessary secondary supplies to finish apparel and accessories.

A field of flax. *(Courtesy of the International Linen Promotion Commission)*

5

TEXTILE FIBER AND FABRIC PRODUCTION

CAREER FOCUS

Careers in textile production require a technical education in textiles and/or engineering. Since most mills in the United States are located in the Southeast, this is the area where most jobs are found. Other opportunities exist in New York City and the Los Angeles area. There are technical career opportunities in research and development, styling, plant technology, engineering, and management.

CHAPTER OBJECTIVES

After reading this chapter you should have attained competence in the following areas:

1. Awareness of the sources of fibers
2. Understanding of the processes involved in the production of fibers and fabrics
3. Knowledge of the roles of mills and converters

*T*extiles is a broad term referring to any material that can be made into fabric by any method. Occasionally, the term *textile industry* is used to cover the whole apparel industry: the production and marketing of textile merchandise from raw materials to the product in the retail store.

More precisely, the textile industry encompasses the production and marketing of fibers, yarns, and fabrics, including trimmings and findings. This production and marketing chain includes the following steps: fiber production, yarn production (spinning and texturing), fabric production, dyeing, printing, and finishing. Defined in this way, the textile industry represents the first level of the fashion industry. Textile production will be discussed in this chapter followed by textile marketing in Chapter 6 and trimmings and findings in Chapter 7.

FIBERS

Before the textile industry can supply fabrics to apparel manufacturers, it must first develop and produce both natural and man-made fibers.

Fibers are the hairlike raw materials that are spun into yarns and then made into fabrics. Fiber characteristics such as fineness, moisture regain, elasticity, luster, or crimp are inherent and, therefore, affect the properties of the yarns and fabrics made from them.[1]

Total world fiber production is continually growing. Production is now 39 billion kilograms per year as compared to 22 billion in 1970 (only one half of worldwide fiber production is for apparel).[2]

The vast differences between the *natural* and *man-made* fiber industries have resulted in markedly different operational and organizational forms, even though the final goal of both groups is the same—to produce fibers that fill consumer needs.

NATURAL FIBER PRODUCTION

Used for thousands of years, natural fibers are derived from either animals or plants.

Natural Fiber Producers

The natural fiber industry is dependent on animals and living plants. Thus, the production of natural fibers depends on climate and geography, and in most countries the majority of crops are produced by thousands of small farmers. For thousands of years, farmers around the world have worked independently to raise and harvest crops or raise and shear animals to obtain fibers. They sell their fibers at local markets to wholesalers, who, in turn, sell the fibers at central markets to textile mills.

The most widely used *natural fibers* are cotton, wool, flax, and silk. Others include ramie, jute, sisal, and hemp. There is a trend toward blending natural fibers to create new textures, such as linen with cotton, cotton with wool, or silk with cashmere.

Cotton

Cotton has long been the world's major textile fiber. It comprises about one-half of world fiber production or approximately 22 billion kilograms annually, but this amount fluctuates. A vegetable fiber, it grows best in tropical and subtropical climates. Leading cotton-growing countries are China followed by the United States. Uzbekistan, India, and Pakistan also produce large cotton crops.

In the United States, 14 states in the South make up what is known as the Cotton Belt, with Texas having the largest acreage under production. The *Cotton Belt* stretches from the Southeast through the Mississippi Delta to Arizona and California.

The cotton plant has blossoms that wither and fall off, leaving green pods called *bolls*. Inside each boll, moist fibers push out from newly formed seeds. The boll ripens and splits apart, causing the fluffy cotton fibers to burst forth.

There are 13 steps in manufacturing cotton yarn. Basically, the cotton is picked and *ginned*, an operation that separates the fiber from the seed. Then the fibers are cleaned and then straightened by the *carding* process.

Cotton fiber may be processed on a *combing* machine that removes short fibers, resulting in a smooth, uniform yarn. The quality of cotton depends on the length and fineness of the fiber or staple, long-staple cottons being the best quality. Among American cottons, Sea Island is considered the finest, followed by Pima.

Cotton harvesting. *(Courtesy of the Cotton Council)*

Cotton is washable and durable, holding up well after many launderings. But because it has no elasticity, it wrinkles easily. However, wrinkle-resistant finishes have recently been created that make cotton easier to care for. Cotton absorbs dyestuffs easily to produce a wide range of vivid colors. It also absorbs moisture, which makes it feel cool against the skin in hot, humid weather. For this reason, cotton has traditionally been a summer fabric. Yet cotton is very versatile and can be made in both light weights for summer and heavier weights for winter. Cotton fabrics range from the light and sheer (such as voile and batiste) to the heavy and thick (corduroy, flannel, and chenille) to the strong and sturdy (denim).

Flax

Flax is made from the fibrous material in the stem of the flax plant. Flax is harvested by pulling up the plants in order to preserve the full length of the fibers. Extracting the fibers from the flax plant is a lengthy and complex process. Flax seeds and adhesive substances that bind the fibers together must be removed by a process called *retting*. Then, in the *scutching* process, the fibers are separated from the outer bark and the woody inner core of the stem. Further processing can include *hacking* or *combing* and drawing the flax into a continuous ribbon of parallel fibers ready for spinning into yarn to make the fabric called *linen*.

Linen is the oldest known textile, dating back as far as the Stone Age. At one time linen was used extensively for bedding; this explains why we still call sheets, towels, and tablecloths collectively "linens." Flax was an important crop in the United States until the invention of the cotton gin in 1792 made cotton cheaper to produce.

The scutching process. *(Courtesy of the International Linen Promotion Commission)*

Today, flax makes up only 2 percent of world fiber production or approximately 600 million kilograms annually. Eighty percent of the world's flax is grown in Russia; France is the largest producer of flax in the Western world. Because the United States no longer grows flax, there are no quotas on its importation.

The cool, crisp, lightweight qualities of linen make it especially suited for summer clothing. Renewed interest in texture and natural fibers has repopularized linen and linen blends as well as linen look-alikes in the form of rayon and other fiber blends.

Ramie

Ramie is a formerly rare fiber that is now being used for apparel because its importation into the United States is not restricted, as there are no domestic commercial growers. A vegetable fiber similar to flax, it comes from the 5- to 6-foot stems of a nettlelike shrub. Ramie grows best in a semitropical climate and is imported primarily from India, China, and the Philippines.

Ramie is even stronger than flax and has a smooth, lustrous appearance. The fibers dye easily but are brittle and more difficult to spin and weave than other fibers. Therefore, it is most often combined with cotton to soften it.

Wool

Wool fiber comes from the fleece of animals, most commonly sheep. The *fleece* is removed by the use of shears or clippers in the *shearing* process. Wool fleece is a natural and renewable resource: after a year the wool has completely grown back and is again ready for shearing.

Although wool is commonly understood to be fiber from the fleece of sheep, some other animal fibers are also classified as wool. They include angora, camel's hair, cashmere, mohair, llama, alpaca, and vicuna. With fashion's focus on texture, specialty fibers, such as mohair, angora, and cashmere, have renewed popularity.

Wool fiber has an unusual ability to absorb and evaporate moisture. The crimp structure of wool fibers allows it to return to its natural position after stretching, which gives it resiliency. When woven or knitted, the crimp structure creates air pockets, which give it insulating properties. Because it is warm, wool has traditionally been used for fall and winter suits and coats. Yet it can also be woven or knitted into lightweight fabrics such as challis. Wool fibers are firm, yet soft and resilient, making wool fabrics resistant to wrinkling and comfortable to wear. Machine-washable, wrinkle-resistant wool

Shearing a Merino sheep in Australia.
(Courtesy of the Wool Bureau, Inc.)

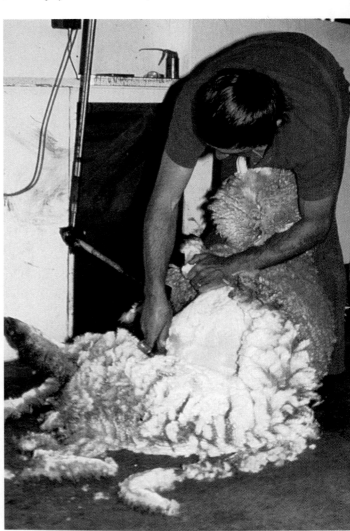

has been developed for use in trousers. Other new developments in wool fabrics include blends of cashmere, wool, and angora; metallic sparked suitings; and lightweight velour fleece.

Raw wool is *carded* (cleaning the fibers by separating and laying parallel) and *combed* to separate short fibers from long ones. The long fibers are spun into smooth, compact *worsted* yarns used for fabrics such as gabardine or crepe; short fibers make up the soft, dense *woolen* yarns used in textured tweeds and flannel.

Australia is by far the world's largest wool producer, followed by New Zealand. Although more than 1.9 billion kilograms of clean wool are processed each year, this represents only 4 percent of world textile fiber production.[3] The supply of wool changes yearly; sometimes there is a stockpile and other times a shortage.

Silk

Silk is the only natural fiber that comes in continuous *filament* form as opposed to short staple lengths. *Silk* is the protein filament secreted by a silkworm to make its cocoon. The silkworm, the forerunner of the silk moth, uses the cocoon as a shell to protect itself during its transformation from caterpillar to moth. Silk harvesters unwind the filament from the cocoon onto silk reels. A typical cocoon will produce 600 to 2000 meters of continuous fiber, making silk the only natural filament fiber. It takes over 500 silkworm cocoons to make a blouse.

The time and labor needed to cultivate silk make it a rare and therefore expensive fiber. World production of silk fiber is a mere 0.2 percent or only 60 million kilograms annually. Asia produces 95 percent of the world's raw silk filament fiber. Asia has decreased exports of raw silk and increased production and exports of finished silk fabrics. The most famous quality silk fabric mills are in Como, Italy, and Lyons, France, but the Koreans are learning their techniques.

There are four kinds of silk fibers: *Cultivated silk* comes from the domesticated silkworm. The filaments are almost even in size, their fineness indicated by a unit called *denier*. Cultivated silk is used for the finest silk fabrics, such as crepes, taffetas, and satins. *Wild* or *tussah silk* comes from the wild silkworm. Less secure environmental conditions cause the filaments to be coarser and more uneven. Therefore, fabric made from wild silk is not as smooth as that made from domesticated silk. *Douppioni silk* is the filament from two or more cocoons that have grown together so that the fibers join at intervals. Yarns made from these fibers have thick, uneven nubs from the joinings. Such yarns are used in shantung (a rough-textured silk made from uneven yarns). *Schappe* and *bourette (waste) silk* are composed of short fibers from damaged cocoons and are not strong or long enough to be used on their own. Yarn spun from waste silk also has irregular slubs (uneven yarns); it is used in rough-textured silks.

Silk has always been used for the finest garments. The silk fiber is triangular and reflects light, giving silk its unique luster. Because it takes dyes with exceptional depth and clarity and has a luxurious feel, it adds elegance to any garment. Silk also has insulation properties, making the wearer feel cool in summer and warm in winter. Silk drapes exceptionally well, is very strong yet lightweight, and is comfortable as well as beautiful.

MAN-MADE FIBERS

The phenomenal growth of the textile fiber industry would have been impossible without the development of man-made fibers.

Chemists began to experiment with synthetic fibers as early as 1850. In 1884 a Frenchman named Hilaire de Chardonnet patented a fabric he called "artificial silk," which is known today as *rayon* He discovered that silkworms use cellulose from mulberry leaves to make real silk, and he reproduced the process chemically. Rayon was first produced chemically in the United States in 1910, but not until 1939 was the first completely chemical fiber, *nylon*, introduced by DuPont.

Originally, the term *synthetics* was used to denote all chemically produced fibers. In the world market today, however, the term *synthetic* covers only the noncellulosic fibers. A true synthetic is made from the carbon atom of oil or coal, while viscose and acetate are rejuvenated cellulose. The textile industry refers to all chemically produced fibers together as *man-made* or *manufactured fibers*.

Man-made Fiber Producers

Large chemical companies such as BASF (Badische Anilin und Soda Fabrik), Courtaulds Fibers, Inc., DuPont, Hoechst-Celanese, and Zeneca (formerly ICI) pioneered the development of man-made fibers. The fiber divisions of these companies do extensive research and development of both fibers and fabrics and work closely with their customers, the textile mills, and provide technical services to manufacturers and retailers.

Strong competitive pressures from imports forced the U.S. textile industry to reorganize, consolidate, and focus on the things that they do best. This specialization has led to international mergers and acquisitions. For example, Linsing of Austria bought the rayon division of BASF and is now the world's largest rayon producer. DuPont bought Zeneca's nylon facilities and, in turn, Zeneca purchased DuPont's acrylic division.

Man-made fiber production depends mainly on the supply of petroleum products; therefore, it is subject to shortages and ever-increasing prices. In contrast with natural fibers, man-made fibers are produced by a few chemical companies, whose huge facilities enable them to take full advantage of mass production. These plants are located in areas where the combined cost of raw materials, labor, energy, and transportation is the lowest possible.

The growth rate of man-made fibers far outstrips that of natural fiber production. In 1960, man-made fiber production was only 3.511 billion kilograms or 22 percent of world fiber production as compared to over 17.6 billion kilograms or 46 percent of world production today (however, only about one-third of this amount is used for apparel).[4] This growth is due to many factors: fiber research and development by chemical companies, new technical developments in making new varieties of fibers, the scarcity and expense of some natural fibers, and increased production facilities in Asia. The United States produces less than one-quarter of that amount, having lost some of its share of the market to foreign competition.

The United States as a single nation leads the world in man-made fiber production, followed by Taiwan, Japan, Korea, and China. However, if you combine the Asian countries, their output far exceeds that of the United States. Asia and the United States are followed by Western Europe (primarily Germany and Italy) and Russia.[5]

Of utmost importance is the use of man-made fibers in blends, either with each other or with natural fibers. Blends capitalize on the best qualities of each fiber. For example, a polyester might be blended with cotton to add easy-care properties to the look and feel of the natural cotton. Polyester might also be blended with rayon to create a less expensive substitute for flax.

Cellulosic Fibers

Derived chiefly from the pulp of wood, cellulosic fibers create a *hand* (the feel, body, and fall of a fabric) more like that produced by natural fibers compared to chemical noncellulosic fibers. They include rayon, acetate, and triacetate.

Rayon

The first man-made fiber to be developed, rayon is composed of rejuvenated cellulose derived from wood pulp, cotton linters, or other vegetable matter and dissolved into a viscose spinning solution. Rayon has become very popular because it is a soft, lustrous, versatile fiber that can be treated and finished to produce a wide range of characteristics. There are new developments of silklike rayon microfibers. However, soaring wood prices have made rayon expensive, and the caustic materials needed for the wet-spinning process cause pollution. The rayon fiber industry is incurring heavy costs to conform to more stringent environmental standards.

Lyocell (CF0001)

Lyocell is the generic designation in the United Kingdom for a new type of solvent-spun cellulosic fiber developed by Courtaulds, known commercially as Tencel. In the United States it is currently known generically as CF0001 until the Federal Trade Commission gives it a generic name. Lyocell is twice as strong as rayon, both wet and dry, and is a good blending partner with cotton, wool, acetate, and polyester. It takes color well and its hand can be altered to resemble silk or cotton. Like rayon, Lyocell is produced from wood pulp. However, Lyocell is manufactured using a solvent spinning technique in which the dissolving agent is recycled, thus reducing waste that is harmful to the environment.

Acetate and Triacetate

Acetate (diacetate) and triacetate have been adopted as less expensive, less polluting (they can be dry spun) alternatives to rayon as they are also soft and lustrous, although not quite as strong as rayon. Both are cellulose chains treated with acetic anhydride. However, only two-thirds of the chain is treated to produce diacetate. The entire chain (all three parts) are treated to produce triacetate. Then both kinds (acetate and triacetate) are dissolved in a solvent to make dry spinning possible. Triacetate can be heat-set to give it easy-care properties, but it requires such strong solvents that it is no longer produced in the United States. Diacetate can be dissolved in solvents that are easier to handle and therefore is more widely produced.

Noncellulosic or Synthetic Fibers

Made from chemical derivatives of petroleum, coal, and natural gas, synthetic fibers used in apparel include nylon, polyester, acrylic, spandex, and polypropylene.

Nylon

One of the most durable man-made fibers in spite of its extreme light weight, nylon is made of a long-chain synthetic polymer that has recurring amide groups. Scientists have learned to vary the shape and width to develop nylons with a crisp, even, silky hand. The filaments can also be textured to produce a soft, supple hand. Nylon is not only strong but also flexible, washable, and colorfast. In apparel it is used primarily in hosiery, lingerie, bathing suits, and active sportswear.

Polyester

A long-chain synthetic polymer (composed primarily of dihydric alcohol ester and terephthalic acid), polyester is the most widely used man-made fiber in the world. Fiber forms produced are filament, staple, and tow (short or broken fiber). The production process resembles that of nylon. There is a wide variety of polyester fibers that differ in, among other variables, their shape, whiteness, type of crimp, and whether they are solid or hollow. Polyester is highly wrinkle resistant and easy to care for. It was one of the first fibers to be developed in fabrics with permanent-press features. It is often blended with natural fibers to lend easy-care properties to them. New developments include microdenier polyester. It is used in many types of apparel, including textured knits and wovens, permanent-press blend fabrics, shirtings, suitings, and sleepwear.

Acrylic

A long-chain synthetic polymer (composed mainly of acrylonitrile units), acrylic fiber is thermoplastic, allowing fabrics to be heat-set for wrinkle resistance and permanent pleating. Because of the composition and cross section of

New uses for nylon include this quilted suit from Prada. *(Courtesy of Prada)*

the fiber, fabrics made of acrylic have a high bulk-to-weight ratio. This provides warmth in fabrics that are lightweight, soft, and resilient. End uses of acrylics include knitwear, fleece activewear, suits, and coats. Acrylic fiber is often used to simulate fur.

Spandex

A long-chain synthetic polymer comprised of segmented polyurethane, spandex can stretch over 500 percent without breaking and return to its original length. Its elastic properties are unequaled by any other fiber, and it does not deteriorate as rubber does. Because of its tremendous stretch, spandex is generally blended with other fibers in small percentages of 2 percent to 20 percent. When blended, spandex is essentially invisible. This characteristic makes it an excellent fiber for use in swimwear, hosiery, and active sportswear. Spandex is very popular and is blended with cotton, nylon, rayon, and even flax to create stretch fabrics. It is used in stretch wovens as well as knits and even stretch satin for evening wear! It is most often seen advertised under the DuPont brand name of Lycra.

Modern man-made fibers, such as nylon, spandex, and polypropylene, help to keep skiwear flexible, warm, and dry. *(Courtesy of Fila, Inc.)*

Polypropylene

An olefin fiber made from polymers, polypropylene is very strong and resilient. It provides greater coverage per pound than any other fiber, yet it is so light that it actually floats. While major uses of polypropylene are industrial and carpet applications, its good insulative properties make it desirable in high-tech activewear where moisture transport is important.

Generic and Brand Identification

When a completely new fiber is developed, the U. S. Federal Trade Commission assigns it a generic name, such as *polyester*. Many companies produce polyester, but they each call it by a different name in order to promote it independently. A *brand name* or *trademark* (identifiable symbol) is registered and is owned by the manufacturer. For example, Dacron is DuPont's brand name for polyester, while Trivera is Hoechst-Celanese's brand name. The Textile Fibers Products Identification Act requires that end products carry labels listing the generic names of the fibers used and the percentage of each.

It is possible to work within the basic generic composition of an existing generic fiber and modify it, both chemically and physically, to change the properties of the fiber to create variants. *Variants* are specialty fibers for special applications. For example, Hoechst-Celanese created a silklike, lustrous polyester they call *Ceylon* to use as a silk substitute. Another variant called *Linenesque* was created with a new texture suitable for blending with rayon to imitate linen. Not all variants are intended to imitate natural fibers. Some are blended with natural fibers to add easy-care properties to them. Others are engineered to add stretch, moisture wicking, or other comfort properties. *Thermax* is DuPont's brand name for its insulating hollow-core polyester. There are also variants of other man-made fibers.

Man-made Fiber Production

In very simple terms, all man-made fibers are extruded from a viscous solution of cellulose (purified wood pulp) or from chemical raw material. Originally, the chemical substances exist as solids and therefore must be first converted into a liquid state. The raw materials are converted into flakes, chips, crumbs, or pellets, which are then dissolved in a solvent, melted with heat or chemically converted into a syrupy liquid, and pumped through the tiny holes of a spinneret to form continuous filaments. The process of extrusion and hardening is called *spinning*, not to be confused with the textile yarn operation of the same name.

Unlike natural fibers, the man-made fibers can be extruded in different thicknesses, called *denier*. These long fibers can be left as continuous filaments or cut into staple (short, uniform lengths) to be blended with other fibers.

Man-made fibers were first created to imitate the texture of natural fibers, duplicating their crimp, length, and thickness. Since then, scientists have learned how to vary the shape, composition, and size of fibers to achieve pleasing aesthetic effects and higher levels of performance.

The newest man-made fiber development is *microfibers*, which contain individual filaments that are less than one denier thick, twice as fine as silk. Used primarily in polyester, this luxury fiber is giving polyester a renaissance. It can be used alone or combined with silk, worsted wool, or other fibers.

TEXTILE YARN AND FABRIC PRODUCERS

Textile mills and converters are the producers of yarns and fabrics and the suppliers to the apparel industry.

There are over 4307 apparel-related textile plants (yarn, fabric, and finishing) dispersed throughout the United States and approximately 593,000 people are employed in domestic textile production.[6,7] Although textile mills exist in almost every state, the Carolinas and Georgia together account for more than half of all industry employment. Much of the industry has moved to the Southeast to be close to the source of cotton and where overall expenses, especially labor, tend to be lowest. The textile industry is also growing in the Los Angeles area. However, because New York City is the nation's fashion capital, most textile companies have offices there, as well as sales representatives all over the country (see Chapter 6).

Textile Mills

Mills are the producers of yarns and fabrics. Some mills produce only yarns; others knit and weave fabric from their own yarns or from purchased yarns. Certain mills produce unfinished fabrics called *greige* (pronounced "gray") *goods*, which are sold to converters to be finished, or they may produce both greige goods and finished fabrics. Small mills usually specialize in one type of fabric, such as velveteen or corduroy. Large companies create separate divisions to do the same thing, grouping similar fabrics under one division.

The various stages in textile production may or may not be handled by firms under common ownership. Firms have tended to grow either forward or backward into the production or marketing chain to form large *vertical mills*, which perform all processes, from top to bottom (fiber to fabric). However, these operations are separated in specialized facilities. Milliken and Burlington are examples of vertical mills.

Mills have had increased capital expenditures for the latest technology to offset the low labor cost advantage of imports. Because of the huge investment they have in machinery and technology and the expense of changing it, the large mills tend to serve the mass market with volume fabrics. In domestic mills, everything is computerized: the spinning and texturing of fibers and yarns; high-speed weaving and knitting; and automated material handling, dyeing, and finishing. Their commitments do not allow the flexibility of keeping up with fashion trends and the pressure for constant change.

Converters

Converters do only the finishing stages of production. They can be a division of a vertically integrated textile company or independent. Converters *source* (find the best quality goods at the best price) greige goods from domestic or worldwide mills. They design prints or buy them from a studio and specify colors and finishes. They usually contract out all printing, dyeing, and finishing processes to specialized factories rather than owning production facilities. This gives them the flexibility to be able to change methods or products to keep up with changing fashion. Therefore, the converter is an important supplier of fashion-oriented fabrics to manufacturers. Examples of converters include Abraham, Brittany, Channel, Charter, and Pressman-Gutman.

YARN PRODUCTION

Once a fiber is produced, yarn production is the next step in creating a garment.

Textile manufacturers choose a yarn-making technique that can best achieve the texture, hand, or drape desired. Yarn can be made as coarse as rug yarn or finer than sewing thread. Finished yarn is then sold to fabric producers to be used for weaving and knitting.

stitches per inch on the finished fabric may be more or less than the number of needles per inch. A 5-cut machine with 5 needles is the most commonly used for bulky knits. However, the resulting knit fabric can have as little as 3 stitches per inch or as many as 9 stitches depending on the amount and size of yarn fed into the machine. The more needles there are, the finer and closer the knit loops are. A fine jersey might be made on a 28-cut machine. The most common cut-and-sew jerseys and double knits are 18 to 24 cut.

Weft and *warp* knitting are the two basic methods of knitting fabric.

Weft Knitting

When the loops run horizontally across the width of the fabric, the process is called *weft knitting*. Weft knits can be made on either flatbed or circular machines, and circular knits may be either single or double knit. In single knits, all the stitches in a given course or row are made with a single yarn. In double knits, the stitches in a given row may be made by interlocking two different yarn feeds. Weft knits are made in a wide variety of single and double knits and generally have more stretch than warp knits.

Jersey is the basic construction of all weft knits. The front and the back of the garment are different in appearance. The rows of stitches running across the garment are called *courses* and the ones running vertically are called *wales*. Jersey is the most common stitch used in fine-gauge fabrics and stretches equally in length and width. Popular uses include pantyhose, underwear, and full-fashioned sweaters (see Chapter 10 for sweater and knitwear production). There are many variations on the jersey construction that are made by differing needle arrangements.

◆ **Purl** knit is actually the reverse side of jersey and used primarily for sweater knits.

◆ **Rib**-knit fabrics have a distinctive lengthwise rib on both sides of the fabric for added stretch in the width. A combination of jersey and purl stitches, it is most often used in sweaters, socks, knit accessories, or trims such as neckbands or cuffs.

◆ **Interlock** knit looks like jersey on both sides of the fabric. The stitches alternate a half movement up or down to create a zigzag horizontally across the fabric.

◆ **Knit and welt** uses the front and back beds of the knitting machine to create a welt.

◆ **Float-jacquard** knits have a pattern on the face side. Yarns not being used on the pattern float on the back until they are needed again.

◆ **Full-jacquard** knits also have a pattern on the face side, but there is another simple pattern on the back instead of floats. This requires the use of both the front and back knitting beds and makes a double fabric, which is heavier.

◆ **Novelties**, including *tuck* stitches, *miss* stitches, and *pointelles*, can be created with other needle arrangements.

Warp Knitting

In *warp knitting*, multiple yarns are used and the loops run vertically and zigzag across each other to form the fabric. Each stitch in a row is made by a different yarn that is fed from a sheet of yarns wound on a beam. Patterns and inlays can be introduced by various needle arrangements. The Missonis in Italy are famous for their beautiful warp knits. Warp knits include tricot and raschel.

Tricot knit fabrics are usually made with fine-denier filament yarns. They are soft, drape well, and are somewhat elastic. Popular uses include women's lingerie and uniforms for nurses.

Raschel is the most complex warp-knit machine capable of making lacy open stitches. Yarns may be heavily twisted filament yarns or spun yarns. Uses of this knit include thermal underwear, swimwear, shapewear, knitted lace, and crochet.

Nonwoven Fabrics

Nonwoven (or *engineered*) fabrics are made by either bonding or interlocking fibers, filaments, or yarns into a web or sheet by mechanical (pressure, needle punch, or needle tufting), chemical, thermal (heat), or solvent means. Examples of such fabrics include nonwoven interfacings such as Pellon. Felting is a process for making matted fabrics, such as nonwoven felt. Nonwoven fabric production usually includes four stages: (1) fiber preparation, (2) web formation, (3) web bonding, and (4) post-treatment. Nonwoven fabrics constitute one of the fastest growing segments of the textile industry.

Production Centers

Italy and Japan produce the most woven woolen apparel fabrics and Italy the most woolen knitwear. Better cottons come from Italy and Switzerland. However, the largest cotton fabric producer is China, followed by Eastern Europe and then India and the United States. The United States produces more denim than any other country. Linen fabrics are produced in Italy, Belgium, Northern Ireland, France, China, and Poland. Italy produces the most printed silks, but only one-third of the total world silk fabrics. The other two-thirds come from Korea. It is difficult to calculate the production of fabrics from man-made fibers because so many are blends and most industry and trade associations calculate production only in their own countries. The three major global centers of man-made and blend fabrics are Asia, Europe, and the United States.

DYEING

Dyeing can be done at any stage of fiber, yarn, or fabric production. Some of the most important methods of dyeing are the following:

Producer colored   Producer or solution dyeing, used for man-made fibers, adds the pigment or color when the fibers are still in solution before the filaments are formed.

Stock dyeing   The dyeing of loose fibers before yarn processing.

ENVIRONMENTAL CONCERNS

The growing demand for more environmentally friendly products has generated a new awareness and ingenuity at each level of the textile industry.

The American Textile Manufacturers Institute has established an Environmental Excellence program to set up an awareness and action program. This includes environmental targets and audits to encourage recycling and environmentally efficient manufacturing and finishing processes. As a result, many textile firms now budget and plan for environmental improvements.

Alternatives in Cotton Growing

New standards are being set for the growing, processing, printing, and dyeing of natural cotton fabrics. Sally Fox, president of Fox Fibers, has developed naturally colored brown, green, blue, and pink cotton that eliminates the need for dye. New strains of cotton are being developed that are insect and water resistant and require little if any chemical insecticides or fertilizers. Organic farming techniques promise chemical-free cotton fibers.

Recycled Polyester

Recent developments in recycled products include EcoSpun by Wellman Inc., recycled soda bottles and polyester manufacturing waste that are cleaned, chopped, melted, and spun into fiber and used mostly in fleece for outerwear.

Alternatives in Fiber and Fabric Production and Finishing

Various companies are working to develop nontoxic pesticides, environmentally friendly alternatives to PVA and finishing detergents; citric-acid cleaners to replace phosphate and chlorine; natural oils to supplant petroleum lubricants; bifunctional, fiber-reactive dyes to decrease water use and chemical waste; resins to replace formaldehyde; and enzymes to replace acid washes.

"Green" Jeans

Formerly, the textile industry was *dumping* approximately 70 milion pounds of scrap denim a year into American landfills. Now, North Carolina State University in conjunction with Burlington Industries has developed a method to reclaim cotton waste and convert it into yarn for reweaving. The new material, called Reused Denim, is made of 50% reclaimed denim yarn and 50% virgin cotton yarn.[8] Companies are also making efforts to reclaim other scrap.

Costs of Environmental Improvements

The expense for all these improvements causes problems. Some American textile producers are against environmental improvements due to the expense. The costs to American and European textile companies to maintain health, safety, and clean air and water are astronomical. It is therefore very difficult for environmentally responsible producers to compete with the low prices from mills in Taiwan and China where producers do not pay to clean up their environment.

American textile manufacturers want to require imported textile products to be made under the same environmental, health and safety standards to ensure fair competition as well as a clean environment throughout the world.

SUMMARY

Textile producers, the suppliers to apparel manufacturers, are an integral part of the fashion industry. Textile fibers are the basis for fabrics. They are classified as natural (cotton, flax, wool, or silk) or man-made (cellulosic or noncellulosic). Yarns are made from fibers or filaments and are usually woven or knitted into fabrics. The fabrics are then dyed or printed and finished in preparation for shipment to manufacturers.

The phenomenal growth of the textile industry would not have been possible without the development of man-made fibers. These fibers have revolutionized the industry, especially in the areas of yarn and knit production and fabric printing. The industry is making advances in the development of environmentally friendly production. The textile industry is now dominated by a few large companies for only they have the capital for the modern technology needed to survive in today's competitive international textile market (see Chapter 6).

CHAPTER REVIEW

Terms and Concepts

Briefly identify and discuss the following terms and concepts:

1. Textiles
2. Natural fibers
3. Flax
4. Ramie
5. Worsted yarns
6. Synthetic fibers
7. Man-made fibers
8. Cellulosic fibers
9. Lyocell
10. Microfibers
11. Generic fiber names
12. Man-made fiber spinning methods
13. Spun yarns
14. Filament-yarn texturing
15. Plain weave
16. Twill weave
17. Warp knitting
18. Types of dyeing
19. Printing techniques
20. Finishing methods
21. Mills
22. Converters

Questions for Review

1. Why is a study of textiles important to someone working in apparel production?
2. What determines the quality of cotton?
3. What are the two basic ways of making fabric?
4. How is knit yardage made?
5. Give examples of textile dyeing methods that can be used at three different levels of fabric production.
6. Why were specialization and consolidation important in the textile industry?
7. What is the difference between a mill and a converter?

Projects for Additional Learning

1. Examine the fiber-content labels in the clothes in your wardrobe. How many garments are made from natural fibers? How many from man-made fibers? How many from blends? How does the fiber content affect the care of the garment?

2. Visit a local fabric store and find examples of a plain weave, a twill weave, a satin weave, a novelty weave, a warp knit, a circular knit, and a nonwoven fabric. Ask for tiny swatches of each or purchase the smallest amount possible to illustrate your findings.

NOTES

[1] Joe Sammartino, sales manager, Milliken & Co., interview, February 1995.

[2] Bertye Worsham, Cotton Incorporated, interview, February 1995.

[3] John E. Eckert, director, Technical Center, The Wool Bureau Inc., interview, January 26, 1995.

[4] "World Fibre Production," 7 *Wool Facts* booklet, International Wool Secretariat, London, March 1992, table 2.

[5] *Wool Facts*, tables 23 and 24.

[6] Dave Link, director, American Textile Manufacturers Institute, interview, April 19, 1995.

[7] "U. S. Industrial Outlook," U. S. Department of Commerce, Washington, D. C., January 1994, p. 9-1.

[8] "Scrap Denim Spun into 'Green' Jeans," *Apparel Industry Magazine*, February 1995, p. 16.

A Cotton Incorporated fashion marketing presentation in Thailand.
(Courtesy of Cotton Incorporated)

6

TEXTILE PRODUCT DEVELOPMENT AND MARKETING

CAREER FOCUS

In textile product development there are career opportunities in research, design, and merchandising. In marketing, positions range from entry-level junior sales representative to account manager, sales manager, marketing manager, and director of marketing. There are also the support areas of advertising and public relations to consider. Most of these opportunities are in New York City, Los Angeles, or other textile centers.

It is also essential for manufacturers and retailers to understand the marketing forces that transform fibers into fabrics and then move these fabrics into the hands of the apparel designers and manufacturers.

CHAPTER OBJECTIVES

After reading this chapter you should have attained competence in the following areas:

1. Understanding of the impact of imports on the domestic textile industry
2. Understanding of the importance of product development for both fibers and fabrics
3. Knowledge of the promotional tools of the textile industry

*T*extile producers respond to consumer demand through their product development and marketing efforts. Textile consumers include the fabric manufacturers who use fibers, the apparel manufacturers who use fabrics, and the end users who buy apparel.

Product development covers the research, merchandising, and styling involved in creating new and updating existing products.

Marketing incorporates the entire process of planning, promoting, and selling of goods, in this case textiles.

Much has changed and will continue to change in textile marketing. This chapter discusses the impact that foreign competition and consumer demand have on the industry. It also describes how the industry is reacting with product development, new technologies, and new marketing strategies for fibers and fabrics. Product development, design, and marketing activities are centered in textile and fashion capitals such as Paris, Milan, Como, Lyon, London, Tokyo, New York, and Los Angeles.

THE GLOBAL TEXTILE MARKET

Globalization has made a huge impact on the textile industry.

One major trend in the textile and fashion industries is globalization. Nowhere is this more evident than in the textile industry. Ever increasing amounts of textile products are being imported into the United States because of the availability of cheaper labor abroad. American manufacturers compete with labor rates of as little as 25 cents per hour in China, Thailand, Pakistan, and India and 15 cents an hour in Indonesia.[1]

Imports Cause Trade Imbalance and Loss of Jobs

Fierce competition from imports has caused the American industry to lose over 50 percent of its domestic market and has resulted in buyouts, takeovers, and consolidations to salvage what was left. Since 1980, imports have increased from 4 billion square meters to 12.4 billion; the textile trade deficit has increased from $5 billion to $25 billion; the industry has lost at least 350,000 jobs, and 1000 plants have closed.[2] This corresponds to the enormous growth of the textile industries of Japan, China, Taiwan, Korea, and India.

Even American textile converters are joining the stampede to import, as they find that fabrics produced and finished overseas are sometimes 25 to 30 percent cheaper than those produced domestically.[3] They also find quality improved and lower minimum requirements. However, they also find that producing overseas requires longer lead times. For a complete discussion of imports and global trade, see Chapter 2.

Exports and Overseas Investment

American textile producers find that one way to compete in the global economy is to export. With the devaluation of the dollar against other currencies, this is becoming a viable way to create new business. Also, just as foreign producers have opened facilities here, some U.S. textile companies, such as Burlington, Cone Mills, Dan River, and Guilford Mills, are among those that are investing in Mexico.

COMPUTERS IN TEXTILE MARKETING

Computer technology has helped textile producers to cut down on wasted time in the textile marketing chain.

In an effort to combat imports with faster response to consumer needs than imports can provide, textile and computer experts developed a computer strategy called Quick Response (QR). As discussed fully in Chapter 2, QR is an attempt to reduce wasted time in ordering and distribution between textile and apparel producers by forming cooperative alliances between them via electronic data interchange (EDI), the exchange of data between two parties by means of computer. This strategy requires a willingness to supply on a reorder basis and the flexibility to sell smaller quantitites of fabric.

Crafted With Pride

In conjunction with Quick Response, textile producers formed the Crafted with Pride in the USA council to promote domestic-made goods. The council points out that the American textile industry has the advantage of its close proximity to the American consumer. Domestic suppliers should be more convenient, dependent, and expeditious. Purchasing U.S.-made textiles allows shorter lead time in ordering. However, many people now feel that Crafted with Pride is outdated, that value, cost, style, color, fabric, and fashion are the real factors that influence consumer purchasing, not the country of origin.

NEW MARKETING STRATEGIES

To compete with imports, textile producers have developed new marketing strategies.

The American textile industry was built on producing large volume, streamlining the product in order to be efficient and offering quality at a reasonable price. In response to consumer demand, textile producers have had to overhaul their marketing strategies completely. With so many diverse life-styles and resulting market niches, textile firms realize that they have to be market driven (responding to market or consumer needs) rather than manufacturing driven.

Textile manufacturers are trying to provide innovative styling, better quality and flexibility and to respond more quickly to the market. However, to be fashionable and flexible, it is necessary to produce smaller quantities, which costs more per yard. The new strategies are more difficult; it is easier and less expensive to go on making the same thing. Innovation, which requires creativity and not just improved technology, has become an important part of the business.

FIBER PRODUCT DEVELOPMENT AND MARKETING

To meet consumer demand, fiber producers do extensive research and product development. Textile marketers then promote and sell these fibers to yarn or fabric producers.

In the past, the marketing role of the natural-fiber producer was relatively simple. The crops or animals were raised, harvested or sheared, and the fibers sold at local markets to wholesalers who in turn sold the fibers at central markets. Sheep farmers and cotton growers did not have to be concerned with fabric and garment promotion; there was no competition.

Man-made Fibers. The development of man-made fibers and new marketing strategies changed all that. The giant chemical companies that make man-made fibers invest a great deal of time and money in the research and development of new fibers and variants. This process may take several years (see Table 6-1). Several fiber companies may research the same problem simultaneously and might develop similar, competitive fibers. Then these chemical companies try to create a demand for the new fibers among yarn and fabric producers and apparel manufacturers and educate the consumer on the value and uses of these fibers.

Natural Fibers. The need to compete with man-made fibers forced natural fiber producers to form associations to promote their own fibers. Supported by growers, they include Cotton Incorporated, the International Wool Secretariat (the Wool Bureau in the United States), the Silk Institute, and the International Linen Promotion.

Cotton Incorporated has a research center in North Carolina and its headquarters in New York City where it utilizes advertising and promotion to build demand for cotton. The International Wool Secretariat (IWS) has a huge research facility in Ilkley, England, and worldwide offices such as the Wool Bureau for promotional activities. All the

Researching new fiber finishes in a textile laboratory. *(Courtesy of the International Wool Secretariat, England)*

TABLE 6-1
Timing of Product Development in the Textile and Apparel Industries
(The industry constantly strives to shorten lead times.)

Activity	Length of Time Before Retail Selling Season
Development of new fibers and variants	Several years
Fabric development (fiber firms working with mills to research and develop new fabrics)	1 to 2 years
Color predictions (fiber level)	18 to 20 months
Presentation of new fabric lines by fabric producers (Interstoff, Premier Vision, Ideacomo, etc.)	1 year
Shopping fabric lines (by designers and merchandisers)	8 months to 1 year
Apparel design and line development	6 to 9 months
Apparel collection openings, market weeks, showing lines to retail buyers, taking orders	4 to 6 months
Apparel production	1 to 5 months
Shipping to retail stores	1 week to 1 month
Apparel for sale in retail store	0

natural fiber associations work to improve fiber quality and processing, support fabric development, and promote their fibers to the trade and consumers.

Sales Promotion

To foster sales, fiber producers make their products known to potential consumers. The man-made fiber industry has concentrated on consumer brand recognition and uses of new fibers or variants. Natural fiber associations also want the public to be aware of the attributes of their fibers. Both use trademarks or *logos* (symbols) for identification, such as the Wool Bureau's ball of yarn symbol.

To prepare for international textile trade shows such as Premier Vision or Interstoff, fiber producers may have sample fabrics and garments made up to display. These samples show yarn and fabric producers how the fiber may effectively be used in a fabric.

Advertising and Publicity

The goal of advertising is to make consumers aware of natural fibers or man-made brands. Fiber producers advertise to fabric and apparel manufacturers in trade publications. They may offer *cooperative advertising dollars* (to share the cost of advertising) to fabric producers, manufacturers, and retailers that use their fibers. In this case, the fiber brands must be identified in the ads. These cooperative allowances are based on the percentage of fibers used in the fabrics or may be based on market potential in order to stimulate interest in a fiber.

A still from the Woolmark global television advertising campaign to increase awareness of wool as a contemporary fiber.
(Courtesy of the International Wool Secretariat, England)

Fiber producers may also advertise their brands directly to consumers in consumer magazines or on television. Cotton Incorporated's "Fabric of Our Lives" is an example of a national fiber advertising campaign. Television ads appealed to consumers' emotional association with the product by showing people in real-life situations wearing cotton. The aim of the campaign was to raise consumer awareness and demand for cotton.

Publicity is another way of sending a message to the consumer. In this case there is no cost for media coverage. Fiber producers and trade associations continually provide the press with newsworthy material and photographs in hope of an editorial mention.

Marketing and Customer Services

Fiber producers provide many services to their customers on both the manufacturing and retailing levels in order to promote sales.

Consumer education   Fiber producers continually provide information on their products to apparel manufacturers, schools, and the general public in the form of brochures, exhibits, lectures, audiovisual aids, and films. This information covers every aspect of fibers and fabrics, including history, production, use, care, and benefits to the consumer.

Technical advice   Fiber producers offer advice to yarn and textile mills as well as to garment manufacturers. Fiber producers often commission fabric designers to work up new ideas for them. Samples of these ideas are woven or knitted in short runs, and swatches are sent to the mills. The fiber producers are also able to offer mills production advice.

Hang tags   Some fiber producers provide apparel manufacturers with printed hang tags listing fiber properties and often care instructions. Hang tags can be a useful form of publicity as well as information for the consumer.

Fashion presentations   Fiber producers have been the major source for styling and color directions. Based on their research, fiber producers make trend direction information available to mills, converters, and manufacturers, usually on a semiannual basis. A stylist representing the fiber producer may make presentations to manufacturers showing garments, new and experimental fabrics, and color charts. Presentations are often targeted to specific needs, such as coat ideas for coat manufacturers or men's wear ideas for men's wear manufacturers. Market research and sourcing information may be included. Some companies also produce fashion styling reports.

Color forecasts   Color directions based on color cycles, the economy, the arts, and international fashion trends are researched at the fiber level. These are combined with basic and seasonal colors to round out the color story. Companies decide on the colors that they think will be the most popular and dye yarn or fabric swatches to present to their customers. These are usually made available to fabric producers and manufacturers to help them plan their color stories.

Fabric libraries   An important service of the fiber producers is their fabric libraries, located in major fashion centers such as Paris, London, New York, and Los Angeles. Fabric libraries keep samples of fabrics from every mill or converter using their fibers. A designer can visit the library for an overall picture of what is available. If a designer is looking for a specific fabric, the library can help locate a mill or converter that makes it. Some libraries now bar code the fabric samples. A scanner automatically reads and prints out the name and address of the mill and the contact person. At the same time, the designer's name is sent to the mill or converter so they know of potential customers.

A selection of wool color cards and yarn forecasts.
(Courtesy of the International Wool Secretariat, England)

Fiber Distribution

Natural Fibers

Fibers are sold to mills for yarn spinning and weaving or knitting. The farmers who produce natural fibers sell their goods at the markets organized by their various trade associations. The major markets in the United States are Dallas, Houston, Memphis, and New Orleans for cotton and Boston for wool. Farmers have no control over prices, which are set in the marketplace by supply and demand.

Man-made Fibers

The large chemical companies that produce man-made fibers have their own sales forces and set prices based on their costs. In some cases, when fiber producers and mills are vertically integrated into one large company, the producing company becomes its own market.

Fibers are often sold under certain obligations so that standards of quality may be controlled. After spending a great deal on advertising to build a good reputation for a fiber's performance, the producer wants to preserve that good name. Restrictions on standards are therefore imposed when the fiber is sold under a brand name or a licensing agreement. There are no restrictions if the fiber is sold without the use of a brand name.

FABRIC PRODUCT DEVELOPMENT AND MARKETING

The next step in the textile marketing chain is the development and marketing of yarns and fabrics.

Fabric is becoming the driving force of change within the fashion industry. Karl Lagerfeld commented, "Fabrics bring the big changes now. Lycra, stretch and all that really made things possible that you could not do before, except in couture with 20 fittings."[4] There are many exciting innovations in fabrics, especially in blends that create interesting textures.

Textile Design

Specialization

To focus on a specific target market, fabric producers specialize in one or a few types of fabrics. For example, their collection may center on only one fiber or fiber blend, a certain quality level, only knits, or only prints. Within that specialty, they offer a well-balanced line of fabrics and prices. Textile designers, too, tend to specialize in print, woven, or knitted design. They may work as full-time employees of mills, converters, or design studios or sell their designs to textile companies.

Market and Technical Research

Fabric merchandisers and designers try to anticipate consumers' needs by doing intensive market research. They also study international fashion and fabric trends and work to develop fashionable products having desirable fiber blends, finishes, and other properties. Merchandisers and designers must understand the physical attributes of fibers, the effects that can be achieved with the yarns that they are using, as well as the capabilities and limitations of the weaving looms or knitting machines to be used. They work hand in hand with textile engineers and have to understand textile processes to know if their ideas will work.

Focusing on End Use

Product managers, merchandisers, and designers feel that it is very important to consider the fabric's end use.

◆ Fiber content and yarn sizes that are appropriate for the season and type of garment to be made

◆ Fabrics and prints that are appropriate for the men's wear, women's wear, or children's wear manufacturers that will use them

◆ Fabric prices that will fit into the price ranges of finished apparel

Concerned primarily with texture, textile designers may use CAD systems to help them experiment with visual representations of weave and pattern designs. A well-balanced collection of fabrics is created within the company's product line. Then a color story is chosen for the entire collection or for various groups within it.

Designer Marc Grant paints one of his original textile designs.
(Courtesy of Jeanne-Marc, photographed by the author)

Print Design

Print design ideas come from worldwide influences, including historic and folkloric motifs, wallpapers, old fabrics, architecture, nature, and people's hobbies and interests. Designers may shop worldwide for fabrics or garments as a source of new ideas. Many fabric companies maintain fabric archives to supply designers with ideas from the past for new prints. Print designers must consider the essential elements of color, texture, line, shape, and space. *The motifs* (repeated designs) for a print should have interesting shapes, a pleasing rhythmic pattern, and a harmonious relationship to one another.

Designers are concerned primarily with a two-dimensional surface, the flat fabric. Yet they must keep the three-dimensional end use of the fabric in mind if they are to create practical designs. Print design is a continuous repetition of motifs, and the designer must consider how cutting will affect the pattern.

Different types of prints may be designed for particular segments of the apparel industry. For example, florals and feminine motifs may be aimed at women's apparel, traditional geometrics at men's wear, and small, whimsical prints at children's wear. However, the use of prints is also cyclical; some kinds of prints are more popular than others at a given time.

A textile designer uses a computer-aided-design system to experiment with color combinations in a print repeat. *(Courtesy of Cotton Incorporated)*

Mills or converters may have their own design studios or they may purchase original designs from independent print studios in Milan, Paris, London, Tokyo, or New York. Large print studios may also bring their design collections to New York and other textile centers for trade exposure. The original *croquis* (paintings) are then put into a repeat design for fabric application. Variations, repeat work, restyling, and coloring may be done by the converter's own studio or by an independent studio. CAD systems are sometimes used to make the original design and most often used for repeat work. CAD systems also transfer licensed artwork to be printed on T-shirts and sweatshirts, such as the Disney/Warner characters.

Coloring

A print is usually offered in several colorways. For a new color combination, a croquis is made by the textile firm's design department or by computer. If that is approved, a *strike-off* is run as a test on a short piece of fabric. Minimum yardage requirements for custom colors vary with the printing method.

The Fabric Collection

The textile industry must develop fabrics early enough to allow apparel designers time to find and test suitable goods. Every season, fabric producers prepare a new line or collection of fabrics to show to their customers, the apparel designers, and manufacturers. Designers at Abraham AG, a trend-setting converter in Zurich, for example, create collections of more than 300 fabric designs twice a year.

It is very important for fabric merchandisers and designers to work directly with apparel manufacturers while developing the line. Cathy Cregan-Valent, director of fabric development and merchandising at Omega, explained, "One can make the most beautiful collection; however, if one doesn't have distribution or the ability to place a product in the appropriate market, it doesn't really matter."[5]

It is important for each fabric collection to be unique so that customers will not be tempted to buy something cheaper from another producer. Fabric producers have to be careful not to give swatches away because piracy is widespread. Fabric producers also offer their expertise to apparel manufacturers and sell sample cuts of fabrics for test garments.

Sales Promotion

Fabric producers compete for the business of apparel manufacturers and for retail-level acceptance of products made of their goods. Sales promotion usually focuses on a particular fabric characteristic, quality, finish, or end use. Milliken, for example, advertises Visa, a finish they created, which adds easy-care and soil-release characteristics to their fabrics. They educate the consumer about Visa's properties in order to create consumer demand. The consumer learns to equate Visa with those characteristics and to look for the Visa hang tag.[6] Fabric producers use advertising, publicity, and customer service to make their products known to their customers.

Advertising

Large fabric producers advertise the brand names of their products. Like the fiber producers—and often in cooperation with them—they use television, newspapers, and magazines to reach national audiences. They also join apparel manufacturers and retail stores in cooperative advertising nationally or locally.

A cooperative advertisement between Burlington, the fabric producer, and the Wool Bureau. Note: wool symbol at lower right. (*Courtesy of Burlington Industries, Inc.*)

Publicity

Many fabric producers also provide educational materials to consumer groups, schools and colleges, and the general public. They also supply information on fabric fashions and developments to the press in hope of editorial coverage.

Marketing and Promotional Services

Like fiber producers, fabric companies provide services to their customers on both the manufacturing and retailing levels to promote sales.

Fashion Presentations.   Some large fabric producers also employ merchandising and marketing experts who analyze trends and pass the information on to manufacturers and retailers. They may invite customers to fashion presentations where they present photographs, fabrics, and/or garments from Europe, as well as the new fabrics from their own company and ideas on how to use them. Fabric presentations and the fabrics they promote exert a great influence on apparel design.

Other Services.   Other services might include printed or visual materials, hang tags, brochures, in-store fashion shows, sales training sessions for retailers, and consumer education.

Fabric Markets

Twice a year, textile producers from all over the world display their lines at the following important international yarn and fabric shows:

Pitti Filati ("Pitti Yarns" originally shown at the Pitti Palace)   Held in July and January in Florence, Italy, this is the foremost international yarn show.

Yarn Fair International   This is New York's yarn show held each August and February primarily for Americans who are unable to go to Florence.

Premier Vision ("First Look")   With approximately 650 exhibitors and 40,000 visitors, this market, held in March and October in Paris, has become increasingly important as an early source for fashion fabrics.

International Fashion Fabric Exhibition (IFFE)   Showing fabrics from about 380 fabric producers, IFFE is held in New York in March and October; it is scheduled between Premier Vision and Interstoff to give European textile producers a chance to do business in the United States.

Interstoff ("International Fabrics")   Held in April and October or November in Frankfurt, Germany. Interstoff offers buyers and designers an opportunity to see the complete lines of over 1000 exhibitors.

Ideacomo ("Ideas from Como")   Primarily an exhibit of Italian silks, this market follows Interstoff in April and November in Como, Italy.

Los Angeles International Textile Show (TALA)   Sponsored by the California Mart and the Textile Association of Los Angeles, TALA shows fabrics from approximately 140 producers each January and August.

There are also fabrics shows in other major cities. Textile trade organizers often try new shows, such as Interstoff Asia, to try to make buying con-

The denim-couroy exhibits at Premier Vision fabric fair in Paris.
(Courtesy of Sophie Xuereb Communications)

venient. Textile producers visit these shows to see the latest directions in fabrics. Manufacturers and their designers visit the shows to buy fabrics and gather ideas about how to use them.

There are two official fabric seasons per year; however, the market is becoming increasingly seasonless and new fabrics are continually being developed.

Selling

Twice each year, fabric producers present their new lines to their customers. To get response to the line, fabrics are first *presold* to key customers. Then market weeks are held in the showrooms of each fabric producer. Worldwide fabric producers have showrooms in major fashion centers. In New York City, these showrooms are on Sixth Avenue or in the Seventh Avenue garment district area. Designers and merchandisers from apparel companies across the country come to fabric showrooms in New York or Los Angeles to see the new lines.

Sales Representatives

Each fabric company also has sales representatives who visit manufacturers and their designers, showing them suitcases full of *headers*, head ends of fabrics. Most salespeople in the textile industry, especially for large companies, are salaried employees of the firms they represent. Independent sales agents or representatives may handle several textile lines and are paid by commission, usually 3 percent of the price of fabrics sold and shipped. Salespeople are assigned specific manufacturers to call on. They try to make contacts to gain new accounts, as well as to show and sell fabrics to regular customers.

Jobbers

Jobbers are independent agents who purchase leftover fabrics at considerable discounts from manufacturers and resell them. They may buy from several sources and put together their own line, or they may buy goods in hope of selling them later at a good markup during a period of peak demand. Buying leftover fabrics clears warehouse space and gives operating cash to the textile producer. Another role of jobbers is to buy up unsold goods for resale to discount stores or other outlets.

Brokers

Also independent agents, textile brokers act on behalf of apparel manufacturers. When there is a need for a particular kind of fabric at a certain price, brokers try to find it. They may first have to find the greige goods and then have a converter finish it to order. They work on a commission based on the sale of fabrics.

SUMMARY

The tremendous growth of the Asian textile industry and its low production costs due to cheap labor have caused keen competition for the U.S. textile industry. The United States is fighting imports with new marketing strategies to meet consumer demand and new technology such as Quick Response to speed distribution in the marketing chain. Product development has become very important, and the industry is striving for innovation and flexibility. The industry promotes fibers and fabrics with brand-recognition advertising and customer services. International fabric markets and sales representatives provide the link to the apparel manufacturer, the next level of the fashion industry.

CHAPTER REVIEW

Terms and Concepts

Briefly identify and discuss the following terms and concepts:

1. Imports
2. Marketing strategies
3. Logos
4. Cooperative advertising
5. Consumer education
6. Hang tags
7. CAD systems
8. Motifs
9. Strike-off
10. Brand recognition

11. Customer services
12. Interstoff
13. Premier Vision
14. Headers
15. Jobbers
16. Brokers

Questions for Review

1. Why have textile imports taken such a big market share in the United States?
2. What has been the textile industry's response to imports?
3. How does modern marketing differ from textile marketing in the past, when only natural fabrics were available?
4. How do natural fiber producers compete with the giant chemical companies?
5. What types of advertising do fiber producers use?
6. How are styling and color direction influenced by fiber producers?
7. What influences print design?
8. What are the major fabric markets in the world?
9. What function do jobbers and brokers perform?

Projects for Additional Learning

1. Select a print that you like from a book on historic costume or art. Trace (or modify to update, if necessary) and recolor the print in the current season's fashion colors.
2. Shop a local department store to compare fabrics used in designer or contemporary fashions.
   a. What fabrics look the freshest and most exciting?
   b. What kinds of fabrics (knits, wovens, prints, solids) are used the most?
   c. What are the predominant colors?
   d. Examine hang tags and labels for fiber content. What kind of fiber is used more frequently in the garments—natural or man-made?
   e. Can you identify the fiber brand names and generic names on the labels?
   f. Can you identify fabric producers by information on the labels?
   g. Is enough information provided for the consumer about the fibers and fabrics?
   h. Summarize your findings in a written report.
3. Shop a local department or specialty store and examine country-of-origin and fiber-content labels in 20 garments.
   a. Among the garments made of cotton, what country of fabric origin predominates? Where is each garment made?
   b. Find the same information for garments made of wool, silk, ramie, and man-made fibers.
   c. Make a chart showing fiber content, country of fabric origin, and country where made. Make separate sections for (1) foreign fabric and labor, (2) imported fabric but American labor, and (3) American fabric and labor.
   d. Do you see a pattern forming? What conclusions can you draw from these data?
   e. Are all garments adequately labeled?
   f. How do prices compare between garments made overseas and those made in the United States? How do quality and detailing compare?

NOTES

[1] "Textile Report," *Women's Wear Daily*, January 28, 1992, p. 27.
[2] Ibid.
[3] "Converter Game Plan: Offshore Sourcing," *Women's Wear Daily*, December 13, 1994, p. 24.
[4] As quoted in "King Karl," *Women's Wear Daily*, November 20, 1991, p. 8.
[5] Cathy Cregan-Valent, director, Fabric Development and Merchandising, Omega Textiles, interview, February 15, 1995.
[6] Joe Sammartino, apparel sales manager, Milliken & Co., interview, February 1995.

Lace trimmings are important to the Jessica McClintock look.
(Courtesy of Jessica McClintock)

7

TRIMMINGS, LEATHER, AND FUR

CAREER FOCUS

There are many job possibilities in the trimmings industries very similar to those in the textile industry: stylists, merchandisers, technicians, and marketers. Much of the domestic leather and fur industry has been lost to imports, but there are opportunities in marketing.

Designers and manufacturers who use trimmings have to learn about them to use them properly. Apparel manufacturers need trimmings buyers. Retailers need to know the sources and characteristics of the fur and leather that they sell.

CHAPTER OBJECTIVES

After reading this chapter you should have attained competence in the following areas:

1. General knowledge of how threads, interfacings, narrow fabrics, zippers, buttons, and belts are produced and used
2. Understanding of the sources of fur and leather and the steps in processing them

*T*o complete our discussion of the raw materials of fashion, this chapter presents a survey of trimmings, leather, and fur.

Trimmings, covered in the first half of this chapter, are the secondary supplies necessary to complete a garment. The category of trimmings is very diversified, comprising both textile and nontextile areas. Thread, interfacing, and narrow-fabric manufacturing are extensions of the textile industry having similar production and marketing procedures. Zipper and button manufacturing, however, are entirely separate industries with their own resources and production methods.

Leather and fur sources and treatments are explored in the second part of the chapter. Leather and fur were used for clothing long before textiles were developed. Even today, leather and fur are important materials for the fashion industry. Leather is used for jackets and coats as well as fashion accessories—shoes, handbags, gloves, and belts—whereas fur is primarily a garment material.

TRIMMINGS

Designers and trimmings buyers need to know the best uses of a wide array of available trimmings.

Trimmings, or *sundries*, are the necessary supplies used to finish and adorn both garments and accessories. The huge array of decorative trimmings includes buttons, buckles, frog closures, belts, braids, ribbons, fringe, bows, laces, emblems, and sequins. Often functional trimmings, such as threads, needles, elastics, tapes, fasteners, interfacings, and shoulder pads, are classified as *notions*.

Use of trimmings varies with each segment of the industry. For example, men's wear manufacturers use more interfacings, construction tapes, and basic buttons, whereas activewear, swimwear, and underwear manufacturers use the most elastics. Women's wear designers use a wider variety of decorative ribbons, laces, and buttons.

Threads

Thread is supplied by yarn producers. Formed by spinning and twisting textile fibers or filaments together into a continuous strand, *thread* holds a garment together and its quality is vital to the durability of apparel construction.

Until recent years, cotton and other natural fiber threads met requirements of durability, appearance, and sewability because the majority of fabrics available were also made of natural fibers. However, the advent of man-made fibers brought about the development of many new fabrics, including knits. Because of their new characteristics, these fabrics demanded a stronger, more elastic thread. To meet these specifications, polyester threads were developed.

Thread choices available today include the following:

Cotton, used in cotton and wool garments

Silk, used in silk garments and men's wear

Nylon, a monofilament used to sew rayon or nylon fabrics

Rayon, or rayon wrapped around a nylon core

Polyester and polyester blends:

A polyester core wrapped in cotton (to give flexibility to the cotton)

Three-ply 100 percent spun polyester

Long-staple polyester

Threads are wound on cones in 1200- to 30,000-yard lengths for factory use. The Thread Institute has suggested metric conversions that approximate current yard lengths, but no one in the industry uses them.

Manufacturers use various thread sizes (based on thickness) according to fabric and quality needs. A metric system called *tex* has been suggested for measuring thread size. Based on the weight of the raw material, the tex number increases as the size increases; average thread sizes range from 10 to 500.

Elastics

Elastic is used often in today's clothes, in swimwear, underwear, activewear, pull-on pants and skirts, and stretch cuffs. Its use is part of the ease of dressing that many people appreciate in comfort apparel.

Elastic is made from a man-made rubber called *elastomer* or from *spandex*. Elastic strands are covered (wrapped) with polyester, cotton, or acetate. They can be woven, braided, knitted, cut into flat strands, or made into thread.

Elastics are available in widths from 1/8 to 3 inches to fit manufacturers' needs. Types of elastic include the following:

◆ **Knitted** elastics are the most commonly used because they are the least expensive. They are widely used in 3/4- to 2-inch widths as for waistband tunneling.

◆ **Narrow braided** elastic is usually used for wrist and neck in 1/4- and 1/2-inch widths.

◆ **Webbed** elastic wrapped in colored thread is used for decorative purposes such as stretch belts.

◆ **Woven** elastic is the highest quality product but also the most expensive and, therefore, used infrequently.

◆ **Elastic thread** (a strand of elastic wrapped in cotton, rayon, or polyester) is sewed into fabric to add stretch, as in shirring or smocking. It can also be used as loops for buttons.

Interfacings

The most essential kind of inner construction is *interfacing*, a layer of fabric placed between the garment fabric and its facing fabric. Interfacings have always been an important part of garment production, especially for structuring and support in tailored jackets and coats. They are also used to reinforce details such as collars, lapels, cuffs, pocket flaps, buttoning areas, and waistbands. Although interfacings are actually fabrics, they are usually sold to manufacturers by the trimmings suppliers.

Formerly, interfacings were made primarily of linen, burlap, or horsehair. Now, natural and man-made fibers and blends are used to make interfacings.

Types of Interfacings

Stable interfacings have no give and are designed to add stability to tailored garments. Stable interfacings can be either woven or nonwoven textiles. *Woven* interfacings are made by interweaving yarns at right angles. *Nonwoven* interfacings, made of yarns held together by fusing or bonding, have no grain and therefore can be cut in any direction.

Stretch-knit interfacings have been developed to support knit fabrics, but because interfacings are inherently intended to stabilize, they really do not give, especially when fused.

Stable and stretch interfacings are available in both fusible and sew-in forms. *Fusible* (heat bonded) interfacings have become important labor and time savers.

Weights of Interfacings

Basically, interfacings are available in three weight categories: light, middle, and heavy. The choice depends on the weight of the garment fabric as well as the support and effect desired. Ideally, interfacing is never heavier than the actual garment fabric. Heavyweight fleece and thermal interlinings are also used in jackets and coats to give additional support and warmth.

Narrow Fabrics

Narrow fabrics include narrow laces, ribbons, braids, other woven and knit decorative bands, pipings, and cordings. Woven, knit, and braid trims are produced by narrow fabric manufacturers. Formerly, most of the trims sold in the United States were imported from Europe. Now the imports come from Asia, but the domestic narrow fabrics industry has been able to compete. Narrow fabric manufacturers are small companies heavily concentrated in Pennsylvania and New York.

Narrow fabrics are either functional or decorative. The decorative trims industry is a fashion-oriented business, although there are really no seasonal lines. The fashion for trims is cyclical, like any other fashion. When ethnic looks are popular, decorative trims are in great demand.

Trim Types

There is a great variety of trim types, specially made for different uses and methods of application.

Appliqué An individual motif that can be attached singly or in multiples as a trim (this term is also used for a technique to attach the edges of a motif to fabric)

Banding   Narrow fabric having two straight or decorative edges that make it ideal for borders, edging, insertion, or accenting a design line

Beading   Openwork trim, usually lace or embroidery, through which a ribbon may be threaded (this beading is not to be confused with beads used to create banding or edging for evening wear)

Binding   Prefolded trim that encloses a raw edge, finishing and decorating it at the same time

Edging   A trim having one decorative edge and one straight edge

Galloon   Lace, embroidery, or braid having two shaped and finished edges; it can be used as a banding, border, or design-line accent or can be applied like insertion

Insertion   A trim with two straight edges (also a method of applying trim by inserting and sewing it between two cut edges of fabric)

Medallions   A chain of trims with individual motifs that can be used continuously as banding, edging, or galloons or clipped apart and used as appliqués

Laces

The popularity of handmade laces led to the invention of lace-making machines. Although narrow-textile manufacturers primarily produce bands of lace, their methods can be applied as well to the production of lace fabric. Laces are used primarily for lingerie or bridal gowns, but like other decorative trims, they recurrently play an important role in fashion. Today, there are basically four types of machine-made lace.

Barmen lace has its roots in Germany and Cluny, France. The Barmen machine runs on a Jacquard system. *Jacquard* is a weaving system that utilizes a highly versatile pattern mechanism to produce intricate designs. Yarns are plaited together to resemble heavy, crocheted lace.

Leaver lace, named after Englishman John Leaver who developed the machine, is sheer bobbin lace. Also Jacquard programmed, the Leaver machine twists threads into a giant web that can have up to 180 bands, each connected by auxiliary threads. To separate the bands, auxiliary threads can be hand-pulled (as is usually done in Europe) or dissolved in an acetone solution.

Raschel knitted lace is less expensive than Leaver because of the high speeds at which it can be produced. This lace is also made in a giant web, formed by linking chains of yarn. The bands are separated by pulling drawstrings.

Venice lace is made on Schiffli (see the following section) embroidery machines. The Schiffli machines are also controlled by a Jacquard system.

Embroidery

Although embroidery is not confined to narrow fabrics, it seems appropriate to discuss its production after that of laces. As an all over or as a trim, embroidery has been used most often in lingerie and blouses. While there is some competition from imports, there are several hundred embroidery companies located in northern New Jersey.

Schiffli is a continuous embroidery used on fabrics or for trims. Often a manufacturer will send out fabric panels to have them embroidered and

A computer-automated embroidery machine.
(Courtesy of Saurer Textile Systems, Charlotte and Switzerland)

then insert them into garments, as on a blouse front. The newest Schiffli machines are huge and highly automated but require some labor to operate the machines, sew sections together, or cut and fasten threads. Schiffli machines are also used to make embroidered eyelet (cut-work embroidery) trim or fabric and lace.

Framework embroidery is used when a single motif is needed on a garment. Multihead machines, operated by a computer, embroider up to 20 pieces, such as a pocket, at one time.

Ribbons

Ribbons are another category of narrow fabrics. Many ribbons are woven at one time on looms with 2, 4, 6, 8, 16, 24, or 48 spaces. The width of the ribbon and the volume of production determine the size of machine to be used. Satin and velvet ribbons are made much like their fabric counterparts. Grosgrain is woven on a belting or dobby loom.

Throwaway or **craft** ribbon is woven on a broadloom and cut into bands. This type of ribbon is usually reserved for the gift-wrapping market. However, if the edges are embossed, it may be used in less expensive garments and accessories.

Solid color ribbons can be piece dyed after weaving to match manufacturers' color specifications. Patterns such as stripes or plaids may be woven

The Bobbin Show in Atlanta. *(Courtesy of Bobbin Blenheim)*

The trimmings industries are also cooperating with Quick Response initiatives in order to speed up ordering, production, and distribution to apparel and accessory manufacturers. The Sundries Apparel Findings Linkage Council (SAFLINC) has established universal codes and linkage systems throughout the industry.

THE LEATHER INDUSTRY

Designers, merchandisers, and manufacturers of leather apparel and accessories must know the sources, properties, and best uses of leather. Retailers, too, are interested in the quality of the product that they sell.

Although much older than the production of fiber and fabrics, the processing of leather is not as sophisticated—and it takes much longer. Lately, however, production methods have improved, greatly increasing the supply and variety of leather. However, as with textiles, the domestic industry has shrunk considerably due to competition from imports.

Leathers are preserved animal hides and skins, by-products of the meat industry. Cattle hides provide the most leathers, but deer, goat, pig, and sheep skins are also widely used. The world's largest exporter of cattle hides is the United States, most goatskins come from India and China, and most sheep skins from Australia. Developing countries, particularly those with abundant raw material supplies such as Argentina, Brazil and India, impose export controls or taxes in order to encourage the growth of their own tanning and leather products industries.

Hides and skins are differentiated by weight. *Skins* come from smaller animals, such as goats, deer, pigs, and calves, and weigh less than 25 pounds. *Hides* come from large animals such as steers, cows, buffalos, and horses, and weigh over 25 pounds each.

Printed cowhide coat from Prada.
(Courtesy of Prada)

Leather Processing

Tanneries purchase and process skins and hides and sell the leather as their finished product. Companies usually specialize because processing methods depend on the nature of the skins treated and the end use of the leather. New equipment and technology have made the U.S. tanning industry more productive than any in the world. However, due to competition from cheap labor in developing countries, the tanning industry in the United States has shrunk to only 110 facilities clustered in New York, Massachusetts, California, Wisconsin, Pennsylvania, New Jersey, Texas, and Tennessee.[4]

The process by which hides and skins are made into leather can take up to six months and requires extensive equipment and skilled labor. There are three basic steps in leather processing: pretanning, tanning, and finishing.

Pretanning

Pretanning is basically a cleaning process. Skins are cured to prevent them from rotting. Hides are cured by applying salt, soaking them in brine or just drying them. The cured hides are soaked in water to rehydrate them and to remove dirt, salt, and some proteins. Hides and skins must also have hair and fat removed by additional treatments, which differ with each type.

Tanning

Tanning involves the application of various agents that protect the hide or skin against decomposition. Treatment methods include soaking and powdering. The choice of agents depends largely on the end use of the leather. Tanning agents include vegetable products, oils, minerals, and chemicals.

Vegetable tanning is generally done in large vats filled with tanning solutions made from water and tannin. Tannin is a bitter substance obtained from the roots, bark, wood, leaves, or fruits of various trees and shrubs and produces a firm, heavy leather.

Oil tanning, using codfish oil that is rubbed into the skin, produces relatively soft and pliable leathers such as chamois.

Mineral tanning is performed with a tanning solution of chrome salts. Chrome tanning is much faster and is also more resistant to heat and scratching.

Chemical tanning, a newer method, uses agents such as sulfonic acid.

Combination tanning is the use of a combination of agents to obtain the desired effect. For example, many leathers are pretanned with chrome and then retanned with vegetable tannins.

Finishing

Finishing produces the desired thickness, moisture, and esthetic appeal. After excess water and wrinkles are removed from the tanned leather, it is shaved or split into uniform thickness.

Color is applied to leather by brushing or by tray, drum, spray, solvent, vacuum, or tank dyeing. Special effects may be created by dabbing on color with a sponge, applying color through stencils, sprinkling, spraying, or tie-dyeing.

The dyed leather is treated with oils and fats, which provide lubrication, softness, strength, and waterproofing. The leather is then dried to fix the dyes and oils permanently. Dried leather is conditioned with damp sawdust to obtain uniform moisture content and then stretched for softness.

Finally, the leather is coated with a seasoning or finish that improves its properties or character. For example, urethanes are used to add shine to patent leather.

Leathers may be further treated with buffers, rollers, or presses to achieve glazed, matte, and embossed effects. Tanners in China and Korea add distressed finishes to less expensive pigskin and goatskin to make them look richer in order to compete with the more supple lamb- or calfskin.

Environmental Concerns

The Environmental Protection Agency (EPA) has established standards to control the polluting wastes that tanners discharge, such as sulfides, chromium, and acid. Control of these wastes requires expensive primary and secondary treatment facilities. The industry is developing and adopting new tanning systems that will use nontoxic metal salts and other organic tanning materials to replace the chromium. The industry is also encouraged to adopt low-solvent or solvent-free finishes.

Leather Promotion and Marketing

Like the fiber and fabric producers, the leather industry promotes its products to apparel manufacturers, fashion editors, retailers, and consumers. Promotion is done by the company or through trade associations such as the Tanners Council. However, individual tanners, unlike fiber producers, are not known by the public. Retail advertising for leather products may mention the type of leather and the designer, but not the producer. The footwear industry is the tanning industry's largest market.

Leather markets are concentrated in Western countries. The United States imports more processed leather than it exports. It exports leather, but for nonapparel use, to more than 80 countries, primarily Japan and Hong Kong. It imports leather primarily from Argentina and Italy. The major importers of finished leathers are the European Community and South America. Major exporters are Japan and China.[5] International trade in leather is over $1 billion per year.

Rising world population and incomes, along with new fashions for leather, have contributed to an ever increasing demand for leather. To protect and expand their markets, leather producers must constantly strive to develop new leather finishes and colors.

THE FUR INDUSTRY

The fur industry is another supplier of raw material for the fashion industry. Many apparel designers also design collections for fur manufacturers.

Fur is the hairy coat of a mammal. However, except in the case of lamb, fur is not a by-product of the meat industry. From prehistoric times, people have used animal fur for both its warmth and its attractive appearance. Because fur has long been associated with wealth and prestige, the demand for luxury has played a major role in the development of the fur industry.

This section discusses the characteristics of various furs, the processes involved in preparing fur pelts for their use in the manufacture of fur garments, and the marketing of furs.

The fur industry consists of three major groups: pelt producers or trappers, fur processors, and companies that produce fur garments for consumers (fur garment production is discussed in Chapter 11).

Fur Sources

The industry must first obtain the pelts or skins of fur-bearing animals. Furs come from wild animals and, more often, fur farms or ranches.

The international fur market is focused mainly on mink production. Scandinavia produces 45 percent of the world mink supply, Russia 31 percent and the United States 10 percent.[6] The major animals raised or trapped for the United States fur business are (in descending order of importance) mink, mostly bred; fox, trapped and bred; and sable, imported from Russia and Canada, where it is trapped. Other furs, used in smaller quantities, include muskrat, skunk, opossum, lamb, and rabbit.

Wild Furs

Wild furs for commercial use come from over 80 countries on all six continents, but mainly from North America, which has the greatest variety (40 different types).

Endangered Species.   In the late 1960s, individuals, international organizations, and governments became concerned about the possible extinction of endangered species. As a result, some countries enacted legislation restricting or prohibiting the commercial use of particular animals, including certain monkeys, seals, and leopards.

Trapping.   Wild fur-bearing animals are usually caught in baited traps. There is public concern about the agony animals suffer in this slow, painful death. There is new legislation against certain kinds of traps to try to make trapping more humane. In some areas, seals are clubbed to death, a practice that has caused protests and efforts to prohibit the commercial use of wild seal fur.

Fur Farming

Fur farming has greatly increased the supply of fur. General livestock methods are adapted to the keeping and breeding of animals for their pelts. Research in management, feeding, and breeding techniques has resulted in the production of quality furs in thousands of mutations. Mink has become the most popular fur, accounting for approximately 60 to 70 percent of today's fur trade. Silver fox is also raised mainly on farms.

Fur Processing

After manufacturers purchase pelts at auctions or from wholesale pelt merchants, they usually contract with fur dressing and dyeing firms to process them. New York City is the largest fur-processing center in the United States.

Inspecting fur pelts.
(Courtesy of the Deutsches Pelz Institute, Germany)

Dressing

Fur skins are dressed to make them soft, pliable, and lighter weight, as well as to preserve their natural luster. Dressing processes vary with the nature and condition of the skin, but there are usually at least four distinct steps:

Preliminary cleaning and softening of the pelt

Fleshing (cleaning) and stretching

Leathering, a tanning process using oils or other solutions

Finishing, to condition and and bring out the natural beauty of the fur

Dyeing

Dressed pelts may be sent out to a dyer. The modern use of chemical compounds known as fur bases has enabled fur dyers to produce a wider variety of colors. Although not all furs are dyed, dyeing has led to the use of many skins that were unattractive in their natural colors. New colors are an important selling point among fur retailers. Dyers often keep their techniques secret from competitors to maintain a market edge. Following the dyeing process, the pelts are now ready for garment production, a process covered in Chapter 11.

Environmental Concerns

As in the leather industry, an effort is being made to control the polluting wastes from dressing and dyeing processes.

Ethical Concerns

The People for the Ethical Treatment of Animals (PETA) organization has raised the public antifur consciousness (as PETA's campaign is aimed at manufacturers and designers, its activities are discussed in Chapter 11). Roger Caras, president of the ASPCA, said, "To the best of my knowledge, fur farms in this country are either finished or dying…. But that doesn't mean the fur industry is history." Domestic pelt production has been dwindling for years. The number of mink farms, for example, has declined from 1027 in 1988 to 502 in 1994.[7] Still, the use of shearling lamb is acceptable to many people because lambskin is a by-product of the meat industry.

Marketing

Trappers normally sell their catches to collecting agents, who in turn sell them at auctions or to wholesale merchants. These merchants maintain stocks of furs, selling them to manufacturers as they are needed.

Fur farmers and ranchers, however, sell their pelts at public auction directly to the wholesale pelt merchants, manufacturers, or commission brokers (who buy for merchants or manufacturers). Major fur auction centers are located in New York City, Frankfurt, St. Petersburg, and Montreal. Pelt prices can fluctuate sharply, because price is dictated by supply and demand.

SUMMARY

Trimmings are the materials needed to finish and decorate apparel and accessories. Decorative trims include buttons, ribbons, laces, braids, and belts. Functional trimmings include thread, interfacing, zippers, tapes, and elastic. Thread, interfacing, and narrow fabrics are an extension of the textile industry. Each of these trims is a separate industry with its own resources and markets and is a study in itself.

Leather and fur, the oldest body coverings, are still an important part of the fashion industry. Animals, either wild or raised on farms, are the sources of both leather and fur. Tanning (for leather) and dressing (for fur) are similar treatments: they clean, preserve, and bring out the natural beauty of the skin, hide, or pelt. Although modern technology has speeded processing and made it somewhat easier, leather and fur production are still basically time consuming craft industries.

CHAPTER REVIEW

Terms and Concepts

Briefly identify and discuss the following terms and concepts:

1. Trimmings
2. Sundries
3. Notions
4. Interfacing
5. Narrow fabrics
6. Jacquard system
7. Schiffli
8. Passementerie
9. Cut-up belt trade
10. Leather types
11. Tanneries
12. Fur dressing

Questions for Review

1. Briefly explain the difference between decorative and functional trimmings.
2. Discuss the various types of interfacings and their uses.
3. What categories are included in narrow fabrics?
4. Describe the four basic kinds of machine lace.
5. Describe the three basic types of zippers and their construction.
6. Discuss the various natural and man-made materials used to make buttons.
7. Explain how belts are produced for the cut-up trade.
8. Briefly discuss the basic steps in leather processing.
9. Discuss the animal rights controversy and how it affects the fur industry.
10. Discuss the steps in the dressing of furs.

Projects for Additional Learning

1. Select one category of trim (lace, for example) and find a variety of samples at fabric stores. Ask if you may have or purchase just a small piece of each. Describe the pattern or construction of each type. Show examples (photos or actual garments) of their end use.
2. At the library, trace the origin and development of a specific trim. Explain the differences between how it was made by hand originally and how it is mass produced today.
3. Visit a local department or specialty store and find five garments that use decorative and functional trimmings. List every trim on each garment.
   Discuss how the trims affect the total design of the garment. How do you think the manufacturers balanced the added cost of the trimmings with fabric and labor costs?
4. Write to a national animal protection agency such as API (Animal Protection Institute) or PETA (People for the Ethical Treatment of Animals). Find out what members are doing to promote animal rights. What impact do prevailing political attitudes and economic conditions have on the sale of furs?
5. Visit a furrier or fur dealer. Learn to identify various furs by their characteristics.

NOTES

[1] Thomas L. Allison, director of engineering, Talon, Inc., letter, February 27, 1995.

[2] Ibid.

[3] Giles S. Brown, Rochester Button Company, letter, April 6, 1995.

[4] "U. S. Industrial Outlook 1994," U. S. Department of Commerce, Washington, D. C., January 1994, p. 34-2.

[5] Ibid., p. 34-3.

[5] "Mink Market Share," *Fur World*, November 26, 1992, p. 5.

[7] Sarah Ferguson, "Radical Chic '94," *New York Magazine*, November 7, 1994, p. 66.

Part Three

THE MANUFACTURING OF FASHION

Part Three concentrates on the core of the fashion industry, the manufacturing sector. Chapter 8 gives an overall picture of the international centers of design and manufacturing as well as a brief discussion of major designers. The three major divisions of a manufacturer are product development and design, production, and marketing and sales. Each is related to and dependent on the others. Chapter 9 discusses product development, merchandising, and the entire process of design and sample development. Chapter 10 goes on to the production of apparel and Chapter 11 covers the design, production, and marketing of accessories and furs. Chapter 12 deals with the wholesale markets, sale, and distribution of fashion merchandise, the meeting ground of manufacturers and retailers.

The Christian Dior salon on the corner of rue François Premier and avenue Montaigne in Paris. *(Courtesy of the House of Dior)*

8

INTERNATIONAL FASHION CENTERS

CAREER FOCUS

Every professional in the fashion business wants to be informed about what is happening in the fashion capitals around the world. Retail buyers want to know what designers are showing in their latest collections. Designers, their business partners, other manufacturing executives, and promotional organizations are all involved with fashion in the major centers of the world.

CHAPTER OBJECTIVES

After reading this chapter you should have attained competence in the following areas:

1. Knowledge of the names of well-known international fashion creators
2. Explaining the reasons for French fashion leadership
3. Understanding the growth in importance of the prêt-à-porter
4. Understanding the reasons for the importance of New York as a fashion center
5. Knowledge of the role of international and domestic fashion centers

*T*his chapter introduces the major fashion capitals of the world, the centers that are most influential in creating, manufacturing, and marketing new fashion. You will read about the specialties of each and about the creators who have made them into fashion centers. Fashion centers develop as a result of concentrations of resources, supplies, skilled labor, and creative people. All designers are influenced by what other designers and artists are creating. Excitement about a new idea acts as a catalyst for more creativity. This is why many creative people gravitate to major creative centers.

GLOBAL NATURE OF FASHION

It becomes more and more difficult to discuss fashion by individual city or country.

Three cities have emerged as major fashion capitals: Paris, France; Milan, Italy; and New York City in the United States. Other noteworthy but less influential centers include London, England; Tokyo, Japan; various cities in Spain and Germany; Montreal and Toronto in Canada; and Los Angeles and San Francisco in California. American designers score high when it comes to marketing savvy and making saleable clothes that appeal to the whole U.S. population. However, retailers still believe that "real creative originality is abroad."[1]

However, it is increasingly difficult to describe the characteristics of fashion by country or fashion capital. There is no longer clear division between what is foreign and what is domestic; the fashion industry is becoming a worldwide exchange of ideas, talent, material, and products. Ideas come from all over the world, textiles are exported from one country to another; production is done almost everywhere, and nearly every country contributes in some way.

Designers move to other countries to work. Karl Lagerfeld, a German, works in Paris. Should we consider him a German designer or a French designer? Gianfranco Ferré, an Italian, designs the Dior couture collection in Paris. Brian Rennie, a Scotsman, designs for Escada in Germany and Todd Oldham, an American, is a design consultant for them. Keith Varty and Alan Cleaver, Englishmen, design for Byblos in Italy. John Galliano, an Englishman, shows his collection in Paris. Rifat Ozbek, from Turkey, works in London and also shows his collection in Paris. The list is endless.

The job of the international designer is not an easy one. Ferré commutes between Milan and Paris. Oscar de la Renta communtes between New York, Balmain in Paris, and his home in Santo Domingo. Lagerfeld designs five collections: his own signature line, Chanel couture, Chloe, a less expensive KL line produced in Germany, and Fendi in Italy. Some designers have time for little else than designing or promoting their designs. They supervise large design teams for several collections, visit factories, attend store openings, and make worldwide public appearances.

Promotion and Licensing

Designer names become famous because of extensive press coverage, their own promotional efforts, and success in the marketplace. With fame come requests for *licensing*, a process through which manufacturers are given permission to use the designer's name (see Chapter 12). Their fashion empires grow to the point that successful international designers have become stars.

Business Partners

A successful fashion business is not built on a good designer alone. The top designers have astute business partners like Pierre Bergé at St. Laurent, Giancarlo Giametti at Valentino, or Peter Strom at Ralph Lauren. These people manage the finances, operations, and marketing sides of the business to enable the designer to concentrate on creativity.

Ownership

One trend in the fashion business is to try to build powerful conglomerates. Frenchman Bernard Arnault owns Dior, Givenchy, and Louis Vuitton and has also backed Lacroix. Company ownership has become so complicated that it is often difficult to judge the origin of a collection. The Cerruti 1881 line, for example, originates in Italy, but the production and distribution rights have been purchased by Escada, a German firm.

FRANCE

Paris has long been the foremost city of world fashion and it has managed to keep its position in spite of fierce competition.

Paris is the capital of France and the Hollywood of the fashion world. Fashion is one of France's top three export industries and the second most important in employment with 140,000 workers (less than half of what it was 10 years ago).[2] This compares with a total of 1,130,000 employed in the apparel industry in the entire European Economic Community. Paris became the capital of fashion because it has the necessary resources and a creative atmosphere. But, in addition, the French government has always supported and encouraged *les mains de France* (the hands of France), giving the needle trades much deserved respect.

There is also tremendous cooperation among the French design firms, fabric mills, and the auxiliary shoe, hat, fur, trimmings, findings, and embroidery industries. A designer who needs special fabrics finds the mills willing to weave or print just a few meters as a test run. Shoe manufacturers plan designs to complement designer garments, and button and trim manufacturers will create items for the exclusive use of one designer. Oscar de la Renta describes the situation as "the extraordinary support system and all the little artisans that make Paris special."[3] Having such an atmosphere, Paris is understandably looked to for fashion leadership.

Recognizing Paris as a fashion center, many fiber and fabric associations, promotion agencies, and information sources have established their main

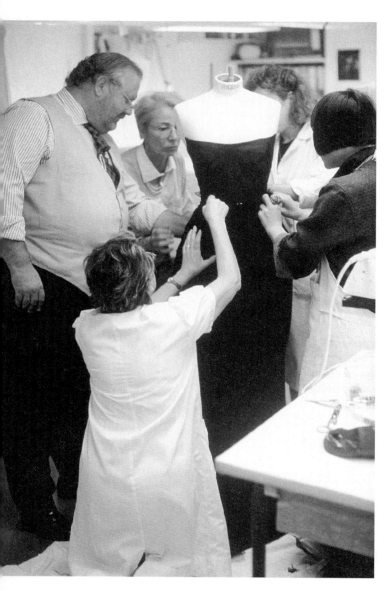

Italian designer Gianfranco Ferré fitting a gown with his assistants at Christian Dior in Paris, where he designs the couture collection.
(*Courtesy of Christian Dior, photo by Sylvie Lancrenon*)

fashion offices there. Among the designers from other countries who are now showing their collections in Paris are Valentino from Rome, Kansai Yamamoto from Japan, John Galliano from London, Helmut Lang from Germany, and Dries van Noten from Belgium. Paris attracts talent from around the world, which in turn keeps Paris the center of fashion.

The Couture

"Fashion is a very important economic sector for our country, and couture is the flagship of French fashion and the radiance of France," explains Dominique Strauss-Kahn, the former French minister of industry.[4] Couture is simply the French word for fine custom dress design, made to measure for a particular customer. A *couturier* is a male couture designer, a *couturière* his female counterpart. *Haute couture* (the most exclusive couture) is reserved for the very best design and highest quality of fabrics and workmanship. In houses where the original couturier is no longer living, former assistants or other designers have taken over design responsibilities, such as Ferré for Dior. Some houses have one designer for the couture collection and another for the prêt-à-porter line.

Maison.   A couture business is called a *maison* (house). The couture houses and adjacent *boutiques* (retail shops for ready-to-wear and accessories) center in the avenue Montaigne and the Faubourg Saint-Honoré in Paris. The private client comes to the *salon*, an elegant showroom in the same building as the design studio, to see sample garments in the collection.

High Costs.   When a client orders a dress or suit, it is made up in her exact measurements, with several fittings. Construction usually takes weeks. However, many people today find that this is a dying art. Fewer than a thousand women in the world can afford to buy couture from $10,000 to $20,000 for a suit or up to $50,000 for an elaborate gown!

It costs approximately $1 to $2 million a year for a large house to produce its couture collections. Collection costs include fabrics, labor, specially made accessories, and the expenses of the show itself: models, catwalk, sound systems, rental of a theater, and dinners for buyers.

Publicity.   However, these costs are offset by government support and publicity. The French government gives support to the couture in order to promote exports. Government-owned French television gives the couture free exposure. This kind of publicity is more prestigious than costly advertising and helps to compensate for the costs of producing a collection. The publicity is especially important because it generates sales of ready-to-wear, perfume, and licensing businesses, thereby helping to keep the couture alive.

Creative Opportunites.   The couture is regarded as offering the opportunity for the purest form of creativity in fashion, providing the "research and development" for the French fashion industry. Emanuel Ungaro explained, "We have the freedom for creation in couture…. It is our duty to serve as a laboratory for fashion and a guide to ready-to-wear."[5] The clothes of some couturiers are audacious, but this is usually done to attract attention. Other couturiers feel that it is their responsibility to make pretty clothes that are flattering and saleable. Christian Lacroix remarked, "Haute couture runs the risk of being suffocated by its own traditions. If it is to survive, it must be firmly anchored in daily life." [6]

Parisian Couturiers

Karl Lagerfeld for Chanel (Shah-nell') brought international attention back to the couture when he took over as artistic director for the house in 1983. He also designs the Karl Lagerfeld, Chloe, and KL ready-to-wear collections, as well as furs for Fendi of Italy. Lagerfeld won the International Wool Secretariat design competition in 1954 at age 16 and was hired by Pierre Balmain as an assistant. He was designer for Chloe for 19 years before Bidermann Industries offered to back him in his own line. Because

German designer Karl Lagerfeld in Paris, where he designs his signature collection, Chanel couture, Chloe, furs for Fendi of Italy, and the KL collection for Steilman of Germany. *(Self portrait courtesy of Karl Lagerfeld)*

he is the major international trendsetter, he is often referred to as "King Karl" by the fashion press. "When Karl speaks, the fashion world listens."[7]

Yves Saint Laurent (Eve Sahn' Law-rahn') is still considered a master of couture. He is a steady, major influence in the fashion world, setting trends in a restrained, sophisticated way with a good sense of timing. He began his career by winning the wool design competition at age 17 and a post as assistant to Dior. He opened his own business with Pierre Bergé in 1962 at the age of 26 and now has over 200 licenses. The Metropolitan Museum presented a retrospect of his work in 1984.

Christian Lacroix (La-kwa'), who also helped to bring excitement back to the couture, is known for his extravagant costume looks, silhouettes, colors, and pattern mixes. Born in Arles in 1951, he studied art history, intending to become a museum curator. Chance brought him to Hermès in 1978 and he became the artistic director of Jean Patou in 1981. In 1987, Bernard Arnault, president of Financière Agache, offered to back him in his own couture house.

Gianfranco Ferré for Dior (Fer-ray'), an Italian, was chosen by Bernard Arnault to replace Marc Bohan at the house of Dior in 1989. He does his own ready-to-wear line in Milan (see Milan).

Emanuel Ungaro was born in 1933 and learned his trade in his father's tailor shop. At 22, Ungaro left for Paris and eventually spent 4 years with Balenciaga and a year with Courrèges. He opened his own salon in 1965 and added a men's wear collection in the late 1970s.

Oscar de la Renta for Balmain, a well known American designer, has joined the ranks of the international commuter designers to design couture in Paris.

Other couturiers include Michel Goma for Balenciaga, Pierre Cardin, Carven, Tom Van Lingen for the reopened house of Jacques Fath, Louis Feraud, John Galliano for Givenchy, Lanvin, Oliver Lapidus for Ted Lapidus, Guy Laroche, Hanae Mori, Dominique Morlotti, Patou, Paco Rabanne, Gerard Pipart for Nina Ricci, Rochas, Erik Mortensen for the house of Scherrer, Per Spook, Torrenté, and Philippe Venet. Also Italian designers Valentino and Versace show their couture collections in Paris.

Fédération Française de la Couture.   In France, only those on the selective Couture-Creation list of the Fédération Française de la Couture are considered members of the haute couture; membership is based on high standards of excellence and special requirements. The federation includes three branches: couture, women's ready-to-wear, and men's wear. Under their auspices, the Chambre Sydicale dictates rules about workrooms and collections.

Ateliers

To qualify for the Couture-Creation list of the Chambre Syndicale de la Couture Parisienne, a house is required to have at least one *atelier* (workroom) in Paris with a minimum technical staff of 15, not including the director. A couturier may have anywhere from 20 to 400 employees in one or a combination of several ateliers. To get established, novice couturiers are allowed a 2-year transition period during which they need have only 10 employees.

In large houses, where there is much work to be done, *modelistes* work under the head designer, executing the individual designs. The modelistes are the liaison with the ateliers, where they supervise construction of the *toile*, or sample garment.

Ateliers are separated into *flou*, where they make dresses, and *tailleur*, where they specialize in the tailoring of suits and coats. Each atelier is headed by a production manager or chief technician called the *premier d'atelier* (pre-me-ay' dah-tel-yay'). Under the manager are the shop assistant(s), fitters, *midinettes* (seamstresses, classified as first hands or second hands), and apprentices.

Prêt-à-Porter

Prêt-à-porter (pret-a-por-tay') is French for "ready-to-wear." Most French fashion is mass produced, as it is in most cases. Mass production makes fashion less expensive. In this case, identical garments are manufactured in various sizes and colors. The customer needs only to try one on in a store to see if it fits, purchase it, and take it home immediately.

As couture garments became more expensive, mass produced garments became more and more fashionable. By the 1960s, designer ready-to-wear became as influential as couture. The couturiers suffered from the competition and were no longer financially successful. Therefore, the couturiers began to produce their own prêt-à-porter collections.

Today designer prêt-à-porter creations cost as much as couture used to. Whereas a couture creation might now cost from $5000 to $50,000, the upper end prêt-à-porter range is roughly $1000 to $5000. However, despite its price, a prêt-à-porter garment brings no exclusivity with it. There is the same experimentation involved in creating original sample garments for a ready-to-wear collection as there is for a couture garment, however, the mass production of these samples makes ready-to-wear a profitable business.

Prêt-à-Porter Designers

Most of the couturiers also have prêt-à-porter collections.

Karl Lagerfeld is a major ready-to-wear trendsetter both with his signature collection and his Chloe collection. **Yves St. Laurent**, **Christian Lacroix** and **Emmanuel Ungaro** also have important prêt-à-porter lines.

In addition, there are designers who have built their reputations on ready-to-wear. Some of the most well known are the following:

Jean-Paul Gaultier, known as the *enfant terrible* ("terrible child" due to his extreme creations) of the French fashion world, began his career with Pierre Cardin and Jean Patou. He began his own collection in 1978, adding a men's collection in 1984 and Junior Gaultier in 1988.

Claude Montana created his own company in 1979. He designs both men's and women's collections produced in Italy, a leather collection, knitwear, furs, shoes, and accessories.

Thierry Mugler began his company in 1974. In addition to women's wear, he has licensed collections of knitwear, activewear, men's wear, and accessories. He is also a professional photographer and has designed costumes for the theater.

Additional prêt-à-porter designers (some from other countries who work in Paris) include Agnes B, Azzedine Alaia, Anne-Marie Beretta, Barbara Bui, Jean-Charles de Castelbajac, Corinne Cobson, Jean Colonna, Ann Demeulemeester (Belgian), Marithe and Francois Girbaud, Jerome l'Huillier, Michel Klein, Herve Léger, Lolita Lempicka, Marcel Marongiu, Popy Moreni, Myrene de Premonville, Sonia Rykiel, Martine Sitbon, Sophie

Sitbon, Frank Sorbier, Kenzo Takada, Chantal Thomass, and Dries Van Noten (Belgian).

To reach a wider audience, most designers also have a less expensive *diffusion* line such as Ungaro's Emanuel line. There are also many less expensive prêt-à-porter lines shown in group exhibitions at the Porte de Versailles. Some of these companies, such as Naf Naf, Et Vous, Chipie, and Chevignon, do not publicize the names of their designers, but have become world famous and influential.

ITALY

Italian fashion is very popular with Americans, for it suits a casual life-style better than the more extreme French fashion.

The Italian fashion industry and its influence on the world have grown enormously. Around 1940 only 30 fashion manufacturers operated in Italy, their production limited basically to men's wear. The Italians built an international fashion reputation on beautiful fabrics, styling, knitwear, leather goods, tailoring, and quality production. To expand its markets, Italy's fashion industry is export driven. Fashion is now Italy's second biggest industry (next to tourism). Clothing and textiles have become Italy's biggest export after shoes. The Italian fashion industry is primarily devoted to ready-to-wear and accessories.

Milano (Milan) has become the center for *moda pronta* (ready-to-wear) because it is close to the fabric sources of Como, Biella, and Torino. Italy also has a smaller fashion center in Florence, as well as fashion and accessory companies scattered around the country.

Designers, manufacturers, and fabric companies work cooperatively, often as integral parts of a large vertical company. Many of these fashion companies are part of family-owned textile firms. They are able to invest heavily in the newest technology and spacious, modern factories that help Italy maintain its reputation for high-quality production. Some of the largest Italian-based apparel companies, such as Benetton, Fendi, Ferragamo, and Marzotto, are family owned.

Italian Designers

Giorgio Armani, born in 1934, wanted to become a doctor. However, he gave up his studies and became assistant men's wear buyer for Rinascente, an Italian department store. Later he was hired by Nino Cerruti to choose fabrics for one of his manufacturers, where he learned apparel production. In 1974, he created his first collection under the Armani label with partner Sergio Galeotti and added women's wear in 1975. His multi million dollar empire includes Emporio Armani (stores and a less expensive collection), A/X Armani Exchange (basics and jeans), Mani (Italy only), and licenses. His tailored style set international trends in the 1980s.

Domenico Dolce and Stefano Gabbana began working together in 1982. Dolce learned his craft working in his family's clothing factory in Sicily. Gabbana studied graphics in design school. They met in 1980 while working for a Milanese designer. In 1985, they presented their first women's collection under the Dolce & Gabbana label and have since added men's wear, knitwear, lingerie, and swimwear.

Gianfranco Ferré, born in 1944, studied architecture and today is considered the architect of Italian fashion. He gave up architecture to design accessories and later presented his first collection of ready-to-wear under the Baila label in 1974. His first women's collection under the Ferré name was shown in 1978 and his men's collection was introduced in 1982. He was selected in 1989 to design couture for Dior in Paris, but continues his ready-to-wear collections in Italy.

Romeo Gigli (Ro meh' o Gee lee), known for his *minimalistic* style, first studied architecture in Italy and then learned tailoring in New York City. He presented his first collection in 1983 and has since added men's wear. He now has a diffusion line called G. Gigli and has chosen to show his women's wear collection in Paris.

Valentino Garavani (who uses only his first name professionally) was born in 1932 and started at age 17 to work for Guy Laroche and Jean Desses in Paris. He opened his own house in Rome in 1960, and shortly thereafter Giancarlo Giametti became his business partner. Because he is Italy's most successful couturier, Valentino has been considered the main link with Paris and now shows his collections there. Oliver is his primary ready-to-wear line. He is a fastidious worker and is known for his elegant collections.

Gianni Versace, born in 1946, studied design in hopes of a fashion career. He worked as a tailor's buyer and later designed for Complice, Genny, and Callaghan. In 1978 he set up his own women's wear business with members of his family and added men's wear in 1979. He continues to design for Genny and has started a couture collection, which he shows in Paris. His secondary collections include Versus and Istante.

Giorgio Armani at the Emporio Armani shop in Milan. *(Courtesy of Giorgio Armani)*

Although most Italian designers have built their reputations in ready-to-wear, Valentino and Versace both have couture collections that they show in Paris with the French couturiers.

Other internationally known designers and manufacturers in Italy include Laura Biagiotti; Scott Crolla for Callaghan, Nino Cerruti, who put Italian men's wear on the map; Extempore by Itlierre; the Fendi sisters—Anna, Franca, Alda, Paola, and Carla—who produce both furs and apparel; Salvatore Ferragamo's sons and daughters—Ferruccio, Fiamma, Massimo, Giovanna, Fulvia and Leonardo—who have added other accessories and ready-to-wear to the original shoe business; Alberta Ferretti; Genny Holding SpA, which owns Genny, Byblos, and Complice; Tom Ford for Gucci; Mariuccia Mandelli, who owns Krizia with her husband Aldo Pinto; Max Mara; Rosita and Tai Missoni, who design elegant knitwear; Miuccia Prada, who expanded a successful accessory collection to include apparel; Sportmax; Englishmen Keith Varty and Alan Cleaver who design for Byblos; and Zegna men's wear.

UNITED KINGDOM

London has an international reputation for men's tailoring and has occasionally enjoyed the spotlight for trendy fashion for young women.

London, the capital of England, Great Britain, U.K., enjoys a diversified reputation for fine men's tailoring, classic woolen and cashmere apparel for women, and innovative young fashion.

Savile Row

London has long been the respected world center for classic men's business attire because of its famous Savile Row tailors and shirtmakers. Famous tailors include Anderson & Sheppard, Gieves & Hawkes, H. Huntsman & Sons, Henry Poole (the oldest Savile Row firm), Turnbull & Asser, and Bernard Weatherill. A *bespoke* (custom-tailored) suit may cost between $2000 and $4500 and takes three to four weeks to fit and tailor.

Chester Barrie, also in Savile Row, is respected for high-quality ready-made suits. The best known men's ready-to-wear lines include Roger Dack, Duffer of St. George, Griffin Laundry, Richard James, and Paul Smith.

Gieves & Hawkes tailors at No. 1 Savile Row, London. *(Courtesy of Gieves & Hawkes)*

Women's Apparel

The young designers of the 1960s, such as Mary Quant, Jean Muir, and Zandra Rhodes, made London a fashion capital, but designers have had a difficult time maintaining that reputation since the fading of "swinging London." The 1970s gave the junior fashion world the British *Punk* look, and English designers were popular in the early 1980s, but London has not been able to recapture its former glory. In the early 1990s, the focus of young fashion in London shifted from the Kings Road to around Covent Garden.

Well-known London *off-the-peg* (ready-to-wear) designers include Ally Capellino, Caroline Charles, Toby Clark, Paul Costelloe, Bella Freud, Flyte Ostell (Ellis Flyte and Richard Ostell), Nicole Farhi, David Fielden, John Galliano, Ghost, Abe Hamilton, Katharine Hamnett, Margaret Howell, Betty Jackson, Nicholas Knightly, Lisa Johnson, Roland Klein, Patricia Lester, Ben de Lisi, Alexander McQueen, Terence Nolder, Benny Ong, Rifat Ozbek, Jenny Packham, Arabella Pollen, Edina Ronay, Paul Smith, Helen Storey, Catherine Walker, Vivienne Westwood, and Richard Nott and Graham Fraser for Workers for Freedom. Some of London's best-known designers are showing their collections in Paris or Milan. The British Fashion Council was formed to try to mount a single women's wear exhibition for London Fashion Week to strengthen the United Kingdom's position in the market.

Couture designers include Bellville-Sassoon, Linda Cierach, Anouska Hempel, Bruce Oldfield, and Zandra Rhodes. Hardy Amies continues as the Queen's couturier.

The British also have an international reputation for classic apparel, woolen country clothing, trench coats, and cardigans from such companies as Aquascutum, Austin Reed, Burberry, Daks-Simpson, Jaeger, Mulberry, and Laura Ashley. McGeorge and Pringle are well-known names in cashmere sweaters.

Britain's apparel industry employs approximately 240,000 people. North of Oxford Street in London, in the area around Margaret Street, lies the West End "rag trade" district, which supports a conglomeration of fashion suppliers, studios, and showrooms. Actual manufacturing, originally confined to London's East End, has now spread all over England, Scotland, and Wales, with a concentration of high-quality cashmere and wool knitters to be found near Hawick in Scotland. However, as in other countries, many manufacturers have garments produced in Italy, Eastern Europe, or Asia.

GERMANY

More and more buyers are adding Germany to their European shopping trips. A "Made in Germany" label has enjoyed a strong quality connotation and now is becoming known for styling.

Unlike France, Germany's fashion industry is decentralized. Apparel companies are located all over the country, with large centers in Munich, Berlin, Krefeld, Düsseldorf, and Hamburg. The industry employs over 200,000, the largest group of workers in the German consumer goods industry, in over 2500 firms.

German designer Wolfgang Joop in his design studio.
(Courtesy of Wolfgang Joop, photo by Bernd Isemann)

Internationally known designers and fashion brand names include Iris von Arnim, Bassler, Willi Bogner, Hugo Boss, Marc Cain, Comma, Escada, Hauber, Wolfgang Joop, Helmut Lang, Rena Lange, Rene Lezard, Mondi, Caren Pfleger, Uta Raasch, Jil Sander, Uli Schneider, Klaus Steilmann (the largest women's clothing manufacturer in Europe), Strenesse, Susanne Wiebe, and Windsor.

Germany is also the home of international trade fairs such as IGEDO and Interstoff, as discussed in Chapter 12.

SPAIN

Spain is seen as Western Europe's fashion frontier and Spanish designers are enjoying some international attention.

The Spanish fashion industry consists of about 5000 firms and approximately 150,000 employees, a large percent concentrated in the Catalunya area. The burgeoning industry has little international business or merchandising experience because it has been run from small shops and factories. Members of the Cámara de la Moda Espanola are scattered throughout the country. One problem in promoting Spanish fashion is that half of the designers show in Madrid and half in Barcelona. Efforts are being made to try to consolidate government-sponsored presentations of men's wear in Barcelona and women's wear in Madrid.

Well-known designers include Armand Basi, Lydia Delgado, Manuel Marino (for the Roberto Verino label), Antonio Miro, Palacio and Lemoniez, Jesús del Pozo, Nacho Ruiz, Victorio & Lucchino (actually José Victor Rodriguez Caro, and José Luis Medina del Corral), Angel Schlesser, and Joaquim Verdu. Spain is also an important producer of leather products, particularly shoes, and also moderately priced knitwear.

JAPAN

Tokyo, the capital of Japan and the center of its fashion industry, enjoyed the position of major international trendsetter in the 1980s.

Until World War II, Japanese women still wore the kimono. As they started to take jobs in the postwar period, practical Western dress became a necessity. In the 1950s and 1960s the Japanese became eager for Western-style clothes, most notably those from Paris. Their fascination with the West continues as many large apparel firms have licenses to manufacture European and American fashions in Japan.

The first generation international Japanese designers, Hanae Mori and Jun Ashida, held shows in Paris in the 1960s. In the 1970s, Kenzo Takada became an international success working out of Paris. Since then, other designers such as Junko Koshino, Mitsuhiro Matsuda, Issey (Kazanaru) Miyake, Rei Kawakubo (Commes des Garçons), Kansai Yamamoto, and Yohji Yamamoto have gained international recognition. Their creations have given full play to the Japanese aesthetic sense, which is rooted in a culture in which Western garments were not traditionally worn. In the 1980s, these designers influenced Western fashion with their unusual shapes, somber color combinations, asymmetrical balance, layering, interesting textures, and use of natural fibers, particularly cotton.

Most Japanese manufacturers are small or medium sized, but there are a few operating on a very large scale, including Renown, Onward Kashiyama, Sanyo Shokai, and World Company. These firms not only produce Japanese designs and license European and American designs, but also have been buying production facilities and apparel companies in the West.

CANADA

Canadian designers blend European and American styling and export many of their products to the United States.

The apparel industry is the eighth largest industry in Canada, employing more than 80,000 people and accounting for an estimated 2000 apparel firms. The Canadian Apparel Federation has been established to promote the industry.

Although quite diversified, Canada's apparel industry is particularly known for exports of men's tailored clothing, outerwear, furs, leather goods, and children's wear. Pre-NAFTA, in 1989 a free-trade agreement was already made between the United States and Canada. Since then, exports to the United States have doubled.

Two of the largest Canadian manufacturers, Freed & Freed International and Nygard International, are located in Winnipeg. Well-known companies in Vancouver include Mr. Jax (designed by Ron Leal and now owned by Koret), NETO leathers, and Virani. The two largest fashion centers are around Montreal, Quebec, and Toronto, Ontario.

Montreal

Montreal, Quebec, is Canada's largest fashion center with 57 percent of the apparel work force.[8] The Place Bonaventure is the center for fashion industry showrooms and buyers' weeks.

Well-known Montreal area designers and collections include Jean Airoldi, Helene Barbeau, Angela Bucaro, Simon Chang, Leo Chevalier,

Montreal designer Michel Desjardins on the runway after his collection showing. *(Courtesy of the Toronto Ready-to-Wear Canadian Designer Collections, photographed by Ola Sirant)*

Toronto designer Brian Bailey on the runway after his collection showing. *(Courtesy of the Toronto Ready-to-Wear Canadian Designer Collections, photographed by Ola Sirant)*

Denomme & Vincent, Michel Desjardins, Robert Krief, Dita Martin, Jean Claude Poitras, Hilary Radley, Michel Robichaud, Marie Saint Pierre, and Debbie Shuchat.

Toronto

The Toronto area is Canada's second largest fashion center with 31 percent of the work force. Over 500 textile or fashion companies in Ontario employ 26,000 people. In Toronto itself, more than 14,000 people work for 300 fashion-related companies concentrated in the King-Spadina Fashion District. Toronto also plays host to the Toronto Ready-to-Wear Designer Collections in February and September.

Toronto-area designers and collections include Lida Baday, Brian Bailey, Dominic Bellissimo, Marilyn Brooks, Stephan Caras, Tricia Cochrane, Judy Cornish and Joyce Gunhouse for Comrags, Roger Edwards, Debora Kuchme, Paula Lishman, Linda Lundstrom, Mariola Mayer, Pat McDonagh, Franco Mirabelli, Price Roman, Anne Seally, Alfred Sung, Donna Stephens, Michael Tong, Nancy Young and Karen Gable for Zapata, and James Yunker.

THE UNITED STATES

American manufacturers are largely headquartered in New York City followed by California and other smaller regional manufacturing centers.

New York

American designers and manufacturers naturally understand the domestic market best and make most of the fashion that we wear. American fashion blossomed during World War II, when communications to Paris were cut off. Since then, an American style, especially for sportswear, is now appreciated around the world.

New York became the American garment center because creative talent, supplies, and skilled labor were concentrated there. At least two-thirds of American fashion manufacturing is still located in New York: fabric showrooms, designing, manufacturing headquarters, the major markets, and apparel showrooms.

The Seventh Avenue Garment District

Most fashion originates in the vicinity of Seventh Avenue on Manhattan Island in New York City. Seventh Avenue gives its name to the whole garment district, which runs north to south from Fortieth to Thirty-fourth Streets and east to west from Fifth to Ninth Avenues. Many buildings in the garment district are known for certain apparel specialties. For example, 550 Seventh Avenue has traditionally housed high-fashion companies, one on each floor. Crowded into this area are over 2500 manufacturers and contractors. In New York City there are an estimated 4500 factories located primarily in Chinatown, Manhattan, and Sunset Park, Brooklyn.

The fashion industry employs 250,000 people in design, manufacturing, distribution, and related activities. Approximately 95,000 of these people work in garment manufacturing. Fashion is still the largest manufacturing industry in New York City and the second largest employer after the financial sector.[9] To preserve manufacturing in the city, owners of these buildings are now blocked from converting more than half of their space from manufacturing to offices.

Seventh Avenue is anything but glamorous. The streets are jammed with trucks and taxicabs, young men speaking foreign tongues push racks of fabrics or clothing from suppliers to manufacturers, and sales representatives pull suitcases on wheels from appointment to appointment. Inside old buildings, design studios, showrooms, and offices crowd each building on every block. There is a sharp contrast between the plush showroom in front, for the outside world to see, and the cluttered design rooms in back. Yet this place is the fashion capital of the United States and one of the major fashion capitals of the world!

Enterprises such as the Garment Industry Development Corporation and the Fashion Center Business Improvement District are working to establish a permanent fashion center for shows and an adjacent museum, incentives in the form of tax breaks to upgrade or expand manufacturing facilities, a Made in New York promotion program, and to clean up the garment district to make it more pleasant to work in and more attractive to out-of-town buyers.

Company Size and Ownership

Traditionally, fashion businesses were small, family owned and operated. Their small size allowed flexibility in both design and production, which is needed to respond quickly to market needs. Today, however, the sizable advertising and marketing budgets of the large companies make it difficult for small companies to compete. As a result, small companies have been bought up by larger ones so that the number of apparel firms has decreased. However, overall production has increased with the growth of the larger companies. Liz Claiborne, one of the world's largest women's apparel companies, has many divisions, including Lizwear, Lizsport, Elizabeth, Liz Claiborne petites, Dana Buchman, Claiborne men's wear, and accessories.

American fashion companies also reflect globalization. Many foreign companies have invested in the United States, purchasing companies or production facilities. Takihyo, a Japanese firm, backed Donna Karan so that she could start her own business. The industry is full of similar examples.

Fashion manufacturing has crossed gender lines. Except for some men's suit companies, many companies have expanded to produce both men's and women's fashion. Ralph Lauren started in men's wear and added women's; Liz Claiborne did the opposite. Most sportswear and outerwear companies produce for both sexes.

Designers

In companies that produce moderate- or lower-priced clothing, the designer's name is usually unknown to the public. The company may use a fictitious name, such as "Ellen Tracy."

On high-priced clothing, designers who have proven themselves may have their names added to the company's label, such as "Linda Allard for Ellen Tracy."

Some designers are able to start their own businesses under their own names. They may have started small like Ralph Lauren did with neckties. Or if they have a good reputation working for a manufacturer, a financier might offer to back them in their own business. If their collections are successful, if they have skillful business and financial partners, quality production, and clever advertising, their names become well known.

As in show business, however, designers are only as good as their last production. A designer is often a star today and forgotten tomorrow; the picture changes every season. It is increasingly difficult to name the most important American designers because they change from year to year. Reading fashion publications regularly is the only way to keep informed about current designer favorites and best-selling styles.

American designer Donna Karan at her collection opening.
(Courtesy of Donna Karan Studio © Donna Karan)

Well-known American Designers

Geoffrey Beene. Born in Louisiana in 1927, Beene is a consistently innovative designer. He originally studied to be a doctor, but complained that "every disease we studied I got." He began his career in the display department of I. Magnin in Los Angeles. In the 1940s, he studied fashion in New York and with Molyneux in Paris. He designed for Teal Traina from 1958 until he started his own collection in 1963 with partner Leo Orlandi. He later added men's wear and Beene Bag sportswear. One of the first American designers to show in Europe (in 1975), he has over 30 licenses.

Bill Blass. Born in Indiana in 1922, Blass worked as a sketcher for David Crystal in the 1940s. He worked as designer for Maurice Rentner, later became a partner, and then in 1968 bought out the business. To his women's day and evening collections, he has added Blassport sportswear and men's wear. With 30 domestic and 70 international licenses, Blass has had the longest continuing success of any American designer.

Tommy Hilfiger.   In 1969, Tommy began his business with a small store in Elmira, New York, his hometown, with a $150 investment. In 1980, he moved to New York City and designed for Seventh Avenue companies. In 1985, he was backed to manufacture his own men's wear collection. His company has enjoyed tremendous growth in both men's tailored clothing and sportswear and boys' wear since then.

Donna Karan.   Born in 1948 in New York to parents in the "rag trade," Donna (Faske) Karan left Parsons to become Anne Klein's assistant. After Anne Klein's death in 1974, Karan became head designer with Louis Dell'Olio. This was the first time that an American fashion company was able to continue successfully without the original designer. In 1985, Tomio Taki offered to back Karan in her own business featuring luxury sportswear. Her bridge collection called DKNY (Donna Karan New York) has been extremely successful.

Calvin Klein.   Born in New York City in 1942, Klein always wanted to design clothes. He studied at the Fashion Institute of Technology and worked at Millstein sport and suit company on Seventh Avenue. In 1968, he and his friend Barry Schwartz opened a coat business and got their first order when a buyer from Bonwit Teller accidentally got off the elevator on the wrong floor. He expanded into sportswear, men's wear, jeans, and accessories. He was the first American designer to open his own shops in London and Milan.

American designer Ralph Lauren at a collection opening. *(Courtesy of Ralph Lauren)*

Ralph Lauren.   The perfect example of a designer who was able to build an empire on a life-style, Lauren was born in New York City in 1940 and began his career as a salesclerk at Brooks Brothers. In 1967 he started to design ties and by 1968 had established Polo men's wear with backing from Norman Hilton. The Polo name is perfect for his classic, Ivy League look in expensive fabrics. Lauren built the rest of his multimillion-dollar business on licenses for women's wear, a less expensive men's wear collection called Chaps, boys' wear, girls' wear, accessories, and home furnishings. In 1986 he opened a $14 million retail store on Madison Avenue and has Polo shops in stores across the country.

Nicole Miller.   Born in Texas in 1951, but raised in Massachusetts, Miller studied at the Rhode Island School of Design and in Paris. In 1982, she started a women's wear collection with partner Bud Konheim. What began as a way of getting rid of excess fabric turned into a huge additional business of whimsical men's ties, shirts, and boxer shorts in witty prints. She now has Nicole Miller boutiques in Mexico, Canada, Argentina, Spain, and Korea.

Isaac Mizrahi. Born in Brooklyn, New York, on October 14, 1961, Mizrahi studied at Parsons and apprenticed with Perry Ellis. He opened his own women's wear business in 1987 with partner Sarah Haddad-Cheney and added a men's wear collection in 1990. Mizrahi also likes to design costumes for the ballet and films. In 1992 he won his third Council of Fashion Designers of America (CFDA) Designer of the Year Award.

Oscar de la Renta. Born in 1933 in the Dominican Republic, de la Renta studied painting, sketched for Balenciaga in Madrid, and afterward became assistant to Castillo at Lanvin. In 1962 he designed for Elizabeth Arden in New York and in 1965 became partner at Jane Derby where he took over the business in 1966. His work, which enjoys a reputation for elegance, includes evening wear, suits and dresses, sportswear, men's wear, accessories, and the less expensive Miss O collection. Now he also designs couture for Balmain in Paris, the second American to do couture in Paris.

Adrienne Vittadini. Born in Hungary, Vittadini moved to the United States as a young girl and studied fashion in Philadelphia. After gaining experience at Louis Feraud in Paris, she designed knits for Rosanna and Kimberly in the United States. In 1979 she struck out on her own with women's knit sportswear, activewear, and more recently dresses. She is involved with the design of her own fabrics as well as apparel.

Other successful designers with signature collections in both men's and women's wear include Joseph Abboud, Victor Alfaro, Linda Allard for Ellen Tracy, Badgley Mischka (Mark Badgley and James Mischka), Marc Eisen, Han Feng, Carolina Herrera, Marc Jacobs, Andrea Jovine, Betsey Johnson, Gemma Kahng, Norma Kamali, Randy Kemper, Michael Kors, Byron Lars, Bob Mackie, Mary McFadden, Robert Merloz, Josie Natori, Todd Oldham, Mary Ann Restivo for Burberry, Patrick Robinson for Anne Klein & Co., Cynthia Rowley, Cynthia Steffe, Anna Sui, Zang Toi, and Joan Vass. Couture designers include John Anthony and Arnold Scassi.

More moderately priced brand names have increased in importance. Major brands, such as Liz Claiborne, Jones New York, or Kenar, are recognized nationally and have grown into multimillion and even billion dollar enterprises. They all have talented design staffs who are specialists in their field, and many graduate to having their name on a label.

Regional Fashion Centers

The United States has approximately 22,000 apparel manufacturers employing over a million people.[10] Although New York City remains the largest fashion center, the trend toward decentralization is increasing. Some manufacturers have left New York City in search of a cheaper labor supply and more space. Other companies have started up in regional locations. The result is the growth of regional fashion centers.

California

California is the second largest apparel manufacturing state, with about 5000 manufacturers and contractors and one-fourth of the nation's apparel production. The California clothing industry has a reputation for innovative styling and the advantage of close proximity to sourcing in Asia.

Los Angeles. At least two-thirds of California's fashion companies are headquartered in Los Angeles County, making it the second largest U.S. apparel center.

Successful designers in Los Angeles include Katayone Adeli for Parallel, Christine Albers, Michele Bohbot for Bisou Bisou, Francine Browner, David Dart, Dennis Goldsmith, Tina Hagen, Karen Kane, Carole Little, Georges Marciano for Yes, Jonathan Martin, Leon Max, Dorothy Schoelen for Platinum, Allen Schwartz for ABS, Shelli Segal for Laundry, Bonnie Strauss, and Richard Tyler (winner of the CFDA 1994 Designer of the Year Award). Nationally known brands from the Los Angeles area include Bugle Boy, B.U.M. Equipment, Cherokee, Cross Colours, Anne Cole swimwear, Guess, L. A. Gear, Rampage, St. John Knits, and Speedo.

San Francisco. The nation's third largest fashion city is home to approximately 400 apparel companies. The garment industry is San Francisco's second-biggest industry and its biggest source of manufacturing jobs.

San Francisco is headquarters for the world's largest apparel manufacturer, Levi Strauss, which also manufacturers Dockers. Other manufacturers include Esprit, the Gap (actually a private label retailer) and its subsidiary Banana Republic, Byer, and Koret. Recognized local designers include Michael Casey, Isda Funari, Nick Graham for Joe Boxer, Jessica McClintock, Lat Naylor, Celia Tejada, and Eileen West.

Much of the California designers' success is based on their ability to promote a certain life-style approach to fashion. California is especially known for sportswear, swimwear, and contemporary dresses. Sales of the California look keep growing as Americans become more leisure conscious and as population shifts toward the sunbelt.

Australian-born, California designer Richard Tyler accepting the Perry Ellis Award at the CFDA Awards Gala at Lincoln Center, New York City. *(Courtesy of the Council of Fashion Designers of America)*

Other Regional Centers

Other important apparel manufacturing and design centers are scattered throughout the country.

Seattle, Washington, has become the fourth largest apparel manufacturing center. Companies such as Brittania, Generra, and Union Bay have made it an important men's sportswear center. Outerwear manufacturers include Pacific Trail (now owned by London Fog), Helly Hansen, and Roffe. Eddie Bauer produces sportswear and outerwear for its own catalog and stores.

Portland, Oregon, area manufacturers include Nike, Jantzen, Pendleton, Hanna Anderson, and Columbia Sportswear.

Dallas, Texas, is home to designers and companies such as Susan Apple, Michael Faircloth, Haggar, Jo Hardin, Rebecca Harrison, Holly Holman, Jerrel, Ginnie Johansen, Megan Moore, Ann Tobias, and Howard Wolf. There are approximately 1800 textile, apparel, footwear, and accessory manufacturers and wholesale businesses in the state of Texas.[11]

Miami, Florida, has a large number of children's wear, swimwear, sportswear, and activewear manufacturers.

Philadelphia, Pennsylvania, is the headquarters of Jones New York, Albert Nipon, J. G. Hook, and has many children's wear manufacturers.

Chicago, Illinois, the home of Hartmarx and Rochester, New York, headquarters for Hickey-Freeman, have long been known as centers for men's wear.

St. Louis and Boston are smaller centers for apparel and accessory manufacturing. Osh Kosh and Jockey are located in Wisconsin, Lee jeans and sportswear in Kansas, London Fog in Maryland, and Wrangler in North Carolina. As regional manufacturing develops, each center becomes less and less specialized. The spreading of fashion centers throughout the United States and the world is helping to balance fashion influence and to diversify styling.

Many large corporations own manufacturers located around the country. VF Corporation, for example, is based in Pennsylvania but owns Wrangler of North Carolina, Jantzen of Oregon, Lee of Kansas, and Vanity Fair of Pennsylvania.

Other well-known brand names such as Jaclyn Smith (Kmart) or Kathie Lee (Wal Mart) are actually private label names belonging to retailers. The line is getting blurry between manufacturers and retailers because so many retailers are producing their own merchandise and many designers are opening their own stores. Private label is discussed with retailing in Chapter 13.

SUMMARY

Fashion has become a global phenomenon. Due to a concentration of resources, supplies, skilled labor, and creativity, Paris grew to be the fashion capital of the world. It built its reputation with the couture, but profits now come from prêt-à-porter. Today, Paris shares the European spotlight with Milan, whose designers and fashion brands have achieved similar international success. London, the focus of youthful fashion of the 1960s, remains noteworthy for its Savile Row tailoring. Also in Europe, German and Spanish designers are gaining global respect. In the far East, Tokyo designers had great impact on fashion in the early 1980s. Canada has its style centers in Montreal and Toronto. New York, especially the area around Seventh Avenue, is the fashion capital of the United States and continually gains international recognition. Los Angeles and San Francisco make California the second largest U.S. center. Fashion has become big business and the top designers are the fashion stars.

9

PRODUCT AND DESIGN DEVELOPMENT

CAREER FOCUS

The creative side of manufacturing offers highly competitive positions as designers, merchandisers, product managers, and pattern makers. In a large company, a designer, a merchandiser, and their assistants are assigned to each product group. A recent college graduate may obtain employment as an assistant in one of these areas.

CHAPTER OBJECTIVES

After reading this chapter you should have attained competence in the following areas:

1. Understanding line development by item or by group
2. The ability to explain the important elements and principles of design and their application to line development
3. The ability to describe the process of creating a sample garment

*T*he manufacturer's design or product development department plans and creates new styles, within the company's image or identity. This chapter begins by explaining how a manufacturer's line is developed. To prepare for this, it is very important to first read Chapters 2, 3, and 4 to understand target customers, design influences, and resources. The chapter then goes on to discuss fashion design elements and principles, including color and fabrication and the creation of the sample line.

PRODUCT DEVELOPMENT

Management, merchandisers, designers, and their assistants are involved in the development of a line or collection of the fashion manufacturer's product.

Appealing to a Target Market

Each apparel manufacturer is defined by its customer and identified by its particular style. This involves finding a *market niche* around a particular life-style or need, ideally a part of the market that is not served adequately or successfully by another manufacturer. Christian Lacroix reflects on his own creative methods: "As I look for my line, I ask myself what will be the life-style of the woman of my next collection."[1] Manufacturers identify their customers as a group, develop a product that fits that identity, and stay with it.

Maintaining an Identity

A designer or manufacturer that develops and is recognized for a particular style, yet incorporates current trends into that style, attracts buyers year after year. Lacroix, Ralph Lauren, and Jessica McClintock are excellent examples of designers with a distinctive style. Lauren himself said, "It's the most important thing for designers...to have an identity..."[2]

Traditionally, manufacturers specialize in a particular styling category, price range, gender, and size range of apparel. As a company grows, it expands by adding diversified lines. Many manufacturers have broadened their product lines to include other style categories or size and price ranges, but they have separate divisions and/or label names for each. For example, sportswear firms such as Carole Little have added dresses. Liz Claiborne started with women's sportswear and later branched out to include dresses, suits, accessories, and men's wear. Both Ralph Lauren and Giorgio Armani began with men's wear and later added women's wear collections. The addition of large-size and petite divisons offers manufacturers tremendous growth opportunity because no new design is necessary, just additional patterns. As manufacturers diversify, however, they must maintain a consistent identity oriented toward their customers. Giorgio Armani reiterates, "Coherence is always the secret, I believe, behind a great company."[3]

The Product Development Team

Responsibilities for product development, design, and merchandising vary from manufacturer to manufacturer. *Product development* is the process of market and trend research, merchandising, design, and development of the final product. In a large company, a designer, a merchandiser, perhaps a product manager, and their assistants are assigned to each division.

◆ When the designer is president of the company, the designer is obviously in charge. Manufacturers that are design driven, like Liz Claiborne or Ellen Tracy, have designers in charge of product development.

◆ In companies that are merchandising driven or numbers oriented, like Levi Strauss, merchandisers or product managers direct development of the line. However, in most companies it is a team effort among management, designers, and merchandisers.

Merchandising

Merchandising is planning to have the right merchandise at the right time in the right quantity and at the right price to meet the needs of the company's target customers. The merchandiser or product manager is basically a process manager, developing the blueprint of the line. Merchandising activities, which vary from company to company, usually include setting financial goals, budgets, and price points, making the merchandising plans, planning line size, planning fabric purchases, sourcing, scheduling production, controlling product flow, and presentation of the line.

Merchandiser Charles Sommer shows a new shirting to product development director Michael Alexin, second from right, at a styling meeting for Dockers at Levi Strauss. Also attending are merchandiser Anna Hanley, Designer Jerry Tinker, and design assistant Marie Richardson. (*Photographed by the author*)

The Merchandise Plan

Each season, merchandising has to decide how many groups of apparel or accessories are needed to meet both the demands of retailers and the financial goals of the manufacturer.

The previous year's actual sales are used as a basis for projected *sales goals* for each group. Spreadsheets are created to show what needs to be produced and sold per month to reach sales and profit goals.

Next, the merchandiser has to determine the *line concept* and the approximate *number of styles and fabrics* required to meet those sales goals. Price points are established so that fabric and labor cost limits can be determined. In the value-oriented 1990s, manufacturers have tried to lower prices by offering less expensive fabrics or cutting labor costs.

Scheduling

Merchandising is responsible for integrating all the phases of product development, including design and production. The merchandiser sets up a schedule of deadlines for styling, finished samples, and production, working *backward* from the required shipping dates.

Seasons

Each season, the design and merchandising departments of each division are responsible for creating a new line, the seasonal collection that the manufacturer will sell to retail store buyers. The terms are synonymous:

◆ **Collection** is used primarily in Europe and for high-priced apparel in the United States.
◆ **Line** is used more often in the United States for moderately and popularly priced fashion.

Work on a new line begins approximately eight months before the selling season (a velvet dress to be worn in December must be designed in May). Designers and merchandisers work on two or more lines at once, designing a future collection while solving problems of the one that is about to be shipped. It has become a continual process of creating new merchandise, a "seamless" product development.

Most women's wear companies produce four or five seasonal lines a year: spring, summer, transitional, fall, and holiday or resort. Men's sportswear firms also have four line releases a year as compared to men's suits, which have just two. Children's wear firms have three or four, depending on the product focus. Most manufacturers have staggered delivery dates for each group within the line. Managing delivery dates in this way means that manufacturers are shipping to stores monthly, providing them with continual fresh merchandise.

Some manufacturers are now trying to fit their lines into the financial calendar of the retail stores with a line per quarter: January to March for spring, for example. This makes it easier for the retailer to plan buying and deliveries. Manufacturers that have their own catalogs also do not follow traditional seasons. Instead, they plan their lines around planned catalog mailing dates.

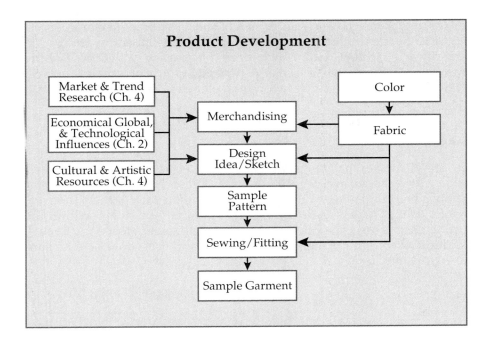

DESIGN DEVELOPMENT

The designer creates the styles for the collection, giving form to fashion ideas.

The emphasis on uniqueness has made creativity in design more important than ever. Couture and top ready-to-wear designers are able to enhance their creativity with expensive fabrications and beautiful workmanship because they are able to sell at higher prices. Their skill enables them to create trends. Mainstream designers must know how to adapt trends and timing to suit their own customers and select fabrics that fit into their price range. They are responsible for concepts, styling, and colors. Designers must also supervise pattern making, fit, and sample making and see their lines through to a successful completion.

Concept Boards. To begin work on a collection, many designers use concept boards to show their ideas to the management team. They make a collage of color and fabric swatches, sketches of ideas, and *swipes* (idea photos) from magazines that capture a mood or theme. When the ideas are approved, designers refine and develop specific ideas into themes for groups and individual garment designs.

Groups

Lines are divided into groups of garments. Liz Claiborne, for example, does six to eight groups in each line release in each division. Each group has a specific *theme* based on a fabric, color, or a particular fashion direction.

Ideas for the theme come from research and environmental influences. Sometimes the idea for a single garment may inspire an entire group. The styling of each garment within each group has variety, yet carries out the central theme. To present a visually pleasing group of dresses, gowns, sportswear, suits, or coats, a few common elements are needed, such as a fabric or color story.

Dresses

Groups of dresses may begin with an *anchor*, a best seller from the previous line with a change of color and/or fabric. Often dress designers emphasize only a few silhouettes, called *bodies*, interpreting each of them in several prints, or they will feature one print in a variety of styles. Within the group, the garments must offer a variety of silhouettes, sleeve treatments, necklines, and/or other details. Women's suits and coats are also merchandised in this manner.

Suits and Outerwear

Men's suits are treated as individual units sharing only a basic silhouette. The manufacturer's objective is to include a variety of colors and suitings in the line, providing a wide choice for both the retail buyer and the consumer. The prime factors in styling men's suits are fabric and silhouette. There is generally little detail change from season to season. The ideal suit is a timeless classic.

Women's suits, on the other hand, may be fashion oriented or classic. They are merchandised rather like dresses with a variety of silhouettes, collar treatments, details, and fabrications.

Sportswear

Sportswear differs from dress or suit design in that individual pieces are designed to be worn together. A balanced mix of skirts, pants, jackets, and shirts or blouses and other tops are included in each group. There may be a basic jacket and a fashion-forward jacket, various skirt lengths, a basic pant and an updated version, and shirts plus other kinds of tops with a variety of necklines.

- ◆ **Coordinated sportswear** is designed to mix and match interchangeably, and is sold as a package to the retailer, as opposed to
- ◆ **Separates**, which do not show an obvious relationship and are sold individually to the retailer.
- ◆ **Men's sportswear** is also merchandised in groups. A group may include pants, jackets, vests, shirts, and sweaters. Fabrication mixes are very important.

The number of pieces or styles in a group is determined by the statement the company wishes to make and the variety of pieces needed to complement one another. The designer must think through what the customer can wear with what. A top has to go with more than one jacket and/or bottom. Multipurpose clothing is very important in today's market.

In large companies, like Levi Strauss and Eddie Bauer, designers are specialists in one category of the group such as bottoms or "lowers," knit tops, or woven tops. The design director is then responsible for the cohesiveness of the group.

Fashion versus Basics

Every group must have a balance of fashion and basics. Even if the manufacturer is not a designer business, fashion pieces give the company credibility by showing retail buyers that the company is aware of fashion trends. However, basics are often what brings in the orders. Even designer lines such as Ralph Lauren make most of their sales and profits on one or two hot basics such as khaki pants or polo shirts. Tommy Hilfiger says that he begins with basics for the core of his men's wear collection and then adds newness and fashion to that.[4] The strength of basics is also obvious at Levi Strauss. Although they offer many varieties of fits and colors in jeanswear, their biggest seller is still the 501 basic jean.

An Esprit Kids sportswear group.
(Courtesy of Esprit)

Items

Some manufacturers produce single *items* that do not relate to each other. Items are popular style categories that a consumer can use to update an existing wardrobe. Each garment must be strong enough to sell on its own, not depending on the strength of other garments in the group. Such garments are usually produced at moderate or budget price ranges at the request of retailers for private labels (see Chapters 12 and 13) and/or by a knockoff house.

Knockoffs

A *knockoff* is a copy of someone else's design, usually a garment that is already a best-seller for another manufacturer. Knockoff companies simply buy a particular garment, make a pattern from it, order large quantities of the same or similar fabric, and have the garment manufactured. Production and fabric costs are lower because of the huge quantities made. The knockoff producer must have (1) an acute awareness of what garments are selling well at the retail level, (2) rapid production capabilities to capitalize on the success of the style while it lasts, and (3) lower prices. Now, in an age of instant global communications, copies often reach stores before the originals and at a fraction of the cost.

Some designers try to copyright their designs. Copyright is nearly impossible, however, because of the fast pace of the industry. By the time a design is granted a copyright, the garment is no longer in fashion. Yves St.

Laurent sued Ralph Lauren for copying, but this is very rare. To protect their profits, some designers copy their own designs at lower prices, in lower-priced fabrics, a season later.

Copying becomes an even more serious problem when it involves *counterfeit merchandise*, imitations with fake labels intended to deceive the consumer. Fake Gucci and Ferragamo accessories and Levi jeans are seen all over the world. The U.S. government confiscates this merchandise when they discover it. It is difficult to control internationally, however, because a designer or brand name must be registered separately in every marketplace. The cost of registration plus legal fees is very high when it must be paid in every country. In January 1995, an agreement was reached between China and the United States to protect trademarks, and the World Trade Organization is also working to stop counterfeiting.

Design Elements

Keeping the theme of the group in mind, a designer must incorporate into each garment a pleasing combination of all the elements of good design: color, fabric, line, and shape. The ingredients of design, which are essential to every art form, are not a recipe for success and cannot substitute for experience. The designer does not think of these elements consciously; the use of them just becomes automatic. Also, fashion changes continually; there are no hard and fast rules.

Color

Color is the first element to which consumers respond, often selecting or rejecting a garment because of its color appeal. Therefore, designers must consider their customers and provide colors that are both appealing and flattering.

People connect certain colors with holidays and seasons. They expect to see earth tones in fall clothing, jewel colors for the holidays, the pastels of flowers in the early spring, and refreshing white for the summer. All manufacturers include some of these colors in their lines.

Color Dimensions.   Color has three different dimensions: hue, value, and intensity.

Hue enables us to tell one color from another, such as red from blue or green.

Value refers to the use of darks and lights; it is the variation of light strength in a color. The value scale runs from white to black. White is pure light; black is the total absence of light. Adding white lightens a color and adding black darkens it. The lighter values are called *tints* and the darker ones *shades*. Every garment has value contrasts, even if only those created by normal gathers and folds. Strong value contrasts (pure black against pure white is the strongest) achieve a dramatic effect.

Intensity is the relative brightness (strength) or paleness (weakness) of a color. Bright colors are considered high intensity; pale ones are low intensity. For instance, when paint is paled by adding water, the intensity of its color is lowered. Within the blue hue, marine blue is high intensity and soft pastel blue is low intensity.

Warm Colors. We classify red, yellow, and orange as warm colors because of their association with fire and the sun. Warm colors are stimulating, aggressive, and lively. Red is associated with matters of the heart: valentines, love, and romance; it is also exciting, fiery, and dangerous. A popular color for sportswear and evening wear, it is one of the few colors used in high intensities for clothing in every season. Yellow is bright, sunny, cheerful, friendly, and optimistic, but it can be a difficult color to wear because it conflicts with many skin tones. Orange combines the sunniness of yellow and the warmth of red. It is often a difficult color to wear as intense orange can be irritating and overpowering. Usually, it is best toned to a softer peach or apricot or limited to use in activewear.

Cool Colors. Cool colors, as the term implies, are refreshing in contrast to warm colors. The cool colors—blue, green, and purple—remind us of the sky and the sea. Blue is quiet, restful, and reserved. Denim blue and navy have become wardrobe classics. For that reason most manufacturers include it in at least their spring or summer line. Green is a refreshing color, suggesting peace, rest, calm, and quiet. It is used primarily in a dark value in fall sportswear lines or mixed with neutrals to create earthy olive or loden. Purple, historically associated with royalty, has come to represent wealth, dignity, and drama.

Neutrals. For sophisticated fashion, neutrals such as beige, tan, taupe, brown, white, gray, and black are even more popular than the colors just mentioned. The reason is probably that they present a pleasing background for the wearer without competing for attention. Neutrals are part of every season's fashion picture, as either a strong fashion statement or a way to round out a color story.

An unusual combination of colors in a Christian Lacroix design. *(Courtesy of Christian Lacroix, Paris)*

White is associated with purity and cleanliness. Because it reflects light, it is cool in the summer. In Western culture black has been connected with villains and death. However, it has come to be regarded as a sophisticated fashion color. Both black and white have become classic fashion "colors."

Color Relationships. There are no hard and fast rules for the use of colors. Rather, colors are considered harmonious if they are used so that one color enhances the beauty of the other. Colors are now combined in many more unusual ways than ever before. Ethnic influences on fashion have changed our view of color combinations, making us more receptive to new ideas. In addition, colors run in fashion cycles just as styles do. Color combinations that look right to us now will not work with the new looks a few years hence.

Color Naming. An exciting color name can be important in promoting a fashion look. Fashion colors sometimes reappear with new names that make them seem fresh. "Plum" of one year might return as "aubergine" in another. Oil-paint color lists, as well as books featuring the names of flowers, trees, wood, fruit, vegetables, spices, wines, gems, and animals, can provide color-name ideas. To create moods, colorists and fashion journalists use exotic names such as "China Blue" or "Poison Green."

Color Selection. Colors must be selected for each group and for individual garments. As trendsetters, couture and top ready-to-wear designers have the privilege of basing their color story on whatever inspires them. Mainstream fashion designers may rely on color selections provided by color and design services, trade associations, or fiber companies. The colors common to these sources indicate trends. By basing a color story on these trend forecasts, the designer is assured that the group will be in the mainstream of fashion. Usually, designers select some trend colors and combine them with their own color choices.

The colors in a print fabric may also inspire a color story. Color choices must reflect season, climate, and type of garment. Active sportswear, for example, employs many more vivid colors than business attire. Every line should include a range of colors that appeals to a variety of customers.

Within the line, each group is usually formulated around a color plan consisting of as few as two colors or many colors. Color must also flow well from one delivery date to another, so that they look good together on the selling floor of a store. The group may then be anchored with neutrals, darks, white, or black. In any case, the color story must be meaningful, not just a group of unrelated colors. The color story might be all brights, or all muted, or a balance of darks and lights.

Fabric

Color is interpreted in the medium of fabric. Fabrics are the designer's artistic medium, in that fashion design is essentially sculpture in fabric in relation to the body.

Fabric Selection. *Fabrication* is the selection or creation of an appropriate style for a fabric—or the reverse, the selection of the right fabric for a design. Next to understanding the needs of the customer, choosing a fabric suitable for a particular style is probably the most important aspect of designing. The designer chooses fabrics on the basis of fashion trends, quality, performance, price, and suitability.

Fabrics themselves often inspire garment design. For example, the softness and drapability of a jersey might inspire gathers in a dress. Christian Dior wrote, "Many a dress of mine is born of the fabric alone."[5] Other designers work the other way around, first getting an idea, perhaps developing it in a sketch, and then finding the appropriate fabric for it. However the designer works, he or she must ultimately decide which fabric will work best with a design, or vice versa. Designers must develop the ability to picture a design already made up in the fabric. This ability comes through observation and experience.

Many firms build a line or even an entire reputation on one fabric, such as denim or stone-washed silk. In sportswear, a *base fabric* is selected for jackets and lowers. In jean-swear, of course, the base fabric is always denim. An assortment of fabrics (solids and prints) is chosen to go with the base fabric. The designer or merchandiser must be sure to include a variety of weights, textures, and prints in a line, as well as a balance of fashion and classic fabrics.

Fabric Characteristics. Fabric suitability is determined by characteristics such as fiber, weave, texture, performance, hand, pattern, and color.

Texture is the sensuous element of design. It is the surface interest of a fabric, created by the weave and by light reflection. Our eyes appreciate the play of light on smooth or rough surfaces, we feel the surface with our hands, and sometimes we can even hear the texture, such as the rustle of taffeta. Combinations of textures, such as suede with jersey (rough with smooth), create interest in a garment. Texture has been a very important element in the 1990s.

Performance refers to a fabric's wearing and cleaning properties based on fiber content, weave, and finish. Fabric performance is an important consideration regarding the *function* of the garment, especially in activewear and outerwear. A ski jacket must keep a customer warm in subzero conditions, for example.

A contrast of textures in a Bill Blass suit.
(Courtesy of Bill Blass)

Weight and hand dictate the silhouette of a garment. *Weight* is the heaviness or lightness, thinness or thickness of a fabric. *Hand* is the feel, body, and fall of a fabric. A designer must know how a fabric will behave and whether it will carry out an idea. A garment must be styled in a fabric that is compatible with the desired silhouette.

Firm fabrics like worsted wools, gabardines, and linen are needed to carry out a tailored look. These fabrics have both the crisp look and the fall necessary to achieve the desired effect. Interfacing, a fabric sewn or ironed into the garment's inner construction, is used to give additional stiffness to finished edges such as necklines, collars, cuffs, and buttoning areas.

Soft fabrics like crepe, jersey, chiffon, and challis are ideal for draped designs that delineate body shape. Additional fluidity can be achieved by cutting fabric on the bias grain, so that the diagonal of the fabric falls vertically in the garment. However, bias is difficult to lay out on a *marker* (pattern layout) and thus expensive to produce. Softness may be increased by the additional use of gathers, shirring, smocking, and unpressed pleats.

Fabric weight varies with the type of garment. For example, blouse weights are lighter than bottom (skirt or pant) weights. Manufacturers often buy fabrics in specific weights, such as a 5-ounce shirting or an 11-ounce denim. The weight is determined by the square yard for wovens and by the linear yard for knits.

Fabric weight must also be appropriate for the season. Heavier, warmer fabrics are needed for winter and light, cooler ones for summer. Specific natural fibers have traditionally been considered appropriate for certain seasons. Wool is used for fall and winter because it is heavy, bulky, and warm. Linen and cotton are used as warm-weather fabrics because they are light, cool, and washable. However, there are now seasonless fabrics and fashions. A fabric such as jersey can be worn year round. Cotton, traditionally a summer fiber, can be woven into warm, bulky fabrics such as corduroy for fall and winter garments. Wools can be woven into lightweight voile for spring.

Prints and Patterns.   The *scale* of a pattern must complement the design. To show a large print to its best advantage, it should not be cut up with seams and details, but rather allowed to be the most important element of the garment; construction should be kept simple. On the other hand, if a design idea consists of seam lines and details, then the fabric must be of secondary importance. The scale must also be considered when choosing a fabric to use for large sizes versus petites. Scale is particularly important in children's wear because the garment pieces are small.

The *repeat* of a print is the amount of fabric necessary for a floral or geometric pattern to duplicate itself totally. Large repeats are not usually suitable for trims or for children's wear. In addition, garments to be made in border prints must be carefully thought out so that fabric is not wasted in production cutting.

The designer must recognize patterns that require special matching because they increase the amount of fabric used and therefore the cost. Bold plaids and irregular stripes must match when sewn together.

One-way prints and pile fabrics also use more yardage, because all the pattern pieces must be cut in the same direction. Many fabrics today are directional, and the manufacturer cuts them all one way to prevent variations in color.

Environmental Concerns.   Many designers are concerned with the condition of our polluted environment and want to do their part in trying to improve the situation. Companies such as Patagonia, Ecotex, Ecosport, or Esprit with their Ecollection are trying to fill the need for environmentally responsible apparel. Patagonia, for example, uses fabrics made out of recycled plastic bottles.

These companies feel that it is the fashion industry's responsibility to make environmentalism fashionable because fashion is an important communicator of values to people. To do this, manufacturers must choose organic cotton, naturally colored cotton, linen, wool, tencel, or recylced materials that are treated with low-impact or bifunctional dyes, enzyme washes, and other safe finishes. Some companies are returning to natural materials for buttons and using nonelectroplated metal trimmings.

Reviewing Fabrics.   The designer's involvement in fabric selection for a manufacturer varies. Sometimes designers have the entire responsibility for fabric selection; in a large company they often work with a fabric merchandiser, especially when an entire group is built around one particular fabric. The fabric merchandiser may also research the textile market for trends and sources and follow through with fabric purchases.

Before a new season, the designer and/or merchandiser studies fabric trends by reviewing the fabric market. The designer may visit one of the international fabric trade fairs, such as Premier Vision. This is the best way to keep abreast of the newest fiber or fabric developments.

Designers and merchandisers also frequently travel to a major fashion capital such as New York, where most textile mills and converters have headquarters, for an overall picture of the season's textile offerings. Moreover, at these centers the designers can discuss their ideas directly with textile designers and technicians. Designers often work directly with mills or converters to develop a new pattern or fabric. Fabric mills or converter sales representatives also call on the designer at work. Each season designers try to see as many fabric representatives as possible to learn about the variety of fabrics available.

Price Considerations. Fabric quality and, therefore, price must be consistent with the price of the line. An expensive designer collection is made of the finest fabrics; a moderately priced line requires less expensive materials. A general rule is that fabric and trimming costs must balance labor costs. More expensive fabrics may go into understated, simple garments whose construction is less complicated. Garments requiring more yardage have to be cut from less expensive goods so that they will not exceed the price range of the line. By using a less expensive fabric, the designer can afford to put more money into labor or trimmings.

Sample Cuts. Color or swatch cards sent by textile companies help designers and merchandisers to make fabrication decisions. To test the fabric, the designer orders a 3- to 5-yard cut of a fabric to make a test garment. If the designer and merchandiser are very enthusiastic about a fabric, they may initially order enough for many samples—perhaps 100 yards or more. They also have to consider the availability of the fabric for orders and production. They may have to commit to a fabric order before even having a collection to show. Once fabrics have been selected, the designer can begin to create styles.

Line

After selecting the fabric, the designer must consider the other design elements. In this section, the term *line* refers to the direction of visual interest in a garment created by construction

A peony and black wool suit by Linda Allard for Ellen Tracy. The black button detail accentuates the line from the black collar, along the jacket opening, down to the black trim and skirt.
(Courtesy of Ellen Tracy)

An intriguing shape of jacket and neckline and perfect proportions make this Richard Tyler suit special.
(Courtesy of Tyler-Trafficante)

details such as seams, openings, pleats, gathers, tucks, topstitching, and trims (it is confusing that the apparel industry also uses the term *line* to refer to a collection of garments). Line direction should flow from one part of the garment to another and should not be meaninglessly cut up.

Straight lines suggest crispness, such as that of tailored garments; curved lines imply buoyancy. However, a garment designed with only straight lines is too severe; a garment with all curves is too restless. Curves need the steadying influence of straight lines. For optimal beauty, the two should work together. Straight lines are softened by the curves of the body, and full curves must be restrained to be compatible with the human form.

Lines have the power to create moods and feelings. Vertical lines remind us of upright, majestic figures and suggest stability. Horizontal lines are like lines at rest; they suggest repose, quiet, and calm. Soft, curving lines express grace, and diagonal lines imply powerful movement and vitality.

Shape

Another function of line is to create shape. We use the term *silhouette* to describe the outline of the whole garment. Because the silhouette is what we see from a distance, it is responsible for one of our first impressions of a garment. Silhouettes tend to repeat themselves in cycles throughout history. At times a more body-conscious, natural (hourglass) silhouette is popular. At other times rectangular, inverted triangle, or tubular shapes that de-emphasize body contours may be prevalent.

A silhouette should be related to body structure, but some variation is needed to add interest. Sometimes one part of the silhouette, such as sleeves, hips, or shoulders, predominates. Of course, the final effect is heavily influenced by the fabric used. *Bodies* (industry jargon for silhouettes) that do well in one season are usually updated in a new fabric or color for the next season.

Lines also divide the total area into smaller shapes and spaces by means of seams, openings, pleats, and tucks. A good silhouette is composed of parts that in themselves have interesting shapes. Parts may be square, round, oval, rectangular, triangular, or irregular. The minute a waistline is added, a garment is divided into two new shapes: a bodice and a skirt. The sleeve becomes another shape. These parts create new spaces for smaller details, such as collars and pockets. The pattern of the fabric can create even smaller shapes.

Design Principles

Whether design elements are used successfully depends on their relationship to one another within the garment. *Design principles* serve as guidelines for combining elements. Designers may not consciously think of these principles as they work, but when something is wrong with a design, they are able to analyze the problem in terms of proportion, balance, repetition, and emphasis to create a harmonious design. These principles are flexible, always interpreted within the context of current fashion trends.

Proportion

Proportion is simply the pleasing interrelationship of the size of all parts of the garment. Proportion sometimes follows natural body divisions and sometimes creates its own divisions. When conceiving a style, the designer must consider how the silhouette is to be divided with lines of construction or detail. These lines create new spaces, which must relate in a pleasing way. Generally, unequal proportion is more interesting than equal. Many mathematical formulas have been proposed as guidelines, but the best results come from practice in observing and analyzing good design. Standards of proportion change with fashion cycles along with the evolution in silhouette and line.

Karl Lagerfeld uses resourceful repetition of collar shape and button detail in this symmetrical Chloé dress. *(Courtesy of Chanel, Paris)*

The height and width of all parts of a design must be compared. Individual sections of a garment, such as sleeves, pockets, and collar, must all relate in size to each other as well as to the total silhouette. A jacket length and shape must work with the length and shape of the skirt or pants.

Background space is just as important as the detail or shapes within it. A large, bold shape against a plain background is dramatic. Areas broken into small shapes suggest daintiness. Each detail or shape within the silhouette should complement the whole.

The spacing of trimmings, pleats, and tucks must have meaning in relation to the total design. Trimmings must not be too heavy or too light, too large or too small to harmonize with the space around them. Every line, detail, or trim changes the proportion because it breaks up the space even more. The designer continually experiments with subtle variations in proportion: line placement, hem length, and size and placement of trims.

Balance

Balance refers to "visual weight" in design. A garment must be balanced to be visually pleasing.

Symmetrical Balance. If the design composition is the same on both sides of the garment, then the design is considered *symmetrical,* or formally balanced, following the natural bisymmetry of the body. Just as we have two eyes, two arms, and two legs, a symmetrical garment must have exactly the same details in just the same place on both sides. Formal balance is the easiest, most logical way to achieve stability and is therefore, the most commonly used in design. Even slight deviations, when minor details are not exactly alike on both sides, are considered *approximate symmetry.* A sensitive use of fabric, rhythm, and space relationships is needed to keep a symmetrical design from being boring.

Asymmetrical Balance. To achieve a more exciting, dramatic effect, asymmetrical, or informal balance, can be used. Asymmetrical design composition is different on one side of the garment compared to the other and is achieved by a balance of visual impact. A small, unusual, eye-catching shape or concentrated detail on one side can balance a larger, less imposing area on the other side. Striking line, color, or texture can appear to balance larger masses of less significance. Technically, asymmetrical designs make pattern layout more difficult and therefore more expensive.

Repetition

Repetition, or a sense of movement, is necessary to create interest in a design and to carry out the central theme. This can be achieved by the repetition of lines, shapes, and colors to give direction. We can see rhythm of lines and shapes in the repetition of pleats, gathers, and tiers or in rows of trim, banding, or buttons. The dominant color, line, shape, or detail of the garment may be repeated elsewhere with variation. The sense of movement must be felt, even if subtly.

The use of repetition is one of the most helpful guidelines in designing. A design line, shape, or detail repeated in another area of the garment helps to carry the theme throughout the whole design. In dress design, for example, a V neck might be repeated upside down in bodice seaming or in an inverted pleat in the skirt. Soft gathers at the neck could be repeated at the hip to unify the design.

Emphasis

Emphasis, or a center of interest, draws attention to the focal point of a garment. This point is the central theme; the rest of the garment is of secondary importance. A center of interest must create more visual attraction than any other design element in the garment, and all other elements must support it by echoing its design message with weakened impact. A center of interest should be related to the total structure of the garment. Such a focal point can be achieved by accenting with color, significant shapes or details, lines coming together, groups of detail, or contrast. A combination of these methods gives the focal point added strength, as does placing the decorative emphasis at a structural point. Karl Lagerfeld does it simply with rows of gold buttons for Chanel.

In the designing of sportswear, each piece is considered a part of the whole. Although some pieces are simple basics, they create a background for or complement another piece such as a jacket, which creates the center of interest.

maker to solve construction problems. Factory construction methods must be tested as the garment is sewn. Some manufacturers such as Adrienne Vittadini have their samples made abroad at the same factory where production will be done due to the need for specialized equipment and to test factory production.

Fit

The next step is to test the sample for fit and total effect. The ability to create a good fit is the most important skill needed in the development of the garment. It is necessary to see how the garment fits not only on a dress form but also on a model to test comfort and ease of movement. Donna Karan likes to try on her samples herself.

The Designer Work Sheet

Records are kept on all styles as they develop. Each designer fills out a work sheet containing information that guides the production department in figuring costs and in ordering *piece goods* (the factory term for fabrics) and trimmings. Many companies now have computer-generated design work sheets. In this case, each department responsible (such as fabrics, trims, design) enters their own information into the computer.

The work sheet includes the following information:

1. The date the garment was designed
2. The selling season for which the garment is designed

Designer Nicole Miller works with samplemakers on the development of a garment. *(Photographed by the author)*

DESIGNER WORKSHEET

DATE   STYLE No. *1025*
DESCRIPTION *Floral print dress*   SEASON *spring*
                                                  SELLING PRICE: *$ 61.52*

SIZE RANGE *4-14*   COLORS *blue on white ground*
MARKERS
MARKER YARDAGE: ALLOWANCE:

1. MATERIAL	YARDS	PRICE	AMT.		SKETCH
print	*4.75*	*3.85*	*18.29*		
Lining					
TOTAL MATERIAL COST			*$18.29*		

2. TRIMMINGS	QUANT.	PRICE	AMT.
Buttons *#20 covered*	*6*	*.03*	*.18*
Pads			
Embroidery			
1½" wide satin ribbon	*1.7*	*.25*	*.43*
Belts			
Zippers			
Pleating, Tucking			
¼" elastic	*.7*	*.05*	*.04*
interfacing	*.15*	*1.05*	*.16*
fusing			*.50*
label			*.12*
shipping			*.08*
TOTAL TRIMMINGS COST			*$1.51*

3. LABOR		
Cutting		*2.00*
Labor		
grading and marking		*.75*
sewing $126.00 per dozen		*10.50*
pressing		*.75*
Payroll Taxes & Health Fund		*.46*
Trucking		
TOTAL LABOR COST		*$14.46*

4. **TOTAL COST**   *$34.26*

REMARKS

ADAMS PRESS, 830 SO. BROADWAY, L. A. 14, MADISON 7-2151   FORM NO. **32**

3. The sizes in which the design will be made

4. The style number assigned to the design (each manufacturer has a code of numbers representing season, fabric, and pattern)

5. A short description of the garment

6. A working sketch of the design to make it easy to identify the garment

7. The colors or color combinations in which the design is offered

8. Fabric swatches of what is used in the garment

9. Material descriptions, including each fabric type and source, width, and price per yard

10. Marker width, usually 1 inch narrower than the fabric

11. Trimmings information: the kinds, sources, sizes, and prices of buttons, zippers, braids, lace, belts, elastic, and so on; special fabric treatments done by outside contractors, such as pleating, spaghetti straps, and ties, are also included

12. Labor costs for grading, marking, cutting, and sewing; these may be listed either on the designer work sheet or on a separate cost sheet figured by the costing department (see Chapter 10)

The work sheet becomes an *adoption sheet* when the final line is selected.

LINE SELECTION

Regular **line-in-process** *meetings are held to analyze the development of the line.*

Designers develop many designs for each line, which are then edited. A designer must be objective in judging each design and develop an unbiased, critical eye—a difficult task when judging a personal creation. Adrienne Vittadini feels that the hardest lesson she had to learn was "detaching myself from the emotional tie—that each garment is your baby."[7]

Editing

From all the samples, management, the designer, and the merchandiser choose the best for the line. Successful buyers and sales representatives are often asked for their opinions because of their familiarity with customer preferences and retail merchandising expertise.

Some styles are weeded out, leaving only the most successful combinations of fabric, style, and price. Some companies feel that they need a closely edited line so that combination possibilities are not confusing to the customer. Some large companies like to give their customers more options. Escada, for instance, typically shows 600 pieces per collection; Adrienne Vittadini, 200 pieces; and Ellen Tracy, approximately 160 pieces. Recently, collections have tended to be carefully edited to reduce their size.

Reassessment of the Merchandise Plan

At this point, merchandise plans might be *reassorted*. If a group is particularly strong, styles or colors could be added. The dollar merchandise plan we discussed at the beginning of this chapter could be revised so that it states the exact number of styles adopted, the actual price of fabrics chosen, and the yardage estimates for each style.

Line Presentation

Just before the scheduled line-release or collection-opening dates, the line is presented to the sales force. The designer or merchandiser must explain the line concepts, current fashion trends, and new developments in fabrications, to the sales representatives, who can use this background information when showing the line to retail buyers.

A consistent visual image created by a well-developed theme is a good selling tool on both the wholesale and the retail levels. Visual impact is what makes the line competitive once it is displayed in a retail store. The designer cannot be there to explain each style idea to the customer, so the product must speak for itself.

Product and design development is a challenge. Not only must designers be creative; they must understand production and also know what sells. Claude Brouet, fashion director of Hermès, said, "There are plenty of designers with great talent, but one also needs to understand production, distribution, and on-time delivery. If you don't have those, even the most beautiful collection will be useless."[8] The ultimate blame for a bad season (assuming that economic conditions and the sales force remain the same) falls on the designer and the product development team.

Duplicates

Duplicates are copies of the sample garments chosen for the line that are made to keep in the showroom to show to buyers or to give to sales representatives to take on the road. These are usually made in the factory to test production.

SUMMARY

In this chapter we discussed product development, merchandising, and design. The company establishes an image and a product to appeal to a target market. The merchandiser prepares plans to achieve sales goals and meet consumer needs. The design department creates a seasonal line of items or groups. The designer considers color, fabric, line, shape, proportion, balance, rhythm, and focal point in each design in order to develop pleasing garments. After a sketch and first pattern are complete, the sample garment is made as a test of the design and fabric. Finally, the line is selected and prepared to show at wholesale markets.

CHAPTER REVIEW

Terms and Concepts

Briefly identify and discuss the following terms and concepts:

1. Collection or line
2. Seasons
3. Merchandising
4. Dollar merchandising plan
5. Designer
6. Items

APPAREL PRODUCTION

CAREER FOCUS

There is an interesting variety of job possibilities in apparel production. Entry-level positions are usually available in shipping and quality control. Technical training in both patterning and computers is needed for positions as pattern makers. Engineers are needed for computer-aided manufacturing. For those interested in materials, there are positions as fabric and trimmings buyers. Numbers-oriented people might like to work in cost analysis and production planning. Experience brings promotions to managerial positions in each production area.

CHAPTER OBJECTIVES

After reading this chapter you should have attained competence in the following areas:

1. Explaining the costing of a garment
2. Describing, in order, the steps in garment production
3. Understanding of the various types of contracting
4. Understanding of all the uses of computers in manufacturing
5. Explaining the differences between men's tailoring and men's sportswear production
6. Describing the two commercial methods of knitwear production
7. Understanding of the importance of quality control

*P*roduction is another of the three integral phases of fashion manufacturing: design, production, and sales. Without design, there would be nothing to sell; without sales, there would be no reason to produce. Conversely, sales would not continue if orders were not filled properly and delivered on time. This chapter focuses on apparel production, from patternmaking to quality control.

After the collection or line is shown at a market, orders are sent to the factory. Styles that receive insufficient orders are dropped from the line. To keep its retail customers, each manufacturer tries to maintain a consistent price structure, quality of styling and construction, and timely deliveries.

COSTING A GARMENT

The production cost of a garment must be determined in order to set the wholesale price, the price that retailers pay for goods that they purchase from manufacturers.

Costing Functions

There are two separate costing functions: the precost and the final costing.

Precost

The *precost* is an estimate made before the garment is adopted into the line. From the outset, the designer must keep fabric and labor costs for each garment within the limits set by the company for a particular line's price range. The designer keeps a record of all material costs on a designer work sheet. Then, either the designer or the costing department can roughly estimate the wholesale cost to determine whether the garment fits into the line's price structure.

Final Costing

This is an exact calculation by the costing department, utilizing final figures for materials and labor. The costing department uses the designer's work sheet, an actual sample, and the production pattern to analyze the garment's materials and construction step by step. It may consult the designer for information or to recommend more practical or cheaper ways to make the garment.

Labor costs may be calculated by time studies. Engineers time each operation, such as closing a seam or how long it takes to make an entire garment. Or a prototype may be sent to a contractor for costing. A detailed cost analysis is made for each garment, including expenses for fabric, trims, cutting, labor, overhead, sales commission, and manufacturer's profit. The final cost is plotted on a cost sheet.

TABLE 10-1
Manufacturer's Cost

Wholesale Unit Pricing for a Typical Dress
(each company uses a unique pricing structure)

Direct Cost	Amount	Average Percentages
Fabric (cost depends on quantity purchased)		
4.75 yards at $2.48	$18.29	30
Trimmings	1.51	2
Labor (cost depends on number of garments sewn)	14.46	24
Total Direct Cost	**34.26**	**56**
Indirect Cost		
Design and Manufacturing:		
Design Staff Salaries, Sample Fabrics, Cost of Samples	5.00	8 (8-10)
General Administrative Overhead:		
Office Salaries, Rent, Insurance, Utilities	5.28	9 (8-15)
Sales Commission	4.50	7 (7-10)
Trade Discount	5.00	8
Markdown Allowance, Promotion, or Other Retail Services	2.40	4
Shortages	0.96	2
Total Indirect Cost	**23.14**	**38**
Total Cost	**57.40**	**93**
Profit Before Taxes	4.12	7
Wholesale Price of Dress	**$61.52**	**100**

(refer back to design chapter for work sheet on same dress; see retailing chapter for retail price of the same dress)

The Cost Sheet

1. **Materials**   First, the total amount of yardage of each fabric needed for the garment is estimated and then multiplied by its cost per yard. The sum of these figures is the total material cost per garment. Higher volume allows more flexibility in making the marker and thus a more efficient use of fabric. Material cost is somewhat reduced for high-volume styles, while extra expense has to be allowed for a low-volume style.

2. **Trimmings**   Unit costs are multiplied by the amount of trimmings needed for each garment. The sum of these figures is the total trimmings cost per garment.

3. **Production patternmaking, grading, and marking**   Most companies allow for these costs in the general overhead that also covers the design department. However, if these functions are performed outside by a pattern service, the cost is divided by the total number of units that they estimate will be cut plus a profit for the contractor:

$$\text{total cost} \div \text{units to be made} = \text{cost per unit}$$

If the garment is later recut (because of reorders), there will be no new cost for patterns and grading.

4. **Spreading and cutting**   The cost for cutting done in house is based on the cutter's hourly wage multiplied by the number of hours it takes to cut the style and divided by the number of units cut. If the cutting is done by a contractor, the total negotiated cutting cost is figured on the number of garments to be cut. The contractor adds his or her fee to this amount.

5. **Assembly**   Construction labor includes all sewing including finishing. Some companies break down labor costs by each operation. Information for such a costing structure is gathered through time-and-motion efficiency studies. The cost for each operation, such as the closing of a shoulder seam, is determined. To figure the total costs for a whole garment, the individual operation costs are added. Other firms calculate the average time it takes to sew the whole garment and multiply that by the worker's hourly rate. If the garment is made by a contractor, the contractor's fees must be added to production costs.

6. **Finishing**   Costs must be included to cover final preparations. In designer apparel, this may include some handwork. For most apparel, washing, pressing, and folding are done in house. The cost for packing in preparation for shipping is also figured.

7. **Freight**   The cost of shipping completed garments from the contractor to the manufacturer must be calculated. For domestic shipments, the garments are usually trucked. If the garments are imported, then a percentage of the air or sea freight cost must be added to the cost of each garment. Obviously, sea transportation is cheaper and therefore adds less cost to the garment, but valuable lead time is forfeited. The cost of shipping garments to the retailer is generally paid by the retail store (the receiver). But manufacturers must pay air freight if they are late with their delivery.

8. **Additional costs for imported garments**   These include the quota charge and/or import duty and agent fees.

Wholesale Pricing

The wholesale price is determined by adding the cost of labor, materials, and a markup. The markup covers sales commission (usually 7 to 10 percent), overhead, and a profit, which is necessary for staying in business. *Overhead* includes all the daily costs of running the business. Fixed overhead expenses include rent, heat, lights, trash collection, insurance, salaries, taxes, and legal and auditing services. Variable overhead expenses include advertising, promotion, equipment repair, markdowns of leftover fabrics and garments, and losses due to fire and theft. Companies also have to use a large portion of their profits for capital investment in new equipment and technology.

Most companies add a markup of between 28 and 44 percent of the wholesale price. In other words, they increase the direct cost by 56 to 88 percent. Budget companies usually take the lowest markup and hope to make a profit by volume sales. For example, a blouse costing the manufacturer $21 to produce would cost $35 wholesale with a 40 percent markup.

Cost Merchandising

Another important aspect of costing is whether the garment's perceived value is worth its price. Each garment has to compete on the market with other, similar garments. If two garments are very much alike, the less expensive one is more likely to sell on the retail level. Therefore, both the styling and quality of a garment must be better than those of competing garments.

The price of a garment may be adjusted slightly higher or lower to try to affect its sales potential. Occasionally, a manufacturer uses a *loss leader* (a garment with a low markup) to attract buyers.

Some companies figure an *average markup* so that their garments fit into a price line. For example, shirts often cost out higher than pants and skirts because of expensive fabrications and labor. Therefore, the shirt price may be lowered so that it is more acceptable (a practice called *low balling*), while the skirt and pant prices are raised (*high balling*). In this way the average markup is within an acceptable range.

Many volume manufacturers *re-engineer* some of their first samples to meet their target price points if the garment in question is important to the line. This is accomplished by reducing fabric consumption by altering such features as the sweep of a hem or facings or pockets.

PURCHASING OF PIECE GOODS

Ordering the materials necessary to produce garments is usually done by the manufacturer's fabric or piece goods buyer.

The *piece goods buyer* acts as liaison between the mill or converter and the manufacturer. The buyer must know all the properties of fabrics and have information on prices, availability, and delivery.

Barry Fishman, product engineering manager, Flora Peters, production planner, and Rachel McLean, trim buyer, coordinate purchasing and production scheduling at Koret. *(Photographed by the author)*

Electronic data interchange (EDI) allows the exchange of piece goods ordering information by computer. As discussed in Chapter 2, this linkage has fostered partnerships between manufacturers and suppliers to ease purchasing procedures. Computer software is available that uses sales figures to automatically adjust planned production and the amount of fabric and trim that need to be purchased.

Some things that must be considered in the purchasing of piece goods are discussed next.

Environmental Concerns

Consumer preference for environmentally safe products has led some manufacturers to look for naturally colored cotton; organically grown cotton, linen, wool, and tencel; vegetable-based and water-based inks in prints; fiber-reactive, low-impact dyes; and safe finishes in the fabrics that they purchase. Some manufacturers now have special lines of environmentally friendly clothing.

Volume Purchases

Generally, volume manufacturers purchase goods from large textile companies that can handle big orders. Ordering in quantity may give the manufacturer a cost advantage. The goal of a volume manufacturer is to obtain the lowest-priced goods at the widest width in order to use an efficient marker layout.

Smaller Orders

Conversely, small manufacturers usually deal with smaller textile firms, which can do shorter runs. This often forces U.S. companies to buy imports because their minimums are lower. For example, a manufacturer may be able to buy a minimum of 300 yards of a fabric from Asia versus a 2000-yard minimum in the United States. Domestic textile producers are making an effort to lower minimums.

Ordering

The buyer must calculate the amounts of yardage needed to supply the cutting order. Orders for stock yardage must be based on sales histories and on expectations of future sales. Textile sales representatives encourage manufacturers to make a commitment early in the season to buy a specific amount of yardage. Ordering in advance ensures the availability and on-time delivery of a popular fabric, which may subsequently be in short supply. Volume orders usually require a seven- to eight-week lead time for delivery. Popular fashion fabrics and yarn dyes can require as much as a six-month lead time.

Fabric for Reorders

The manufacturer must also consider the amount of fabric that may be required for possible reorders. A manufacturer takes a great risk by stocking up for anticipated orders. To eliminate some risk, manufacturers often commit for *greige goods* only, to be dyed later. Then, as sales information becomes more precise, colors can be *assorted*. In other words, the greige goods can be dyed in their various colors according to the sales percentage established for each. Designer and bridge fashion manufacturers are usually unable to reorder materials because the fabrics are imports. There is not enough lead time to wait for another fabric shipment.

Trimmings

The fabric or trim buyer buys trimmings and notions, sometimes collectively called sundries. These are the materials used to finish garments or fashion accessories. Other sundries purchased by the trimmings buyer include labels, hang tags, hangers, and plastic bags. The trimmings buyer at Koret, for example, must purchase an average of five different trimmings and notions per single fabric order. Trimmings buyers may attend the Bobbin Show in Atlanta each September or the Trimmings Expo in New York each November to see new products.

Trimmings buyers must find the best trimmings available for each kind of application in each garment. Trimmings must have the same care properties as the fabrics used in the garment. For example, if the fabric can be safely washed, so must the trimmings. Buyers must also make sure that the colors of all trimmings used match and coordinate deliveries from each trim producer so that all trims are in house in time for manufacturing. As trimmings and findings arrive at the plant, they must be sorted and inspected along with fabrics.

Piece Goods Inspection

In some large factories, fabric is measured to make sure that the total order has been received. Special equipment automatically counts the fabric yardage as it rolls from one bolt to another. The fabric is then pulled by rollers over large viewing tables or examined on the cutting table to check for flaws such as holes or shading. Flaws are marked with colored threads or flags at the side of the fabric so that they can be avoided in cutting. In an automated factory, a computer-programmed inspection system locates flaws, color differences, and variations automatically. If there are too many defects, the fabric is returned to the mill. However, this is a time-consuming and, therefore, expensive process.

In most factories, all measuring and inspecting is done on the cutting table. In this case, the spreader has the responsibility of measuring, inspecting, and spreading the fabric in preparation for the cut.

Some apparel manufacturers build strong reputations on the reliability of their products. They perform washing, dry cleaning, steaming, and pressing tests to check tensile strength, durability, color cracking, color fastness, and shrinkage. They also test how the fabric holds up during sewing—whether it pulls or frays excessively.

Coordinating tops and bottoms must be cut from the same dye lot and, at the very least, shipments to the same store must be within acceptable variations of color if from different dye lots.

PATTERNMAKING

Accurate patternmaking is crucial for successful apparel production.

The Production Pattern

In a traditional apparel factory, the production pattern maker relies on the same methods used in the sample room to make patterns: draping, drafting, or flat-patterning from standardized basic blocks. In fact, in many small companies the same person does both the sample and production patternmaking. In production, strict attention must be paid to company size specifications, which are standardized measurements including ease (extra room for movement) for each size. When using fabrics that shrink, such as cotton, patterns have to allow for that shrinkage. Also, the seam lines of each pattern piece must exactly fit the piece to which it will be sewn, with notches marked perfectly for operators to follow. Grain lines, plaid lines, and other annotations are also marked on the patterns.

Computer Patternmaking

At most large manufacturers, patterns are made on a computer. With *computer-aided-design (CAD)* systems, the pattern maker manipulates small graphic patterns on the computer screen with a hand-held control device. Geometry drivers can make an infinite number of changes to the shapes

A pattern maker using Gerber's AccuMark Silhouette pattern development system. The pattern maker works on a backlit patternmaking table with a stylus that automatically records lines in the computer and shows them on the screen.
(Courtesy of Gerber Garment Technology, Inc.)

and sizes of the patterns, including creating new design lines or adding pleats, fullness, and seam allowances.

To allow pattern makers to make patterns manually, another system has been developed allowing the pattern maker to work life size on a sensitized table with traditional tools and a stylis that is attached to the table and the computer. The stylus picks up the lines drawn on the table and shows them on the screen. Changes can also be made directly on the screen.

In both cases, patterns are immediately available for other operations such as grading and marker making.

Grading Sizes

Patterns, like garments, must provide for different sizes. *Grading* is the method used to increase or decrease the sample-size production pattern to make up a complete size range. For example, the sample size 10 pattern must be made larger to accommodate sizes 12, 14, and 16 and smaller for sizes 8 and 6. Each company sets predetermined grade specifications, or rules. For example, a missy manufacturer's grade rules might call for increments of one and a half inches in width and a quarter-inch in length for each size.

Traditionally, the sample-size pattern is held in place over tag or manila board by a grading machine. The operator turns one knob of the machine to move the pattern forward and backward and the other knob to move the pattern sideways to mark points of size change. The pattern is moved for each point of increase or decrease. Each size may be made on a different colored pattern board for easy recognition.

Computerized Grading

Most large manufacturers grade patterns by computer on a CAD system. The pattern maker guides a *cursor* around the edges of the sample pattern on a digitized table. At each of the key points, he or she pushes a button to record a grade point. Each point is cross referenced by a grade-rule table stored in the computer, which enlarges or reduces the pattern automatically according to predetermined increments and in a predetermined direction.

If the pattern was originally made by computer, the data are already in the computer and can be enlarged or reduced automatically. Grade rules must be applied to the pieces at each grading location. Then the computer can print out the pattern in each new size.

Making the Marker

From all the pattern pieces of varying sizes, a master marker is made. The marker is the cutting guide or pattern layout made on a sheet of lightweight paper the same width as the fabric. The purpose of the marker is twofold: to place pattern pieces close together to avoid fabric waste and to accommodate the cutting order. The desired economical use of space is called a *tight marker*, which utilizes the highest percentage of fabric possible. To accommodate the cutting order, patterns are laid out so that each size and color are cut as needed.

Traditionally, manila board patterns, already graded, are traced or photocopied onto marker paper. Grain direction, one-way prints, plaids, stripes, and naps are considered in making the marker. Copies of the marker are made to use in each cut.

Computer Markers

Most large manufacturers make their markers on a CAD system. Miniatures of the graded pattern pieces are displayed graphically on the computer screen. The operator can electronically position the pattern pieces into the most efficient arrangement. Once the marker is completed, a full scale marker is printed by the *plotter* on a long sheet of paper. The pattern maker checks the arrangement on the screen or prints out a mini marker to check. Miniatures of an entire marker can be faxed to locations around the world.

PRODUCTION SCHEDULING

The production manager schedules cutting and garment assembly in time to meet shipping dates.

Issue Plan

A production schedule or *issue plan* is created on a computer to ensure that delivery dates are met. This schedule is a reverse timetable, usually covering six months. The first date on the schedule is a shipping date that will meet the retail store's order requirements. The schedule progresses backward to include completion dates, cutting dates, and even fabric delivery dates. Production scheduling is very difficult because it has to be organized to take maximum advantage of plant capacity as well as meet shipping dates.

Orders for each style must be compiled to determine how many garments of each size to produce. There are two philosophies of production planning: cut to order and cut to stock.

Cut to Order

The safest method of production is to *cut to order*, that is, to cut and produce only against orders. This means waiting until all orders are in and then working quickly to cut, sew, and deliver. As mentioned earlier, an ideal situation for retailers would be to test and reorder. However, this method can work only under model conditions using the newest production technology and with close communication and cooperation between levels of the industry.

Cut to Stock

The method with the greater risk involves cutting against estimates of projected sales or *cutting to stock. Projections* (expected sales) are determined

Cutting Techniques

The marker is put on top of many layers of fabric. Traditionally, the cutter follows the pattern outlined on the marker, using a straight-knife machine with a long, thin blade that vibrates vertically as it is pushed through many layers of fabric. A vertical knife can cut to a depth of 9 inches. For only a few layers, a cutting machine with a rotating circular knife may be used. The cutter must select the correct speed and blade for each type of fabric. For example, a coarse blade edge is used for tightly woven fabrics and a smooth edge for softer fabrics.

Computer Cutting

A numerically controlled cutter reduces labor and improves the accuracy of the cut. A beam structure across the table holds the cutting head. The beam can move up and down the table while the cutting head moves across. Movement is directed by data in the CAD system. The knife in the cutting head vibrates vertically to cut the fabric.

Laser-beam cutting is sometimes used for men's suits, a single layer at a time. The laser, a concentrated light beam, is also directed by a computer. *Water-jet cutting* is being used for some fabrics and leathers, especially in the shoe industry. A thin stream of water, also computer directed, is fired under high pressure through a tiny nozzle to cut the leather.

Die Cutting

Die cutting may be used for garments or parts of garments that do not change from season to season. A die, a device that operates much like a cookie cutter, is made for each piece to be cut. The sharp edges of the die are pressed against the layers of fabric to cut them. A *gang die* can be made by connecting several dies together.

Automated computer cutting showing the cutting head, beam structure, and multiple-layer cut pieces. *(Courtesy of Gerber Garment Technology, Inc.)*

Cutting by Hand

Modern technology notwithstanding, it is quite a contrast to find cutting done by hand in a couture house or in the sample room. Quantity is not necessary in this case, and single-layer cutting makes absolute accuracy possible.

Environmental Concerns

Manufacturers of apparel are giving increased attention to environmental concerns. They are trying to identify ways to reduce and recycle their supplies. Their primary concern is the disposal of fabric scrap, which makes up a large percentage of production waste. One possibility for the disposal of this waste is to use an on-sight incinerator to generate electricity. Some fabric scraps are shredded and spun into new yarn. Levi Strauss has come up with an innovative method to recycle their scrap. They are using their denim scrap to make blue letter paper. However, most environmental improvements and recycling are still too expensive for most manufacturers to implement.

Bundling

The process of sorting cut pieces and tying them together is referred to as *bundling*. Parts of garments and necessary findings must be grouped for the sewing machine operators. Bar-coded identification tickets are attached to each bundle that constantly keep track of work in progress and each garment by size and color. Bundled work is distributed to machine operators in the factory or sent out to contractors to be sewn.

CONTRACTING

Manufacturers are able to purchase patternmaking, cutting, and sewing from outside services or factories.

Most manufacturers do not handle the production of a garment in their own factories. They are responsible for all phases of manufacturing, from design and fabric purchase to selling and shipping, but they may contract out some or all of the production. Just as a manufacturer can purchase designs from a design service, it can also contract out patternmaking, cutting, and sewing.

Many manufacturers contract out all sewing because they do not own any production facilities. These manufacturers do not have to pay wages during slack seasons or to be concerned with hiring, training, or wage demands of personnel. They also do not have to invest in plant facilities and machinery that require large capital investment.

A *contractor* is an independent producer who does sewing for manufacturers. Contractors are hired only as production is needed, and they have equipment and trained operators for specialized work, such as sewing knits, pleating, quilting, embroidery, or piping.

Contracting provides greater production flexibility, but it can involve problems. The manufacturer has less control over quality. There is extra movement of goods, which could result in extra costs and some losses. There may also be communication problems or a possibility of late deliveries.

The production manager selects the contractor who is most reliable and best suited for a particular job. It is very important that the production head work closely with the contractor to make sure that standards and time schedules are met. Most contractors specialize either in a particular quality of sewing or in sewing one type of fabric, such as knits or wovens. Others are specialists in shirring, smocking, ruffling, pleating, or belt making. Some contractors may arrange to work exclusively with one or more manufacturers. A contractor agrees to maintain a certain standard of workman-

Asia

Overseas production started in Hong Kong, which became the capital of Asian apparel manufacturing. Hong Kong companies became specialists in knitwear. Now these workers have become so skilled and well paid that only the highest quality clothing is made there. Manufacturers then sought cheaper labor sources in Taiwan, China, and South Korea. China is now the largest foreign apparel production supplier to the United States.[3] As these countries increased their skills and wages, the Association of Southeast Asian Nations (ASEAN), which includes Indonesia and Malaysia and other newly developed Asian economies including India and Sri Lanka, were found as new sources. Compared with an average hourly wage of $7.55 in the United States, typical hourly wages (in U.S. dollars) are as little as 25 cents per hour in China, Thailand, Pakistan, and India and 15 cents an hour in Indonesia.[4]

Eastern Europe

Countries such as Poland, Hungary, and Slovakia in Eastern Europe, which used to primarily supply the former Soviet Union, are providing cheaper skilled labor for European manufacturers. Some American fashion companies such as Liz Claiborne and Levi Strauss are producing there as well. These countries have had to adjust from working in a command-oriented economy, where delivery schedules were not a problem, to a market-driven economy.

Mexico and the Caribbean Basin

As stores increasingly order closer to season, manufacturers are sourcing closer to home. Mexico is already the world's sixth largest apparel manufacturing country, and under the North American Free Trade Agreement, production will continue to grow. Caribbean and Middle American countries which have enjoyed tax and quota exceptions for apparel that they produce for the United States hope that NAFTA will be widened to include them (NAFTA is discussed in Chapter 12). Sourcing is mainly in the Dominican Republic, Mexico, Costa Rica, Guatemala, Honduras, Jamaica, Colombia, and El Salvador.

Overseas Production Methods

Importing, or bringing merchandise in from other countries, involves numerous negotiators: an agent to represent the manufacturer in the country where production is done, a customs broker to assist in processing the import application papers with the U.S. government to bring the goods into the United States, and a freight-forwarding agent to handle shipping. Manufacturers must rely on a good agent or company representative to keep control of quality, prevent late deliveries, and handle difficulties in communication caused by language differences. Price negotiations are usually made in U.S. dollars because of the fluctuations in international currency exchange rates.

Manufacturers must allow approximately thirty days for sea transportation or three days for air delivery from Asia or Europe, plus trucking within the United States. An extra four days to two weeks must be allowed for customs clearance.

To produce overseas, manufacturers must send patterns, specifications, and samples as guidelines. All details must be exact and clear. Precise records and open lines of communication are a necessity. When production is done overseas, fabric is shipped directly to the contractor who does the cutting and sewing. There are three basic methods of producing clothing overseas: a production package; cut, make, and trim; and offshore assembly.

Production package   A manufacturer purchases a production package through an agent. In this case, everything originates in the production area, including raw materials, production, finishing, labeling, packaging, and shipping. Using an agent is the most expensive method, but it is advantageous because the agent takes responsibility for production, quality control, and the delivery schedule. A manufacturer may also have its own representative abroad to find raw materials, work with agents and contractors, and oversee production, quality control, quotas, duties, and shipping.

Cut, make, and trim   A manufacturer may buy fabric from one country, silk from China, for example, and then send it elsewhere to be cut, sewn, finished, and labeled.

Offshore assembly   Fabric is purchased and cut in the United States and sent to Mexico or the Caribbean countries for sewing. This classification, *item 9802* in the Harmonized Tariff Schedule (still referred to as the *807 program*) is being encouraged to promote the use of American textiles. For this reason there is a *guaranteed access level* (large quotas) for this classification. Duty is charged only on the portion of labor done offshore.

Some American manufacturers have purchased or opened their own production facilities in Asia, the Caribbean, or Mexico. Asian firms are counteracting by investing in America and the Caribbean.

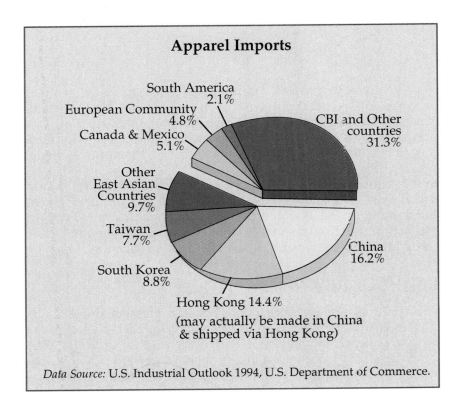

Apparel Imports

South America 2.1%
European Community 4.8%
Canada & Mexico 5.1%
Other East Asian Countries 9.7%
Taiwan 7.7%
South Korea 8.8%
Hong Kong 14.4% (may actually be made in China & shipped via Hong Kong)
China 16.2%
CBI and Other countries 31.3%

Data Source: U.S. Industrial Outlook 1994, U.S. Department of Commerce.

Pros and Cons of Sourcing Abroad

The advantage of contracting overseas has been to keep production costs down. However, even though labor is inexpensive, obstacles such as customs duties (tariffs), quotas, freight costs, lengthy lead times, and maintaining production controls at a distance, or having executives move overseas to supervise, are making it less advantageous than it formerly was. Also, many hidden costs are involved, such as travel to and communications with foreign countries. The trend toward increased overseas production continues, however. Manufacturers are continually seeking new sources of cheap labor.

Understandably, unions are fighting overseas production because it takes jobs away from U.S. laborers. To compensate, unions charge union manufacturers a "damage" fee for production that they do overseas. However, as to the future of domestic production, except for immigrants, the historical wellspring for garment industry workers, young people in America are not interested in this work.

The domestic textile industry wants to keep production here where U.S. textiles will be used. Many manufacturers would like to bring production back to the United States, especially to save lead time, but find that U.S. textile mills are not flexible enough. Some manufacturers feel that U.S. fabrics are good but limited and that minimum orders are often too high. So manufacturers seek both cheaper labor and more fabric choices abroad (see Chapter 12 for general information on imports).

GARMENT ASSEMBLY

The next step in production is the actual assembly or sewing of quantities of garments.

Assembly Operations

The steps involved in garment assembly are called *operations*. A man's suit can have as many as 200 different sewing operations. No two manufacturers use all the same methods, but all follow the same basic order. A supervisor analyzes a garment's construction to determine the best and fastest way to sew the garment. An *operation sheet* is drawn up, listing all necessary operations in sequence.

The introduction of specialized operations or new machinery requires additional training of operators, which results in higher production costs during the training period. As apparel manufacturing remains labor intensive, manufacturers and contractors find it necessary to rely on their operators as individual skill centers or as part of a small production team.

Individual Incentive Systems (Piecework)

Many sewing machine operators, finishers, and pressers are paid on a *piecework* rate. That is, they are paid a set amount for each operation that they complete, rather than by the hour. Rates vary with the difficulty of the operation. As proof of work completed, the operator signs the identification ticket or removes one segment of it. Actually, most companies pay a guar-

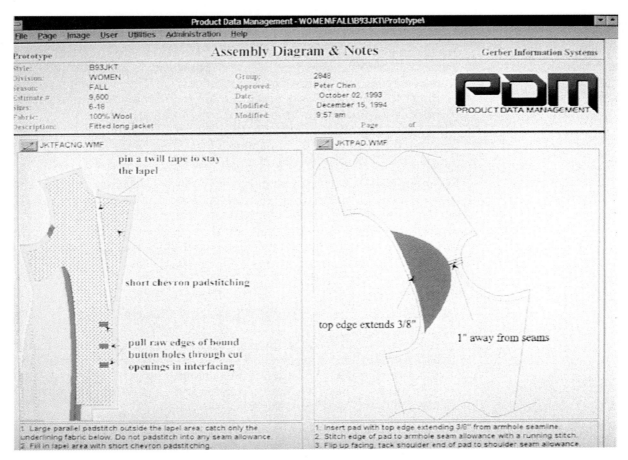

Gerber's product data management (PDM) system showing assembly diagrams and notes for a jacket interfacing. *(Courtesy of Gerber Garment Technology, Inc.)*

anteed wage, with piecework acting as an incentive for operators to work faster and therefore earn more.

Assembly Systems

Sewing operations must be performed in sequence. There are three methods of construction: the progressive-bundle system, the tailor or whole-garment system, and the modular manufacturing system.

Progressive-bundle systems, used most often for sportswear, require each operator to repeat one assembly task, such as closing a shoulder seam or stitching on a pocket. Referred to as *section work*, machine operators are grouped to follow the order of production; they pass the garments in units of 20 to 30 (typically in dozens) from one section to the next as each operation is completed. The advantage of progressive-bundle systems is that the work area can be designed to complete a specific operation utilizing the best machinery and trained operators for that job.

Whole-garment systems use a single operator to sew a whole garment together. This system is similar to the one used for sewing sample garments. In this case, finishing tasks may be performed by another operator who specializes in these operations.

Computer-integrated manufacturing (CIM) can connect these systems and share data for total automation. For example, a manufacturer can network data from a CAD patternmaking, grading, and marking system directly to a CAM cutting system by computer.

Computer simulation allows for the viewing of a manufacturing floor plan on a computer screen prior to actual implementation. Through simulation studies, the type and number of machines and the number of operators needed may be determined before the assembly process begins.

Flexible manufacturing is simply a variety of strategies used by one manufacturer. Not all garments lend themselves to traditional or automated technologies; a flexible system uses a combination of methods.

The **American Textile Partnership** (AMTEX) is working together with the National Aeronautics and Space Administration (NASA) and the Department of Energy (DOE) to transfer their technology to the apparel industry. The areas of targeted research are analysis, simulation, and integration; automation; improved materials and processes; environmental quality and waste minimization; and energy efficiency.

This unit production system allows operations to be performed without removing parts from the hanger, thereby reducing production time.
(Courtesy of Gerber Garment Technology, Inc.)

Power Sewing Machines

Three main types of power sewing machines are used in traditional factories: the lock-stitch, the chain-stitch, and the overlock machine.

The **lock-stitch machine** sews a straight seam on the same principle as a home sewing machine. This machine makes it possible for the top thread to go under the bottom thread around a bobbin, creating a lock. This is the most secure stitch possible, but it leaves an unfinished seam, undesirable in fabrics that ravel easily. Also, of course, operations must be stopped frequently to rewind the bobbin.

The **chain-stitch machine** works on a principle similar to crocheting: it makes a series of loops pulled through one another. The top needle goes in and out of the fabric, making loops underneath that catch into one another. The chain-stitch is not as secure as the lock-stitch but, because the chain-stitch machine does not have a bobbin, the operator does not need to stop in midoperation to rewind it.

The **overlock or serging machine** is based on the same principle as the chain-stitch machine. It was created to make an edge finish as well as to sew seams. In one operation it sews the fabric together, cuts off the fabric to make a smooth edge, and wraps thread around the edge. A simple overlock machine has one needle and two loopers (which look like thick, bent needles) and works with three spools or cones of thread. The needle and loop-

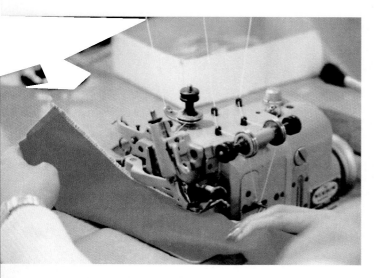

The overlock machine creates a finished edge as it makes a seam. *(Photographed by the author)*

ers work together in a reciprocating pattern, the loopers moving back and forth from the needle to the fabric edge. This stitch is ideal for knits because it gives with the stretch of the fabric.

The **safety overlock machine** is a combination of the chain-stitch and the overlock. The safety factor is that if one row of stitching comes out, the other still holds the garment together. With a total of two needles, three loopers, and five cones of thread, it functions as two machines in one. It provides the straight chain-stitch needed for factory assembling plus an edge finish.

The **blind-stitch hemming machine** is also based on the chain-stitch. The hem is folded back and caught by the needle at even intervals.

Button machines sew buttons onto a garment. Button placement is marked on the fabric. A sew-through button is placed in a holder, which moves the button back and forth while the needle sews it onto the fabric underneath. A shank button is held in position sideways so that the needle can go through the shank on its back. Some machines have a *hopper*, a feeding device that automatically positions the button.

The **buttonhole machine** is essentially a zigzag lock-stitch machine with automatic devices to control the width and length of the buttonhole and to cut it open.

Programmable Sewing Machines

Programmable sewing machines are very expensive and used only by large manufacturers. Automating sewing is a difficult task due to handling different types of fabrics as they are sewn. Moving silk through a sewing machine is very different from moving wool, for example.

Generally, operators must first load fabric pieces into the sewing machine and press a button to start the sewing. Fully automated machines are microprocessor controlled and sensor activated, with an arm to grasp the cloth, align the fabric, and move it through the machine. Programmable machines have been very successful surging or seaming basic pieces in garment assembly.

However, the clothing industry remains labor intensive for two reasons. First, textiles are floppy and soft, which makes it difficult for robots to handle them and for computers to simulate their shapes. Second, since the industry is fashion sensitive, automated machinery must be able to change as fashion changes.

Finishing

Tailoring, the unseen quality handwork formerly done inside collars and lapels to form and hold their shape, has virtually disappeared because of the high cost of skilled labor. Most "tailoring" today is done simply by fusing or machine basting interfacings into the garment to give it shape.

Hand finishing is usually seen only in couture garments. In better garments, some hand finishing is necessary, such as sewing in linings or sewing on buttons, but this too is becoming rare. In moderate- and lower-priced garments, all finishing is done by machine.

PRODUCTION OF MEN'S SUITS

The production of men's suits is one area where tailoring is still used.

Traditionally, the men's clothing industry has been divided into firms that produce tailored suits, coats, and trousers and furnishing producers that make shirts, ties, underwear, and sleepwear. Tailored garment production used to dominate the industry, but with the trend toward casual dress for men, there has been a growing demand for sportswear. The production of men's sportswear is similar to that of women's.

Production of a man's suit, however, can require over 200 steps. Inner construction to give a suit shape and body makes production lengthy, complicated, and costly. Formerly, the industry used a numbered system to rate the quality of men's suits, on a scale from 1 for machine made to 6 for hand-tailored suits. This rating is no longer used because hand tailoring has virtually disappeared. Modern technology has introduced automation into an industry that was traditionally handwork oriented. Fusible interfacing has replaced hand-applied canvas in chest pieces, shoulders, lapels, collar, and buttoning areas to supply the required body and shape. Hand tailoring can be found in only the most expensive suits, such as Hickey-Freeman and Oxxford in America, or custom-made and other high-quality suits made in Europe and Hong Kong.

A fitting at Savile Row tailor Gieves & Hawkes.
(Courtesy of Gieves & Hawkes, London)

Production Steps

The basic steps in the mass production of men's suits are as follows:

◆ Fuse interfacings and jump-baste chest pieces and bridal tape on lapel crease for support

◆ Press, line, and stitch on pockets

◆ Sew around edges or perform a bagging operation (explain)

◆ Join main pieces together

◆ Set in sleeves

◆ Set in linings by machine or, in the case of an unlined jacket, bind seam edges

◆ Sew buttons and buttonholes

PRODUCTION OF KNITWEAR

The production of knitwear requires special skills and machinery.

There are two commercial methods of knitwear production: cut-and-sew and full-fashioned.

Joining sweater pieces on a linking machine at a knitting contractor in Hong Kong.
(Courtesy of Katrena Bothwell Meyer)

Cut-and-sew is a method by which garments are made from knitted yardage. This type of knitted garment requires the same patterning as that used for woven fabrics, except that no darts are needed because knits move and conform to body curves depending on the amount of stretch in the fabric. Stretchability is the key to knitted garments; therefore, an overlock stitch is used, because it is flexible and gives with the fabric. Knitted braids and bands must be used as trims and finishes because all components must have the same stretchability.

Full-fashioned knits, mostly sweaters, are actually shaped on the knitting machine. The specifications for each piece are programmed into the knitting machine, which forms the shape as it is knit by adding or dropping stitches at the edge of each piece to widen or narrow it. Then the pieces are joined together. Most full-fashioned production is done in the Orient because manufacturers saw the potential of cheaper labor there and invested in specialized machinery. Factories in the Orient provide both affordable prices and variety of production.

Computers have also changed the production time and cost of knitting. Computer-aided design (CAD) systems permit designers to see a pattern or garment design, on the computer screen or printed out on paper, without having to knit a sample. Knitting machines tied into the computerized design screens will accept pattern and stitch changes in minutes rather than hours, allowing greater freedom for experimentation. Adrienne Vittadini remarked, "With knits, you are also a textile designer; you need technical knowledge to achieve what you want and you must know how to use the machinery."[5] Each type of sweater, whether it is intarsia, jacquard, shaker, cable, or pointelle, has a different lead time, quantity and weight of yarn required, gauge (stitch size), finishing treatments, and special skill and machinery needed to produce it.

Pattern is introduced by Jacquard and intarsia knitting systems. *Jacquard* patterns are created by various needle arrangements on electronic knitting machines. *Float Jacquard* shows the pattern on the face of the sweater while the yarns are carried on the back side until needed again for the pattern. To create a *full Jacquard*, both the front and back beds of the knitting machine are used, creating a heavier, double knit. The main design appears on the front with another simple pattern on the back to avoid floats. For *intarsia* patterns, the yarn is knotted and cut off in back when no longer needed for the pattern on the front.

Some sweaters are also hand knitted or crocheted. Hand knits have the greatest variety of stitches and detailing. However, because of the time needed to make them, they are very expensive. Hand-knit garments for commercial marketing are usually made abroad, where labor is cheaper and more readily available.

PREPARATIONS FOR SHIPPING

Pressing enhances a garment, quality control eliminates imperfections, and filling orders promptly facilitates on-time deliveries.

Dyeing and Washing

To ensure a perfect color match between garments to be worn together, manufacturers can dye the finished garments. Benetton was a pioneer in this method.

In jeanswear, washing is sometimes a way of finishing the garment. For a bleached look, environmentally friendly enzyme and stone washes have replaced acids.

Pressing or Folding

Pressing vastly improves the look of a garment. It can hide a multitude of imperfections, such as puckered seams and collars that do not lie flat. Garments are pressed during the course of construction as well as at completion. Pressing equipment is sometimes used to shape pieces before sewing, for example, to fold under pocket edges.

Steam irons are used for areas not easily accessible. Various *buck* pressing machines, like those seen at a dry cleaner, are used on tailored garments to flatten jacket edges, crease trousers, and so on. There are also various shaping devices to aid in pressing. A *steam-air form finisher*, which looks like a puffy dress form, can be used to steam dresses into shape. Automated pressing is done by computer-controlled pressing equipment.

One popular trend in sportswear today, especially for denim, is to simply wash and fold the items.

Quality Control

Quality control is the standardization of production using specifications as guides. The last garment sewn should be the same as the first garment. A sample maker can make one garment neatly and accurately, but in the mass production of 500 or 1000 dozen garments it is harder to control quality. To make sure that production has been done correctly and to prevent returns, both work in progress and finished garments are inspected either totally or by random sampling. Quality controllers not only check for poor sewing and uncut threads, but also spot-check measurements against original specifications. If there are mistakes in first stock, the production manager tries to correct them at the sewing or cutting source.

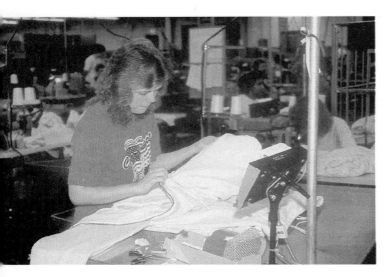

Quality control is an important part of apparel production. *(Courtesy of the National Cotton Council)*

Production standards are very important and must equal the manufacturer's reputation and warrant the garment's price. It means nothing to have a beautifully designed garment if it is not produced well. Inferior garments may be rejected by the store and returned to the manufacturer, or they may look so unappealing on the hanger that customers will not buy them. Either event would mean loss of reputation and future sales.

Garments returned to the manufacturer are analyzed to find the reasons for their return. Computer bar coding or numbers on each garment's label identify the factory or contractor where the garment was made, enabling construction mistakes to be traced to their source. Besides construction mistakes, reasons for returns include poor fabric and fabric shading. The manufacturer tries to prevent these mistakes in future shipments. Manufacturers have realized the need to improve the quality of their products as consumers become more demanding.

Labeling

Labels are the sources of identification for garments. Along the production line, various labels must be attached to the garment. These include manufacturer and/or designer identification, fiber content, care instructions, country of origin, size, and a union label if made in an American union shop. Federal law requires listing fibers in order of percentage used, along with cleaning or washing instructions.

Labels can help to establish the company's image. They tell the consumer the name of the brand and/or designer. Some people are attracted to a particular label or brand because of its reputation for quality or fit. The brand label is usually made on satin or twill ribbon and sewn inside the center-back neck, inside the waistband, or somewhere on the inside of the garment. It has even become fashionable to put labels on the outside of sportswear garments. Jeans often have a leather-like printed patch sewn on the outside.

A label showing fiber content, care instructions, and country of origin must also be included in the garment. This information is usually on a separate, small label under the brand label.

There are pages of government regulations concerning fiber-content and country-of-origin labeling. The predominant fiber in the garment is listed first along with its content percentage, followed by the other fibers in decreasing order of content. Care instructions are recommended and can be very specific. These instructions not only protect the consumer but also protect the manufacturer against returns made by consumers who do not care for their garments as instructed.

A country-of-origin label is required by customs if the garment is made outside the United States. The label must say "made in (name of country)" or "made in USA of imported fabric." A "Made in USA" label is reserved for garments made entirely in the United States of American fabric. Items made partially in a foreign country and partially in the United States must disclose these facts; for example, a tag might read "assembled and sewn in the USA of components made in (name of country)."

In addition, sportswear often has pressure-sensitive labels showing sizes on the outside of garments, particularly where they are folded. *Flashers*, printed cards that give product information, may be stapled to the outside of sportswear.

Hang tags, a printed paper tag, may be hung from the garment by plastic staple, barb, or string. Hang tags are designed to draw attention to the garment and are hung on the side of the garment so that the customer can see them easily. They usually show the brand name, perhaps style number, color, size, and other product information. Sometimes hang tags are provided by the fiber or fabric producer to promote their fibers or finishes. Manufacturers are often requested to *preticket* garments with bar-coded price tags provided by the retailer and to have the merchandise "hanger ready."

Filling Orders

If production work has been done by contractors, the completed garments are usually returned to the manufacturer for shipment to retail stores. At a central shipping point, garments are checked for quality and then divided into groups according to style, size, and color and put into *stock*, a storage area where they may be hung on racks or stacked on shelves.

A store orders a certain quantity of units on a form that includes entries for style number, color number, and price per unit. First, the order is analyzed for a credit rating. The next step is to see what is available in stock to fill the order. This checking is now done much more easily and efficiently by computer automation. Orders can be transmitted by EDI and then automatically translated into invoices. EDI partnerships with retailers have paved the way for manufacturers to cut down the time that garments are held up in stock (see Chapter 2). Large orders and orders from important regular customers are filled first. Merchandise is pulled from stock to fill orders in the correct style, size, and color.

Garments are folded into shipping boxes and marked with the means of transportation specified by the retailer. A *packing slip* (an invoice without prices) is enclosed in the box, while the actual invoice is mailed separately for payment. Manufacturers often use bar-coded "128" cartons, which can be scanned at the retail distribution center to reveal the contents without opening the box. The boxes are labeled with addresses and then moved by trolley or conveyor belt to be loaded on the delivery truck and sent to the retailer. On-time deliveries are extremely important to prevent cancellation of orders. On the basis of reliable production and delivery standards, a manufacturer builds and keeps a reputation for dependability that accompanies its reputation for innovative styling.

SUMMARY

In this chapter we discussed garment costing, pricing, and production scheduling. We have seen how garments are manufactured, from piece goods purchase and inspection, through patterning, grading, marking, cutting, assembly, and finishing, to quality control. Many manufacturers use domestic contractors to do all or part of their production and foreign contractors or off-shore production to reduce labor costs. Domestic factories try to compete with the newest computer technology, including inventory control, electronic data interchange, and Quick Response strategies, as well as computer patternmaking, grading, marking, spreading, cutting, and assembly systems. Men's suits and knits present unique methods of garment production. Quality control and on-time deliveries help the manufacturer to maintain a good reputation for dependability.

CHAPTER REVIEW

Terms and Concepts

Briefly identify and discuss the following terms and concepts:

1. Wholesale pricing
2. Cost sheet
3. Cost merchandising
4. Loss leader
5. Grading
6. Tight marker
7. Issue plan
8. Cut to order versus cut to stock
9. Piece goods
10. Contracting
11. Global sourcing
12. Laser-beam cutting
13. Offshore assembly
14. Piecework
15. Progressive-bundle assembly system
16. Computer-integrated manufacturing
17. Modular manufacturing
18. Unit production systems
19. Tailoring
20. Cut-and-sew knits
21. Full-fashioned knits
22. Quality control
23. Preticketing

Questions for Review

1. Explain the difference between costing and pricing a garment.
2. What are some of the things to consider when purchasing piece goods?
3. Discuss the differences between the cut-to-order and the cut-to-stock methods of production.
4. Explain the difference between making and grading patterns by hand and by computer.
5. Describe the differences among three cutting methods.
6. Describe three ways in which computers aid apparel manufacturing.

7. Explain various systems of garment assembly.

8. Why do manufacturers use contractors?

9. Discuss the three major methods of overseas production.

10. How has the construction of men's suits changed over the years?

11. Explain the two methods of producing knit garments.

12. Why is quality control so important?

Projects for Additional Learning

1. If there is an apparel manufacturer or contractor in your area, try to make an appointment for a factory tour. Observe production methods. Do operators do section work, or does one person sew one whole garment together? What computer technology is used in the factory? What production methods are unique to the product? Compare the wholesale price range of the garments being produced with the quality of production.

2. Visit a local store and compare imported ready-to-wear with domestically produced items that retail at the same price. Consider fit, styling, and quality. Which is better? Why? What conclusions can you draw from this comparison?

3. Investigate a major apparel manufacturer by interviewing managers, reading the company's annual report, reading trade newspaper articles about the company, or writing to the company for information. Write a profile of the company, including ownership (see Appendix 2), type of garments produced by each division, type of customer to which they appeal, type of production, price line, and where products are sold.

NOTES

[1] Nancy Marx Better, "The Secret of Liz Claiborne's Success," *Working Woman*, April 1992, p. 96.

[2] "ATMI Calls '92 a Better Year," *Women's Wear Daily*, December 30, 1992, p. 8.

[3] "U. S. Industrial Outlook 1993," U. S. Deptartment of Commerce, Washington, D.C., January 1993, pp. 32-7.

[4] "Textile Report," *Women's Wear Daily*, January 28, 1992, p. 27.

[5] As quoted in Vittadini press release, 1993, p. 2.

Beatrice Amblard sews a Hermès bag.
(Courtesy of Hermès, Paris, photographed by the author)

11

ACCESSORY AND FUR MANUFACTURING

CAREER FOCUS

Each category of accessories is a separate industry. Each area needs its own product developers, merchandisers, designers, pattern makers, production engineers, marketers, and sales representatives. In the fur industry, production jobs are limited, but marketing careers are possible in major fur centers.

CHAPTER OBJECTIVES

After reading this chapter you should have attained competence in the following areas:

1. Discussing the unique design considerations of various accessories
2. Describing production methods for the major accessories.
3. Knowledge of accessory design and production centers
4. Discussing aspects of marketing for accessories
5. Explaining fur garment production

*T*his chapter discusses manufacturing as it particularly applies to accessories and furs. Handbags, shoes, belts, gloves, and furs have in common the age-old use of animal skins as a raw material. There are separate sections covering the styling and production of shoes, handbags, belts, gloves, hats, scarves, hosiery, jewelry, and furs, because each type of accessory has its individual methods for design and production. Although fur coats and jackets are wearing apparel, we discuss them separately from other garments because of the specialized methods used in their manufacture.

FASHION ACCESSORIES

Accessories are an important, integral part of the total fashion business.

Accessories such as shoes, handbags, belts, hats, and jewelry are designed to coordinate with apparel to create a total fashion look. The fashion for particular accessories is usually at the mercy of apparel designers and how they accessorize their designs on the runways. Over the last several years the accessories industry has become one of the most exciting segments of manufacturing and retailing.

Each category of accessories is an industry unto itself. The shoes and hosiery businesses are dominated by large companies. The handbags, glove, scarf, millinery, and jewelry industries are comprised of many small firms in New York City and all over the country. Like the apparel business, accessory manufacturers have been faced with increasing competition from imports. Because production is labor intensive, even domestic producers source in Asia and Latin America for cheap labor.

Fashion Trends

The popularity of various accessories is cyclical. As fashion changes, so does the need for certain accessories. The fashion for belts is related to waist interest in apparel. Accessories such as jewelry and scarves become more important when clothing is classic and simply styled. Fashion in hats is related to hair styles. There are currently simultaneous trends for conservative elegance and casual looks. Accessories manufacturers are catering to both.

Product Development and Design

Designers, merchandisers, and product managers of accessories must be aware of fashion trends in order to make accessories that successfully complement apparel. They may attend the Premiere Classe accessories show, which is held twice a year in Paris. They are also influenced by the same factors as apparel designers (see Chapter 4) and develop their seasonal collections in much the same ways. Accessory manufacturers have anywhere from one to five seasonal lines per year, depending on the type of accessory and its price range. Within each line, groups usually have a theme based on function, fabrications, quality, and/or price range. Designers are also aware of how design elements and principles affect their products.

Diversifying Products

To balance product lines in the face of fashion cycles and to increase business by capitalizing on strong brand images, many accessory companies have diversified into other areas. Ferragamo (shoes) now makes handbags, jewelry, and even ready-to-wear. Hermès has added ready-to-wear to their famous line of scarves and leather goods. Nike and Reebok have taken advantage of their shoe brand reputations by adding sport apparel to their businesses. Robert Lee Morris is designing a 100-piece collection of jewelry, belts, and small leather goods for Warner Brothers, has licensed scarves to Collection XIIX, and is involved in a joint venture with a Swiss watch company, in addition to producing his own collections of jewelry and handbags.

Apparel designers want accessories that are specifically created to go with their apparel collections. For this reason, leading apparel companies such as Donna Karan have added accessories to their product lines by opening their own accessory division, through licensing arrangements, or through joint ventures with accessory manufacturers. Even though the designer name is on the product in the store, it is produced and sometimes marketed by an accessory manufacturer that has expertise in that area. Designer accessory marketing benefits from their apparel advertising and the resulting consumer name recognition.

Production

The differences in function and fabrication are why production is so vastly different in each accessory area. Production methods are discussed separately under each category.

Except for hosiery, the accessory market is very involved with importing. High-end accessories from foreign manufacturers such as Ferragamo and Gucci are imported by retail stores. There are also importers who bring in merchandise to sell under retail store private label names. Many U.S. manufacturers also have their own accessory products produced in other countries where labor is cheaper: in Asia, especially China, the Philippines, Eastern Europe, and South America.

On the other hand, as long as the dollar remains low in relation to major foreign currencies, some American accessory manufacturers have had success in exporting. Nike, Reebok, and Betmar are just a few examples.

Marketing

Marketing methods vary from company to company depending on type of accessory and price range. Most manufacturers show their new collections in their New York showrooms during market weeks. They also may have showrooms in major market centers around the country, such as Los Angeles, Dallas, Atlanta, or Chicago, as well as sales representatives who call on retail store buyers across the country. Manufacturers may also show their products at the Fashion Accessories Expo or Accessories Circuit three times a year in New York City: showing spring and summer merchandise in January; fall merchandise in May; and holiday and resort in August.

In an effort to control merchandising and image and have direct access to consumers, many accessory companies have opened their own retail stores. In Europe, it is common for accessories companies such as Ferragamo, Gucci, and Aigner to have their own retail stores. Also, American shoe companies have traditionally had their own retail stores in order to stock sufficient inventory and maintain trained sales staffs. However, retailing is a new idea for most accessory manufacturers in the United States. Now accessory companies, such as Nike, Kleinberg Sherrill, Carlos Falchi, Robert Lee Morris, and Carolee, are opening their own specialty stores. These stores provide accessory manufacturers with increased brand awareness, the opportunity to present their entire collection unedited by a buyer, and to make customer contact.

Accessory manufacturers also have merchandise representatives who work at multibrand retail stores to educate sales associates, arrange merchandise displays, and help customers. Accessory designers may make personal appearances in stores to promote sales and test consumer reactions to new styles. Large retail stores may also have their own private labels made for them by accessory companies.

Store accessory departments have traditionally been on the main floor. Now many retailers have opened accessories shops on their ready-to-wear floors next to apparel to help to sell accessories and to help the consumer to find a complete outfit in one area.

Footwear

Footwear, including shoes, sandals, and boots, is the largest volume producer in accessories. More than 7 billion pairs of shoes are produced worldwide each year. Both functional and fashionable, shoes come in assorted materials, including calf, kid, suede, and reptile skins, imitation leathers, and fabrics such as canvas or nylon.

Trends

Today the shoe industry caters to both dress and casual trends. As a result of the enormous popularity of sport shoes, comfort has become an important element of shoe design. A number of popular shoe brands, from Florsheim to Ferragamo, have tried to combine style with the comfort of athletic shoes.

Due to a heightened interest in the outdoors by baby boomers and their families and the "grunge" look, rugged hiking boots have become a fashion statement. Brands such as Timberland and British-owned Doc Martens have become very popular as a result.

Design of Leather Fashion Shoes

Most dress shoe design direction comes from Europe. Creative international shoe designers such as Manolo Blahnik and Robert Clegerie set international trends for women's fashion shoes. Design for sport shoes is based on function and ideas often come from "the streets." Shoe designers study fashion trends so that their shoes will coordinate with apparel.

Many shoe company designers or *line builders* (product managers) attend the shoe fairs in Dusseldorf, Germany, and Bologna and Milan, Italy, to get

Test of a paper shoe pattern on a wooden last. *(Courtesy of Ferragamo, Florence, Italy)*

ideas for a new shoe collection. Like an apparel merchandiser, the line builder begins with concepts for groups and works with designers who develop individual shoe styles. Designers are primarily concerned with materials, color, shape, and proportion. They must consider the view of the shoe from all angles. Many shoe companies are using computer-aided-design (CAD) systems that are capable of both two-dimensional design (design of uppers and size grading) and three-dimensional design (design of the last and projection of the drawing on the last).

Sometimes the line builder will buy *prototypes* (sample shoes) from a *modelista* (model maker) at a studio or shoe fair; otherwise, the line builder might forward a designer's sketches to a modelista, who makes the first model at the factory. If the line builder and modelista live in different countries, ideas and samples must be sent back and forth. The sample shoes are edited to form a balanced collection. Duplicates are then made for the sales staff, showroom, and trade shows.

Leather Sourcing

Leather sourcing is usually close to production: Italian leather for shoes produced in Italy, South American leather for Brazilian-made shoes, and Chinese leather for Asian-made shoes. However, leather is sometimes sourced in one country, sent to another for production, and marketed in a third country.

Production of Traditional Leather Shoes

Traditional shoe production is complex, involving various measurements for length and width combinations. The full range of women's shoe sizes includes 103 width and length combinations between sizes 5 and 10. Shoes for the American market are made on American lasts. European shoes have only one width, whereas shoes exported to the United States usually come in four widths.

Another factor contributing to the complexity of shoe production is the skilled labor needed to complete the number of operations performed. Two to three hundred operations can go into the production of a finely made fashion shoe. If a shoe is factory made, 80 different machines could be involved in its production. Shoe parts must be joined together for a smooth, perfect fit. Whether a shoe is handmade or mass produced, there are usually 10 basic steps:

◆ **Making the last**   A foot-shaped form called a *last* is created. The original last is made of wood and requires as many as 35 different measurements. A shoe factory needs thousands of lasts, one for each size, width, heel height, and basic style. Duplicate polyethylene lasts are made from the master.

◆ **Patternmaking**   A pattern is created based on measurements taken from the last and from the original *pullover model*, which is sewn and tacked onto a last, or a designer's sketch. A trial shoe is made from this pattern. The line builder further assesses and refines style selections at this time, and the final line is closed or "frozen." Trials are duplicated as samples for sales representatives.

◆ **Cutting**   Paper patterns are converted into steel dies that cut the leather. Modern factories use programmed continuous cutting machines or water-jet cutters to cut the leather. Some shoes are made of vinyl or fabric.

◆ **Stitching and fitting**   The upper portion of the shoe is made. Buttonholes, topstitching, all other upper design details, and linings are added.

◆ **Lasting**   The shoe upper is pulled over the last and attached to the innersole.

◆ **Bottoming**   The sole is attached to the upper by sewing, cementing, vulcanizing, nailing, stapling, or molding. Most shoe soles are cemented to the uppers.

◆ **Heeling**   Heels, premolded in plastic and covered with leather or wood, are attached.

◆ **Finishing**   The finished shoes are polished and the last is removed.

◆ **Treeing**   Shoes are dried and receive a final inspection. Tissue and sticks are put into the shoes to help them retain their shape.

Large companies have a competitive edge because they have the capital necessary to invest in the most advanced machinery and computer technology. Widespread use of *computer-aided shoemaking systems* enables manufacturers to speed production, improve quality, and keep labor costs down. Programmable machines are now available for nearly every aspect of production, including sewing, folding, and lasting.

Domestic shoe production has declined so that there are only 379 manufacturers operating 461 plants in the United States with employment at approximately 48,200.[1] The small amount of domestic shoe production left,

Attaching the leather shoe upper to the last. *(Courtesy of Bally of Switzerland)*

primarily of men's shoes, is done in New England and the Midwest. These firms include better classic men's shoes such as Johnston & Murphy, Allen-Edmonds, Cole-Haan, and Alden and moderate shoe lines such as Florsheim, Bass, Dexter, and Bostonians. In the future, it seems that weaker firms will continue to close while stronger ones will consolidate plants and invest in new technology to narrow the gap between foreign and U.S. labor costs.

Imports

The greatest impact on the U.S. shoe industry is the increasing number of imports. As there are no quotas on shoe imports, they have reached a new high of 88 percent of the 1.1 billion (non-rubber) pairs purchased in the United States.[2]

The highest quality women's fashion shoes, such as Robert Clegerie, Manalo Blahnik, Andrea Pfister, Patrick Cox, Prada, Bruno Magli, and Ferragamo, are made by hand in Italy with the finest leathers. Apparel designers such as Calvin Klein have shoe collections made by Italian shoe manufacturers, in this case Diego Della Valle, in joint ventures or via licensing arrangements. Some women's manufacturers such as Magli and Ferragamo also make men's shoes, as do men's shoe companies including Borri and Lorenzo Banfi.

Bridge lines such as Adrienne Vittadini, Anne Klein II, Via Spiga, Amalfi, or DKNY may be made in Italy or Spain. Better shoes, including Liz Claiborne, Nickels, Caressa, or Pappagallo, are typically made in Spain, Brazil, or China.

Moderate, budget, and sport shoes are usually made in China, Korea, or Malaysia. Manufacturers are always seeking new, cheaper production sources. Some companies buy production time in overseas factories. Others own facilities in Italy, Spain, or South America.

Marketing

Most shoe importers, such as Schwartz & Benjamin, are essentially *marketers*. They buy or license the designs and contract production. They operate this way because they feel that they have the knowledge of what products their customers want and the ability to market the shoes in their own country.

Shoe companies may have shoe lines in all price ranges and categories. For example, Nine West has acquired the Amalfi, Bandolino, Cobbie, Easy Spirit, Evan-Picone, Joyce, Pappagallo, and Selby brands from the former U.S. Shoe Company.

Due to the large inventories needed to stock shoes in all styles, colors, sizes, and widths, many shoe manufacturers own their own stores. Nine West and Florsheim, for example, have their own shoe stores. Some also lease departments from department and specialty stores, but this practice is on the decline.

MICAM, the prestigious international shoe fair, is held in Bologna in March to show fall styles and in Milan in September to show spring styles. Other important international markets include the GDS footwear show in Düsseldorf, Germany; MIDEC in Paris, France; and FICC in Elda, Spain. The Fashion Footwear Association of New York (FFANY) and the National Shoe Fair (for volume and lower-priced shoes) are held four times a year in New York. The largest shoe show is organized by Western Shoe Associates (WSA) in Las Vegas each February and August. Buyers shop for early spring styles in June, for spring and summer in August, for early fall in December, and for fall and holiday in February. Shoe manufacturers use educational tools such as seminars to educate sales personnel as well as consumers with regard to quality and styling. Some shoe companies such as Ferragamo or Nine West also manufacture handbags.

Handbags

A handbag must be both decorative and functional; it must hold necessities conveniently as well as fit into the fashion picture. Large bags, such as totes, satchels, portfolios, or backpacks, tend to be more functional; smaller bags such as clutches or envelopes are usually decorative. Handbag styles range from classic constructed types to soft shapes. Leather, including suede and reptile, still represents approximately half of handbag material; vinyl, fabric (tapestry, rug prints, needlepoint, metallics, nylon, and canvas), and straw make up the other half.

Major trends include backpacks, slings (half-bag, half-backpack), outdoor looks, and structured geometric looks that are classic and elegant. As part of the demand for functionality, backpacks have become mainstream fashion, made in luxury alligator to nylon. Influenced by Prada of Italy, nylon and microfiber bags are available at all price levels.

Product Development and Design

The elements of fabrication (leather or fabric), silhouette, and color are the most important components of handbag design, as well as current trends in ready-to-wear and footwear. From an initial sketch, a sample is made from muslin or imitation leather. A final sample is made up in leather or fabric with appropriate supportive stays (made of treated paper). Felt, foam, and fabric interlinings are layered around the paper stays to give the bag a nice hand and cushion. Ornaments, closures, and/or handles must be chosen to complement the shape and fabrication. Linings differ with each type of bag and each fabrication.

The product development team, designer, pattern maker, samplemaker, production manager, and assistants, critique the sample. The most successful are chosen for the collection. Groups may be based on fabrications, silhouettes, or themes. Usually, a variety of silhouettes is included, perhaps in various fabrications (types of leather). Whimsical or fashion-forward pieces are included. Several groups create a well-rounded collection.

Production

When the final line is chosen, cutting dies are made from the pattern and used to stamp out leather. The leather may also be cut by water jet, and luxury handbags are cut by hand. Rising prices and reduced availability of leather in recent years have had a great impact on the styling and production of handbags. Fabric bags are cut by methods similar to those used in the apparel industry.

Handbag designer Marcia Sherrill in her New York showroom. (*Courtesy of Kleinberg Sherrill Accessories, photographed by Nora Feller*)

Luxury Handbags. The type and quality of workmanship varies greatly. At the top of the luxury market are Hermès handbags, which are entirely handcrafted. Production is limited and is allocated by the number of hours it takes to make a bag. For example, it takes 16 hours to make a "Kelly handbag," which costs over $3000.00. Each bag is dated and stamped with the craftsperson's initials. Distribution is limited in order to maintain exclusivity.

Kleinberg-Sherrill is the only American luxury handbag company that actually produces in the United States. Most other luxury handbags are made in France or Italy, including Chanel, Bottega Veneta, Donna Karan, Paloma Picasso, Prada, Fendi, Ferragamo, and Calvin Klein. Judith Leiber's minaudier (hand-molded metal) evening bags are made in New York.

Designer and Better Handbags. In the production of better handbags, both fabrics and leathers may be stitched by machine, but much of the assembly of linings, ornaments, handles, and closures must still be done by hand. Although this handwork is expensive, some handbags are still made in the United States, primarily in New York, Maine, Connecticut, Massachusetts, and Florida. However, to keep costs down, many manufacturers source worldwide for the cheapest labor. Of the imports, better handbags are made in Hong Kong. Other handbag production sources include South America, Indonesia, South Korea, China, and India.

American accessory designer lines include Carlos Falchi, Carey Adina, Kenneth Cole, and Sharif; apparel designer accessory line examples are Anne Klein or Donna Karan New York (DKNY); and bridge brands are Bally of Switzerland, Coach, Etienne Aigner, or Donney & Bourke.

Moderate and Inexpensive Handbags. Moderate bags are sometimes made of leather but usually of vinyl or fabric. Examples of moderate brands are Liz Claiborne and Esprit.

Moderately priced bags are primarily imported. Handbag imports have risen to 76 percent of U.S. consumption, mostly from China.[3] To keep prices down, many stores create *private label* handbags in all categories. The retailer works directly with a manufacturer, labels the handbags with the store's private brand, and eliminates the cost of wholesale marketing.

Marketing

There are two major handbag markets per year—in May for fall and in November for spring. Smaller markets are in August, March, and January. Collections are shown in New York and other market center showrooms as well as at the Fashion Accessories Expo.

Belts

The fashion for belts in women's wear is *apparel driven* (corresponding to waist interest in apparel styling). In women's wear, a return to classic apparel means a rise in belt sales. Fashion belts are made of lightweight leathers and suedes, metallics, woven cord, metal chain, fabrics, and elasticized fabrics. Men's belts are strictly functional and must withstand everyday wear, so they are traditionally made of heavy 5- or 6-ounce leather.

Many apparel companies, such as Chanel, Donna Karan, Isaac Mizrahi, Calvin Klein, Ellen Tracy, and Liz Claiborne, have belts manufactured to accessorize with their clothes. Accessories companies such as Hermès, Ferragamo, and Gucci also make belts to coordinate with their handbags. These firms try to carry a design element throughout their accessory lines. A chain belt might repeat the design of a chain strap on a handbag or a handbag clasp might be copied as a belt buckle. Judith Leiber, for example, has used an animal clasp on a belt to go with an animal design handbag.

Production

Leather and imitation leather materials are cut on *strap-cutting* machines or on computer-aided cutting machines. These machines cut the material into long, straight lengths of any desired width. Shaped belts are made either by die cutting or from Plexiglas patterns. With die cutting, the pattern is made into a die resembling a cookie cutter. A *clicker* machine presses the sharp edges of the die through the leather. Plexiglas patterns are used like paper patterns for single-layer cutting. The cutter must carefully cut around the patterns, using only flawless pieces of leather. Computer-automated cutting has helped to speed up production and ensure accuracy.

The cut leather is next sewn or laminated to a backing with a *walking-foot* machine or on computer-automated machines. Belt buckles, made from metal, wood, or plastic, come mostly from Italy (for high-priced lines) or Taiwan. Sterling silver buckles also come from the Southwest for western-inspired styles. Holes are made at one end of the belt by a foot-press or kick-press machine. The holes, the slit for the buckle, and the shape of the tip may also be cut by a die. In addition, a die can emboss a pattern onto the leather. Belts are finished with trims such as stitchery, cording, nail heads, or rhinestones and may have an edge finish.

Industry Organization

Belt manufacturers tend to be small firms. The industry is centered in the New York metropolitan area because of that city's proximity to suppliers, but production is also growing in California. A large investment in equipment is needed to finish leather well, but some of the operations can be contracted out.

Imports

As in the manufacture of other accessories, belt production has moved to a large extent overseas. Many belts are now made in China, Taiwan, Korea, and Hong Kong.

Markets

As with handbags, belt markets are held five times a year in New York and market center showrooms. Belt manufacturers also show at the Fashion Accessories Expo.

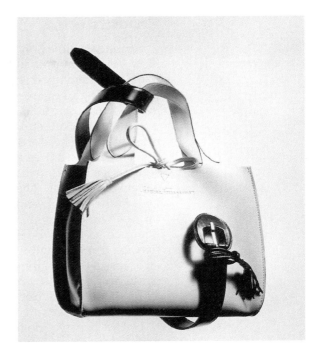

Salvatore Ferragamo handbag and belt. *(Courtesy of Ferragamo, Italy)*

Gloves

Gloves are both functional and fashionable. They are needed to protect hands in work or sports or from the cold. The fashion aspect is cyclical; gloves are more in demand when fashion apparel is elegant.

Product Development and Design

Glove manufacturers have only one line per year, which is shown in November for the following fall and winter. This means that designers must work up to 2 years in advance of the retail selling season. The timing is very difficult since designers want their gloves to accessorize with apparel, particularly outerwear. Therefore, they have to be aware of apparel trends as well as glove styling directions. Designers may travel to Europe to study apparel as well as the Italian glove market for ideas. Some wholesalers, such as Shalimar, simply buy gloves directly from factories in Italy, Portugal, or Romania.

Like other accessories and apparel, glove collections are usually divided into groups. The basis for the groups might be function, such as dressy or sophisticated, tailored or classic, outdoor or country. Groups are also often based on materials: deerskin, pigskin, suede, shearling, cashmere knits, wool knits, fleece, or nylon. Linings are the second most important component and may be made of silk, cashmere, microfibers, olefin and polyester insulating fabrics, fleece, or wool.

Within each group there is usually a variety of colors. Black remains the most popular color for dress gloves, but brights are also included in glove collections. Natural colors predominate in casual leather gloves and a variety of colors in fleece or ski gloves.

Production

American glove production was originally centered in Fulton County, New York. Domestic industry employment is now only about 2300.[4] Glove firms have remained small because of their specialized, handcrafted operations. Most gloves are still produced by a painstaking process that requires many hand operations.

Fine gloves are still table cut from patterns one at a time because it is most precise. There are pieces for the front and back of the hand, the thumb, the *fourchettes* (pieces that shape the fingers between front and back), and sometimes *quirks* (small triangular pieces sewn between the fingers in expensive gloves). The leather is kept damp during cutting and sewing. Due to the curved seams, a glove maker can only sew up to 12 pairs a day on a sewing machine, a French Pique machine, or by hand. Gloves are hemmed and may be lined with knit, pile, or thermal fabrics. Dress gloves may be trimmed with real and fake fur, buttons, bows, braid, embroidery, lace, tassels, and zippers. Finished gloves are rolled or layered in damp cloths and then fitted on heated brass hands, called *laying off* boards, which press them to take out wrinkles and straighten seams. Finished gloves are buffed to a glossy finish.

Less expensive gloves are made with less expensive materials and may have less pieces. They can be cut faster with patterns made into iron dies. In this case, a clicker machine presses the sharp edges of the die through the leather. Some gloves are knit, but even those are labor intensive because the fingers are closed by hand.

Some glove companies also produce scarves, hats, socks, or mittens. Aris Isotoner, for example, has added slippers, socks, and umbrellas to its product lines. Major U.S. manufacturers include Aris/Isotoner, Fownes, Gates, and Grandoe. LaCrasia and Carolina Amato make high-fashion gloves. Glove companies continually work on production innovation, water-proofing techniques, and washability.

Imports

Glove imports are steadily rising. Italy has been a traditional leader in the glove industry; some Italian glove companies produce their own lines as well as gloves for major designers. Portolano, for example, also produces for Moschino, Fendi, and Barry Kieselstein Cord. Many European and American glove manufacturers have either purchased plants or use contractors in China, Hong Kong, or the Philippines. Grandoe, for example, has their own plants in the Philippines, China, and India.

Marketing

Glove manufacturers show their dress lines in November and sport styles in January each year in their own New York showrooms and/or take part in one of the accessories exhibitions. Many glove lines are not marketed under the manufacturer's name but carry the retailer's private label. Grandoe, for example, makes gloves for the L. L. Bean, Nordstrom, and Saks Fifth Avenue labels. Gates makes gloves for Eddie Bauer. For branded gloves, manufacturers often provide hang tags with product care information and in-store training to educate salespeople in order to promote sales. Like other accessory manufacturers, some glove companies are opening their own stores. LaCrasia, for example, has its own store called Glove Street.

Hats

In the past, the most important accessory was a hat. A woman bought a new hat to add a bright spot to her wardrobe; a businessman was never seen on the street without one. The trend toward more casual life-styles and bouffant hairdos of the 1960s changed that, and the millinery industry suffered a severe setback. Of course, functional hats to protect against the weather remained a necessity.

Today, hats are enjoying a comeback at a tremendous growth rate of 12 to 15 percent a year since the mid 1980s.[5] Part of this rise in sales is due to fashion and is also driven by an increased demand for sun protection.

Product Development and Design

Hat manufacturers produce two seasonal collections per year. The spring collection is centered around a wide variety of straws and fabrics such as cotton and linen. Fall collections are dominated by felt and fabrications of velvet, velveteen, fake fur, and corduroy.

Hat collections are usually divided into groups organized around fabrications, color schemes, themes, or price ranges. Hat designers are aware of fashion trends, especially color projections, and use many of the same design sources as apparel designers.

Designers and Manufacturers

Successful hat designers include Lola Ehrlich, Louise Green, Deborah Harper, Melinda Hodges, Eric Javits, Marina Killery, Kokin, Frank Olive, Deborah Rhodes, and Patricia Underwood. Most hat designers also have less expensive lines such as Rhodes' Mocha. Leading apparel designers such as Donna Karan, Ralph Lauren, and Calvin Klein also have hat lines to complement their clothing. These are usually made for them by hat manufacturers as joint ventures.

A romantic hat design by Louise Green.
(Courtesy of Louise Green Millinery Company)

There are a few large manufacturers such as Betmar, Commodore, and Liz Claiborne, but most are small. Other manufacturers include Hoodlums, Korn & Korn, Madcaps, S & S Hat Co., Toucan, and Two Girls NYC. Most specialize in hats alone but there are exceptions, such as Liz Claiborne, which is primarily an apparel company, and now Kokin, who has just designed his first ready-to-wear collection.

There are over 100 hat manufacturers in the United States located primarily in New York City and the Los Angeles area, but also found in Chicago, Texas, and Florida. World centers include Paris, Milan, Germany, England, and Australia.

Blocking a hat form by machine. *(Photographed by the author at Sonni Hats)*

Production

Traditionally, fine hats were referred to as *millinery*. Designer millinery is made of the finest materials. Natural straw, imported from China, Indonesia, Japan, Equador, or the Philippines, or felt is first steamed and then hand blocked over wooden forms. *Blocking* makes the straw or felt into the shape of a hat. The edges are hand trimmed and then wired or bound with ribbon. The best quality ribbons, flowers, and other trims are applied by hand.

Hats in the inexpensive to moderate price range are machine blocked on metal forms. New machinery from Italy automatically regulates the heat and timing for steaming and blocking. Decorative trims are applied by hand.

Soft hats and caps are made from fabrics. Patterns are made for the crown and brim of the hat and used to cut the fabrics. The pieces are sewn together, some over stiffening material, and then hand trimmed.

Marketing

Market dates vary according to where the hats will be sold to retailers. Market weeks for spring lines are in August and for fall lines in January. The manufacturers show their lines in their New York showrooms, followed by regional markets. They may also show their collections at the Fashion Accessories Expo or Accessories Circuit in January, May, and August. Some designers show at the same time as the apparel shows. Manufacturers also have sales representatives at major market centers such as Los Angeles, Atlanta, Chicago, and Dallas. The Millinery Information Bureau gives annual "Milli" awards for outstanding hat design.

At retail stores, hat designers are using sales training and personal appearances in the stores to promote their designs. Many upscale stores create comfortable areas with chairs, mirrors, and special lighting for their customers to try on hats. Some stores are opening hat shops on apparel floors to help customers to accessorize their clothing purchases.

Scarves

The popularity of scarves, shawls, and stoles, like other accessories, is cyclical. The customer wants variety, so it is necessary for a company to produce many designs. Design is usually based on historic textiles, fine art, and ornate architecture, as well as apparel trends. A collection includes groupings based on motifs, fabrications, color, and scarf shapes. Motifs are painted to fit the variety of scarf shapes.

Scarves can be made of silk, wool, cashmere, cotton, and man-made fibers. Fabrications include challis, sheers, metallics, and knits that can be printed, embroidered, or beaded.

16 to 50 color screens are used to make a Ferragamo scarf. *(Courtesy of Ferragamo)*

Production

Scarf production is similar to textile production. The difference is in the printing and finishing. A small percentage of scarves, those made of the finest fabrics, are made in Italy or France. Most of the printing is done by silk screen, which lends itself to the square or rectangular shape of the print. Hermès, which make the finest scarves, uses an average of 24 color screens and up to 50 screens for their highest quality! Less expensive scarves use only 4 to 10 color screens. The printed fabric is cut and then hand rolled, machine rolled, flat hemmed, or fringed.

Most scarf production occurs in Asia, where expertise as well as inexpensive labor can be found. Many American manufacturers buy their fabrics in Japan, Korea, or China and have the scarves printed there as well. Many scarves are cut and sewn from fabrics available on the market. Microfiber polyester and rayon are currently popular, especially in novelty textures such as chiffon with a velvet pattern woven in it.

Designers such as Ralph Lauren and Donna Karan also have scarves made for them. Collection XIIX manufactures Anne Klein, Ellen Tracy, and Robert Lee Morris scarves as well as their own brand. Successful moderate resources include Collection XIIX, Echo, and Liz Claiborne.

The high price of silk, the cost of labor, and the demand for scarves has caused rising prices. Retailers have to order early to get on-time deliveries because of the long lead time involved in overseas production. Scarf manufacturers have developed videos and brochures on how to wear scarves to help the customer and promote sales.

Hosiery

Hosiery serves as a fashion accessory and has the practical function of keeping legs and feet warm. Major changes in the recent history of the women's hosiery business include the development of nylon stockings in 1940, which were stronger and more uniform than silk, and the development of pantyhose in 1965, which liberated women from gartered stockings, were more comfortable, and dominated the industry almost overnight. Today, hosiery is manufactured in a wide range of knits, colors, and categories such as sheers, support, opaques, tights, and socks. The men's business, of course, is all socks.

Trends

Manufacturers of women's hosiery are now offering consumers more variety in large and petite sizes for better fit, figure-enhancing products such as control-top pantyhose, better fit with spandex, and multicolor patterns using polypropylene with nylon. Recently driven by the trend to casual dressing, the sheer hosiery business has decreased, while tights and casual socks have grown to a major part of the business. The fashion for pattern or color on the legs is cyclical and does not necessarily coincide with variations in skirt length.

Product Development

The number of seasonal hosiery lines varies from two to four depending on the manufacturer and the price range. Some companies specialize in sheers and tights or socks, others make both. Collections are usually grouped by construction categories, such as pantyhose, control-top pantyhose, support hose, stockings, thigh-highs, and socks. Constant research is done to develop better constructions and a variety of nylon and spandex combinations. Within these groups there is an assortment of colors and, in the case of socks, a variety of patterns.

Production

Hosiery is produced in knitting mills where machines run 24 hours a day. Pantyhose and socks are both knit on automated circular knitting machines with special techniques to shape the heel. Sock machines use thicker yarn and fewer needles. Knitting machines have become more productive, capable, and flexible, with electronic patterning enabling individual control of every stitch. The steps involved in hosiery production are knitting, dyeing, drying, *boarding* (a heat-setting process), pairing (for stockings and socks), labeling, and packaging.

There are approximately 800 hosiery mills in the United States, located primarily in North Carolina. The second largest accessories industry, it is dominated by large companies such as Berkshire, Ithaca, Kayser-Roth,

Pennaco, and Sara Lee. Sara Lee owns both Hanes and L'eggs and has the Donna Karan, DKNY tights, and Liz Claiborne licenses. Kayser-Roth owns No-Nonsense, Burlington, and Hue Hosiery and has the Calvin Klein license. Pennaco's brand is Round the Clock. Ithaca produces the Evan-Picone and Vanity Fair (VF Corporation) lines. Sock manufacturers include Bonnie Doon, Burlington, Gold Toe (Great American Knitting Mills), Hot Sox, and Trimfit. Designers and designer brands such as Giorgio Armani, Kenneth Cole, Christian Dior, Givenchy, Donna Karan, Calvin Klein, and Ralph Lauren have hosiery and socks produced for them by licensing arrangements.

Marketing

Hosiery manufacturers also maintain sales headquarters and showrooms in New York City and sales representatives to work directly with their retail clients around the country. There are two main markets, in March for fall and in September for spring. More fashion-oriented lines such as Calvin Klein from Kayser-Roth may be shown four times a year with apparel collections. Basic hosiery lines change little and are constantly replenished in the stores.

The hosiery business is extremely competitive. Hosiery manufacturers have huge national advertising budgets. They also invest in other promotional material, such as informative packaging, point-of-sale visuals, in-store events, and merchandisers. Merchandisers help to stock shelves, train salespeople, and generally do whatever is necessary to assure that their products are well placed in the sales area. Kayser-Roth, for example, invested $1 million in their promotion program called RSVP.[6]

Stock replenishment is especially important in the hosiery business. Manufacturers take responsibility to see that stores consistently maintain complete inventories of all sizes in each style category. Manufacturers are using Quick Response systems such as electronic data interchange (EDI) and bar coding to keep track of and continually replace inventory.

A witty Hanes hosiery ad. (*Courtesy of Sara Lee Hosiery and Saatchi & Saatchi Advertising*)

Jewelry

Because jewelry is made from metals and stones, it is a completely different industry from the other accessory industries that use leather or fabrics. It would take an entire book to describe the many facets of the design, production, and marketing of jewelry. Here is an overview of fine, bridge, and costume jewelry.

Fine Jewelry

Fine jewelry is made of precious metals and gemstones; it is made by hand or with settings reproduced by casting. The quality of craftsmanship, the beauty of the design, and the value of the metals and gemstones determine the cost. Because fine jewelry is usually a life-long investment, its design is often classic. However, "Cable television sales of jewelry have made fine jewelry a fashion statement," according to Mary Solkin, vice-president of merchandising for Andin International, one of the largest fine jewelry manufacturers.[7]

Metals.   Only precious metals such as 10-, 14-, or 18-karat gold, platinum, and sterling silver are used to make fine jewelry. Since precious metals in their pure state are generally too soft to retain shape or to hold stones securely, they are combined with other metals. Gold alloys are made with copper, silver, palladium, or nickel. Gold content is expressed in *karats*: 24 karats is pure gold; 14 karats is 58.3 percent gold. Platinum is mixed with silvery metals such as palladium. Silver must be 925 parts per thousand of silver to be considered sterling. *Goldsmiths* use these precious metals to create jewelry and make settings for precious gems.

Gemstones.   Precious gems are hard, natural stones selected for their beauty and cut or polished for use in jewelry. Gemstones include diamonds, rubies, emeralds, sapphires, alexandrites, aquamarines, topazes, tourmalines, garnets, jade, opals, lapis lazuli, turquoise, and real pearls. Extoic stones, such as tanzanite, are currently popular. Price depends on clarity, color, rarity, and size. The weight of gemstones is measured in carats, a standard unit of 200 milligrams. The term *carat* comes from the seeds of the carob tree that were once used to balance the scales used for weighing gems. Gemstones are found mostly in Asia, especially Thailand. Jewelers may also use synthetics or "created" stones that look like gemstones.

Diamonds.   Diamonds have traditionally been the most valuable and coveted of gems, as Lorelei Lee sang in "Diamonds Are a Girl's Best Friend." Diamonds are the strongest natural element known: a diamond can be cut only with another diamond. Eighty-five percent of the world's diamond production is controlled by DeBeers, a huge South African conglomerate.

Stonecutting.   Transparent stones such as diamonds and aquamarines are cut by a *lapidary* (stonecutter) into symmetrical facets to show off their beauty. At least 50 percent of a rough gem is wasted in cutting. Stonecutters have developed new shapes such as the "trillion," a triangular shape. *Cabachon* stones—the unclear stones such as jade, opal, and coral—are domed, carved, or left in their natural state. Cabachon rubies and sapphires are also treated this way, a process that results in star rubies and sapphires. Although computers have recently been programmed to direct the cutting of gemstones, it is by and large still a craftsperson's field. Major stonecutting centers are in Antwerp, Belgium; Tel Aviv, Israel; London; New York City; and Idar-Oberstein, Germany.

Bridge Jewelry

Bridge jewelry is a category between fine jewelry and costume jewelry defined by lower price points than fine jewelry. However, it is still made of precious metals, such as vermeil (a process of electroplating gold over silver) or sterling silver, 14-karat gold trim, and semi-precious stones and cubic zirconia (faux diamond) stones.

Costume Jewelry

Costume jewelry is mass produced to provide consumers with a variety of jewelry to coordinate with each look in their wardrobes.

Classic costume jewelry simulates the look of fine jewelry, using base metals such as brass, palladium, aluminum, copper, tin, lead, or chromium, *electroplated* (coated or bonded) with gold or silver. When shapes are cut or stamped out of the sheet, the edges must be covered with gold. Freshwater or faux (glass or plastic) pearls and enameling are also used to make classic costume jewelry.

Fashion jewelry is more trendy and utilizes metals that imitate gold and silver, as well as materials such as wood, plastics, leather, beads, glass, or clay. Fashion jewelry is often colorful and styles change seasonally in keeping with apparel design. This jewelry is not created to look "real," but rather to make a fashion statement.

Product Development and Design

Like any successful fashion company, jewelry manufacturers try to identify their target customer and find a market niche. They develop a special look, perhaps concentrating on certain materials.

Jewelry design is often inspired by architecture, fine art, and nature, such as flowers and leaves. Designers often go to the International Jewelry Show in Basel, Switzerland, each April to study jewelry trends and/or attend the Tucson Gem and Jewelry Show in Arizona each February to see what stones are available. Jewelry designers also pay particular attention to the jewelry that designers show on the runways with their apparel collections.

Major jewelry categories are rings, necklaces, earrings, and bracelets. A manufacturer might further subdivide categories into diamond, gold, precious, and semi-precious jewelry, or copies thereof, and then into price ranges. Each collection features a balanced variety of designs and materials based on the seasons and how the jewelry will be worn. As in apparel design, the designer may first develop story boards around themes for various groups within the collection.

Jewelry Production

There are as many techniques of making jewelry as there are jewelry types. Artisans use various methods of carving, grinding, drilling, filing, hammering, and welding metal into desired shapes. There are also many ways to mass-produce jewelry by using sheet metal, metal cast in molds, and wire.

Flat shapes are usually stamped out of sheet metal and may be decorated with embossing or engraving.

Casting is a process used to produce three-dimensional shapes. Rubber molds are used to cast low-temperature metals, such as tin alloys; *lost-wax casting* is used for high-temperature metals, such as gold, silver, and brass (for both fine and costume jewelry). In the latter method, wax is first formed in the rubber mold and a new plaster mold is made over the wax forms. The wax is then burned out and molten metal is forced into the plaster mold. Finally, the plaster mold is broken open to expose the shaped pieces of metal, which are then snipped off of a supporting tree structure and polished.

Electroform is a process that applies gold electrostatically around a base metal core. The metal is then chemically dissolved, creating a hollow shell of gold with a seamless surface.

Wire is used to make chains and various necklaces and bracelets. Band rings may be made by slicing tubes of metal. Fake jewels and pearls are made from glass.

Designs may be applied with enamel. Enamel work is distinguished by the way it is applied; methods include cloisonné, champlevé, basse taille, and painting.

Resources

Fine Jewelry. Italy, New York, and Israel are international centers for the creation of fine gold jewelry. There are appoximately 2000 jewelry firms in the United States, found mostly in New York, Rhode Island, and California. The two largest fine jewelry firms in the United States are Town & Country Corporation and Andin International. Contemporary fine jewelry designers include Elsa Peretti, Paloma Picasso, Henry Dunay, and Michael Good.

Bridge and Costume. There are approximately 750 costume jewelry firms in the United States. Production is concentrated in Providence, Rhode Island, and New York, but there are small firms all over the country. There is growing competition from imports from countries such as South Korea, Taiwan, Singapore, and Hong Kong.

Dominique Aurientis, Angela Cummings, Ted Meuhling, Robert Lee Morris, and Jay Strongwater are well-known bridge jewelry designers.

Jewelry designer Robert Lee Morris at work in his studio.
(Courtesy of Robert Lee Morris)

Designer costume jewelry manufacturers include Carolee, Carol Dauplaise, Chanel, Ciner, Erwin Pearl, Judith Jack, Kenneth Jay Lane, Miriam Haskell, and St. John.

Among branded jewelry lines are Anne Klein II by Swank, Christian Dior, Liz Claiborne, Marvella, the Monet Group (also Trifari and Marvella), Napier, Swarovski, Victoria Creations, and the 1928 Jewelry Company. Designers license their names to companies that have the expertise to manufacture jewelry. For example, Victoria Creations produces licensed Karl Lagerfeld and Bijoux Givenchy lines as well as Richelieu, its own pearl brand, and Worthington for J. C. Penney.

Marketing

New jewelry collections may be shown at the Jewelers of America Show in New York each February and July or at the United Jewelry Show in Providence, Rhode Island, each March, June, and September. Some costume jewelry firms bring out new collections five times a year in January, March, May, August, and November. Fine jewelry manufacturers usually have two collections a year. Manufacturers have showrooms in New York City and major market centers, as well as sales representatives.

Large jewelry vendors are emphasizing consumer and sales staff education to promote multiple sales. Trifari, for example, has full-time fashion accessory consultants on the selling floor who are paid in part by Trifari and in part by the store. Erwin Pearl has over 40 merchandisers to train sales staff, ensure that jewelry is displayed properly, and help customers. Jewelry designers, such as Henry Dunay and Carolee Friedlander, also make personal appearances at stores to promote their jewelry and get customer feedback. Manufacturers also use booklets to show the consumer how to accessorize with jewelry and what styles look best on what facial structures and necklines.

Another trend in the business is specialty retail stores devoted solely to costume jewelry. Some jewelry manufacturers, such as Erwin Pearl, have opened their own retail stores, too.

Watches

Watches have become a fashion accessory. Watches have intricately detailed mechanical works, usually hand- or self-wound, and some are quartz powered. Many include alternative functions such as the phase of the moon, the corresponding time halfway round the world, chronograph capacity, which indicates time intervals, perpetual calendars, and/or an accumulator that indicates elapsed time. Watches may be shock resistant and/or water resistant.

Luxury watches have become status symbols. Many watches are 18-karat gold and some are covered with diamonds. The most expensive brands include Breguet, Blancpain, and Patek Philippe and can cost up to a million dollars. Other top-end luxury watches include Audemars Piguet, Gerald Genta, Ulysse Nardin, and Vacheron & Constantin. Less expensive luxury watches are Rolex, Ebel, Cartier, Baume & Mercier, Corum, Piaget, and Omega. Switzerland produces 95 percent of the world's luxury watches.

In 1967, a Swiss firm produced the first quartz watch, which was copied by Japanese and American fashion watch companies. Most fashion watches now use a battery-activated quartz crystal, computer chip, or electronic motor.

By the late 1970s, the Swiss share of the world market had dropped from 43 percent to 15 percent due to competition from less expensive watches made in Japan and Southeast Asia.[8] Unable to compete, many Swiss watchmakers were going bankrupt until the Société Suisse de Microelectronique et d'Horlogerie (SMH) developed the colorful, pop-art Swatch in 1982. By limiting the number of components needed to make a good watch and by using synthetic materials, SMH was able to keep costs to a level low enough for mass production. The Swatch set a fashion direction for a whole new market of fashion watches at popular prices.

Fashion watches are one of the most exciting accessory categories. New brands are continually appearing as consumers buy watch wardrobes to accessorize every style of dressing. Popular fashion watches include Swiss Army, Fossil, and Guess. Watch companies manufacture for various brand names. E. Gluck, for example, produces Anne Klein and Looney Tunes; Timex produces Nautica, Joe Boxer, and Timberland; and Callanen Group produces the Guess line. Timberland, Armitron's Instalite, and Guess' Waterpro are examples of new lines of casual, outdoor looks.

FUR MANUFACTURING

Furs were the earliest form of clothing and, like leather accessories, are made from animal skins.

In Chapter 7 we discussed the processing of furs. Some manufacturers buy furs directly at auctions and contract out the processing operations or have their own vertical operations. Other manufacturers buy processed furs from merchants. Once the pelts have been processed, the actual production of fur garments can begin.

Product Development

As in the styling of cloth coats, fur designers plan a collection of coats and jackets for their one season a year, winter. They may specialize in one type of fur or plan a variety of furs within their collection. Groups may be planned around themes. Designers also plan a variety of silhouettes, neckline treatments, and closures to please a variety of tastes, and some manufacturers also make accessories such as hats to go with their coats and jackets. Creating a good fit and maintaining a light weight are important considerations for the designer. Collections are still dominated by classic, timeless styles due to the expense to the consumer. However, many designers add interest to a collection or build an entire reputation around trendy looks and innovation.

Styling Trends

Fashion trends influence the design of fur garments and the popularity of specific furs. Trends include shearling, sheared fur, dyed fur, recycled fur, knitted fur, and reversible leather-fur or cloth-fur coats. Saga has even developed washable mink, which has great merchandising appeal. There is an increased use of both fake and real fur as trim on cloth coats, suits, or jackets. These trends are causing a blurring of the boundaries between textile and fur garments and attracting new, younger customers.

Industry Organization

Fur garment styling centers include Milan, Paris, Frankfurt, Hong Kong, Montreal, and New York. Famous fashion names in fur manufacturing include Alixandre, Ben Kahn, Christensen, Corniche, Danzl, Grosvenor, Fendi, Maximilian, Revillon, Solecitti, Theo, Yves St. Laurent, and Zuki. Some well-known apparel designers, such as Ferre for Mondialpelli or Montana for Christensen of Copenhagen, create styles for fur manufacturers on licensing arrangements.

New York

Only a very small percentage of coats is still produced in New York. The old-fashioned family furriers have virtually disappeared. The area of New York City between Sixth and Eighth Avenues and Twenty-sixth and Thirtieth Streets is the center for the creation of luxury fur coats in the United States. Furs designed by Valentino and Karl Lagerfeld are manufactured in New York.

World Centers

On the world market, Hong Kong is the largest producer of fur garments, followed by Canada, Greece, and China.[9] Imports from Greece and China tend to be low end (low priced) and must be purchased in volume and ordered farther ahead of selling season.

A sheared beaver coat designed by Zuki of Canada.
(Courtesy of the Fur Council of Canada, photo by Ugo Camera)

Production

No two fur pelts are totally alike; the furrier must match pelts according to quality and color to achieve uniform texture and color in the finished garment. The sewing of furs requires much skill and does not lend itself to mass-production techniques.

The two basic methods of fur manufacturing are the skin-on-skin technique and the letting-out technique.

Skin-on-Skin Method

In the less costly skin-on-skin method, one full skin is sewn next to another in a uniform alignment. This method is often used to sew together

Stapling damp sections of a coat into shape. *(Courtesy of the Deutsches Pelz Institute)*

the leftovers of expensive furs, such as paws and flanks, into less expensive garments.

Letting-out Method

Luxurious furs, such as mink, are often manufactured by the letting-out method, which accentuates length, reduces width, and enhances draping. This technique involves splitting each skin in half lengthwise and then slicing every half pelt into diagonal strips 1/8 to 1/4 inch wide. The strips are then rematched and sewn together to form a narrower, longer skin that can run the full length of the garment. The result is a slimmer, longer pelt that is often more beautiful than the original. A let-out coat might have anywhere from 1000 to 20,000 seams, which is one reason that fur coats are so expensive.

Sewing

The strips are sewn into sections according to the coat or jacket pattern. They are first dampened, stretched, and stapled onto the pattern on a wooden board. After the sections are dried into shape they are sewn together.

The next operation is called *glazing*. The fur is again dampened and the hairs are combed in the desired direction. Gums and other materials, which often increase the luster of the fur, are applied to hold the hair in the desired position. Then the fur is slowly dried and the lining is sewn in.

Innovative Methods

Some fur designers and manufacturers have innovative methods for creating fur garments and accessories. Paula Lishman of Canada, for example, cuts fur pelts into strips and then weaves, crochets, or knits these strips into garments. The company Roots makes accessories such as backpacks out of recycled fur.

Fur Labeling

The United States Fur Labeling Act requires that the label (as well as related advertising) contain the following information: animal name, country of origin, type of processing and dyeing, whether the furs have been reused, and whether the garment contains paws or tails. If the garment resembles another fur, it must be labeled with the name of the actual pelt used.

Markets

Annual fur fairs are held to show retail buyers fur collections from manufacturers around the world. International fairs include the Tokyo Fur and Fashion Fair in February, Fur Industries International Salon (SIIF) held in Paris in March, Milan's Comispel in March, Fur & Fashion Frankfurt in April, Montreal's show in May, and New York in June.

The demand for furs depends on a number of variables: climate, the world supply of mink, economic conditions, nonexclusivity of fur due to cheaper coats, and sympathies with animal rights activists. Animal-rights group People for the Ethical Treatment of Animals (PETA) have an active campaign against the fur industry with a steady barrage of confrontations, wacky stunts, and carefully orchestrated media events. Super models like Christy Turlington and Cindy Crawford posed in the buff for a PETA ad that read, "I'd rather go naked than wear fur." Certain designers, including Giorgio Armani, Donna Karan, Calvin Klein, and Ralph Lauren, have given up designing furs in general. However, Karan and Klein still make shearling coats and jackets because shearling is a by-product of the meat industry.

The United States and Italy are the largest markets for furs, followed by Japan. Once profitable markets in Britain, Germany, and the Netherlands have fallen off. Harrod's of London has closed its fur salon. A symbolic blow to the Canadian industry was the closing of the fur salons of the Hudson Bay department stores, a company that was built around the fur trade in Canada.

SUMMARY

Fashion in accessories is cyclical and related to apparel styling. Many apparel designers create accessories to complement their clothing. In the shoe business, a modelista makes the first models of shoe designs and then the line builder organizes them into a balanced collection. The production of shoes is a complex process from last making to finishing. Manufacturers are using computer-aided machinery to speed up production and save labor. In handbag production, dummies are first made to test a design. Expensive bags are made by hand of quality leather, while less expensive bags are made of imitations or fabrics and are imported. The manufacture of belts is done at many small companies. Glove production involves many hand operations; most gloves are imported. Designer hats are hand blocked and made of the finest materials, while less expensive fabric hats may be cut and sewn. High-end scarves are made in Italy, with many color screens on the finest fabrics, while less expensive scarves are made in Asia. Hosiery manufacturing is dominated by large knitting mills. Fine jewelry is made of precious metals and gemstones and tends to be classic in design. Better costume jewelry is vermeil or gold filled and is made out of sheet metal, cast metal, or wire.

Most of the accessory manufacturers are small firms, because highly skilled crafts are involved in production; however, the shoe and hosiery industries are dominated by large companies. Domestic production of shoes, handbags, gloves, and scarves has been overshadowed by imports from countries where labor costs much less.

The fur industry produces coats, jackets, and hats, as well as trimmings for textile and leather apparel. The largest centers of fur production are Hong Kong, Canada, and Greece. There are two methods of fur production: skin-on-skin and letting-out. Because the latter is especially tedious and time consuming, the coats and other fur garments so produced are very expensive.

CHAPTER REVIEW

Terms and Concepts

Briefly identify and discuss the following terms and concepts:

1. Accessories
2. Last
3. Line builder
4. Modelista
5. CAD
6. MICAM
7. Hermès
8. Clicker machines
9. Millinery
10. Blocking
11. Gemstones
12. Cabachon stones
13. Carat versus karat
14. Lapidary
15. Vermeil
16. Casting
17. Electroform
18. Letting-out method

Questions for Review

1. How do fashion cycles influence accessory production?
2. Discuss the pros and cons of an apparel firm expanding to include accessories collections.
3. Why are certain countries specializing in dress shoe production while others lead in casual shoe production?
4. Explain the major steps involved in traditional shoe production.
5. How are computers used in mass shoe production?
6. Name five important shoe designers or manufacturers.
7. What is the role of imports in the U.S. shoe market?
8. Briefly describe handbag production.
9. Explain how belts are apparel driven.
10. Name three well-known hat designers.
11. What is the difference between fine millinery and inexpensive hats?
12. What is used to make the finest scarves?
13. What are the basic steps in hosiery production?
14. Why is most of the hosiery business still in the United States while many other accessories are produced overseas?
15. What materials are used to make fine jewelry?
16. What is bridge jewelry?
17. Briefly explain two types of jewelry production.

18. How has the Swiss watch industry responded to competition from low-priced watches?
19. What is the effect of imports on accessory manufacturing?
20. Why has fur manufacturing remained basically free of mass-production techniques?
21. Discuss the differences between the two main fur manufacturing methods.
22. How do animal rights activists influence the fur industry?

Projects for Additional Learning

1. Arrange to visit the fur salon in a department or specialty store. Ask to see and feel a variety of furs. Note the fashion styling of today's furs. How do you feel about fur as wearing apparel?
2. Visit the hat department of a local specialty store. Note the differences between hats and fine millinery and the variations between functional and fashion styling. How do the millinery looks tie in with the apparel trends in the store?
3. Look for shoe advertisements in a fashion magazine. Collect pictures of five popular dressy styles and five popular casual or sport styles. How has function affected styling?

NOTES

[1] "U. S. Industrial Outlook," U. S. Department of Commerce, Washington, D. C., January 1994, pp. 34-7.

[2] Ibid.

[3] Ibid., pp. 34-9.

[4] Ibid.

[5] Casey Bush, Millinery Information Bureau, interview, March 1995.

[6] Rosemary Feitelberg, "Resources Pitch in at Retail," Women's Wear Daily, January 30, 1995, p. 6.

[7] Interview, April 23, 1995.

[8] Andrew Rosenbaum, "Switzerland's Watch Industry: Changing with the Times," Hemispheres, June 1994, p. 39.

[9] "The Changing Market Share," Fur World, March 15, 1993, p. 4.

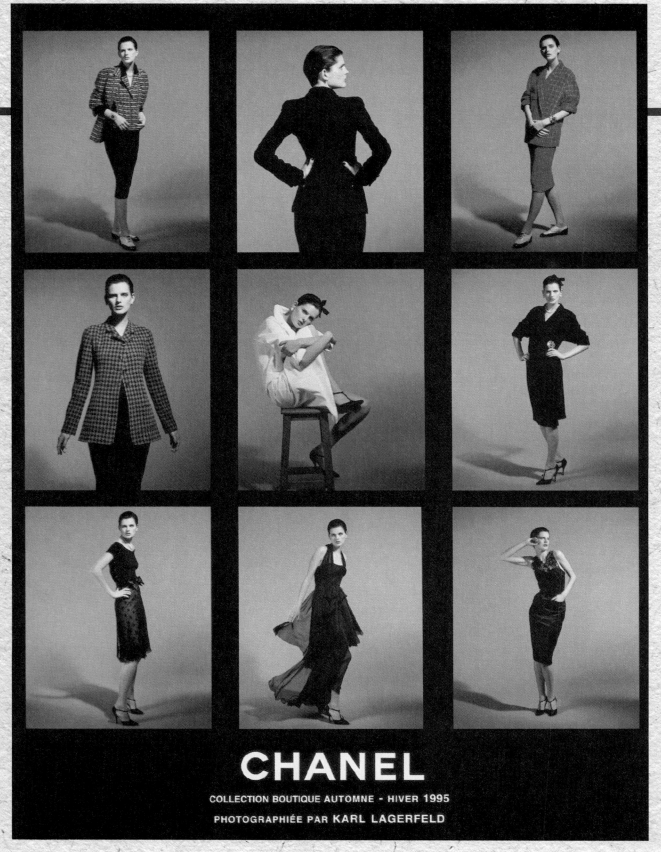

Chanel collection promotional photographs.
(Courtesy of the designer and photographer, Karl Lagerfeld)

12

WHOLESALE MARKETING AND DISTRIBUTION

CAREER FOCUS

Providing the key link to the retailer, marketing specialists try to establish contacts and a good rapport with the stores that they supply. Marketers include manufacturing management, designers, merchandisers, sales representatives, customer service representatives, merchandising representatives, all the various people involved in sales promotion and advertising, catalog directors, publicists, writers, photographers, video producers, models, fashion show coordinators, television fashion specialists, and trade association personnel.

CHAPTER OBJECTIVES

After reading this chapter you should have attained competence in the following areas:

1. Knowledge of major international markets of apparel
2. Understanding of collection openings, line releases, and market weeks
3. Understanding of distribution policies
4. Knowledge of various aids to selling
5. Understanding of the forms of sales promotion
6. Understanding of the use of EDI in distribution

*I*nternational wholesale apparel and accessory markets are the means of distributing the manufacturer's finished products to retailers. A *market* is the potential demand for a product or the place, area, or time at which buyers and sellers meet to transact business. In this chapter we refer specifically to the *wholesale* fashion market, where the sellers represent fashion manufacturers and the buyers are fashion retailers. This material is presented from the *manufacturer's* standpoint, whereas Chapter 14 discusses buying from the retailing point of view, as part of their merchandising process.

Traditionally, fashion markets have located close to suppliers and manufacturers; therefore, most market centers are also production centers. However, newer market centers have been created in various locales for the convenience of buyers.

We refer to the domestic market (the United States), to the regional markets within it, and to the international or global market (see Chapter 2). This chapter discusses major international fashion centers, New York, and regional fashion centers and their role in buying and selling on the wholesale level. Although it is usually possible to buy year round, specific weeks are scheduled for collection openings or for the purpose of bringing buyers and sellers together.

INTERNATIONAL MARKETS

Markets, the time and place where buying and selling occurs.

After each manufacturer's collection or line is designed, it must be presented to retail buyers so that they can buy for their stores. This presentation can be accomplished by various means, including fashion shows, market weeks, showroom presentations, and contacts with sales representatives.

The terms *collection opening* and *line release* are synonymous; both signal the first opportunity for buyers to see fashion merchandise for a new season. The term line release is used by most fashion manufacturers to indicate that their new seasonal merchandise is ready to be seen. Collection openings are held by designer houses and involve extravagant showings.

European Collection Openings

Couture

Paris continues as the world center for couture. Even Italian couture designers Valentino and Versace show their couture collections in Paris. The spring collections are shown in January and the fall collections in July. Collections are now largely shown at a new fashion center beneath the Place du Carrousel near the Louvre.

The couture is highly regulated by the French Ministry of Industry and the Fédération Française de la Couture, which have eased the regulations governing couture. Designers have to show a minimum of 50 pieces in a collection; new couturiers have to show only 25 pieces for a 2-year transition period. *Houses* (couture companies) may show or send videotapes of the collections to private clients instead of having 45 informal fashion shows per season, which was a waste of both time and money. Still, it costs approximately $1 to $2 million a year for a large house to produce their two couture collections because costs include expensive fabrics, labor-intensive handwork, especially made accessories, high-paid models, catwalk, and high-tech sound systems.

To compensate for the losses, the French government gives support to the couture in order to promote exports. Government-owned French television gives the couture free exposure. This kind of publicity is more prestigious than costly advertising and helps to generate sales of ready-to-wear, perfume, and licensing businesses, thereby helping to keep the couture alive.

Prêt-à-porter Collections

European designer ready-to-wear openings are held twice a year: fall collections are shown in March and spring collections in September or October. They are shown earlier than couture to allow time for mass production. Ready-to-wear collections may also be shown in company showrooms, and many manufacturers now show 4 or more collections per year.

Gianfranco Ferré at his collection opening at Christian Dior in Paris.
(Courtesy of Christian Dior)

Paris is such a draw that designers from other countries such as Romeo Gigli from Italy, Jil Sander from Germany, Kansai Yamamoto and Issey Miyake from Japan, and Katharine Hamnett from London show their collections in Paris. The Paris prêt-à-porter shows are generally preceded by shows in Milan. The French, Italians, and Germans want to consolidate their show schedules to make them run sequentially, possibly eliminating London. A buyer needs over two weeks to see the shows in Paris, Milan, and Düsseldorf. Buyers complain that the Paris shows are spread over too many days, that many shows do not start on time and are too long, and that many of the clothes are for editorial purposes only.

Buyers of better merchandise and approximately 2000 journalists from all over the world flock to see the individual showings of many designers. These fashion shows are by invitation only and have become very theatrical. Most buyers see 10 shows a day, from early morning until late at night, taking notes to remember styles. After analyzing the collections from the point of view of their stores' needs, buyers place orders, usually through *commissionaires* (representatives) or their own buying offices in each city. Deliveries are staggered so that new merchandise arrives periodically in the stores to capture customer interest.

The French prêt-à-porter shows are not limited to the designer collections. There are other shows and groups of exhibitors spread out all over Paris, organized by various fashion associations. While the Chambre Syndicale designer shows are usually at the Louvre, there is a large show at the Porte de Versailles. There are also other exhibit groups called Paris sur Mode, Atmosphere d'Hiver, and Tranoi. Some manufacturers show in hotels or restaurants.

In Milan, both the Milano Collezioni Donna (Milan women's collections) and Modamilano are together at the fairgrounds with some overflow in hotels. In Germany, the first women's ready-to-wear show of the season is Collections Premieren Düsseldorf (CPD).

Market Weeks and Fairs

The collection openings are held in their respective fashion centers as part of market weeks or fairs. Markets are held in specially built buildings called fairgrounds, convention centers, or hotels. A market can last from three days to two weeks. Many Americans do not understand that European trade fairs are markets and not just expositions. In Germany, businesses often sell 75 percent of their merchandise at these markets. Markets are an excellent opportunity for the manufacturer to reach new stores, establish new accounts, and, in turn, help retailers looking for new resources.

IGEDO (Interessensgemeinschaft für Damenoberbekleidung, or interest group for women's wear) in Düsseldorf, Germany, which also produces the CPD shows, has developed into the world's largest women's wear market. Manufacturers from 73 countries show their fashion lines to over 200,000 buyers each year at four markets.

Men's Wear

The Salon International de l'Habillement Masculin (SEHM; men's and boys' wear) takes place in Paris each January and September. The Milano Collezioni Uomo (Milan men's designer collections) and the Pitti Immagine Uomo (men's wear) in Florence take place each January and June. Other markets of men's clothing are held in London, Cologne, and Copenhagen in January or February and again in August or September. There are collection openings, fashion fairs, or market weeks going on somewhere the year round. Table 12-1 presents a calendar of the world's most important fabric, apparel, and accessories fairs and market weeks.

TABLE 12-1
IMPORTANT INTERNATIONAL FASHION MARKETS AND COLLECTION SHOWINGS
(Some of the hundreds of fashion-related markets happening year round throughout the world)

January	
Pitti Uomo and Uomo Italia (men)	Florence
Milano Collezioni Uomo (men)	Milan
Designer Men's Wear Collections	Paris
Fashion Accessories Expo and Accessories Circuit	New York
Hong Kong Fashion Week	Hong Kong
National Association of Men's Sportswear Buyers (NAMSB) Show (men's)	New York
Couture collections (spring)	Paris
Market Week (women's ready-to-wear for summer and transitional)	New York
Los Angeles market (summer)	Los Angeles
Pitti Bimbo	Florence
Prêt-à-Porter Paris	Paris
Salon de la Mode Enfantine (children)	Paris
Village Premiere Classe (accessories)	Paris
SEHM, Salon International de l'Habillement Masculin (into February)	Paris
February	
Herren Mode Woche (men) and Interjeans	Cologne
CPD, Collections Premieren Düsseldorf	Düsseldorf
FFANY, Fashion Footwear Association of New York and National Shoe Fair	New York
WSA (Shoe Show)	Las Vegas
International Fashion Week and Imagenmoda (women's ready-to-wear)	Madrid
Mode Woche München (women's ready-to-wear)	Munich
Toronto Ready-to-Wear Collections (women)	Toronto
Market Week (women's ready-to-wear for fall)	New York
WWD/MAGIC (men's and women's)	Las Vegas
March	
International Jeanswear and Sportswear	Miami
Prêt-à-Porter Designer Collection Shows	Paris
Milano Collezioni Donna and Modamilano (women's ready-to-wear)	Milan
British Fashion Week	London
IGEDO (women's ready-to-wear)	Düsseldorf
Mode Femme	Montreal
Premier Vision (fabrics)	Paris
MIDEC, Mode Internationale de la Chaussure (shoes)	Paris

MIPEL (leather accessories)	Milan
GDS (shoes)	Düsseldorf
MICAM (shoes)	Bologna
SIIF, Fur Industries Salon	Paris
Fur and Fashion Frankfurt	Frankfurt
NAMSB Show (men's wear)	New York
Market Week (women's ready-to-wear for fall II, holiday) (into April)	New York

April

American Designer Collection Shows (women's ready-to-wear for fall)	New York
Los Angeles Ready-to-Wear market (fall I)	Los Angeles
Interstoff (fabrics)	Frankfurt
Fall Fashion and Accessories Market	Montreal

May

Fashion Accessories Expo and Accessories Circuit	New York

June

ESMA-Eurotricot (knitwear)	Milan
Milano Collezioni Uomo (men)	Milan
Pitti Uomo and Uomo Italia (men)	Florence
Pitti Bimbo and Moda Bimbo (children)	Florence
NAMSB Show (men's wear)	New York
Market Week (women's ready-to-wear, holiday)	New York
Los Angeles market (fall II, holiday)	Los Angeles

July

Mode Enfantine	Paris
Designer Men's Wear Collections	Paris
Couture collections (fall-winter)	Paris
Hong Kong Fashion Week	Hong Kong
Market Week (women's ready-to-wear for resort, into August)	New York
CPD, Collections Premieren Düsseldorf (women's ready-to-wear)	Düsseldorf

August

Fashion Accessories Expo	New York
Los Angeles Ready-to-Wear Market (resort)	Los Angeles
Herren Mode Woche (men) and Interjeans	Cologne
WWD/MAGIC	Las Vegas
Mode Woche München	Munich
FFANY, Fashion Footwear Association of New York and National Shoe Fair	New York
WSA Shoe Show	Las Vegas
Salon de la Mode Enfantine (children)	Paris

September

Prêt-à-Porter Paris	Paris
Premiere Classe (accessories)	Paris

SEHM, Salon International de l'Habillement Masculin (men)	Paris
MIDEC, Mode Internationale de la Chaussure (shoes)	Paris
IGEDO (women's ready-to-wear)	Düsseldorf
GDS (shoes)	Düsseldorf
MICAM (shoes)	Milan
International Jeanswear and Sportswear	Miami
IMB, International Clothing Machine Fair	Cologne
Bobbin Show (technology and trimmings)	Atlanta
Premier Vision (fabrics)	Paris
International Fashion Week and Imagenmoda (women's ready-to-wear)	Madrid
Prêt-à-Porter (spring women's ready-to-wear)	Paris
October	
British Fashion Week (women's ready-to-wear)	London
Milano Collezioni Donna and Modamilano (women's ready-to-wear)	Milan
Prêt-à-Porter Designer Shows	Paris
Interstoff (fabrics)	Frankfurt
NAMSB Show (men's wear)	New York
Market Week (women's ready-to-wear for spring)	New York
Fashion Accessories Expo and Accessories Circuit	New York
American Designer Collections (for spring)	New York
November	
Los Angeles market (spring)	Los Angeles
December	
ESMA, Eurotricot (knitwear)	Milan
FFANY, Fashion Footwear Association of New York and National Shoe Fair	New York

DOMESTIC MARKETS

Domestic market weeks and trade shows in New York City, California, and other regional centers are the most important wholesale markets for U.S. retail buyers.

New York

New York remains the major fashion market of the United States. 22,000 apparel buyers visit the city each year for five market weeks and trade shows.

7th on Sixth

Seasonal designer collections are usually presented as fashion shows. The Council of Fashion Designers of America (CFDA) organizes the "7th on Sixth" show of women's wear in large tents in Bryant Park adjacent to the

At a Bill Blass collection showing.
(Courtesy of Bill Blass)

New York Public Library. There are approximately 60 shows at Bryant Park and 30 other shows elsewhere. Fall collections are shown in March-April and spring collections in October.

Women's Wear Line Releases

Line releases for better women's fashion usually occur five times a year:

- Summer merchandise is shown in January.
- Early fall merchandise is shown in late February or early March.
- Fall II merchandise is shown in late March or early April.
- Holiday and/or resort merchandise is shown in August.
- Spring merchandise is shown in November.

Buyers usually see lines for most merchandise in manufacturer's showrooms, in hotels, or in rented spaces around New York City. Many out-of-town buyers from department and specialty stores travel to New York because many popular lines are "sold up" before any regional markets begin. New York designer shows and market weeks are followed by regional markets.

Children's Wear

Formerly shown only twice a year, children's wear has now become so fashion oriented that it is shown three or four times a year depending on the type of apparel. Dress manufacturers, for example, have major lines for holiday and spring. Sportswear manufacturers have three or four lines. Some trendier 7 to 14 manufacturers have new lines almost monthly.

Manufacturers of children's coats show their lines in January, fall apparel lines are shown in February or March, holiday from March to May, and spring-summer from August to October. Many children's wear companies only show their lines in their showrooms. The International Kids Fashion Show is held in New York featuring fall fashions in March and spring in August. The Florida Children's Guild Show is in Miami in September.

Men's Wear

- The Designers Collective Show features upscale tailored suits and coats in late January for fall and in late August or early September for spring.

◆ The National Association of Men's Sportswear Buyers (NAMSB) has increased shows to four times a year since the sportswear market has grown so much. Summer lines are shown in January, fall lines in March or early April, holiday and resort in June, and spring lines in October. These shows are followed by regional markets.

◆ The Clothing Manufacturers Association (CMA), a men's wear trade organization, arranges tailored clothing market weeks in January for fall lines and August or September for spring.

Showrooms

Sample merchandise is shown to prospective buyers in over 5000 *showrooms* of the Seventh Avenue manufacturers, often next to design studios. A showroom is a place where manufacturers' sales representatives show samples to prospective buyers. In designer showrooms, fashions are modeled; in medium-to-lower-priced apparel showrooms, clothes are displayed on hangers. The showroom is outfitted with display racks, sometimes mounted on the walls for greater visibility, and with tables and chairs for the clients' comfort. Showrooms provide continual exposure for the line. They can be located on the same premises as the factory or in a mart, or they can be set up in a hotel room or market-week pavilion. The showroom is the primary setting for selling merchandise to retail buyers.

Apparel showrooms are usually grouped in buildings according to merchandise classification and price range. Grouping by apparel type was organized for the convenience of the buyer who does not have the time to travel all over town, yet must see everything offered in a particular category and price range. For example, the prestigious addresses of 530 and 550 Seventh Avenue have traditionally been designer addresss. Broadway houses showrooms for moderately priced women's wear. Lingerie and intimate apparel are centered on Madison Avenue. Children's wear showrooms are grouped around Thirty-fourth Street and Sixth Avenue and at Abraham & Straus plaza, at Thirty-third Street and Sixth. One large building at 1290 Avenue of the Americas has showrooms representing approximately 75 percent of domestically produced men's clothing. The Empire State Building houses showrooms of men's furnishings. The buildings are becoming less specialized, however, as showrooms relocate because of lease losses or the need for more space.

Garment District Improvements

The fashion industry and the city are trying to work together to improve conditions for the fashion industry in New York.

◆ They hope to establish a permanent fashion center for shows, exhibitions, and a museum.

◆ They would like to offer tax breaks for expanding or upgrading manufacturing.

◆ They want city endorsement of marketing programs to promote the fashion industry.

◆ They have formed the Fashion Center Business Improvement District (BID) to enhance the garment district.

National Trade Show

MAGIC, the Men's Apparel Guild in California has grown from a regional market to a national one. MAGIC produces the largest men's apparel trade show in the world with over 5000 brands and 60,000 buyers attending! The interesting thing is that it is no longer held in California and it is not held in a permanent mart. It takes place at the Las Vegas, Nevada, Convention Center each February and August. In 1995, MAGIC cooperated with *Women's Wear Daily* to show women's wear at the Las Vegas Hilton Hotel. The combined show is called WWD/MAGIC.

Regional Market Centers

Regional markets are used primarily by small store owners who have neither the time nor the money to travel to New York. Some of these regional markets have developed because the area is also a manufacturing center. Large buildings called *marts* have been built in these centers to house showrooms. These showrooms represent local manufacturers as well as representatives of manufacturers from all over the United States and foreign countries. Within the marts, showrooms are grouped according to category for the buyers' convenience. For example, men's furnishings showrooms may be grouped on one floor, women's lingerie on another, and so forth. Regional markets are known for moderate and budget apparel because of the needs of the stores that buy there. In the case of Las Vegas, however,

Aerial view of showrooms at MAGIC.
(Courtesy of the Men's Apparel Guild in California)

A seminar for buyers offered at the Dallas Apparel Mart.
(Courtesy of the Dallas Apparel Mart)

trade shows are held in the convention center or hotels, but there are no permanent fashion showrooms. The major regional centers are as follows:

Los Angeles   Los Angeles has become the nation's second largest fashion market center and is a showcase for California designers. First opened in 1964, the recently renovated 13-story, 5-building California Mart complex is the largest apparel mart in the United States with 1500 permanent showrooms housing 10,000 lines.

Dallas   The Dallas Apparel Mart is part of the Dallas Market Center Complex. Opened in 1964, the mart now has 1200 women's and children's showrooms and 300 men's wear showrooms. The Apparel Mart hosts the annual Dallas Fashion Awards each October.

Chicago   The Chicago Merchandise Mart, serving the Midwest, opened in 1977 and has approximately 800 permanent showrooms exhibiting 4000 lines.

Atlanta   The Atlanta Apparel Mart, which serves the Southeast, opened in 1979 and now houses 1200 permanent showrooms.

Miami   The Miami International Merchandise Mart, opened in 1968, has over 300 showrooms. Due to its strategic location, it has emerged as a wholesale center for the Americas, with many Latin-American and Caribbean buyers attending its 16 trade markets each year.

San Francisco   The Fashion Center, serving the northwest, is a 6-story, atrium-style building of 740,000 square feet. The center sponsors the Golden Shears Awards to bay area designers.

Other regional marts are the Denver Merchandise Mart, Colorado; the Carolina Trade Mart, Charlotte, North Carolina; the Miami Merchandise Mart, Florida; the Northest Trade Center, Woburn, Massachusetts; the Radisson Center, Minneapolis, Minnesota; and the Trade Center, Kansas City, Missouri.

All the regional fashion marts offer year-round market weeks, fashion shows, and educational seminars on subjects such as visual merchandising, management, and fashion show production. Other facilities include restaurants, auditoriums, hotels, hair salons, health clubs, printing services, and parking. To attract retailers and stimulate business, regional marts have developed aggressive new strategies. *Megamarts* (combined women's, men's, children's, and accessory markets) have been created for *crossover buying* so that buyers can make fewer or shorter trips to market and save travel costs. Other incentives include free or discounted hotel accommodations and air fares and more events throughout the year aimed at specific market niches.

DISTRIBUTION

Manufacturers decide on a distribution policy to ensure proper merchandising of their apparel and accessories.

Distribution Policy

Manufacturers' merchandise quality and prices must be at the proper level to attract their target customers and therefore certain types of retail stores. For example, manufacturers of designer fashion sell to better department stores and fine specialty shops. Manufacturers of moderate-priced apparel and accessories sell to a wider variety of department and specialty stores. Popular and budget-line manufacturers sell to discount and other price-oriented retailers.

The manufacturer must plan distribution so that (1) the proper stores buy the merchandise, (2) the merchandise is represented in desired geographical areas, (3) one store does not create unfair competition for another, and (4) the estimated business volume is obtained. The manufacturer may have an *open distribution* policy, selling to anyone who can pay for the goods (which is most common), or a *selected distribution* policy, limiting the number of stores in an area that may buy. When Giorgio Armani opened Armani Boutiques in West Germany, he took the Emporio Armani line away from 150 clients who had carried it before in order to keep his clothes more exclusive. Manufacturers such as Hermès and Chanel limit the actual number of garments or accessories that they produce and distribute in order to maintain exclusivity. Retailers often compete to be allowed to buy designer lines.

Brand Names

Brand names have become very important in the fashion business. *Brand names* identify products made by a particular manufacturer. Brand names must fit the image that the manufacturer wants to project, reflect the style and mood of the clothes, and appeal to the intended customer. The ultimate goal of the manufacturer is to establish the identity of a particular brand to such an extent that consumers prefer that brand compared to all others—a phenomenon sometimes referred to as *consumer franchising*. When this is achieved, brand name recognition and the resulting consumer demand almost dictate retail buying choices.

Retailers who wish to buy popular brands often must fulfill minimum-order requirements that are aimed at ensuring proper merchandising of the collection. Consumer franchising makes it difficult for other manufacturers in the same product area to compete, because retail budgets are already allocated to the popular producers. However, while the label is an element in the consumer's decision making, it has to be backed up by quality and value.

Manufacturers support *brand integrity* with quality control, licenses kept to a minimum for purposes of control, appropriate advertising campaigns, in-store fixtures to create a consistent image, and service to retailers and consumers. Successful manufacturers clearly identify and maintain a tight focus on their target customer and do not expand their scope beyond that image and what they can effectively manage and deliver.

Building a Brand or Designer Name

Manufacturers diversify to strengthen their brands and to build their businesses. First they make sure that they are focused on their target market and that their brand has a strong identity. There are several ways manufacturers can diversify. They can become multiproduct manufacturers, export their merchandise, or open their own retail stores.

Multiproducts

Manufacturers often add new lines in other categories to build their business.

◆ They may add secondary lines at lower prices, such as designer-label manufacturers who have added bridge lines. Almost all name women's wear designers have added them.

◆ A sportswear manufacturer may start a dress line, or vice versa; a woman's wear company might start a men's line or the opposite. Calvin Klein and Donna Karan, originally women's wear designers, have gone into men's wear; Ralph Lauren, first a men's wear designer, added women's wear.

◆ Manufacturers often add large sizes and/or petites to a missy size range. This is lucrative because new lines can be achieved by simply grading patterns to the new size ranges.

◆ Or they may branch out to include accessories in their product lines. Donna Karan, Liz Claiborne, Guess, and many other designer names and brands have added various accessories to complete their fashion statement.

As manufacturers grow into multiproduct companies, they have to be sure to stay focused on a particular target customer age range or life-style in order to retain brand integrity. They may oversee the manufacture of these new products themselves (as do Donna Karan, for domestic products, and Liz Claiborne) to maintain tight control over product and marketing or form joint ventures or licensing agreements.

Tommy Hilfiger at the launching of his new fragrance. *(Photographed by the author)*

Licensing

Licenses provide a means of diversification for the designer or brand without the risk of capital investment or the responsibility of production. Under licensing agreements, popular designers and brand-name manufacturers give other manufacturers permission to use their names and/or designs. For this the designer or brand name is paid a royalty, a percentage of wholesale sales.

Licenses make it possible for designers to produce a line of coats or accessories to complement and complete their fashion statement, things that they could not make in their own company for lack of expertise or capital. The licensee has expertise in production and marketing of a particular product but in exchange gets the designer image to trade on. The licenses are supported by brand name and designer advertising, and vice versa.

Anne Klein, Adrienne Vittadini, Ellen Tracy, and Nicole Miller license their names to produce accessories. There are a few designers who have hundreds of licenses; Pierre Cardin has 840, Yves St. Laurent has 200, while Karl Lagerfeld has only 30 and Nicole Miller a mere 15. Ralph Lauren licenses his women's wear collection, fragrances, eyewear, hosiery, leatherwear, Chaps men's wear, luggage, and handbags. Guess licenses watches, knitwear, eyewear, infant's wear, boy's wear, legwear, and shoes.

However, manufacturers are wary of indiscriminate licensing for a broad range of products because they must be careful to maintain control of design, quality, marketing, and image.

Joint ventures

Joint ventures are a form of partnership between designer or brand manufacturers and specialty producers. For example, a coat manufacturer and a designer could arrange a joint venture to produce that designer's coats. It is a give-and-take relationship in terms of merchandising and marketing the line. The designer has more control and the licensee has less risk since payment is usually on the basis of profits.

Exports

American manufacturers are slowly learning to be exporters. As domestic markets are not growing, it is one of the few ways to expand. Santo Versace, chairman of Gianni Versace SpA, Milan, advised, "Today it is essential to divide the risk among many markets."[1]

Exporting is a new idea for Americans, but as the value of the dollar has declined in international money markets, it has become a viable option. Opportunities exist selling apparel and accessories to overseas retailers or in opening stores abroad. Nicole Miller, for example, has opened boutiques in Canada, Mexico, Spain, Germany, and Brazil, some owned, some franchised.

However, while trade agreements are beginning to eliminate many barriers, manufacturers need to research to understand the foreign consumer, make connections with foreign sales agents or retailing experts, understand customs regulations, and deal with problems of currency fluctuations and credit. Many manufacturers would like more support from the U.S. Department of Commerce. Some designers and manufacturers use licensing as a way to reach certain countries where trade barriers exist and to use local production.

Manufacturers as Retailers

To enhance their image, to merchandise complete collections, to test new ideas, to build brand loyalty, and to expand their businesses, many manufacturers open their own retail stores. This is a fairly new idea in women's wear in the United States but not in Europe, where designers such as Giorgio Armani, Ferragamo, Chanel, or Laura Ashley have traditionally had their own retail stores. In the United States, vertical operations such as Brooks Brothers are fairly common in the men's wear field, and there are many vertical shoe companies, such as Bally or Johnston & Murphy, that operate chain stores. Today, more and more designers and popular brand manufacturers are opening retail stoes that carry only their lines. Firms such as Ralph Lauren, Anne Klein, Adrienne Vittadini, Nicole Miller, Liz Claiborne, Nike, Kenar, Esprit, and Osh Kosh B'Gosh have opened their own stores.

A.B.S., a California apparel manufacturer, has opened retail stores such as their South Beach store in Miami, Florida. *(Courtesy of A.B.S. Clothing Collection, Inc.)*

By having their own stores, these firms are able to sell directly to the consumer and therefore avoid wholesale markets. This arrangement affords the opportunity to display their total concept, including accessories, without having it edited by a buyer, thereby setting an example for retailers. However, most retailers are not pleased that they are in direct competition with their own suppliers.

Factory Outlet Stores

One of the fastest growing forms of retailing is *factory outlet stores*. Formerly the only retailing done by manufacturers, outlet stores were located at production facilities where they sold *overruns* (garments not purchased by a store) or *seconds* (garments with flaws). But now most of the merchandise is flawless, deep in size and selection. Outlet stores have opened around the country in specially created outlet malls. Retailers are naturally unhappy that their own suppliers are underselling them (see Chapter 13 for a complete discussion of retailing).

In-store Boutiques

Some designers are so popular that they are able to demand that their apparel and/or accessories be displayed in a specific strategic location with a prescribed decor. This "store within a store" concept gives the designer or brand prime retail space without having to administer a store. These designers or manufacturers may provide decor and fittings for the entire shop on a cooperative basis.

Catalog Sales

Certain manufacturers avoid retailers altogether by mailing their own catalogs directly to the public. Many manufacturers feel that catalog sales are the wave of the future due to today's busy life-styles, and traditional retailers are understandably threatened by them (see Chapter 13 for more information on catalogs as a retailing concept).

Other Forms of Distribution

Franchising

In a *franchising* agreement, a manufacturer sells the rights to retail a product or product line within an area. Manufacturers benefit from this arrangement because the product must be sold under the brand name and merchandised according to specifications that protect the manufacturer's image. Retailers benefit because they are guaranteed availability of stock and the right to use the brand name in advertising, supported by the manfuacturer's national advertising campaign. The store has no rights to selection from the line but must carry the entire range of merchandise. Escada of Germany, Hermès of France, and Nicole Miller of the United States franchise at least some of their stores.

Leased Departments

Manufacturers sometimes lease space in stores to sell their merchandise, although this practice is becoming rare. This arrangement requires no selling to a retail buyer. Leasing space is especially useful in retailing types of apparel and accessories that require salespeople with particular expertise. Fur, jewelry, and shoe manufacturers, for example, may lease departments because their sales staff must have special knowledge of their products.

Consignment Stores

Manufacturers may sell their merchandise on consignment. In this case, the retailer provides only floor space and personnel but accepts no risks for the merchandise. The merchandise is lent to the store, and the store pays only when the merchandise is sold. The manufacturer must take back any unsold merchandise and try to sell it elsewhere, which, of course, is very difficult. Consignment arrangements have been used by shops featuring new designers and by many vintage apparel stores.

Jobbers

In the fashion industry, merchandise is usually sold directly from manufacturers to retailers. The exception is the *jobber,* a middleman who buys goods from many manufacturers and resells them. These goods are usually overruns or markdowns bought at the end of a season at a large discount to clear the manufacturer's warehouse (especially if the manufacturer does not have an outlet store). Ellen Tracy executive Jay Margolis, commented that, "Jobbers are necessary to the industry because they clean up distribution."[2] They may sell in volume to small retailers or sell to the public in their own outlet stores.

SALES PROMOTION

Manufacturers use sales promotion to make their merchandise known to prospective retail buyers and to the public.

Effective sales promotion can often mean the difference between success and failure. Promotional efforts can take the form of publicity, advertising, and other aids that manufacturers make available to retailers who buy their products.

Collection and Market Week Promotion

The extensive arrangements for collection and market openings are handled by a press attaché, a public relations consultant, or a trade association. For major collections, invitations are sent to journalists the world over, as well as to the designer or manufacturer's best customers. A "run of show" (numbered list of models to be shown) is given out at the show. After the shows and market week, a *dossier* or press kit is prepared and sent to each journalist. The kit includes photographs and sketches of a few pieces from the collection, a press release or analysis of the collection, and perhaps a biography of the designer.

With so many lines for buyers to remember, manufacturers often use gimmicks such as distinctive invitations or souvenirs to draw attention to their product. Promotional items such as shopping bags or T-shirts with the manufacturer's name on them can serve as walking advertisements.

Major fashion shows are very costly ventures. It costs Anne Klein approximately $150,000 to present a seasonal collection to buyers and the press. Typical expenses include 22 models for a full day at $90,000; lighting, set design, and videotaping at $22,000; accessories at $10,000; rental of the facility at $10,000; hairstylist and two assistants at $6000; music at $2500; two makeup artists and two assistants at $6000; and invitations, postage, and programs at $4000.[3] As a result, some designers are making their shows less extravagant or showing only in their own showrooms.

Publicity

Publicity is information given to the public regarding products, policies, personnel, activities, or services. Fashion manufacturers use in-house public relations or publicity staffs, consultants, or agencies to create publicity material and obtain *editorial coverage* of their collections in newspapers, magazines, and on television. Fashion editors of publications and television choose the material for their articles from information and photographs sent to them by the manufacturers. The manufacturers do not have to pay for this coverage.

Advertisers are putting more pressure on publications for editorial coverage. "All things being equal, if we are looking at two items that are equally available nationally, if one of them is an advertiser, we'd use it," says Kimberly Bonnell, *Glamour's* senior fashion editor. Designer Michael Kors explains why editorial coverage is so important, "Advertising establishes your image, but editorial is *it* for prestige—and sales."[4]

Fashion programs on television are also an opportunity for designers to get publicity. "Style with Elsa Klensch" on CNN, Jeanne Becker on VH-1's "FT-Fashion Television" from Canada, and MTV's "House of Style" with Cindy Crawford offer various approaches of giving free publicity to designers and brands. TV events, such as the Academy Awards, also give exposure to the designers of the stars.

Advertising

Advertising is the planning, writing, producing, and scheduling of paid announcements designed to attract potential customers' attention to the manufacturer's merchandise. Manufacturers have in-house staffs or hire outside agencies or consultants to develop and produce advertising campaigns. Large manufacturers of apparel, hosiery, and shoes advertise their brand names nationally or globally. Advertising budgets are usually 2 to 3 percent of projected business volume.[5]

Media

Manufacturers use both trade and consumer media, thereby reaching both markets. They may use traditional print such as newspapers and magazines. Ralph Lauren, for example, uses full-cover multipage ads in both trade and consumer magazines in order to achieve *brand name saturation*.

Television has become increasingly important as an advertising medium for the manufacturer. Television ads, too, are frequently repeated.

A Max Mara advertisement. *(Courtesy of Dente & Christina Associates, Inc.)*

Designers and brands are also advertised in bus shelters. Resourcefully, Emporio Armani is advertising on London Underground tickets! Catalogs are also used as an advertising vehicle.

Image Advertising

Designers and manufacturers may use *image advertising* to make the consumer aware of their names or brands. Image advertising tries to capture the spirit of the product and build brand identity. Companies such as Calvin Klein, Donna Karan's DKNY, Banana Republic, and Guess spend millions of dollars each year on image advertising.

Fashion changes so quickly that it is often impossible to produce an ad for a specific style for national media. In addition, since each store carries different styles from any one line, it may be impossible to advertise one specific style for all stores.

Item Advertising

When *item advertising* is desired, manufacturers choose one outstanding style from their collection to picture in an ad. With image advertisements, they are able to see direct sales response. Dana Buchman, for example, advertises an item twice a year.[6] Levi Strauss advertises just one style of jean.

Cooperative Advertising

Many manufacturers cooperate financially with textile producers and retailers on advertisements in order to make the public more aware of brand names. Manufacturers offer to share costs with retailers who advertise their styles. Manufacturers' ads may also be funded by textile producers if their fibers or fabrics are used. Textile and apparel manufacturers' co-op allocations may provide a retailer with up to 50 percent of its media costs. The cooperative ads carry the names and *logos* (brand or store symbols) of each contributing company.

Photographers and Models

Fashion photographers such as Irving Penn, Steven Meisel, and Bruce Weber and popular models including Claudia Schiffer, Linda Evangelista, and Cindy Crawford have commanded huge sums of money to help shape company images. Models such as Lauren Hutton and Carmen are now being used to project the image of older consumers. Karl Lagerfeld commented that, "Each one with his [or her] own personality helped to shape the visual image of today's fashion."[7]

Other Promotional Aids to Retailers

Manufacturers often provide retailers with aids that they can use in their advertising, publicity, and public relations. Each manufacturer constantly tries to develop more selling and promotional tools. A manufacturer may offer one or more of the following to stores that purchase its merchandise.

Personal Appearances.   Many designers make personal appearances at retail stores at the beginning of the major seasons to draw crowds. The appearance may be accompanied by a fashion show, talk, and/or luncheon.

Designer Trunk Shows.   This is a similar idea to the personal appearance, but in this case the designer brings the entire collection. Trunk shows are hard work but very successful, because the line is not edited by a buyer. There is direct payback because customers can order garments in their own size immediately after a fashion show. Small manufacturers who cannot afford national advertising have found this method to be very profitable for them. There are even some couturiers trying this and arranging for fittings to be done in the stores. Philippe Venet travels to New York regularly, where he shows his designs to private customers by appointment and then returns to Paris to make the clothes in his own ateliers.

In-store Clinics.   Many manufacturers have discovered that their merchandise sells better if it is thoroughly explained to both salespeople and store customers. Therefore, the designer or a manufacturer's representative may visit stores to train and educate the sales associates and/or the customers with demonstrations, slides, and a talk.

Merchandise Representatives.   Because manufacturers feel that stores have failed in their responsibility to train sales associates properly, some have hired consultants to work in the retail store. Some work exclusively for a large store, while others are regional merchandisers servicing a cluster of stores in a particular area. Anne Klein calls them "retail sales executives,"

Ellen Tracy's are "retail merchandisers," JH Collectibles has "merchandise coordinators," and Liz Claiborne calls them "selling specialists." They are trained by the manufacturer to educate both sales associates and customers on how the line should be merchandised, worn, and accessorized. They also check to see that merchandise is displayed properly. They are in the position to give feedback to the manufacturer on competitive lines and customer reactions. It is very costly to maintain these consultants and some manufacturers have cut back on this program.

Videos.   Another trend in fashion promotion and training is to show the collection on video. Specific videos for training purposes demonstrate selling techniques and how pieces work together. Couturiers send videos to their best customers. Accessory firms use videos to show customers in a retail store how to drape a scarf or wear a hat.

Image Books.   Another way to communicate an image, these booklets are mini catalogs that try to give a unique impression of a collection. They may be distributed to retailers, the press, and customers. Dana Buchman and Adrienne Vittadini offer *look books* for customers and/or sales associates to learn about the product and how pieces work together. Depending on the size and number of books sent out, which can be anywhere from 5000 to 250,000 per season, image books cost between $40,000 and $100,000 to produce.

Display Fixtures.   Manufacturers sometimes provide stores with fixtures to enhance visual merchandising. Ellen Tracy, for example, offers stores an *enhancement package*, including mannequins and signing.

Pages from an Adrienne Vittadini Look Book for customers and sales associates to learn how pieces from the collection work together.
(Courtesy of Adrienne Vittadini and Dente & Christina Associates, Inc.)

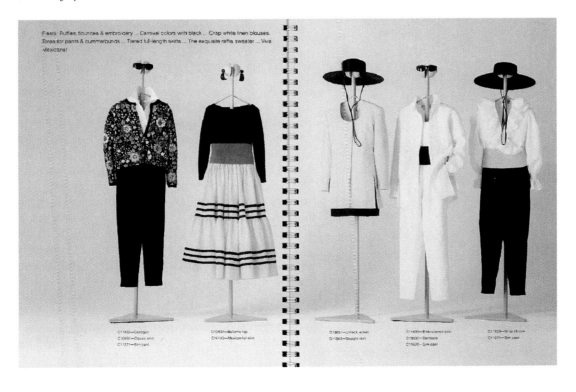

Radio Scripts and TV Commercials. Stores can "tag" media spots provided by the manufacturer with their own names and run them in their local areas.

Glossy Photographs. Photographs of merchandise may be provided to stores to be used for publicity or advertisements. Couturiers also send photographs, sketches, and swatches to their best customers.

Statement Enclosures. Mailing pieces can be provided for stores to send to customers in their monthly mailings.

Hang Tags. To help carry out a designer or brand image, a manufacturer's advertising department or agency may create consistent packaging, including hang tags for their garments or accessories.

Ralph and Ricki Lauren at the CFDA Awards Gala at Lincoln Center, New York City. *(Courtesy of the Council of Fashion Designers of America)*

Associations That Promote Fashion

Trade associations support manufacturers in promoting particular segments of the industry. The American Apparel Manufacturers Association (AAMA), the Council of Fashion Designers of America (CFDA), the Fashion Footwear Association of New York (FFANY), and the Fashion Association (TFA) are examples of the specialized organizations that exist.

The Fashion Group International, Inc., founded in 1931, fosters the careers of women in the industry. Primarily promotional and educational in purpose, it now has over 6000 members with regional chapters in 33 American cities and nine foreign countries.

Fashion Awards

Fashion awards presented by various organizations generate interest in fashion because of the publicity they create.

The Council of Fashion Designers of America presents annual awards in a mimimum of four categories: men's, women's, accessories, and the Perry Ellis Award for new fashion talent. The winners are chosen by a committee of fashion editors and retailers. The CFDA has also organized "7th on Sale" to raise money to fight AIDS. Held every other year, this event took place in New York in 1990 and 1995 and in San Francisco in 1992.

The Dallas Fashion Awards, which began in 1976 as a local awareness program, evolved into a recognition ceremony to honor American designers. Three designers are nominated in many categories and then national retailers can vote for the winners by mail. At the awards dinner, which is a charity benefit, a Fashion Excellence Award is presented to an outstanding figure in retailing.

SELLING

Management and sales representatives carry out the activity of selling fashion merchandise to retail buyers.

In a manufacturer-retailer relationship, the manufacturer is often referred to as the *vendor*. The vendor sales team of management and sales representatives must communicate design and merchandising concepts to retailers. They are also doing more and more *pre-merchandise planning* for each separate account so that the line or collection looks different at each retailer. Vendors recommend what part of the line should be purchased on the basis of the store's image, customers, and needs. Manufacturers often hire retailers to help them give guidance as to distribution.

The sales team can give feedback to the manufacturer's design and merchandising departments regarding retail needs and line evaluation.

There are two basic ways of selling fashion merchandise to retail stores: corporate selling and selling through sales representatives.

Corporate Selling

Most major vendors, including designer companies and large moderate-priced manufacturers, no longer have sales representatives. Fashion distribution to large store chains and groups has become so complex and so important to volume sales that the selling is now done *management to management*. The actual selling at this level is not as important as maintaining consistency of product and a good relationship with the store. Manufacturers and retailers are trying to build partnerships to help each other do better business.

Sales Representatives

Some companies still employ sales representatives ("reps") to call on specialty stores who do not have the time or money to travel to New York. Sales reps are salaried or paid on a commission basis ranging from 5 to 10 percent, paid on orders actually shipped to and accepted by the stores. Most commissioned representatives pay all their own expenses, including part of showroom or market costs, which can run as high as one-third of their income. Independent sales reps carry several small, noncompeting lines. Sales representatives belong to associations that sponsor market weeks and provide other services.

After a line release, sales reps receive duplicate samples and take the line on the road to market weeks around the country and to towns and cities within their assigned geographical territories. The rep usually sets up a presentation in a mart showroom or centrally located hotel room where buy-

A sales rep presenting her line to a buyer. *(Courtesy of Bergdorf Goodman)*

ers from the area can come to see the line. To win new accounts or to introduce a new line, reps have to seek out buyers, because the buyers rarely have time to look for new resources themselves.

Selling Incentives

Retailers look for manufacturers whose styling, quality, and dependability they can trust and from whom they can expect the same level of styling season after season. Retailers expect the following:

◆ Consistent quality

◆ Continuity of styles (a guarantee that all styles ordered will be produced)

◆ On-time deliveries (buyers are shopping later and yet expecting prompt deliveries)

◆ Value

◆ Reorder performance (manufacturer is able to fill reorders when needed)

However, styling, value, quality, and on-time deliveries are often not enough. As there are less and less retailers controlling retail distribution, they have become more demanding with non-key vendors, insisting on contributions for markdowns, advertising, and promotions. The manufacturer may offer or the retailer may demand one or more of the following:

◆ Incentive pricing (to allow for greater profit margins)

◆ Off-price or promotional goods (special buys at low prices, usually offered as a preselected package)

◆ Credit

- ◆ Markdown allowances (credit on goods that had to be marked down)
- ◆ Exchange or return privileges (allowing a retailer to return any unsold garments for credit or a refund)
- ◆ A discount of 8 percent if bills are paid on time (taken even if they pay late)
- ◆ Cooperative advertising allowances
- ◆ Promotional aids such as in-store clinics, designer trunk shows, and brochures
- ◆ Assistance in reordering (for those firms that reorder, reorder forms or direct reordering contact via electronic-data-processing terminals may be supplied)
- ◆ Customer service is usually provided by manufacturers to follow up on orders and ensure customer satisfaction. Liz Claiborne, for example, has 95 customer-service telephone operators who field questions from retailers.

COMPUTER-AIDED MARKETING AND DISTRIBUTION

As we have seen at every level of the industry, computers have become indispensable in marketing and distributing fashion.

Manufacturer-Retailer Relationships

There has been a breakdown in the traditional buy-sell relationship between retailers and manufacturers. Due to competition from imports and declining apparel sales in general, manufacturers and retailers are learning to work together to share risk and information on forecasting, product development, production scheduling, and distribution. They are using Quick Response and electronic data interchange (see Chapter 2) strategies to develop partnerships to exchange information and to quickly adapt to changes in the marketplace.

Sales

Electronic data interchange can automatically put through a purchase-order transaction from retailer to vendor. Through computer networks, orders can be entered via telephone from anywhere in the world. The sales manager can use networks to communicate with salespeople in the field. The computer can instantly report on what is in stock and what delivery dates a customer can expect based on the information that it has sorted and filed.

Customer Service

Computer technology also helps the customer service department follow up on a sale by automatically printing invoices, handling reorders, and even premarking for retailers. It keeps track of shipments and adjusts inventory records automatically. Some manufacturers use round-the-clock merchandise information systems (MIS) that provide up-to-the-minute reports of what is selling and what is not throughout the country. Liz Claiborne, for example, calls theirs *System Updated Retail Feedback* (SURF). This system enables the company to continuously monitor selling patterns and alter production accordingly.

Sales Analysis

At the end of a season, merchandisers and sales managers use computer sales records to compare actual sales figures with the original plan to see if sales and profit goals were met. These records also give merchandisers and designers specific information on what colors, styles, fabrications, and price ranges sold best, which helps them plan future lines.

SUMMARY

The retailer and the manufacturer, who traditionally represent two separate businesses, communicate through wholesale markets. Fashion showings and markets are held in market centers all year long around the world.

Brands and designers expand their businesses by adding product lines, exporting, and opening retail stores. Manufacturers have various distribution policies to ensure that their goods are merchandised properly. Many offer incentives to retailers to buy their merchandise. They also use publicity, advertising, and other promotional aids to foster sales.

Computer technology has helped suppliers, manufacturers, and retailers to form partnerships to try to speed turnaround time for production and distribution and keep records of inventory and sales.

The final test for fashion merchandise is whether the consumer buys it at the retail level. Each season brings a new chance for success or failure. No wonder the apparel industry is a competitive and often nerve-racking business.

CHAPTER REVIEW

Terms and Concepts

Briefly identify and discuss the following terms and concepts:

1. Markets
2. Line release
3. Commissionaires
4. IGEDO
5. MAGIC
6. Showrooms
7. Marts
8. Selected distribution policy
9. Corporate selling
10. Brand integrity
11. Licensing
12. Franchising
13. Factory outlet stores
14. Overruns
15. Jobbers
16. Trunk shows
17. Cooperative advertising
18. Image advertising
19. Brand-name saturation
20. Look books
21. Merchandise representatives
22. Enhancement packages
23. MIS

Questions for Review

1. What role do wholesale fashion markets play?
2. Name five important international apparel or accessories markets or fairs and their location.
3. Name five important international designer collections and the cities where they are shown.
4. What are two regulations regarding couture showings?
5. Why did regional, national, and international fashion markets develop?
6. How does the presentation of a high-priced collection differ from that of a moderate- or low-priced line?
7. Explain the difference between open and selected distribution policies.
8. How and why do manufacturers diversify?
9. Why should the American apparel industry concentrate more on exports?
10. How do manufacturers act as retailers?
11. List five promotional aids that manufacturers offer to retailers.
12. Explain how computer technology aids marketing.

Projects for Additional Learning

1. Analyze the imported fashion merchandise and accessories at a large retail store. Make a list of the countries represented and the merchandise specialty of each.
2. Ask a local buyer if you can sit in when a sales representative shows a line. Is the line presented in groups? Did the sales rep pre-merchandise the line in terms of the store's needs? Do you feel that the line is successful? Why? Summarize your findings in a written report.
3. Sell the line you designed in Chapter 9 to your class, explaining its concepts and features.

NOTES

[1] "The Big Boom," *Focus on Italy Supplement, Women's Wear Daily*, January 1994, p. 6.

[2] Jay Margolis, president and CEO, Tommy Hilfiger, interview, February 1995.

[3] Nancy Lueck, Anne Klein, interview, March 1993.

[4] As quoted by Teri Agins, "Editorial Plugs for Apparel Are in Style," *Wall Street Journal*, October 6, 1992, p. B-1.

[5] Jessica Mitchell, interview, March 1995.

[6] Gail Cook, president and CEO, Dana Buchman, interview, April 1995.

[7] As quoted by Lisa Lockwood, "Fashion's Top Photographers," *Women's Wear Daily*, March 27, 1992, p. 12.

Part Four

FASHION RETAILING

Part Four, the last section of this book, covers all aspects of fashion retailing. It is important to have read Chapters 2, 3, 8, and 12 before reading these chapters. Chapter 13 discusses retailing centers, types of retailing, and retail organizations. Chapter 14 deals with retail merchandising and all aspects of buying and selling fashion. Chapter 15 examines fashion promotion, including advertising, publicity, special events, and visual merchandising. With this section, the book completes its cycle of fashion—from concept to consumer.

Bergdorf Goodman on Fifth Avenue in New York City.
(Courtesy of Bergdorf Goodman)

13

RETAIL STORES

CAREER FOCUS

Retail store line management begins with a chief executive officer (CEO), director of stores, individual store managers, floor and area managers, department managers, and their assistants. Retailing careers are also possible in mail order, computer electronics, and television. Merchandising positions will be discussed in Chapter 14.

CHAPTER OBJECTIVES

After reading this chapter you should have attained competence in the following areas:

1. Understanding of today's retail situation and trends
2. Ability to discuss the various types of retail stores
3. Knowledge of the organizational differences between single-unit and multiple-unit stores
4. Identification of major international stores and famous shopping areas
5. Ability to compare the organizational structure of a small store with that of a large store
6. Appreciation of the growing importance of non-store retailing
7. Awareness of how a store's fashion image is conveyed to consumer groups and manifested in store policies

*R*etailing is the link between the manufacturer and the consumer. Retailers buy fashion merchandise from *vendors*, their suppliers, all over the world and bring it to their stores for convenient selling to consumers. There are nearly 2 million retail firms throughout the United States alone. About 135,000 of these retailers specialize in fashion apparel and accessories; another 70,000 include some apparel and accessories among their merchandise. True success in the fashion business is finally achieved at the retail level by consumer acceptance measured in purchases.

Many factors go into the making of a successful retail store: good management, a convenient location, a pleasant atmosphere, exciting and appropriate stock, buyers with an understanding of customer needs, helpful salespeople, and customer service. The first half of this chapter examines the current retail situation, global retailing, types of fashion retail stores, non-store retailing, and the organization of single- and multiple-unit stores. The end of the chapter covers marketing and the establishment of a retailer's fashion image.

THE RETAILING PICTURE

Enormous changes have occurred in retailing methods, management, and ownership, which will have long range implications for retailing.

The Growth of Consumer Credit

In the 1970s and 1980s, demographics were favorable for retailing, particularly with the influx of women into the work force. The growth of consumer credit, formerly limited to department store charge accounts, and the proliferation of credit cards fostered the growth of retailing. As Leslie Wexner, chairman of the Limited, explained, "Consumers were energized because they not only had the desire to buy, but the capacity to spend."[1]

Retail Bankruptcies and Consolidations

Retailers, too, took on debt to expand operations, through internal growth or by acquisition of other companies, only to discover, when the recession of the early 1990s hit and sales declined, that many did not have enough money to both repay their debts and operate their businesses. Retailers also incurred debt with *leveraged buyouts* in order to transfer control back into private hands. Highly leveraged retailers found it necessary to sell off some of their acquisitions to pay off their debts, were forced into bankruptcy (and had to be restructured), or went out of business.

Across the country, once solid companies have closed their doors, been purchased by other companies, or forced to consolidate. Since 1980, long-established retailers such as Abraham & Straus, B. Altman, Bonwit Teller,

Frederick & Nelson, Garfinkel's, Gimbel's, I. Magnin, and many others have either been acquired and absorbed by other retailers or have closed due to heavy debt, poor management, fierce competition, and/or a poor understanding of their changing customers. Macy's was the third national retailer in a three-year period to seek protection under bankruptcy law; it was then acquired by Federated Department Stores, itself in recovery from near bankruptcy. Many retailers are still consolidating and restructuring and do not know what the future holds.

Too Many Stores

In spite of bankruptcies and consolidations, there are still too many stores for the number of consumers! While there are fewer retail names, there is an increasing number of stores. In the 1970s there was an estimated 7 square feet of retail selling space for every person in the United States; today there are 18 square feet per person.[2] The big are getting bigger. Large chains such as Wal-Mart, the Gap, and Nordstrom keep opening new stores. Allen Questrom, CEO of Federated, observed, "Stores are trying to deal with a highly competitive marketplace with more supply than demand."[3]

Retail Strategies for the End of the Century

Retailers are taking various approaches to compete in the 1990s. Four of these directions seem to be the most successful: value, service, uniqueness, and entertainment. To be successful and improve *productivity* (sales per square foot), a retailer must create a competitive advantage and set itself apart by offering something special.

Value-directed Retailing

After the excesses of the 1980s, the 1990s are often referred to as the *value decade*. Consumers look for value, convenience, and fair prices. Value-oriented retailers include discounters, outlet stores, warehouse clubs, or any retailer where customers feel they are getting their money's worth, whatever the price points.

Jay Margolis, at Ellen Tracy, remarked that "The impact of discounters such as Wal-Mart on retailing has taught us that, while excitement may come from designer merchandise, sales are at lower prices."[4] Bob Connolly, senior vice-president of apparel merchandising at Montgomery Ward, feels that "The winning retailer in the 90s has the proper price/value and assortment relationship. [Retailers] must give the customers what they want, where they want it, when they want it, at a price they think is fair."[5] To have a consistent pricing policy, retailers are attempting to reduce expenses and become efficient in order to keep prices down.

Service-oriented Retailing

Retailers are attempting to become *consumer driven* (to anticipate and focus on the needs of their customers); in fact, to exceed customer's expectations. They are trying to make shopping more convenient and friendly so that customers will enjoy shopping. Many retailers are using capital investments to renovate existing units to create a warm, friendly atmosphere. This service includes maintaining in-depth stock. Service-oriented retailers include Nordstrom, Wal-Mart, and many mail-order retailers such as L. L. Bean and Lands' End (see Customer Service, Chapter 14).

Unique Merchandising

With so much consolidation, uniqueness is often lost because many retailers carry merchandise from the same large apparel manufacturers as only the large manufacturers can supply large chains. Some large stores, such as the May Company, are limiting buying to core vendors only. Many experts believe that as department stores narrow their vendor structures the stores will become too mainstream and boring for their fashion-conscious customers. This may be a boost to designer stores and to small specialty stores that carry merchandise from small manufacturers. Retailers are trying to find new ways to provide unique merchandising (see Chapter 14).

Shopping as Entertainment

In an effort to keep stores alive, many retailers are trying to restore an important aspect of nineteenth-century retailing. Early department stores were so exciting that people went there not only to see but to be seen. Retailers hope to add that excitement back into today's stores. Stores are adding live music, personal appearances, and special events to draw customers. Macy's is one of New York City's foremost tourist attractions, as is Nike Town in Chicago. Entertainment may make it worthwhile for people to come into the stores, but then the merchandise has to be enticing enough to buy.

Global Expansion

Just as globalization has affected manufacturing, many retailers feel that one way to increase market share is through global expansion. Many European firms have stores in the United States. Companies such as Benetton of Italy and Escada of Germany have found the size of the American market attractive and therefore have opened shops here.

Americans are following suit. Since Europe's economic integration in 1992, some American retailers have found that market too enticing to resist with its 325 million inhabitants. Levi Strauss has opened a store in London. The Gap has stores in the United Kingdom and France. Several American designers, such as Donna Karan, have stores in Europe. There is an American Store in the Petrovsky passage in Moscow. Saks Fifth Avenue plans expansion in Europe and Japan.

Japan has already attracted several American retailers, such as Barney's, Brooks Brothers, Talbots, Ralph Lauren, and Charivari. Brooks Brothers has 31 freestanding or in-store shops in Japan.

Closer to home, J. C. Penney, Dillard's, Sears, Price Club, and Wal-Mart are expanding in Mexico. Wal-Mart is opening warehouse clubs in a joint venture with Cifra, Mexico's largest retailer.

In addition to opening stores in other countries, companies are investing in foreign retailing businesses. Marks & Spencer of the United Kingdom owns Brooks Brothers, Aquascutum in the United Kingdom is owned by

Galaries Lafayette in Paris has branches in New York and Singapore.
(Courtesy of Galaries Lafayette)

Renown of Japan, and so on. Most retailers feel that globalization is the only way to survive in the future.

Retailing's Roots in the Cities

Most of the world's top retail stores began in manufacturing and marketing centers such as Paris, London, Tokyo, Rome, Milan, or New York. Certain city streets or areas have become famous for shopping: Fifth Avenue and Madison Avenue in New York City; Oak Street in Chicago; the Union Square area in San Francisco; Rodeo Drive in Beverly Hills; the Faubourg St. Honoré, Avenue Montaigne, Boulevard Haussmann, Rue de Passy, les Halles, and the St. Germain district in Paris; Via Condotti in Rome; Via della Spiga and Via Monte Napoleone in Milan; the Roppomgi and Harajuku districts in Tokyo; and Regent Street, Bond Street, and Knightsbridge in London. Most *flagship* stores, the first or main store of a chain, have remained in the cities and new ones have been added.

In Europe, cities have continued to be the centers of fashion retailing. To further encourage shoppers, many streets have been closed to automobile traffic, creating pleasant walkways between shops. In the United States, there has also been renewed interest in redeveloping retail potential in the cities. Many cities are conducting revitalization projects, including the refurbishing of older department and specialty stores. As a further development, malls have come to American cities. Among these are vertical malls, such as Trump Tower and A & S Plaza in New York City, Water Tower Place in Chicago, and the San Francisco Centre.

Suburban Shopping Centers

The shopping centers that now line many of the world's highways developed as a result of the increase in suburban living, especially the use of automobiles, that followed World War II and have since been fostered by real estate developers. The shopping center was followed by the development of the mall, the closed mall, and finally the regional closed mall.

The rest of the world has followed America's lead in creating shopping centers. The United States now has the most centers, followed by Canada, Australia, England, France, Germany, Sweden, and Switzerland. Approximately 35,000 shopping centers and 1800 larger regional malls account for nearly half of the retail sales in the United States.[6] According to the *Guinness Book of Records*, the West Edmonton Mall in Alberta is the largest shopping mall in the world, with 5.2 million square feet and over 800 stores, including 10 major department stores.[7] Sally Frame Kasaks, CEO of Ann Taylor, points out that "a mall is like a department store, all the specialty stores within it create the same thing."[8]

Traditional Malls

The traditional mall is anchored by at least two department stores with many other small specialty stores. However, with the success of discount stores such as Wal-Mart, many new malls and floundering older malls are using Wal-Mart, K-Mart, Price Club, and other discounters as their *anchors*.

Europa Boulevard, West Edmonton Mall, Alberta, Canada.
(Courtesy of West Edmonton Mall)

A view of the Mall of America, Bloomington, Minnesota. *(Courtesy of Mall of America)*

Diversified Malls

A mall may be diversified with both discount and moderate specialty stores. Ted Kraus, president of TKO, a shopping center management company, explains that "There's a remerchandising of regional malls going on. You may have a mall with a Macy's wing, where you'll have upper-middle merchandise, but at the other end you'll have a Wal-Mart with lower-end stores."[9]

Value Centers

Another type of mall is the value retail center. These malls or strip shopping centers, made up entirely of discount stores, are growing in numbers, size, and popularity. When South Hills Mall in Poughkeepsie, New York, faced overwhelming competition from the new Poughkeepsie Galleria, they decided to convert into a discount center. Now, says U.S. Mall Manager John Mannix, "the customers who visit the Galleria walk around, they ooh and aah, they have their Slurpee at the food court, and then they come to our mall to shop."[10]

Outlet Malls

Manufacturers' outlet stores, formerly located near manufacturing facilities, are now all over the country in specially created outlet malls. Consumers travel to out of the way areas such as Flemington, New Jersey; Boaz, Alabama; Rockford, Michigan; and Freeport, Maine, specifically to shop at their outlet store centers, which have grown up in areas with lower property values, away from traditional department and specialty stores to avoid competition with their own retail customers. The Mills Corporation has the largest individual malls, such as Sawgrass Mills, near Fort Lauderdale, Florida, with approximately 290 stores. Areas such as Orlando, Florida, or Reading, Pennsylvania, have become large outlet shopping centers because they have several outlet malls (see Chapter 12 for more information on outlet stores).

Recreational Malls

Competition has caused some malls to provide entertainment to draw customers and capitalize on the recreational aspects of shopping. Malls are becoming the new amusement parks. The West Edmonton Mall in Alberta incorporates an amusement park, an ice arena, a deep-sea theme park, a golf course, 19 movie theaters, and 110 restaurants and snack bars! The Mall of America in Bloomington, Minnesota, includes 14 movie theaters, an indoor theme park, a roller coaster, and a miniature golf course. At Forum Shops Mall in Las Vegas, Caesars Palace Casino is the anchor usually provided by a large department store. Henry Gluck, chairman of Caesars World, Inc., says, "Our thinking is that in the future, our best competition will be people with more bells and whistles. Just having good prices is not enough."[11]

TYPES OF RETAIL OPERATIONS

Many types of retail operations are continually created to try to serve customers' needs.

To attract customers, a store's image and merchandise offering must appeal to their customers' life-styles or shopping needs. The many different kinds of retail operations to fill these needs include specialty stores, department stores, mass merchants, and nonstore retailers. There are many overlaps among categories, and even retail experts do not agree on how to categorize stores. Retailing is continually evolving; new categories are emerging and old ones are combining.

Specialty Stores

Specialty stores cater to a particular target customer by providing a *narrow focus* or single product category for specific tastes. Specialty retailers carrying just one category of merchandise are called *single-line* stores; those carrying related categories of merchandise are called *limited-line* stores. The limited-line retailer may cater only to men, women, teens, children, the professional woman, the sports enthusiast, or large sizes—the possibilities are unlimited. Single-line stores may carry only shoes or just socks! Most specialty shops buy merchandise within a certain price range as well as in a specific category.

In Europe, specialty stores have continually predominated in fashion retailing. Examples of international specialty stores are Harvey Nichols, Brown's, and Joseph in London; Le Bon Marché and Franck et Fils in Paris; and the traditional small designer shops of Paris, Milan, Florence, and Rome.

Leading multibrand fashion specialty stores across North America include Barney's, Bergdorf Goodman, Saks Fifth Avenue, Charivari, Halls of Kansas City, Holt Renfrew in Canada, Neiman Marcus, based in Dallas, Saks Fifth Avenue, and Ultimo of Chicago. There are also many single-designer specialty stores, both European and American, such as Hermès, Christian Dior, Yves St. Laurent's Rive Gauche, Donna Karan, and Nicole Miller. Many specialty stores, such as The Gap, Ann Taylor, Talbots, the Limited, Gantos, Georgiou, and the Fashion Bug (Charming Shoppes), have added more and more stores and have grown into chains. Ann Taylor has over 275 stores; The Gap operates over 1500 stores worldwide (1384 in the United States), including Gap Kids and Banana Republic. Bud Konheim, CEO of Nicole Miller Ltd., remarked, "There's a Gap on almost every street corner."[12]

Small specialty stores are having a difficult time trying to compete in the 1990s. While they have emphasized personal relations with their customers in the past, today's busy consumer does not have the time to spend hours trying on clothes. Many observers say that the needs of today's customers are not satisfied by the small specialty store that does not have the assortment that a Neiman Marcus or a Saks Fifth Avenue has and that has never lent itself to browsing. On the other hand, the small specialty store may be the only avenue left for the unique fashion made by small manufacturers.

Deep Niche Retailing

There has been a trend toward *deep niche retailing*, more single-line stores that carry only one category of merchandise, in order to obtain dominance in a classification. These stores offer deep inventories of their specific merchandise focus. They may sell only accessories, or only athletic shoes, or ties, or socks! This development is reminiscent of early retailing when consumers went to individual stores for specific needs.

Private Label Retailers

Retailers such as The Gap, Ann Taylor, and Episode are called *private label merchants* because they produce their own clothing, which is sold under the store's name. Ann Taylor, Brooks Brothers, and The Gap are examples of retailers who have established the store's name as an important brand. Corresponding merchants in Europe include Marks & Spencer and Et Vous. Private-label retailers maintain their own design departments or use the services of design studios, such as Mast Industries in Boston or Dominique Peclers in Paris, to design their lines. These retailers usually contract production of their product or may establish joint ventures with factories (see Chapter 14 for more information on private-label merchandising).

Secondary Spin-offs. To please value-oriented customers, several private-label retailers have opened new stores that feature lower-priced lines. The Gap has started a chain called the Old Navy Clothing Company and Ann Taylor is testing a new Loft division.

The Gap is a private-label retailer. *(Courtesy of the Gap)*

Department Stores

The term *department store* comes from the practice of presenting many different kinds of merchandise, each in a separate department. Apparel and accessories for men, women, and children are sold along with household goods such as furniture, lamps, linens, and tableware. The government defines a department store as one that employs at least 25 people and sells three categories of general merchandise: apparel and accessories, home furnishings, and household linens. The traditional definition changed when most stores dropped appliances, toys, and other products that are now handled by individual specialty stores. Department stores usually concentrate 70 to 80 percent of their merchandise in the moderate to upper-moderate price ranges.

Internationally, Seibu in Japan claims to be the biggest department store in the world. GUM in Moscow is the largest in Eastern Europe, Harrod's of London is the biggest in Europe, and Macy's (now part of Federated Department Stores) the largest in the United States. Other leading international department stores include Liberty and Selfridges in London; Galeries Lafayette and Printemps in Paris; Rinascente in Italy; KaDeWe, Karstadt, and Kaufhof in Germany; Matsuzokaya, Mitsukoshi, and Isetan in Japan; and Eaton's in Canada. Well-known American department stores include Bloomingdale's, Strawbridge & Clothier, Hecht, Marshall Field's, Rich's, Dillard's, Bullock's, the May Company, and J. C. Penney. Some researchers also categorize the large specialty stores, such as Nordstrom or Neiman Marcus, as department stores because they carry multiple categories.

Originally, department stores dominated the American center city retail scene and later served as the anchors and magnets that made regional malls successful. However, department stores have suffered from overexpansion,

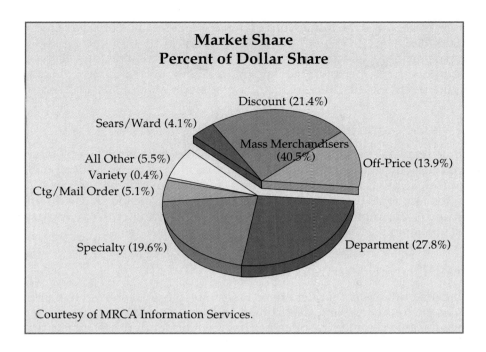

**Market Share
Percent of Dollar Share**

Discount (21.4%)

Sears/Ward (4.1%)

Mass Merchandisers (40.5%)

All Other (5.5%)
Variety (0.4%)
Ctg/Mail Order (5.1%)

Off-Price (13.9%)

Specialty (19.6%)

Department (27.8%)

Courtesy of MRCA Information Services.

leveraged buyouts, the recession, and competition from the discounters, off-price merchants, and specialty stores. Several department stores have responded by spinning off specialty units of their own. However, consumers appreciate the variety—although it can be overwhelming—and the convenience of one-stop shopping.

Mass Merchants

Mass merchandise retailers sell *commodity merchandise* (standard basics) in a multistore format. They have masses of stores and mass-oriented budget-to-moderate prices. Most retail consultants include Sears, Montgomery Ward, discounters such as Wal-Mart, K-Mart, and Target, off-price retailers, and factory outlets as mass merchants. Today over 50 percent of all apparel units are puchased at mass merchants, and sales per square foot are now $200 for discounters compared to $150 for department stores.[13] Due to their ability to buy in volume, mass merchants are able to buy at lower prices and pass the savings on to the consumer. Most of these stores are general merchandise retailers, but we limit our discussion to those that carry fashion apparel and accessories. Sears, for example, has made fashion a priority with its "Softer Side of Sears" campaign.

Discounters

The term *discount store* developed after World War II, when certain stores claimed they could sell merchandise for less because they had lower overhead, that is, lower operating costs: low rent, less advertising, fewer salespeople, and few customer services. Discounters are able to get lower prices by buying large quantities, turning merchandise quickly, and keeping expenses down with a no-frills atmosphere.

Value has become the watchword of the 1990s. Discount stores have more than doubled since 1980 and have taken business away from the traditional department and specialty stores. Led by Wal-Mart, Target, and K-Mart, discounters have become the largest retailers in the United States. Prominent regional discounters include Bradlees, Caldor, Hills, and Ames.

Off-price Retailers

Some retailers specialize in selling merchandise at lower prices by offering special buys, closeouts, overruns (manufacturers' overproduced merchandise), last season's goods, off-colors, and manufacturers' returns. The need for low rents excludes them from high-rent malls and prime downtown areas. Examples of off-price retailers are Burlington Coat Factory, Ross, Loehmann's, Dress Barn, and Marshalls.

Retail Outlet Stores

Since manufacturers' outlet stores and other off-price stores have been gaining market share, some department and specialty stores are attempting to reclaim lost customers by opening their own outlet stores. They feel that it is more profitable to run their own clearance stores than to sell leftover markdowns to jobbers. Macy's, Neiman Marcus, Nordstrom, and John Wanamaker are examples of stores that have their own clearance centers.

Warehouse Clubs

Warehouse clubs, which charge a small membership fee, offer consumers deep discounts on general merchandise in a warehouse setting. While they do offer some clothing on racks, it is primarily casual or active sportswear. With stores ranging from 40,000 square feet to 160,000 square feet, these retailers offer approximately 3000 to 5000 deeply stocked products. Sam's Clubs, owned by Wal-Mart, is the largest with approximately 300 stores in 42 states. The two other largest warehouse clubs, Price Club and Costco, have merged.

Promotional Stores

Any store, be it a specialty store, department store, or mass merchant, that is price-directed is a promotional store (not to be confused with sales promotion, as discussed in Chapter 15). *Promotional stores* offer special buys from manufacturers and frequent sales in an effort to get customers into the store. Many consumers like to buy on sale because they feel they are getting a bargain. Examples of promotional stores are Macy's, the May Company, the Broadway, Mervyn's, and Target. Many stores have become promotional and some are trying to get away from this strategy with consistent value pricing.

Non-store Retailing

Many consumers dislike the inconvenience of traffic, parking, crowds, and going from store to store in search of a coordinating wardrobe. Also, many busy people do not have the time to go shopping. They want to buy clothing and accessories quickly and efficiently. To answer their needs, mail-order, cable television, and computer shopping are offering consumers the convenience of shopping from home.

Mail-order Merchants

Mail-order catalogs provide consumers with the opportunity to compare merchandise and prices while sitting at home. The number of consumers shopping by catalog has almost doubled in the past decade.[14] Consumers like the convenience of ordering by telephone and having merchandise delivered. Apparel catalog retailers include Clifford & Wills, Horchow, Spiegel, Tweeds, Talbots, Bachrach, Eddie Bauer, Land's End, L. L. Bean, J. Crew, Biobottoms, Playclothes, and the Wooden Soldier.

J. Crew, for example, mails approximately 70 million catalogs annually. Arthur Cinader, chairman, explains that "we would be committed to 70 percent of a planned need for an item before the first catalog is in the mail. For example, on a $60 item, we might project $300,000 in volume, and have ordered 3500 units before there's any demand at all."[15]

Many mail-order businesses, including Talbots and J. C. Penney, also have retail stores. Some added stores after their catalog businesses became successful; others were already established retailers. In fact, all retailers are find-

The first proof of a double-page spread, showing needed corrections, from an Eddie Bauer catalog.
(Courtesy of Eddie Bauer)

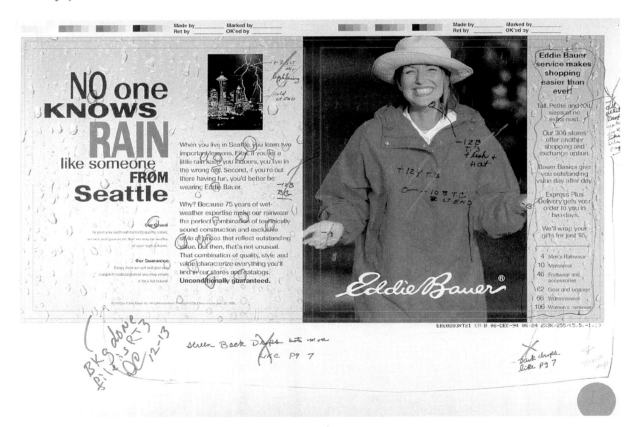

ing that mail order brings them increased business. Mail order is a difficult business, however. Catalogs are expensive to prepare and distribute, postal rates and paper costs have gone up, and sales tax must be figured for many states. Only the best and most focused of the mail-order retailers will survive.

Party-plan Retailing

Often overlooked by the industry, at-home party retailing is a growing vehicle for direct sales of women's wear, children's wear, and jewelry. According to the Washington, D. C., Direct Selling Association, selling products in the home has grown to a $10 billion industry. Sales consultants encourage prospective customers to invite friends into their homes to look at and try on merchandise. The high-priced, high-fashion Carlisle Collection, for example, is sold through a nationwide network of at-home consultants.

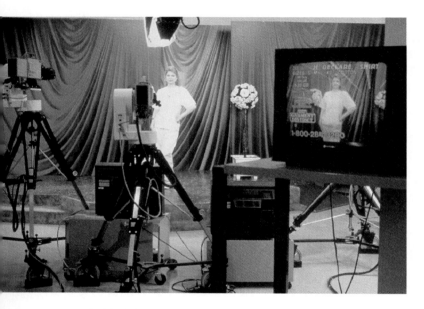

Behind-the-scenes at Home Shopping Network
Courtesy of Home Shopping Network)

Electronic Retailing

Electronic shopping got off to a roaring start with national media attention in the early 1990s, but growth has not been all that was expected. Many retailers have a "wait and see" attitude about getting involved.

Cable Television Shopping. Television allows consumers across the country to see fashion in their own living rooms, order it by phone, and have it delivered. Americans may buy fashion merchandise via cable networks such as QVC/HSN and MTV or via direct-response commercials. Telephone companies are installing fiber-optic telephone lines to make interactive shopping possible.

Computer Shopping. A number of on-line computer information services now offer a shop-by-computer feature. On-line services that require a personal computer (PC), a modem, and a computer-savvy consumer are few but growing. The largest providers of these services are CompuServe, Prodigy, Delphi, and America Online. These services also provide easy access to Internet shopping. In the future, on-line services hope to enable the consumer to seek a specific product in a certain price range from various catalogs and display them on the screen at one time for comparison.

Home shopping, however, is still in its infancy. Once telephone companies complete fiber-optic installation, cable television regulatory issues are sorted out, and more homes have computers and access to the Internet, this form of shopping has potential. Today's video-oriented teenagers and young adults are more likely to embrace electronic shopping and interactive television than their parents. The question remains, will people who may have worked on computers all day want to shop on them at home? If people are too busy to shop in stores, will they have time to watch so much television?

Video Shopping.   Some retailers are also testing video order machines similar to bank automated tellers outside their stores. When the store is closed, a customer can view merchandise on a video screen outside the store and, using a charge card, order the merchandise and have it delivered.

RETAIL ORGANIZATION

There are a number of career opportunities within each area of retail responsibility.

Retailing functions are generally divided into six areas of responsibility: marketing, merchandising, store operations, sales promotion, finance and control, and human resources.

Merchandising has the responsibility for planning, buying, and selling merchandise (see Chapter 14).

Store operations has the responsibility for planning, managing, and maintaining the retail building, protecting the store and merchandise, providing customer services, and coordinating the movement of goods and people within the building.

Marketing directs the focus and image of the store to provide the store's target customer with the right merchandise at the right time and to make a profit doing it. Marketing also includes the responsibility for sales promotion.

Sales promotion informs customers about goods and services through advertisements, displays, publicity, special events, and public relations (see Chapter 15).

Finance controls expenditures and keeps records of money spent and received: accounts payable (goods received but not yet paid for), payroll, taxes, credit (customers' charge accounts), and inventory.

Human resources staffs the store with people who are qualified and trained to handle the work that needs to be done and assures compliance with state and federal labor laws.

The Small Store

Small stores can offer their customers highly personalized service that larger stores cannot provide. They can also get to know the needs of their customers due to frequent personal contact. As many large stores narrow their list of suppliers, it may give a boost to small specialty stores who can buy from small manufacturers, offering their customers unique merchandise.

The typical small store is often managed by one person, usually the owner, who assumes many roles in the store's operation, such as manager, buyer, salesperson, stockperson, and bookkeeper. In some cases, several people jointly run a store, each assuming the responsibility for the jobs he or she is most capable of doing. Problems occur, however, when the people involved have different goals or inadequate experience. Many small retailers in the United States go out of business because of inadequate financing, poor financial management, and competition. Successful stores may grow in size or open additional locations.

The Large Store

In large stores, the retailing functions are divided among managers who are specialists in the performance of their respective jobs. The function of the management team is to set policies and make sure that strategies are being carried out properly. Depending on the ownership, there is usually a chief executive officer (CEO) to oversee day-to-day operations. Several top-level executives are usually in charge of the various functional responsibilities, such as merchandising, operations (store directors), sales promotion, human resources, and finances. The larger the store—by sales, square footage, or number of stores—the more complex the organizational structure.

STORES WITHIN A STORE

The intimate atmosphere of small shops can be created within a larger store.

In-store Designer Boutiques

Popular designers or brands often require that a retail store furnish a permanent location and *real estate* (a certain amount of square footage) within the store for the sole purpose of displaying only their merchandise. The retailer provides space and purchases the product. The designer or brand vendor prescribes how the merchandise is visually merchandised and accessorized. They negotiate with the store regarding creation of boutique environments and may supply the fixtures. For example, there is the Ralph Lauren Polo boutique with its mahogany shelves, fireplace, polo sticks, umbrella stands, shaving mirrors, and other "British gentleman" accessories.

The Donna Karan shop at Saks Fifth Avenue. (*Courtesy of Saks Fifth Avenue*)

In-store boutiques allow designers and brands to present their entire collection and to strengthen their image. They also can present their own accessories together with the clothes. In so doing, they present the consumer with "the world of" Giorgio Armani, Calvin Klein, or Ralph Lauren (many of these same designers and manufacturers also have their own free-standing shops, discussed under Specialty Stores, which compete with these in-store boutiques). Wal-Mart has even opened a "vendor store," where manufacturers are permitted to take charge of selecting and displaying their own merchandise.

This merchandising strategy does not particularly help a store to maintain a cohesive image, except as a store carrying designer names. Retail consultant Walter Levy complained, "When I worked at Bloomingdale's many years back, we had a storewide point of view. Today, it's a series of vendor names along the wall."[16]

Leased Departments

To provide additional services for their customers, many stores lease certain departments to an outside organization better able to handle a particular specialty. Leased departments in retail stores are merchandised, owned, and operated by an outside firm rather than by the store itself. Departments such as furs, shoes, and fine jewelry are sometimes leased because special training for sales associates is necessary. Today, leasing is used less frequently, however, because it is more cost effective for a store to run its own departments.

MULTIPLE-UNIT STORES

Retailers begin as single-unit stores and, if successful, may branch out into multiple units.

Stores that carry on the retail tradition may be classified as *single-unit*, one store only, or *multiple-unit*, more than one store, operations. These range from small, single stores with just a few employees to giant retail firms with thousands of employees. Department, specialty, and price-directed stores can be found in either classification.

The success of the multiple-unit store is based on its ability to buy in large quantities and to distribute the merchandise and operating costs throughout the organization.

Chain Stores

Successful single stores may open additional stores and grow into regional or national status. National specialty stores, such as the Limited, Ann Taylor, Saks Fifth Avenue, and I. Magnin, as well as mass merchants like Sears and J. C. Penney, are chain organizations. Because the term *chain* was formerly associated with low-priced merchandise, many specialty stores simply call themselves *national specialty stores*, even though they are

The Express store on Madison Avenue in New York City is part of a nationwide chain store organization. *(Courtesy of the Limited)*

structured as chains. Some chains have become mega-retailers. J. C. Penney has 1360 stores, and Wal-Mart and K-Mart each have over 2000.

Although most buying is done centrally, allowances are made for regional differences. A store in Connecticut, for example, would need more heavy outerwear in winter than a store in Pasadena, California. Centrally purchased merchandise is distributed to all stores from a central or regional distribution center (see Chapter 14).

Department Store Groups

Many multiple-unit department stores use the term *groups* to describe their organizational structure of a parent store with branches. Several examples include Bloomingdales, John Wanamaker, and the May Company. These department stores originated years ago in metropolitan areas and later opened branches in outlying suburbs to serve customers who enjoyed the convenience of shopping closer to home.

Store groups are either centrally or regionally merchandised. The parent or flagship store is usually the focal point of the group and carries a wider assortment of merchandise than the branch stores. In some cases, however, popular branches now sell more volume than the flagship.

Corporate Ownership

Fashion news often discusses Federated Stores, yet no one has ever seen a store called the Federated! Federated is only one example of a corporate group of retailers. In 1929, seven family-owned stores joined together to form Federated Department Stores. Since that time, many stores have merged or been acquired by larger groups of stores. Federated, for example, now owns Macy's, Bloomingdale's, Bullock's, Jordan Marsh, Lazarus, Burdines, and Rich's. The Limited, Inc., owns the Limited Stores, Lerner's, Lane Bryant, Express, Victoria's Secret, Structure, and Abercrombie & Fitch, among others.

MARKETING

Marketing is the responsibility of everyone in the store from management to sales associates.

Retail management must decide which potential customers it wants to reach and how it wants to reach them. Whether setting up a new store or reevaluating an existing one, management must study the type of people who live in the community, their life-styles, and ultimately their shopping wants and needs. Retail executives determine the target market and tailor the store's image, merchandise focus, and promotional efforts toward their customers.

Retail Target Customers

As in design and manufacturing, the first step in reaching potential customers is to define exactly who they are. No retail store can be all things to all people; it must select one or a few groups of people to serve. *Target market* is the term for the group of consumers the store wishes to attract. Massimo Ferragamo explained, "Today, you can't take the customer for granted and just hope they come floating into the store. We want to know who they are, their likes and their dislikes."[17] As discussed in Chapter 2, a group of target customers is within a general age range, has similar life-styles, and therefore has similar needs and tastes. A department store may try to appeal to several categories of target customers. Separate areas or floors are created for each category, for example, designer, contemporary, or junior.

Database Marketing

As discussed in Chapter 2, retailers use database marketing to learn more about their customers and potential customers. Consultant Walter Loeb pointed out that "Retailers such as Federated and Wal-Mart are using their checkout scanner data to analyze sales on a store-by-store basis to uncover differences in customer buying habits." Sears, for example, has created an ethnic database so that it can react to the needs of individual stores. For example, stores catering to Hispanic customers carry brighter colors; stores with Asian customers carry more petite sizes.[18]

Store Location

The location of a store is very important in relation to its potential customers. *Demographic research* is done to determine what location would best attract target customers. Computerized site-selection programs provide data on area population forecasts, descriptions of households by income, median age of market-area residents, and information about the competition.

Renovations

Rather than building new stores or expanding, many retailers are using capital investments to renovate, strenthening existing units to compete successfully. At the National Retail Federation convention, Michael Gould, chairman and CEO of Bloomingdale's, and Sally Frame Kasaks, chairman and CEO of Ann Taylor, were among the panelists who concluded that renovation is a critical way to reposition a store, generate new traffic, and broaden the customer base without the expense of building a new store.[19]

Fashion Leadership

In conjunction with the target customer, the store must determine what role it wishes to play in fashion leadership. Fashion leadership can be separated into three loosely defined categories:

Fashion-forward stores, such as Barney's, Bergdorf Goodman, Saks Fifth Avenue, or Neiman-Marcus, seek leadership by carrying fashionable merchandise. There are fewer of these stores because the percentage of customers who can afford high quality or have an interest in fashion newness is relatively small.

Main-stream retailers, whose fashion image falls in the moderate fashion and price category, identify with consumers who accept popular fashion. Fashion adaptations are available to them at moderate and upper-moderate prices. Most of the department stores, such as Nordstrom, Macy's, or Dillard's, fall into this category, as do some specialty stores like The Gap.

Mass merchants such as Wal-Mart and Sears usually restrict their fashion offerings to proven styles because they appeal to fashion followers and to people who simply cannot or will not spend more money on their clothing. Mass merchants generally feel that, for their customer, fashion is not the issue. Bob Connolly of Montgomery Ward commented that "Opulent runway merchandise was never intended for the majority of people...."[20] However, some stores, such as Sears, are trying to upgrade their fashion image.

The Retailer's Image

It is important for a retailer to clearly define its *image*, the personality or character that it presents to the public. This image or uniqueness reflects its degree of fashion leadership and its market niche and therefore appeals to its target customers. Ralph Lauren says, "Retailers have to have a point of view. It's the most important thing for retailers to have an identity, a sense of who they are."[21]

In keeping with that image, retailers strive for a store atmosphere that is both a complementary background for merchandise and an inviting environment for the customer. The store's merchandising, interior decoration,

The handbag department at Bergdorf Goodman, a fashion-forward retailer.
(Courtesy of Bergdorf Goodman)

promotion, and customer services develop, maintain, and reflect that image and try to generate excitement about the merchandise in order to create a desire to buy.

SUMMARY

This chapter examined the current retailing situation of closures and consolidations due to fierce competition. Retailers are trying to cope by meeting consumer needs and offering value, service, entertainment, and unique merchandising. Many retailers feel that increased market share can only come from global expansion. There is a renewed interest in inner-city retailing, and malls are diversifying to stay in business.

There are many types of retail operations, including specialty stores, department stores, mass merchants, and mail-order and electronic retailers. There are both single- and multiple-unit stores, some growing into large chains. Store functions include marketing, merchandising, store operations, sales promotion, finance, and personnel. In small stores, all these jobs are handled by only a few people; in large stores, each function is directed by a different executive.

To maintain a competitive position, a retailer must be focused on the needs of its target customer. To appeal to that customer, the store must have a unique yet appropriate image carried out in its merchandise, promotion, and services.

CHAPTER REVIEW

Terms and Concepts

Briefly identify and discuss the following terms and concepts:

1. Retailing
2. Over-stored
3. Leveraged buyouts
4. Fifth Avenue and Madison Avenue
5. Department stores
6. Specialty stores
7. Deep-niche retailing
8. Flagship stores
9. Private-label retailers
10. Off-price
11. Promotional stores
12. Leased departments
13. Electronic retailing
14. In-store boutiques
15. Chain stores
16. Marketing
17. Target customers

Questions for Review

1. What is the purpose of retailing?
2. What is the reason for restructuring and consolidation in retailing?
3. What strategies are retailers using to compete in the 1990s? Which do you think are the most effective and why?
4. How does globalization affect retailing?
5. Explain the different types of shopping malls that have emerged in the United States.
6. How does a department store differ from a specialty store?
7. Explain the differences in organization between a small store and a large store.
8. Why has off-price, discount, and warehouse retailing increased?
9. Briefly explain the growth of mail-order retailing.
10. What impact will electronic retailing have in the future?
11. Describe the basic functions of a retail organization.
12. How can small stores compete with large ones?
13. Why is a store's image important?

Projects For Additional Learning

1. Find out whether one of the department or specialty stores in your community is owned by a retail corporation. Find out what other stores are part of the same corporation (see Appendix 2).
2. Research the history and growth of a large store in your area. Contact the store's public relations department for information and check your college or local library for further information.
3. Watch a fashion presentation on the QVC cable network. Write an analysis of the program, including the effectiveness of the moderator, the presenter, and the merchandise. Was the show successful in terms of sales? What do you think of the future of television shopping?

NOTES

1 "Modes of Retailing," Merrill Lynch Seminar, March 1992.

2 "Out of Fashion," *Wall Street Journal*, February 28, 1995, p. 1.

3 As quoted by David Moin, "Observations," *Women's Wear Daily*, January 20, 1995, p. 5.

4 Interview, February 1995.

5 Letter, May 27, 1993.

6 Howard Rudnitsky, "Battle of the Malls," *Forbes*, March 30, 1992, p. 46.

7 West Edmonton Mall profile, 1995.

8 Interview, April 12, 1995.

9 As quoted by Barbara Solomon, "Malls Mix it Up," *Women's Wear Daily*, March 17, 1993, p. 7.

10 John Mannix, U.S. Mall manager for Sarakreek, owner of South Hills, as quoted in "Battle of the Malls."

11 Interview, March, 1993.

12 As quoted by Gavin Power, "The Bottom Line: Too Many Stores," *San Francisco Chronicle*, January 16, 1995, p. B1.

13 MRCA Information Services as quoted by Ira Schneiderman, "Mass Market Report," *Women's Wear Daily*, February 24, 1993, p. 22.

14 Gretchen Morgenson, "The Fall of the Mall," *Forbes*, May 24, 1993, p. 108.

15 As quoted in a letter from Gerry Hammarth, J. Crew, Inc., May 6, 1993.

16 Walter K. Levy, retail consultant, letter, May 10, 1993.

17 As quoted by Chuck Struensee, "Ferragamo Today," *Women's Wear Daily*, February 11, 1991, p. 7.

18 Walter Loeb, *Loeb Retail Letter*, January 1995, p. 3.

19 As quoted by Dianne Pogoda, "Spruce up to Stir Sales," *Women's Wear Daily*, February 1, 1993, p. 8.

20 Connolly, May 27, 1993.

21 As quoted in "Lauren at 25," *Women's Wear Daily*, January 15, 1992, p. 7.

Retail selling floor of Gieves & Hawkes, Savile Row, London.
(Courtesy of Gieves & Hawkes)

14

RETAIL FASHION MERCHANDISING

CAREER FOCUS

Fashion merchandising is most often directed by store management, merchandise managers, and sometimes a fashion director. However, the actual buying and sell-through of merchandise are the responsibility of buyers and their assistants. Buyers are also involved in sales promotion, as discussed in Chapter 15.

CHAPTER OBJECTIVES

After reading this chapter you should have attained competence in the following areas:

1. Awareness of the buying and selling aspects of merchandising
2. Understanding of buying procedures at the market
3. Comprehension of all aspects of inventory control and evaluation
4. Understanding of the importance of customer service and sales associates

Merchandise is the term used to signify articles for sale; it derives from the word *merchant*, the actual seller or retailer. *Fashion merchandising* includes all the planning and activities necessary to supply the fashion wants and needs of retail customers. In the past, fashion merchandising was usually associated only with women's apparel and accessories. Today, however, stores use aggressive merchandising techniques for men's and children's clothing as well. Fashion influence has also spread to other areas of retailing, from home furnishings to cookware.

This chapter will cover the planning and carrying out of buying and selling, including the responsibilities of buyers. We will follow the flow of merchandise from arrival in the store to purchase by the consumer.

MERCHANDISING ORGANIZATION

Every area of merchandising responsibility needs planning and organization to make it function properly and to ensure successful buying and selling.

Merchandising responsibilities are usually divided between two chains of command. The *buying line* of management has responsibility for merchandise content and assortment; the *store line* is the liaison between the merchandise organization and customers. The goal of both is to sell merchandise.

Responsibilities of the Store Line

The main responsibilities of the store line are to provide customer services, coordinate the movement of goods and people within the store, and operations. Above all, store line executives must work together with merchandise managers, buyers, and sales associates to produce positive sales results. Everything and everyone involved in the operation of the store must be organized to achieve this goal.

The director of stores, an executive vice-president or general manager, heads the store line. The director of stores supervises individual store managers in multiple-unit organizations and they, in turn, usually delegate responsibilities to group sales managers and floor or area managers, who in turn supervise department managers. Department managers and their assistants run the department and supervise sales associates.

Responsiblities of the Buying Line

The merchandise managers and buyers of the buying line must do all the planning and other activities necessary to bring the right merchandise into the store at the right time to satisfy the store's customers.

General Merchandise Managers

The chief executive officer (CEO) of a store or group of stores delegates merchandising responsibilities to several general merchandise managers (GMMs) or corporate merchandise managers (CMMs). The general or corporate merchandise managers are in charge of several divisions. The divisions may be related, such as a general merchandise manager for women's wear, or they may be totally unrelated. For example, a GMM might be in charge of women's sportswear, coats, and jewelry!

Divisional Merchandise Managers

Merchandising responsibility is further segmented into *divisions*, such as women's sportswear or men's furnishings, directed by divisional merchandise managers (DMMs). In the women's area, divisionals might be in charge of missy dresses, missy sportswear, junior dresses, or junior sportswear. Some national retailers, with decentralized buying, have regional merchandise managers (RMMs) instead.

Buyers

Each division is composed of *departments*. These divisions may be based on life-style, styling categories, price ranges, or vendors. Women's dresses might be divided into trendy, traditional, social occasion, and career. Dresses might also be divided into designer, bridge, better, moderate, and budget price ranges. Accessories are subdivided into handbags, hosiery,

Men's wear divisional merchandise manager Tony Brown meets with Polo Ralph Lauren regional manager Ann Peiffer and sales coordinator Darrel Harris at Macy's West. *(Courtesy of Tony Brown, photographed by the author)*

hats, jewelry, and so on. Each department is further segmented into *classifications*. A buyer is responsible for the success of one or more classifications, one department, or several departments.

Fashion Merchandising Direction

Fashion direction is established to maintain cohesive fashion merchandising in line with a distinctive store image. In single-unit stores, the owner usually acts as fashion director and buyer. In large stores or chains, management may give direction, as Gene Pressman does for Barney's, or management may employ a fashion director, such as Kal Ruttenstein at Bloomingdale's. The fashion director is the bridge between corporate marketing policy and actual merchandise buying decisions. He or she works with merchandise managers, buyers, and promotion executives to suggest what merchandise to choose and how to present it.

Along with management and designer collection buyers, the fashion director may attend European and American collection openings to study fashion trends, relates those trends to the store's image, and passes this information on to other buyers as a guide to merchandise planning. The fashion director may also work with buyers to select appropriate merchandise, to develop the store's private label, and to coordinate their buys with merchandise in other departments. A fashion director also prepares seasonal fashion presentations for sales associates so that they can understand the new fashion concepts and the store's merchandising approach and, therefore, better help their customers.

BUYING PREPARATIONS

Careful planning is done to help merchants do efficient and successful buying.

The Merchandise Plan

Management determines a *fashion merchandising policy*, a long-range standard for fashion buying, selling, and related activities. Retailers make up a *merchandise plan* within the framework of the policy, goals, and fashion direction set by management. Actual sales figures and evaluations (see end of chapter) from the corresponding season of the previous year are used as a basis for making up the new plan.

The merchandise plan is a *financial* or *dollar* plan allocating specific amounts of money to each department or division for the purchase of an appropriate assortment of fashion merchandise that will meet consumer demand and sales goals.

The plan also exactly specifies the *units*, or number of garments and accessories, to be purchased to meet these sales goals. Accessory units, for example, are divided according to the number of handbags, belts, scarves, and so on, that should meet demand. The scarf classification would be further broken down into the number of shapes (for example, oblong or square), prints and solids, and desired fabrications. The merchandise plan is further broken down by vendor, by class, and by item.

Merchandise plans may be management or buyer directed.

Management directed   Usually, management determines financial plans for the company as a whole, divides the totals, and assigns sales goals to general merchandise managers. These plans are then further subdivided to divisionals and buyers.

Buyer directed   The buyer may be required to originate the plan by classification or category. The buyer then negotiates with the DMM, who then submits the plan to the GMM and the president or CEO. Very often a combination of the two methods is used, with participants bargaining until an agreement is reached.[1]

Merchandise plans are determined four months to a year before the selling season and cover a six-month period: the spring season (February through July) or the fall season (August through January). The plans are developed on computer spreadsheets, which show what needs to be purchased and sold per month to reach sales and profit goals.

The plan includes sales goals, stock, inventory turn, and purchase plans for a six-month season. Because the only source of income for most retail stores is the sale of merchandise, the projected sales must cover all expenditures, such as the cost of wholesale merchandise, markdowns, inventory shortages, and freight costs, in order to produce gross margin objectives. The *gross margin* is the fundamental income from which operation expenses are deducted to obtain the necessary profit to stay in business.

Planning Sales Goals

To make a realistic estimate of prospective sales, a buyer must consider variations in consumer demand, shifts in population, local retail competition, physical expansion or alterations needed in the store, planned promotional efforts, market and trend analyses, seasonal consumer demand, and economic conditions. For instance, buyers tend to buy conservatively when anticipating a recession. In a good year, they may buy more in hopes of an increase in business.

Planning Stock

The next step in planning is to determine the amount of stock, in terms of dollar investment, necessary to meet consumer demand and thereby support planned sales. The same influences that affect sales also affect the planning of stock. Stock must be brought to a peak just before the expected time of peak selling.

Stock Turn.   A high and quick stock turn rate is the desired result of stock planning. *Stock turn* is the number of times that inventory (merchandise stock) has been sold and replaced during a given period. The quicker stock is turned, the more income and profits the store makes.

Assortment Planning

By stating sales objectives and expenses, the merchandising plan provides the foundation for assortment planning. A merchandise *assortment* is a collection of various styles, quantities, and prices of related merchandise, usually grouped under one classification within a department. The buyer plans to buy a balanced assortment of merchandise to meet consumer demand and appeal to a particular group of target customers.

Buyer Julia Ellard and her assistant Kim Baur at work on a buying plan. *(Photographed by the author)*

The Buying Plan

The *buying plan* is a description of the types, quantities, prices, and sizes of merchandise that a buyer expects to purchase within a specific period of time. The totals state exactly how much may be spent on merchandise in each category in line with sales goals and the dollar merchandise plan.

The more detailed the buying plan, the less confusing buying decisions will be, allowing the buyer to concentrate on the fashion aspects of the merchandise during the seasonal market. The plan must be flexible enough, however, to allow for revision if conditions change; for example, should buyers not find what they want in the market. Retailing executive Joan Bergholt commented, "Buyers must continually adjust to changing business in order to achieve their total sales volume and gross margin objectives."[2]

Open-to-Buy

Considering stock on hand at the beginning of any given month, the buyer has to calculate the amount of purchases that can be made if stock and sales are to be kept in balance. The difference between actual stock and planned stock equals *open-to-buy*, the value of planned purchases. The open-to-buy budget is adjusted according to business. When business is good, stock is low and needs to be replenished. When business is slow, buying has to be reduced. In addition, open-to-buy often has to be based on the amount of space or "real estate" that a buyer has available for specific categories and merchandise or particular vendors.[3]

BUYING

The buyer purchases merchandise in accordance with the merchandising plan and sales and profit goals.

The Buyer's Role

Experience

A buyer's knowledge of merchandise stems from both education and experience. The ability to evaluate merchandise and judge whether it is suitable for a customer develops over years of examining all types of merchandise for quality, styling, and price. Leslie Wexner, founder of The Limited, said that his "experience of being in stores, watching customers' reactions to merchandise and its presentation, and overhearing their comments" helped him develop a retail sense.[4]

Research

Market and trend research becomes second nature to the buyer. In both planning and buying, the following factors are considered:

◆ The store's fashion image and merchandising policies

◆ Market and fashion trends (Chapters 2 and 4)

◆ The effect of economic conditions on demand for certain types and prices of merchandise

◆ Basic stock, merchandise that is in consistent demand throughout the year or the same season each year

◆ The competitors' merchandise offerings

◆ The individual department's ability to house and display the merchandise effectively

◆ The type of promotional activities that are needed to support the merchandise

Analytical versus Creative Aspects of Buying

The buying process is part analytical and part creative. The mechanics involve knowledge of sales histories and development of a merchandising plan. Their increased responsibilities to the bottom line leave many buyers no choice but to be just administrators. As retailers explain in industry jargon, they have had to become "number driven" instead of "merchandise driven." The creative side of buying is the ability to understand the customer, spot trends, and use intuition to choose merchandise with terrific sell-through.

Some retailers, such as Macy's, are experimenting with separating buying functions into a *buyer-planner system*. Under this system, buyers focus on shopping the market and merchandise selection, while planners shape the size of the buy and how it is to be distributed.

Target Customers

The buyer tries to select merchandise from vendors that the store's customers want or need: the right styles, size range, color assortment, and fabrics, all at acceptable prices. Individual preferences must be forgotten in favor of the buyer's knowledge of customer preferences. Buyers need to keep in touch with their customers' life-styles in order to buy merchandise to fit their needs. One San Francisco-based buyer of long formals and evening dresses spent a late spring evening sitting in the lobby of a downtown hotel to see what young people's preferences were in prom dresses.

Buyer Isolation

Unfortunately, many buyers have become isolated from their customers, with offices removed from the selling floor, and in a large chain a buyer cannot visit every store. Several stores, such as Nordstrom and Barney's, however, insist that their buyers spend time on the selling floor.

The Buying-selling Cycle

The buying and selling cycle is related to the fashion cycle of consumer acceptance (as discussed in Chapter 3). Therefore, a buyer's responsibilities involve a complete cycle: planning what to buy; searching the markets and selecting the right merchandise; working with advertising, display, and special events to promote merchandise; training personnel in sales; and marking down leftover merchandise.

The buying-selling cycle is constantly overlapping: new goods come into the store while other goods reach their peak in sales or decline in sales. Thus, the buyer works in two time zones, anticipating future needs and evaluating current sales. In fact, because consumer tastes change constantly, the buyer's job of identifying and interpreting consumer demand is a continuing process.

Broad Assortment Buying.   Ideally, buyers would like to buy a *broad but shallow assortment* of merchandise at the beginning of a season to test consumer reaction and then, as certain styles emerge as best-sellers, to increase stock in depth. By comparing current sales of a particular style with the previous week's or month's figures, a buyer can determine whether sales are rising or declining. If sales of certain styles are on the rise, then more of these looks may be ordered. However, re-orders are often difficult as best-selling merchandise may no longer be available from the manufacturers.

Short-cycle Buying.   Another preference is *short-cycle buying*: to buy closer to the selling season, to be better able to judge market conditions and trends, and to respond to the "wear-now" mentality of today's consumers. Also referred to as *just-in-time* merchandising, short-cycle buying also helps to reduce inventory. Again, this may be difficult due to the availability of merchandise.

Planning Promotions.   Buyers have to plan ahead for *promotions*, special buys at low prices, which are passed on to the consumer. When a particular item is popular, such as cashmere sweaters for instance, a buyer might arrange for a volume purchase at a special price and then pass the savings on to customers. Many retailers would like to cut down on the practice of constant sales and promotions, but it is difficult since consumers now expect them.

Planning Markdowns.   Buyers also have to allow for markdowns in their plans. Many stores mark down prices after the merchandise has been on the selling floor for six weeks to two months. Retailers are speeding inventory turns by marking down clothes faster in order to clear out stale merchandise. Merchandise may be left over because it has passed its peak of popularity, due to broken sizes and colors, or to poor buying decisions.

Retailers often ask manufacturers for *markdown allowances* to help offset their losses. Some manufacturers may even tell the retailer when it is permissible to mark down merchandise to make room for new deliveries. Yet buyers want goods to sell through at full price and would prefer to avoid markdowns.

Shopping the Market

After the buying plan has been established, fashion buyers shop the market to view the merchandise available for the coming season. For the retailer, the manufacturer is the *supplier*, *vendor*, or *resource* of fashion goods.

Buyers from all over the world at the Prêt-à-Porter Paris market.
(Courtesy of Prêt-à-Porter Paris)

Buying trips are generally timed to cover markets that are important for a particular category of merchandise.

Buyers visit different market centers for different needs. Many people imagine a buyer's job to be a glamorous one involving many trips to Europe. However, only designer department buyers, merchandise managers, and fashion directors of large stores attend the European collections. Even then, with packed appointment schedules leaving little time to eat or relax, business travel does not remain glamorous for long. Many French and Italian designers now have New York showrooms so that buyers do not necessarily have to go to Europe.

Designer and contemporary buyers go to New York to see the American collections. Contemporary and junior sportswear and dress buyers also check out the California markets. To find moderate- and budget-priced apparel, buyers may go to manufacturers' showrooms at regional markets. Buyers from Dillard's, for example, are buying half of their merchandise at the Dallas markets. Merchandise may also be bought from manufacturers' sales representatives who call on stores. Some retailers, such as J. C. Penney, even show selected merchandise to their buyers in Texas via CD-ROM.

Line Buying versus Trend Buying

The buyer shops for new fashion from both key resources and new ones. *Key resources* or *core vendors* are those who have maintained a reputation for dependability and whose merchandise sells through because of appropriate styling, quality, and price, such as Ellen Tracy, St. John Knits, Tommy Hilfiger, or Nautica. The buyer regularly buys a good portion of these manufacturers' lines, a practice called *line buying*.

Many retailers are requiring that 80 to 90 percent of all merchandise be purchased from core vendors! Even more restrictive is the *matrix system*, strict centralized merchandising developed by the May Company and Dillard's. Buyers are limited to a list of core vendors and are not permitted to buy from other manufacturers! Of course, this system cuts out small apparel manufacturers, who cannot supply all the stores in a large chain or corporate group and contributes to a lack of choice for consumers.

Buying merchandise for its innovative styling is referred to as *trend buying*. However, because buyers are spending more and more time administering and have less time for actual buying, they are often unable to look for new resources; so new designers and manufacturers have to seek them out. Some retailers are providing *vendor days* when manufacturers can come to the store to show their merchandise. Finding an exciting, unique resource can mean an important merchandising statement for a fashion store.

Market Procedures

Buyers visit the showrooms of manufacturers who produce the specific types and price lines of merchandise that they need. As the entire line is shown to them by management, a merchandiser, or a sales representative, buyers take notes, usually on their lap top computers, recording information about style numbers, descriptions, size and color ranges, fabrication, and wholesale price, using separate discs for each vendor.

Buyers must evaluate whether styling and quality compare favorably with other merchandise that they have seen in the same price range. They must also consider the possible *sales potential* of each style for their stores. At the end of the market trip, a buyer reviews his or her notes on merchandise seen, eliminates the less desirable styles and any duplications, and decides which styles to purchase.

Corporate Buying.   In the case of a major store making a large purchase, buying is often done management to management by a group of executives including the buyer. Wal-Mart, for example, tries to do all its buying in this manner. In this case, the buyer is part of a buying team.

Retailer-Vendor Partnerships

Manufacturers and retailers try to work together toward mutual success. Vendor executives, designers, merchandisers, and/or sales representatives suggest appropriate merchandise for each store's particular customers. Buyers and sales representatives continue to work together throughout the selling season regarding advertising, reorders, markdowns, and sell-through. Buyers also give vendors weekly selling reports.

The Buyer as Editor

Although retailers are not usually fashion creators, they can influence consumer buying to a large degree by their selection of merchandise, which narrows the choice for the ultimate consumer. By determining what parts of a collection are bought and in what quantity, the buyer affects not only the fortunes of a designer's company but also the public perception of the designer's entire line.

Purchase Orders

Placing an order for merchandise is considered a contract between the store and the vendor. Therefore, writing an order commits the store to taking the merchandise if it meets quality expectations and delivery requirements. Generally, the buyer writes up orders on the store's purchase order forms and has them countersigned by the merchandise manager. Purchase orders specify the date of the order, the name and address of the resource, the terms of sale, shipping instructions, the store's shipping address, the name of the department, the quantity ordered, descriptions and prices of styles ordered, and obligations between buyer and seller. Purchase orders are most efficiently done by computer linked with the vendor, which can instantly supply information on what goods are available or are in work and what shipping dates are expected.

Deliveries are timed so that sufficient quantities of merchandise are in the store to meet various peaks in the consumer demand cycle. The vendor is committed to meeting these delivery dates or the order may be cancelled or a discount required.

Automatic Replenishment

In an effort to maintain stock of basic merchandise, retailers are using *automatic replenishment* or *Quick Response*, a strategy that utilizes integrated computer systems that link them to all their stores and to certain vendors. As discussed in Chapter 2, this strategy attempts to speed ordering and distribution and reduce inventories via electronic data interchange between textile and apparel producers and retailers. To implement automatic replenishment, retailers must be willing to adopt a continuous open-to-buy position for *basic* merchandise to let suppliers replenish without any retail management approval or review. Federated, for example, has implemented a sophisticated new computer system with a program called FASST (Federated Accelerated Sales and Stock Turn) whereby suppliers keep each store stocked at all times.

NATIONAL BRANDS VERSUS PRIVATE LABEL

Stores provide their customers with both national brands and house brands to differentiate themselves from the competition.

Stores across the country try to provide their customers with a wide selection of popular national brands. National brands, manufacturers' brands that are available nationwide, help the customer to identify with a consistent standard of styling, fit, and quality from season to season. However, as stores stock more and more national brands, exclusivity tends to decrease and stores look too much alike.

Exclusivity has long been an important aspect of a fashion retailer's uniqueness. Buyers seek distinctive fashion looks from out-of-the-way sources in foreign markets or from little-known, aspiring young designers to give their customers something that no other store has.

Some retailers are working with national brand manufacturers to produce collections for them. Nordstrom, for example, has an exclusive line of Hickey-Freeman shirts.

Private Label

In an effort to save costs and provide quality, value, and uniqueness, most multiunit retailers are selling private label merchandise. Barney's, for example, boasts that almost 70 percent of its inventory is exclusive—much of it created by Barney's under its own label. *Private label* merchandise carries the store's label, such as "Saks Fifth Avenue Real Clothes," or a fictitious name, such as Macy's/Federated's "I.N.C." or "Charter Club." Private labels can be named after a celebrity, such as the Kathie Lee (Gifford) Collection at Wal-Mart. The general public is usually not aware of the difference between a private label and a national brand.

Cost Savings.   Private label merchandise can be produced more cheaply than buying premium national brands. Lower costs allow the retailer higher markups, thereby improving gross margin. Savings are also passed on to the consumer. Terry Lundgren, chairman and CEO of Federated Merchandising Corporation, commented, "We're learning that private label is satisfying our customers' value requirements."[5]

Exclusivity.   Private-label merchandise also provides retailers with merchandise that is exclusive to them. Previously limited to basics such as polo shirts, retailers are now trying to provide quality fashion merchandise under private label. These fashion collections or pieces help retailers to differentiate themselves from their competition.

J. C. Penney's private label "Original Arizona Jeans Company." *(Courtesy of J. C. Penney)*

Major retailers today have hundreds of lines of private-label clothing, which account for at least 20 percent of all men's and women's apparel sold. Private-label accounts for one half of J. C. Penney's merchandise! Many have developed private labels that can compete with national brands, such as J. C. Penney's Original Arizona Jeans Company. Successful private labels become recognized as national brands and have even spawned a new chain of specialty stores, such as Macy/Federated's Aeropostale. As discussed in Chapter 13, some retailers, such as The Gap or Ann Taylor, sell only private-label merchandise.

Retailers as Manufacturers

Retailers have merchandise made directly for them to their specifications by guaranteeing a quantity order. Manufacturing may be arranged in several different ways.

- ◆ Retailers may simply have a "hot" item copied by a contractor for them.
- ◆ They may have a line created for them by a design service, such as Peclers, and then have it produced.
- ◆ They may set up their own design and merchandising department, which works with contractors.
- ◆ They may work with a manufacturer that specializes in private label, such as Cygne Designs, or one that produces both branded merchandise and private label, such as Kasper or Tahari.

BUYING OFFICES

To facilitate buying, many stores are affiliated with **resident buying offices** *located in international and domestic market centers or have their own corporate buying offices.*

Although the term buying office is still used in the industry, its role has greatly expanded to fill a wide variety of functions. In addition to merchandising and market representation, many buying offices now function as market analysts or product developers.

The two primary types of buying offices are independent and store owned.

Independent Resident Buying Offices

Independently owned and operated, these buying offices charge fees to noncompeting stores for market services. The current largest is the Doneger Group, which represents over 800 stores.

Store-owned Resident Buying Offices

There are basically two types of store-owned buying offices: associated and corporate.

The Doneger Group offers customers consultations, market coverage, workshops, design direction, direct mail programs, special merchandise, and other buying information.
(Courtesy of the Doneger Group)

An **associated buying office** is jointly owned and operated by a group of stores. Member stores usually have similar sales volume, store policies, and target customers, but are in noncompeting locations. Operating expenses are allocated to each member store on the basis of the store's sales volume and the amount of services rendered. These offices may also charge a fee for limited services to nonmember stores. Associated Merchandising Corporation (AMC) and Frederick Atkins are well-known examples.

A **corporate buying office** is owned and operated by the parent organization of a group or chain of stores. At Federated, 70 percent of the buying for member stores is done centrally by the parent company, while the other 30 percent is done by individual member stores.[6]

International Buying Offices

Many large retail stores have their own buying offices abroad or use foreign commissionaires. *Commissionaires* are agents representing stores in foreign market centers. A commissionaire is the foreign equivalent of an American buying office. These offices are equipped to handle import-export transactions in the language of the country, check quality control, figure currency exchange rates, provide a consolidated center for shipping, and wade through customs red tape.

Buying Office Services

The buying office is organized along the same lines as a retail store. There are merchandise managers who supervise groups of market representatives. For member stores, market representatives see the lines of new as well as established resources, prepare market analyses, and send out bulletins reporting on new fashion directions, best-sellers, trends, and special price offerings. However, unlike buyers, they do not make final decisions as to purchases and do not place orders unless specifically asked by the buyer of the retail store. Buying offices are not a substitute for buyers, because the buyers still do the actual buying, but instead act as market representatives for them. Buying offices also organize group purchases for small stores so that the total order is large enough to meet the minimum-order requirements of large or important manufacturers.

Buying offices today also offer many other services to their clients, such as color and trend forecasting, product development for private label, sourcing, facilitating imports, advertising and promotional support, and advice and information on all aspects of retailing. They provide members with information by means of reports, newsletters, workshops, and consultations. Some offices, such as Doneger, offer a wide variety of services; others may specialize. AMC, for example, now specializes in product development. Clients also use the buying offices in a variety of ways. Some retailers only want information; others may require help in a specific area.

RETAIL PRICING

Retail selling prices are based on predetermined store pricing policies and on wholesale costs.

Markup

Markup is the difference between the wholesale cost and the retail price of the merchandise. It can be figured as a percentage of retail value or calculated on the basis of cost. Most retailers calculate markup as a percentage of retail price. This method is used because expenses and profits are commonly expressed as a percentage of net sales based on retail prices. The markup must cover markdowns, shortages, operating expenses, and still create a profit. Operating expenses include salaries, travel expenses, sales promotion, and overhead, including rent, utilities, and store maintenance.

TABLE 14-1
Retail Pricing

Pricing of a Typical Moderately Priced Dress
(see Chapters 9 and 10 for wholesale costs)

Retailer's Costs

Wholesale cost ($61.52 less 8 percent discount for prompt payment)	$56.60
Allowance for markdowns (averaged over all dresses in stock)	5.00
Allowances for shortages and pilferage	3.00
Salaries and benefits (averaged per garment)	
Sales staff	7.00
Merchandising and buying staff (including expenses)	8.00
Clerical and stock room staff (receiving, marking, deliveries, and other expenses)	5.00
Advertising, display, and sales-promotion staff	8.00
Administrative staff (executives, credit and accounting officers, including expenses)	11.00
Employee fringe benefits	2.00
Overhead (rent, insurance, utilities, cleaning, and security)	10.00
TOTAL	$115.60
Profits before taxes	8.40
SELLING PRICE	**$124.00** Retail price
	−56.60 Cost
54% Markup	$67.40 Markup

*These are approximate figures; percentages vary depending on the kind of store. Markup percentages vary according to volume and store.

Price Points

Several price points are offered in each department or merchandise category. The term *price range* refers to the span between the lowest and highest price point. Merchandise of comparable quality usually falls into the same price range. Within a price range there must be enough difference between price points that variations in quality at each level are obvious to customers.

RECEIVING

Merchandise purchased by buyers is received into the store or distribution center, entered into stock, and put on the selling floor.

When buyers place orders at the market or with sales representatives, they indicate delivery dates to ensure that the merchandise is in the store at the right time to meet consumer demand. Delivery dates are usually staggered so that new merchandise is constantly on the selling floor.

Merchandise is accepted into a *central* or *regional receiving* and *distribution* location, where it is counted and checked for quality. Merchandise is ticketed according to information stated on the buyer's purchase order. The ticket includes bar code numbers for vendor, season, classification, department, and retail selling price. When this information is recorded in a computer, the data can be used for automatic ticket printing, record keeping, and accounts payable. It speeds distribution when manufacturers preticket merchandise using electronic data interchange.

Retailers try to reconcile differences (*fall out*) between actual shipments and purchase orders and decide whether to accept or reject partially filled orders, substitutions, or late shipments. If the order is unacceptable to the buyer for any of these reasons, it may be returned to the manufacturer or an unfilled order may be cancelled. Retailers use *chargebacks* to withhold payments to vendors to cover manufacturers' mistakes, such as late shipping, missing paperwork, or incorrect assortments.

Central receiving at Marks & Spencer in England.
(Courtesy of Marks & Spencer)

Buyers decide on the proper distribution of merchandise to multiunit stores, often already designated on the purchase order. From central receiving, merchandise is sent to individual stores and on to departments. The department manager also checks and verifies both the count and the information on the price tag. If approved, the merchandise moves into a stock room or onto the selling floor.

RECORD KEEPING

Retailers need to keep control of inventory, what merchandise is in stock and what has been sold, so that they are able to evaluate what to buy in the future.

Unit Control

To track and maintain records of inventory, retailers use a *unit control system*, part of their overall computer merchandise information system (MIS). Unit control is a system for recording the *number of units* of merchandise purchased, on order, received, in stock, or sold. Records are kept of additions to or subtractions from stock, from the time an order is placed with a manufacturer until that merchandise is sold. Information for unit control comes from purchase orders, sales records, and *merchandise transfers* (movement of merchandise from one store to another or elsewhere). Stores use inventory management systems (IMS) for unit control that collect and process merchandise information automatically.

The major advantage of unit control systems is that the records enable a buyer to keep track of consumer demand. If certain styles are selling quickly, the buyer may make additional purchases or even reorder; if styles are selling too slowly, the buyer may make markdown plans. Unit control systems also give a realistic growth picture in inflationary periods, when dollar volume increases may be misleading. Sally Frame Kasaks, president and CEO of Ann Taylor, feels that "it is more realistic to make decisions about merchandise needed per store, per week based on units rather than dollars."[7]

Inventory Control

Inventory control keeps records of the *dollar value* of merchandise on hand. Most stores use the retail method of inventory control, which involves figuring inventory at retail prices rather than on the basis of the wholesale cost.

Computer *inventory control* or *inventory management systems* (IMS) record receipts, sales, additions to and subtractions from stock, stock transfers from one store to another, and even returns by customers in dollars. When merchandise is sold, the point-of-sale terminal automatically feeds this information into sales records and deletes it in inventory records.

Physical Inventory

A *physical inventory* is the actual item-by-item count of all merchandise on hand, taken one to three times annually to confirm computer records and to comply with accounting regulations. In case of discrepancies between the book and the physical inventories, the physical count prevails and the inventory records must be adjusted accordingly.

Stock Shortages and Overages

Discrepancies between computer and physical inventory control are described as stock shortages or overages. Stock shortages mean a lower physical inventory than computer inventory and are due to theft, damage, or clerical error. Shortages are common and allowances must be made in initial pricing to cover these losses. Overages indicate a higher physical inventory than computer inventory and may be due to clerical error, misticketing, or shipment to incorrect location.

CUSTOMER SERVICE

To many consumers, and in many stores, service has become more important than fashion.

American retailers were pioneers in offering customer service. Years ago, Montgomery Ward and John Wanamaker instituted guaranteed-refund policies. Today, stores need more service because fashion is not as strong as it used to be. The success of Nordstrom and Wal-Mart, where customer ser-

The shoe department at Nordstrom, the pacesetting retailer for customer service.
(Courtesy of Nordstrom)

vice is a priority, has paved the way for a renewed interest in improved service in every store. The service in these stores has become the yardstick by which other stores now measure their own level of customer service.

Many retailers are attempting to become customer driven (to anticipate and focus on the needs of their customers), in fact to exceed customers' expectations. Retailers are trying to be more helpful and friendly so that customers will enjoy shopping. Retailers now offer an increasing number of services, such as the following:

◆ Greeters who welcome customers
◆ Special programs for regular customers
◆ Interactive videos that supply information on product location and special prices
◆ Alterations
◆ Gift wrapping
◆ In-store services such as photo finishing, restaurants and snack bars, packaging and mailing, and banking
◆ Free use of fax machines and telephones for customers waiting to be fitted
◆ Appropriate music
◆ Free personal shopping services
◆ Seasoned, helpful sales personnel

- Newsletters or "look" books
- No-question return privileges
- National credit card acceptance
- 800 telephone numbers
- Extended store hours
- Convenient restrooms and comfortable places to sit
- Free local delivery or free parking

RETAIL SALES

Selling techniques have become very important in trying to establish repeat business and customer loyalty.

In many stores, customers have to hunt for assistance. At mass merchants and discount stores, sales help is often limited to cash register clerks. Making sales associates more attentive helps to maximize sales.

Sales Training

Fashion selling requires special training that will give sales personnel merchandise information, confidence, and motivation. In small stores, training is informal, usually based on getting experience on the selling floor. In larger stores and chains, training is likely to be more structured. Chanel, for example, includes intense training aimed at teaching the selling staff how to establish ongoing relationships with customers to build loyalty and repeat business.

Sales meetings are held by the buyer or department manager on a daily, weekly, or monthly basis. The new merchandise is presented, sometimes on models, to show sales associates how garments should be worn and accessorized. The fashion director or buyers explain the selling features of merchandise so that the selling staff in turn can point out quality, fashion, and performance features to their customers. Buyers try to infuse enthusiasm into the sales force, hoping that it will be transmitted to the customer.

The Department Manager

In multiple-unit stores with one buyer in a central location, day-to-day operations, including responsibility for sales and the maintenance of visual merchandising, is generally left to a department manager. Department managers may request more stock of a hot item and give the buyer a projected estimate of quantities that they expect to sell within a certain period. In a small store, the buyer may also function as the department manager.

Selling

Sales, after all, are the key to success in retailing. The retailer's goal is to exceed its own merchandise plan sales goals. Of course, much depends on the buyer's selection of fashion assortments and whether the merchandise is in stock to meet consumer demand. However, success in better fashion retailing also depends on the ability of sales personnel. Sales associates also make the important customer contacts for the store. Jim Nordstrom, co-chairman of Nordstrom's, explains, "We like sales people to tell us what to do, what we need to buy."[8]

Personal Selling

Personal selling is the method involving the most customer contact. In this method, sales associates actively help customers, over the counter or on the floor, to choose merchandise suited to their tastes and needs. Sales associates are encouraged to greet customers at the door and to treat them as guests, tell them about the store's merchandising concepts, and ask questions about their life-styles, needs, and preferences. To build a multiple sale, associates are ready with alternative selections, wardrobe extenders, and accessory suggestions.

Preselling.   After a sale, associates keep files on customers, noting style and color preferences, sizes, and other pertinent information. When new merchandise comes in that seems appropriate for their customers, sales associates call or write a note to their customers. If a good rapport develops, customers are likely to return.

Sales Incentives

To improve customer service, many stores are now offering their sales staffs incentives to increase productivity. These incentives, which may take the form of higher salaries or commissions, help to attract better sales personnel. At Younkers in Des Moines, Iowa, for example, salaries are now based on the productivity of each sales associate. Nordstrom offers their

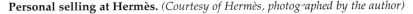

Personal selling at Hermès. (*Courtesy of Hermès, photographed by the author*)

sales associates a 6.75 percent commission, good benefits, and stock options as an incentive. Jim Nordstrom feels that it is also important "to have an atmosphere where people enjoy working."[9]

Vendors are getting much more involved in retail sales. Some manufacturers are supplying *merchandise representatives* to help train salespeople and help customers. For example Ellen Tracy's representatives conduct seminars on merchandising, presentation, and selling. Vendors often supply other aids to selling, such as videotapes, slide shows, or brochures (see Chapter 12).

Cooperative Salesperson Programs

Vendors become directly involved in retail selling by contributing to the salaries of sales associates through various types of programs. Some vendors share the cost of salaries; others pay entire salaries of exclusive salespeople recruited either by the vendor or the retailer. It is difficult, however, to work for two masters.

MERCHANDISING EVALUATION

Evaluation of the success or failure of a season helps buyers to plan for better merchandising for the future.

Merchandise Information Systems

Retailing executives and computer experts work together to develop *merchandise information systems* (MIS) to help retailers make merchandising evaluations based on inventory data. Retailers might use MIS to find out what colors, sizes, or vendors are selling best. They may be able to analyze this information by store or by item, on a daily, weekly, or monthly basis. Each retailer's system is different and yields different information.

How Merchants Use Data

By evaluating exactly what merchandise has been sold, retail executives are better able to plan for the future, thus beginning a new cycle of buying and selling. With this information, they are also able to measure the merchandising impact on the store's profitability. Buyers performance appraisals and bonus awards are also directly related to the achievement of financial goals. These evaluations can be ongoing or periodic processes.

The buyer may compile a *vendor analysis* showing the initial markup, markdowns, and resulting profit percentages gained on products from an individual resource. Although a vendor may have one or two bad seasons, the store will most likely drop a resource whose merchandise consistently gives them no profit.

Sales data can also be very revealing in relation to other important information. When compared with the previous year's data for the same period, the numbers show whether the store's volume grew over the year. When compared with the merchandise plan, the results show how well the store met its objectives established at the beginning of the period and therefore how well planning was done. When compared with inventory on hand and on order, as well as with customer returns, the figures can indicate whether merchandising, planning, and promotional activities were successful.

Sales data are also used to determine important ratios such as average gross sales, sales per square foot, and stock or inventory turnover:

Average Gross Sales

Total dollar sales for a given period divided by the number of transactions for the same period provide *average gross sales*. This ratio indicates the dollar volume per transaction. An increase in the ratio can indicate higher prices, which result from better merchandise, inflation, or larger sales per customer.

Sales per Square Foot

Total sales for a period divided by the number of square feet of selling space of a floor or store provide *sales per square foot*, an internationally used indicator of productivity. In their desire for internal growth, many stores are focusing on raising dollars per square foot in existing units, often through renovation. As a result, new departments may be created or existing ones may have their display space increased or decreased.

Stock or Inventory Turn

Stock turn is basically the number of times the stock is sold out and replaced in a given period. A high turnover is usually very desirable because it speeds the buying and selling cycle and constantly frees funds for renewed use, thus increasing the profitability of the retail operation. A high turn reduces the inventory risk; it increases the choice and selection available to the customer, since new merchandise arrives in the store continually; and it reduces the risk of losses due to outdated styles and resulting markdowns.

Stock turn is calculated by dividing total sales by average stock or inventory. For example, if seasonal sales total $1 million and average stock is $500,000, then the stock turn is 2. These *sales-related ratios* are not only used to evaluate a department or store, but are also very valuable in comparing different stores within a retail chain or in analyzing the success of the competition.

All these indicators are used by buyers and management not only to measure the success of the retail merchandising operation, but also to refine and improve the long-range planning of future merchandising activities. Evaluation and the establishment of new and more accurate goals results in a healthier, more profitable retail operation.

The major drawback of merchandising evaluations is that they cannot determine what styles, colors, or sizes customers wanted but could *not* find at the store. Jim Nordstrom complains that computer technology "never tells the buyer what the customer that walked out empty-handed wanted. It only tells them what they've got that's selling best."[10] So far, this information can be learned only informally through conversations with customers. Retailers hope to gain this information in the future via direct consumer responses fed into databases.

SUMMARY

As merchandisers, retailers must buy the right goods and have them in the store when their customers want them. Merchandising is guided by the fashion director and merchandising managers; responsibilities are divided between the buying line and the store line. Store policies and long-range planning help retailers to do their jobs effectively. The merchandise plan allocates specific amounts of money for the purchase of fashion assortments. In a fashion assortment, related merchandise is balanced between variation and consistency. Assortment planning is expressed as a buying plan that includes descriptions of the types, quantities, prices, and sizes of merchandise needed. Retailers provide their customers with both national brand and private-label merchandise.

Buyers' responsibilities cover both the buying and the selling aspects of retailing. Buyers plan what to buy, search the markets for goods that will meet their customers' needs, promote sales, and supervise merchandising and selling, only to begin the cycle again for a new season.

Computers aid in the planning, monitoring, and evaluation of retail sales. Electronic data interchange allows for automatic replenishment of basic merchandise, computer records of business transactions keep records of sales and inventory, and merchandise information systems help retailers evaluate sales in order to make future merchandising plans.

Customer service has become very important as have sales training and incentives. Customer acceptance is the basis for success and profitability in retailing. Retailers face a constant challenge to serve the public more efficiently and effectively in order to ensure continued growth and development.

CHAPTER REVIEW

Terms and Concepts

Briefly identify and discuss the following terms and concepts:

1. Fashion director
2. Buying line
3. Classifications
4. Merchandise plan
5. Assortment planning
6. Stock turn
7. Open-to-buy
8. Vendor
9. Key resources
10. Corporate buying
11. Line buying
12. Matrix system
13. Resident buying office
14. Private label
15. Central receiving
16. Markup
17. Unit control
18. Personal selling
19. Sales incentives
20. Customer service
21. Markdowns
22. Sell-through
23. Sales per square foot
24. Merchandise information systems
25. Vendor analysis
26. Merchandise representatives
27. Gross margin
28. MIS

Questions for Review

1. How are merchandising responsibilities organized?
2. Explain the differences between the store line and the buying line.
3. How can the merchandise plan be either management or buyer directed?
4. Describe the buying-selling cycle.
5. What are a buyer's responsibilities?
6. Why must a buyer research fashion trends?
7. What is the difference between line buying and trend buying?
8. Describe the difference between broad assortment and short-cycle buying.
9. What is the difference between a national brand and a private label?
10. What are the services of a buying office?
11. Describe inventory control systems.
12. Name five customer services. Are they effective?
13. Discuss the techniques and advantages of personal selling.
14. Explain the difference between promotions and markdowns.
15. Why is merchandising evaluation important?

Projects for Additional Learning

1. Interview a local store's fashion buyer. Ask how and when he or she buys fashion merchandise: At a market? From a sales representative? Through a buying ofice? From a catalog? What type of merchandise is purchased in what way? What is the buyer's favorite method and why? How often does the buyer go to a market center? Which one does he or she attend? Summarize the answers in a written report.

2. Visit the contemporary sportswear department in a retail store and examine the merchandise. Is it all from one manufacturer or has the buyer mixed garments from several vendors to carry out a fabric or color theme? Who are the major vendors in the department? What are the price ranges for jackets, sweaters, skirts, pants, and shirts? Which manufacturers have the most innovative looks? Ask salespeople which groups are selling the best and why they think so. Does the department have a good selection of sizes, colors, and styles? Write a critique of the department.

3. Shop a large department store. Study the three different ways to merchandise the suit look. Compare suits in (a) the missy coat and suit department (the suit is priced as a single unit); (b) the sportswear department (components are priced separately); (c) the dress department (components are priced as a unit, usually a dress with a jacket). What suit styles do you find in each department? Compare the selection (assortment), price ranges, quality, and fit in one department with those in the others. Which department has the best value and selection?

4. In a local store, evaluate a sale rack. Is the merchandise marked down or is it a special purchase (garments purchased at a lower price and offered as a promotional event)? Why was the marked-down merchandise marked down? In your opinion, was it because of styling, poor timing, poor construction, poor fit, unattractive colors, or too high a price? Summarize your findings in a short report.

NOTES

[1] Joan Bergholt, general merchandise manager, interview, January 18, 1995.

[2] Ibid.

[3] Jaime Villablanca, buyer, interview, January 9, 1995.

[4] As quoted by Pete Born, "Wexner Shares Trade Secrets at FIT," *Women's Wear Daily*, February 23, 1989.

[5] As quoted by Sharon Edelson, "The March to the Middle," *Women's Wear Daily*, March 2, 1995, p. 6.

[6] Walter Loeb, retail analyst and consultant, Loeb Associates, interview, April 1995.

[7] Interview, April 1995.

[8] Jim Nordstrom, co-chairman, Nordstrom's, interview, February 27, 1995.

[9] Ibid.

[10] Ibid.

A Bloomingdale's window. (*Courtesy of Bloomingdale's, photo by Willo Font*)

15

RETAIL FASHION PROMOTION

CAREER FOCUS

Fashion promotion provides a wide variety of interesting and creative career opportunities. The advertising director, creative director, ad manager, and copy chiefs supervise layout artists, writers, media buyers, merchandise coordinators, and photographers. Directors of fashion, special events, and/or public relations have regional managers or store coordinators to carry out responsiblities in individual stores. The visual merchandising director of a chain of stores oversees regional or individual store visual merchandising managers and a staff of designers.

CHAPTER OBJECTIVES

After reading this chapter you should have attained competence in the following areas:

1. Understanding of the purpose of sales promotion
2. Explaining the purpose, goals, and procedures of advertising, publicity, special events, fashion shows, and visual merchandising
3. Describing various types of media and their relation to store needs and target customers
4. Describing the buyer's role in promotion

At each level of the fashion industry, the objective is to increase market share and sell products to consumers. *Promotion*, in the broadest sense, is the effort to further those sales by means of advertising, publicity, special events, and visual merchandising. The main purpose of all phases of fashion promotion is to generate more sales by inspiring current customers to buy more and by attracting new customers. The primary challenge of promotion is to get the customer into the store.

Promotion involves communicating a store image or the existence of a product to consumers. It is an attempt to attract the type of customer for whom the merchandise is intended. Therefore, before beginning sales promotion efforts, each fashion business must determine its needs and objectives.

This chapter deals particularly with retail fashion promotion, including planning, advertising, public relations, special events, and visual merchandising. The methods used by retailers to promote fashion vary considerably. Merchants must choose the approach best suited to their customers, merchandise, and the size of their business and budget.

Advertising designer Rob Corder discusses an ad proof with associate creative director Peggi Davis at Macy's. *(Photographed by the author)*

PLANNING AND DIRECTION

The sales promotion director, fashion director, advertising and creative directors, visual merchandising director, merchandise managers, and buyers work together to plan and coordinate promotions.

In small stores, a single person may handle all promotional activities with the help of outside consultants or agencies. In a large store, a sales promotion or marketing director manages or coordinates the joint efforts of advertising, special events, visual merchandising, public relations, and the fashion office. Sometimes the fashion office is part of merchandising or visual merchandising is part of store planning. In any case, the sales promotion or marketing director, fashion director, advertising and/or creative directors, visual merchandising director, merchandise managers, and buyers must agree on what to promote, when to promote it, and how to reach their target market. At planning meetings, managers discuss how to communicate fashion trends and important designer promotions within the context of the store's image.

Stores schedule promotional activities for seasons and holidays throughout the retail calendar year as an integral part of the year's merchandising plan. Promotional events are sometimes scheduled up to a year ahead of time. In spite of all the scheduling, however, new promotions can supersede all the best laid plans. For example, plans for scheduled promotions could be cancelled in order to launch a new fragrance. Sales promotion has to be flexible in order to be current.

FASHION ADVERTISING

The advertising director, creative director, art director, writers, and artists work together to create retail advertising. They may be assisted by similar personnel at advertising agencies.

The largest portion of the sales promotion budget in a retail store is normally allocated to advertising. Advertising involves the planning, writing, designing, and scheduling of *paid* announcements designed to attract customers' attention to a fashion product or event.

Advertising is presented to reach specific target customers or potential customers. Therefore, advertising style must be altered to reach various types of consumers. To the contemporary customer, trendy clothes are sold with sex and sizzle; to the upwardly mobile professional, merchandise is presented in enhanced status images; to the family-oriented consumer, fashion is presented in an atmosphere of hearth and home.

Kinds of Advertising

Stores use three basic types of advertisement: image, item, and promotional advertising.

Image Advertising

Image advertising focuses on fashion image, fashion leadership, community goodwill, a new or remodeled store, or a special event. While it may show merchandise, the goal is to build consumer confidence, community goodwill, create a mood, or create excitement about a new store or event. The "Softer Side of Sears" campaign is a good example of image advertising.

Item Advertising

In today's lean economic climate, advertising must sell merchandise. Therefore, many fashion retailers have abandoned image advertising in favor of single-item advertising. The goal of item advertising is sales as a direct result of the ad. This type of advertising is often done on a cooperative arrangement between manufacturers and retailers. For example, Saks Fifth Avenue advertises items by leading designers.

A Saks Fifth Avenue advertisement. *(Courtesy of Saks Fifth Avenue)*

Promotional Advertising

Promotional advertising is price directed. It might proclaim that a store has low prices or it might announce storewide sales or clearances. Some stores are more promotional than others and, therefore, do more promotional advertising. Macy's, for example, advertises many promotional events, such as its White Flower Day sales.

Scheduling and Planning

The *advertising plan* is based on past experience, present conditions, and future expectations. An advertising plan is a guide for a specific period (such as a week, a quarter of the year, or a season) and for the amount of advertising that a store intends to do in that period to attract customers. Ads are sometimes scheduled up to a year ahead of the selling season, whereas the actual content may be planned closer to the selling season.

A *budget* is prepared, indicating the allocation of funds for advertising production and media. Advertising space in newspapers or time on radio or television must be contracted. A *timetable* is developed detailing how and by whom the ad production is to be carried out in order to meet media deadlines and other requirements.

Media

In advertising, *media* is a general term used to cover all methods of transmitting a sales message. The media include newspapers, magazines, radio, television, billboards, displays, and direct mail. Advertising department or agency media buyers must choose the medium or combination of media to reach a specific target market. Each consumer group has unique tastes, ideas, and interests and consequently responds to different media. Media buyers must choose which particular radio or television station, newspaper, or magazine will reach the appropriate customer for specific merchandise.

Several ads are usually placed in different media to support each other and strengthen the campaign. To balance the spot radio commercial aimed at the car commuter, the store might also place an ad covering the same material in the newspaper for bus and train commuters to read.

Repetition and *consistency* make the advertising message memorable. The same ad heard at the same time every day on the radio or a fashion ad in the same illustration style every week on the same page in the newspaper makes people keenly aware of the store or brand name as well as the fashion message.

Newspapers

Newspaper advertisements, or *run of paper (ROP)*, are popular among most fashion retailers for these reasons:

◆ They provide visual as well as verbal means of telling consumers what merchandise the company has to offer.

◆ They may be offered daily.

◆ Layouts, art, and copy are relatively easy to produce.

◆ Media costs are comparatively low.

◆ They provide a quick turn time from idea to appearance. An idea may be presented at 3:00 P.M. one day and appear in the next morning's newspaper.

Space and Positioning. Media buyers buy space in newspapers that reach the store's potential customers. Day after day, readers in specific geographical areas or trade groups are exposed to the company's fashion message. The producer or retailer can even buy a certain desirable position in the paper, such as the back page of the front section, often paying premium rates to have ads appear the same place each day. For example, Macy's California advertises daily on the front page of one section of the *San Francisco Chronicle*.

Supplements.   The use of preprinted advertising, especially in magazine format inserted into newspapers, is an increasingly successful form of advertising for retailers. Many stores are using the glossy magazine format because, like a catalog, it has a longer "coffee table life."

Vendors, who contribute money toward the cost of this kind of advertising, like the huge circulation and relatively low cost per thousand. Inserts are particularly cost effective when the retailer has many branch stores in an area served by just one newspaper. Related stores under the same corporate umbrella may use the same magazine with only a change of store name on the cover. Macy's West, for example, produces the same Sunday supplement magazine for all the Macy's California, Texas, and Minnesota stores as well as Bullock's. Circulation can be anywhere from a million copies to many millions for stores spread over many states.

Magazines

Stores advertise in magazines that have the same target market as they do. National retailers like Saks Fifth Avenue regularly advertise in fashion magazines because they can benefit from national circulation. These magazines also have regional editions that carry pages of local store advertising. Some retailers also advertise in shelter or general interest magazines to reach certain markets. Metro or regional magazines are used by stores whose target customers live in a specific area.

To provide direct consumer response, some retailers such as Bloomingdale's insert pages of catalog-like advertisements into magazines. Frequently these ads provide 800 numbers to facilitate ordering. Other stores, such as Saks Fifth Avenue, use tear-out response cards inserted next to their ad in the magazine to pull traffic into the store and to track the success of the ad. Customers are requested to bring the cards to the store to exchange for a free gift or a gift with purchase.

Television

Television advertising is growing in popularity as the general public is watching more and reading less. The medium offers the advantage of being able to show how clothing might fit into a real-life situation. However, advertising is hampered by consumers' opportunity to browse channels. Other major drawbacks to TV advertising are the costs of air time and production.

Time Buys.   Purchased by media buyers, the cost of *air time* is determined by the length of the commercial, the time of day and the day of the week it is to be shown, and the size of the audience. Prime time, the most expensive, is between 7:00 and 11:00 P.M. when the greatest number of adult viewers is watching. Air time in a large city with a large viewing audience is much more expensive than air time in a smaller city or town. Media selection is based on how successful stations are at reaching viewers as measured by subjective *gross rating points*.

Production.   A TV commercial might cost anywhere from $50,000 to $500,000 for a 30-second production. Production costs cover fees for the writer, producer, director, talent, voice-over announcer, camera work, location, editing, music, and expenses for wardrobe, props, lighting, film, and developing. Commercials may be produced by broadcast agencies or by local TV stations.

National Television.   National television advertising is used by large national firms that sell and distribute apparel across the country and have large enough advertising budgets to pay for production and buy network television time. Sears, for example, uses TV advertising in its "Softer Side of Sears" campaign to enhance its image. A network television show reaches millions of potential consumers throughout the country.

Cable Television.   Cable television shopping networks, such as QVC, HSN, and MTV, have also become popular vehicles for fashion advertisement and provide an opportunity for direct sales response. See the section on non-store retailing in Chapter 13.

Radio

Because viewers can see the fashion, television has an advantage over radio for apparel advertising. However, radio can make the listener aware of a store location or brand name. Peak radio listening hours, which cost more than other periods, are during drive time, the rush hours when commuters listen most to their car radios. If the target market for a particular campaign is professional men and women, they might be reached most effectively by spot radio ads on various stations at rush hour. Stations are selected for their target market appeal. However, as with television, the wide diversification of formats has made it increasingly difficult to target an entire age range or demographic group on any one station.

A Henri Bendel direct-mail brochure.
(Courtesy of Dente & Cristina Associates, Inc.)

Direct Response

To promote instant sales, there is an increasing trend toward providing the means for direct response in all types of advertising. 800 numbers, which have revolutionized telephone ordering, are provided in many advertisements to encourage immediate response. Telephone companies are spending millions of dollars to install fiber-optic cable to carry digital signals to facilitate interactive shopping.

Direct Mail

Direct mail is a highly effective form of advertising because it is addressed to each individual customer. As discussed in Chapter 2, databases, with information gleaned from customer purchases, can isolate specific groups of customers according to their buying habits, such as frequency of purchases, average dollar amount of purchases, and the exact departments where purchases were made. Stores are able to mail specific statement enclosures or catalogs to target audiences, such as mothers of small children, large-sized customers, or petite women.

Statement enclosures are advertisements, often provided by manufacturers, that are sent with monthly billings to charge customers.

Catalogs have become a tremendously popular form of advertising because of the shopping convenience they provide to working women (see the discussion of mail-order retailing in Chapter 13).

Image brochures are sometimes mailed or given out to customers in the store. These are not catalogs per se because they do not include order forms; they simply communicate a manufacturer's or store's merchandising image to customers.

Billboards

Billboard advertising is sometimes used by retail stores. On a smaller scale, this type of advertising has been adapted to bus shelters that are directed both to car and transit commuters, especially in large cities. This method has proved effective for companies such as The Gap, Esprit, and Levi Strauss.

Cooperative Advertising

Fiber producers, fabric producers, and apparel manufacturers often cooperate with retailers to pay for advertisements that feature their merchandise. Co-op allocations are based on a percentage of net sales to the retailer and may provide a large percentage of media and/or production costs. This additional money enables retailers to make ads larger or to run them more frequently. The resulting increased advertising volume may also help the retailer qualify for a lower media rate. Many retailers would not be able to advertise merchandise without co-op money from producers.

The Advertising Department

Because they do so much newspaper advertising, some large retail stores have in-house advertising departments. The advertising director supervises three areas; art, copy, and production.

Art

The art department is responsible for *layouts*, sketches of how the ad will look. Layouts can be made on computer using software programs such as Quark Xpress or Aldus Pagemaker. Art department or freelance artists execute the final drawings or photographers take pictures. The use of photography is currently popular because its realistic qualities lend themselves to promotional or item advertising. Illustrations are especially appropriate for image advertising, for which the creation of an illusion may be important.

Copy

Copywriters produce the written description for advertisements. The good writer pictures the customer who is reading the ad and writes to him or her. Sales copy, which stresses value, is quite different from high-fashion copy, which emphasizes an editorial fashion message.

Production

The production department puts all parts of the ad into a mechanical composition according to the layout. It is the mechanical technician's responsibility to see that the finished ad is the same as the original idea and layout. This is now accomplished by computer. A scanner is used to digitize photographs or color film. The scans are incorporated into the layout with the copy, store name logo, and any other graphic art to complete the ad.

Traffic

The traffic department is responsible for the flow of artwork and copy between the store, printers, engravers, photographers, newspapers, and radio and television stations. After final approval from the advertising director, art director, and copy chief, the finished document is released. The finished ad can be transmitted electronically via telephone line or modem to newspapers around the world or sent on a Syquest disk by messenger or overnight mail.

Production assistant Rick Thoman creates an ad layout on a computer at Macy's (the glove is to protect the prints and negatives).
(Photographed by the author)

Advertising Agencies

Many retailers use outside advertising agencies to handle projects, even those who have their own in-house staffs. Agencies often help when there is a heavy workload or for a special project such as a magazine format insert. Many stores also use agencies as a cost-effective way of producing timely advertising without having to retain an expensive in-house staff. Payment may be handled by a monthly retainer based on the amount of time the work takes or on a project fee basis.

In large agencies, groups of people are assigned to particular accounts under the direction of an account executive, who acts as liaison between the agency and the client. Agencies also use freelance copywriters, illustrators, and production artists to help them with heavy workloads and special projects. The drawback to using agencies is that it takes time for them to become acquainted with the store's point of view. On the other hand, an agency can offer objective ideas about how to project the store's image.

PUBLICITY

Publicity is usually handled by the directors of fashion, special events, and/or public relations and writers on their staffs.

Publicity is the spreading of information about people, special events, or newsworthy topics through various communications media. There are no media costs for publicity, but for that very reason it is difficult to obtain. It is also considered more prestigious than advertising because it is the result of an editor's choice, rather than the payment of money. Media editors choose the material they will use because they think that it may be of interest to the community and decide how, when, and where the message will be used. Publicity helps promote the sale of fashion merchandise by making a style, manufacturer, retailer, trend, or other aspect of fashion better known to the public.

Publicity Campaigns

Retailers hope to bring their names to the public eye by calling attention to newsworthy developments in their stores. They may create events such as fashion shows or celebrity personal appearances in order to obtain publicity. Stores provide the media with information about such events or topics in the hope that the media will publicize them. A publicity campaign may be handled by the public relations office or the fashion office, whichever is more concerned with the topic or event. Alternatively, it may be prepared by an agency or consultant.

Newspaper fashion editors often use publicity releases and photos to write their articles. Fashion magazines give publicity to retail stores in editorial credits, the mention of the store name as a source of merchandise that is editorially featured. Radio and television also give some publicity, especially to their advertisers. Paying advertisers are becoming more demanding of the media in their requests for publicity.

Press Package.   As part of a publicity campaign, a *press package* consisting of a news release and photographs might be prepared to send to media editors. A *news release* is a written statement of the important facts about a person, place, or coming event. The news release is often accompanied by glossy photographs, which may be provided by merchandise vendors.

Individual Approaches.   To create an aura of exciting news, the publicity director might telephone media editors. To achieve maximum benefits from publicity, public relations or fashion office staff direct publicity to the media whose audience would be most interested in their message. News may be approached from various angles to ensure that each medium gets a unique story. For the Bloomingdale's A/X Armani Exchange campaign, the public relations director told the news story from a fashion perspective—who Armani is, what the shop looks like, why the clothes are different—to fashion editors and approached the store opening from a business angle—A/X shops opening all over the United States—for business editors.[1]

SPECIAL EVENTS

Corporate directors of special events and/or public relations, regional managers, store coordinators, and their staffs need superb organizational skills to carry out a wide variety of special events.

Special events are designed to give customers a specific time and reason to come into the store or to create goodwill. They represent an attempt to replace or renew the personal customer contact that has been lost in many large stores. When well planned and executed, special events can enhance the store's identity, build customer loyalty, and create a sense of community spirit. The retail store as "theater" also caters to the many consumers who enjoy shopping as entertainment. Michael Gould, CEO of Bloomingdale's, commented, "We are in the entertainment business, and if it's pleasant to be in our stores, people will stay there longer."[2]

Most special events are planned and carried out by a special events director and, in the case of a fashion show, in cooperation with the fashion office. In a flagship store, separate offices usually handle each function: fashion, public relations, and special events. In a branch or smaller store, all three functions may be handled out of one office. The special events office must schedule events in conjunction with the advertising department to support store strategies. It schedules guest appearances in the store and sends press releases and invitations for both in-store and community events. These may include fashion seminars, convention tie-ins, community services, the launch of a new designer perfume, and/or fashion shows. One example of a successful event is Macy's Easter Flower Show in San Francisco or their Thanksgiving Parade in New York City.

Fashion Shows

Fashion shows are special events that communicate a fashion story. The selection and organization of the fashions and model bookings may be done by the fashion office, while invitations and other arrangements may be handled by the special events department. There are four possible ways to organize a show: a formal show, a department show, designer trunk shows, or informal modeling.

Formal fashion shows take a great deal of advance planning involving booking models and fittings and arranging for a runway, scenery, light-

Izaac Mizrahi backstage before a fashion show at Saks Fifth Avenue.
(Courtesy of Izaac Mizrahi, photographed by the author)

ing, microphones, music, seating, and assistants. Clothes are generally grouped according to styling, color, or other visual criteria. Models and music are selected to complement the clothes and set a mood. A designer-centered event can cost from $10,000 to $500,000. Because of their cost, these shows are usually reserved for charity events, and stores look for co-sponsors to share costs. For an Italian designer collection show, for example, costs could be split between the store, the designers, and the Italian Trade Commission.

Designer trunk shows are done in cooperation with a single vendor and are a popular way to sell expensive collections. Invitations are sent to the best customers according to records kept by sales associates. The designer or representative travels from store to store with the collection, which is usually shown on models in the designer collections department. Customers get to see the entire collection unedited by a buyer and may order from the samples in their size. While some designers and retailers do 50 percent of their total business through trunk shows, others find them time-consuming, exhausting work and have given them up.

Department fashion shows, on a much smaller scale, are produced in-store to generate immediate sales. Usually a platform is set up right in the department that carries the clothes.

Informal fashion shows are the easiest to produce. A few models walk through the store showing the fashions that they are wearing to customers who are shopping or having lunch in the store's restaurant. The models can take their time and customers enjoy asking them questions. This is often done in conjunction with a trunk show or special promotion.

VISUAL MERCHANDISING

The corporate visual merchandising director, store planning director, architects, regional creative directors, and individual store visual managers and designers create the store's visual image.

Visual merchandising, or visual presentation, is the means to communicate a store's fashion, value, and quality message to prospective customers. Visual merchandising is a team effort involving management, including the fashion director and the sales promotion director; store planning; merchandise managers and buyers; the visual merchandising director, designers, and staff; the sign shop; and the individual department managers and sales associates. The actual presentation work is done by the visual merchandising department, and the daily arrangement of merchandise is carried out by the department manager and sales associates.

Since the ultimate goal of visual merchandising—and of retailing—is to get the customer to buy, visual merchandising must entice the consumer into the store, effectively present the fashions the store has to offer, and show the customer how to wear and accessorize them within the context of fashion trends.

Store Planning and Design

Visual merchandising begins with the store building itself. Although store planning is usually managed by a separate department, it is necessary to discuss it as a background to visual merchandising. Store management, including the visual merchandising director, store planners, and architects, want the store image to be reflected in the design of the store. Many retailers are renovating existing stores in order to generate new traffic and increase market share. They are trying to create a warm, friendly atmosphere in the process.

Departments

The store is divided into departments by fashion category and/or into designer or brand shops. Traditionally, the main selling area is reserved for cosmetics, jewelry, and accessories. The rest of the store is divided into groups of departments and shops that relate to one another by category or price range. Department location is considered and some shops are given prime location to attract attention. Destination departments containing merchandise such as swim suits, lingerie, or coats that customers seek because they are needed can be in secondary locations.

In addition, department relationships, aisle space, and traffic patterns are considered to make the departments and merchandise accessible and to help customers find what they want easily. To comply with the American Disabilities Act, aisles must be wide enough for easy wheelchair access.

Store Image and Target Customers

All this planning must be consistent with the store's image. As many of the same fashions are available at different stores, presentation is an important means of creating the impression of uniqueness. The store's image must also appeal to target customers. For example, attracting the mature customer to a store or department with quality merchandise requires the creation of a warm, comfortable atmosphere. This is often achieved with wood paneling, comfortable seating, paintings, and furniture, such as those found in an elegant home. In the case of basic merchandise, the retailer may appeal to traditionalists by presenting a clean, orderly environment with neatly folded merchandise, such as found at The Gap or Benetton. In the case of the contemporary customer, a store may present a trendy image carried out with glitz, innovative fixtures, and rock music.

Seasonal Visual Merchandising

Seasonal merchandising themes are planned many months in advance in conjunction with the seasons, other store promotions, and arrivals of new merchandise. Planning a theme gives a focus to visual merchandising and a consistent look throughout the store.

A rich, warm, comfortable atmosphere created in Bergdorf Goodman's men's department. *(Courtesy of Bergdorf Goodman)*

Working within this framework, the visual merchandising department makes up a *seasonal calendar* indicating the dates on which specific merchandise is to be featured and the number and location of windows and interior displays that are to show the merchandise. In some cases, the theme may involve a tie-in with a vendor to introduce a new line, such as Anne Klein's men's accessories. The challenge for the visual merchandising department is to blend in with the vendor's concepts while preserving the store's identity.

A Saks Fifth Avenue holiday accessories window.
(Courtesy of Saks Fifth Avenue)

Windows

The visual statements made in downtown store windows or in presentations at a mall store entrance are the customers' first encounter with the store and must effectively and correctly convey the store's image and fashion focus. As marketing executive Virginia Meyer commented, "Store windows as well as interior displays attract, compell, and persuade in a subtle or not so subtle fashion.... A good presentation can and should stop you, get your attention, and maybe even make you smile. In a very broad sense, visual presentation not only helps to sell the merchandise itself but the store [as well]. It becomes a part of the store's personality and is one of the reasons for returning to a store time and again."[3]

"Windows are a uniquely urban phenomenon," explained Steven Kornajcik, corporate senior vice-president for R. H. Macy & Co. "A window is a total environment, a complete statement on its own. It can show humor or be theatrical, anything to attract attention."[4] Windows are usually the most dramatic of the store's visual statements. An attention-getting window can entice a shopper into the store. Many stores use look through windows to make the windows part of the total store environment.

Special event windows tie-in to events and promotions or convey the spirit of a holiday season. They create excitement and interest to see more in the store.

Fashion message windows feature the newest fashion trends and suggest ways to coordinate accessories for those looks. These dramatic windows are created to attract attention and persuade customers to buy a new garment and/or accessory.

Direct-sell windows are used mostly by stores that carry popularly priced merchandise. They show a representative assortment of the store's merchandise accompanied by prices to tempt the customer with a possible bargain.

Interiors

The customer is further exposed to fashion and accessory purchase suggestions by interior presentations that may be located near the entrance to the store, at entrances to each floor or department, or in the various departments on ledges, counters, or platforms. Interior presentations are critical for stores in shopping malls, which may have few or no windows. In this case, visual merchandising must capitalize on the wide store entrance that gives the passing shopper a sweeping view of the selling area, giving entry area displays great impact.

Presentation areas positioned in front of each department or shop set the tone for the area and attract the customer. These displays highlight the most interesting merchandise from the surrounding area within the context of the store theme. Joe Feczko, visual merchandising director for Neiman Marcus, explained, "The inspiration always begins with the merchandise. The props, the colors, the backgrounds are all driven by the merchandise and the item."[5]

Interior displays may take the form of *image* or *life-style* presentations (mannequins posed in a scene and dressed appropriately) or *single items*, shown on a form or stand. Sportswear is usually shown in groups, while evening wear may be shown by individual item. By showing total wardrobing concepts including accessories, displays help to both educate and entice the customer.

A life-style presentation of Ralph Lauren summer fashions at Saks Fifth Avenue.
(Courtesy of Saks Fifth Avenue)

Elements of Visual Merchandising

The elements used to show or enhance the clothes on display include mannequins and other forms, fixtures, ladders, poles, platforms, tables or other furniture, paintings and other wall decoration, tablecloths, banners, posters, counter cards, lighting effects, accessories, and props. Realistic mannequins are most popular because the customer can relate to the way the clothes look when worn on the body. Mannequins change with fashion and are made in the image of the current ideal of beauty. Most of all, visual merchandisers try to enhance merchandise with other merchandise.

Standards Manuals

Stores set standards for consistent visual merchandising. Standards manuals list exact specifications for all display forms, fixtures, and props, for example, the height of a T-shaped stand and how it should be placed on the floor, placement of tables, and so forth. Quarterly addenda update the standards as new ideas are implemented. Sales associates are trained to maintain these standards in each department.

Presentation Packages

The corporate or central visual merchandising office may create presentation packages for branch stores so that the entire group or chain will have the same look. Large presentation packages are assembled for volume stores and smaller versions of the displays for stores with less space. Flexibility allows customizing of packages for seasonal differences in various regions. For example, a theme around fall leaves in Washington, D.C., would not be suitable in Phoenix, Arizona.[6]

In the case of in-store designer or brand boutiques, the vendor has visual merchandising requirements for presenting its line of merchandise. In some cases, the manufacturer supplies the fixtures so that they are the same in every store. It is often difficult to reconcile the individuality of these shops with the store's own identity.

The Department

Successful visual merchandising should invite customers into a department. Fixtures are arranged, usually in a grid pattern, to give access and a clear view of the department from every angle. Visual merchandising must draw the customer to the department most suited to his or her life-style. There is no sign that says, "If you are age 38 to 50, live in the suburbs, and wear an average size 10, go to the 'Miss Macy' department." Yet each department is merchandised with certain life-style statistics in mind. Informational signing and large life-style photographs on the walls, at Wal-Mart for example, help customers find their way.

Because a customer must be able to see fashion in order to buy it, proper fixtures must be used to display stock. The merchandise itself and the way it is presented must appeal to each specific customer. Stock is arranged in an orderly, attractive manner to contribute to the visual effect of the department and to help customers quickly find what they want. Merchandising and design concepts must be presented correctly: coordinates must be shown together and separates and other apparel displayed in groups by color, fabric, or related items. The department manager and sales staff need to rearrange merchandise in order to give greater visibility to slow-selling goods.

Apparel

In an apparel department, assortments may be displayed on *wall racks, rounders* (circular racks), *four-way* or *star* fixtures (with four arms), or *T-shaped stands* (with two arms). Assortment displays must permit customers to see an entire range of colors or styles in each size. To avoid visual monotony, the fixtures are usually mixed. Although wall racks utilize space well and rounders show off a color story, they are not the most desirable means of display because the customer is confronted with nothing but sleeves (or sides of garments). On frontal projection fixtures, such as the four-way or the T-stand, the garments face outward so that the customer can see the fronts. The first hanger on a sportswear T-stand is usually an H-shaped hanger showing a coordinated outfit so that the customer can see how the various pieces work together. Fixtures are becoming more sophisticated and many stores are also creating their own custom fixtures to fit in better with overall store design.

Stores such as Benetton and the Gap have made folding a popular and space-saving way to display merchandise. Store standards dictate placement of shelves or tables and how the merchandise should be folded and grouped. Retailers have found that merchandise on tables sells better because it is more accessible. Sally Frame Kasaks, CEO of Ann Taylor, remarked, "We were able to increase floor capacity 30 percent by folding and stacking apparel in our casual merchandise areas."[7]

Accessories

Much more attention is being paid to visual merchandising of accessories. Traditionally located in the main selling area, accessories are now available on apparel floors so that customers can quickly accessorize their clothing purchases. Accessories can be shown in cases or on shelves or tables or hung on wall display racks. Stores must balance the saleability of accessible, "open-sell" merchandise with the security and exclusivity of case display.

THE BUYER'S ROLE IN FASHION PROMOTION

Because promotion is a team effort, it also requires the involvement of buyers.

Buyers recommend plans for promotions to the heads of the sales promotion department in conjunction with the projected merchandise plan. Suggestions for advertising, displays, special events, and all other types of

A Polo Ralph Lauren shop utilizes wall racks, T-stands, and folding to display merchandise. (*Photograph by Kim Brun Studios*)

promotions are developed with the specialists in these areas, and joint efforts must be coordinated.

Advertising

Buyers request ads on the basis of their merchandise plans. They must provide complete information about the merchandise to the advertising copywriter concerning fabric, colors, styling details, price, and sizes. The garment or accessory itself must be given to the illustrator, layout artist, or photographer. The buyer helps determine the proportion and position of the ad and must carefully check ad copy for accuracy. He or she must then make sure that the merchandise has been delivered and is on the selling floor, with appropriate sign copy, when the ad runs.

Visual Merchandising

Buyers may also request window and in-store displays. They choose garments, perhaps with the fashion director, or accessories that carry out the promotional theme and image of the store. They must also make sure that there is a good selection of that merchandise on the selling floor for possible customer purchase.

Special Events

Buyers may initiate special events and fashion shows. For example, the buyer of a designer collection might arrange with the fashion office for a designer to make a personal appearance to introduce a new collection. The advertising and publicity departments announce this event to the community, giving the public the opportunity to meet a well-known designer. If the results are favorable, both the designer and the store may win new customers.

EVALUATION

All the people involved in sales promotion, directors, managers, coordinators, artists, writers, designers, and buyers, evaluate the effectiveness of their efforts in order to plan for the future.

At the end of a promotional event or an advertising campaign, sales are analyzed and the campaign's effectiveness evaluated. Advertising can be evaluated by sales volume. It is very difficult to analyze sales results in relation to visual merchandising or special events, however. Unless, for example, a fashion show actually takes place in a department and people stay afterward to make purchases, how can the value of the event be measured? Management usually evaluates the effectiveness of a campaign as a whole and makes recommendations for the next year.

SUMMARY

Advertising, publicity, special events, and display help to promote retail sales. Advertising is the use of paid time or space in media such as television, radio, newspapers, magazines, and direct mail. There are no media costs for publicity, but any material used is the choice of the media editors. Special events such as fashion shows draw people into the store and create community goodwill. Visual merchandising is the in-store presentation of a merchandising message. Promotional efforts are coordinated with buyers in each merchandising area. Promotion has its limits, however it is ultimately the consumer who accepts or rejects fashion.

CHAPTER REVIEW

Terms and Concepts

Briefly identify and discuss the following terms and concepts:

1. Sales promotion
2. Advertising
3. Publicity
4. Special events
5. Visual merchandising
6. Life-style displays
7. Image advertising
8. Merchandise or promotional advertising
9. Media
10. Radio and television spots
11. Direct-mail advertising
12. Cooperative advertising
13. Layouts
14. Copy
15. Ad production
16. Advertising agencies
17. Press release
18. Editorial credits
19. Inserts
20. Display packages
21. Standards manuals
22. Trunk shows

Questions for Review

1. What is the purpose of fashion promotion?
2. Explain the difference between advertising and publicity
3. Discuss the types of media used in fashion promotion and give examples of how each reaches target groups.
4. Explain how cooperative advertising works.
5. Why is it essential for a buyer to be involved in retail promotion?
6. Why is visual merchandising important?

Projects for Additional Learning

1. Find and clip from your fashion magazine collection five examples of co-op advertising. Find the names and/or trademark symbols of the fiber producer, fabric producer (if mentioned), manufacturer, and stores.
2. Analyze the advertising campaign of a large chain store. Search through newspapers covering a one-month period and clip the store's advertisements. Are they always on the same page of the newspaper? Do they use photography or an artist's illustrations? Do they have a high-fashion image or popular appeal? Do they show the merchandise to good advantage? Do you feel that the advertisements are effective? What other types of advertisement do they use? Magazines? Television? Billboards?
3. Attend a special event at a local store. What is the purpose of the event? To draw people into the store? To create community goodwill? Describe the event and add your own photographs, if possible. Do you think the event was carried out successfully?
4. Visit a local department store and evaluate its visual merchandising. Do the displays carry out a theme throughout the store? Describe the decor and display techniques, both in windows and in interiors. Is lighting used effectively? Is merchandise attractively arranged? Do you feel that the total image of the store successfully relates to the merchandise offered?

NOTES

[1] Ann Stock, social secretary for the White House, formerly public relations director at Bloomingdale's, interview, April 30, 1992.

[2] As quoted by Dianne Pogoda, "Spruce up to Stir Sales," *Women's Wear Daily*, February 1, 1993, p. 8.

[3] Interview, January 1993.

[4] As quoted by Dianne Pogoda, "At Macy's—Turning Windows Into Worlds," *Women's Wear Daily*, November 30, 1992, p. 12.

[5] As quoted by Rusty Williamson, "Refining Neiman's Vista," *Women's Wear Daily*, Best of Group III/Dallas (May 1990), p. 12.

[6] Roland Theile, corporate visual merchandising director, Nordstrom, interview, April 1995.

[7] Interview, April 1995.

Appendix

CAREER GUIDELINES

How will you fit into the fashion business? Choosing a career—not just a job, but work that you will enjoy and build on for the future—is one of the most important decisions of your life. I hope that this book will help you to make that decision.

This appendix tries to give a realistic picture of fashion career possibilities. It surveys job opportunities in textiles, fashion design, marketing, production, retailing, and promotion. In planning for your career, you should first understand yourself, your talents, and your ambitions. Then apply those abilities and interests to the field that offers you the best employment opportunities.

THE TEXTILE INDUSTRY

If you enjoy working with fabrics, you will find several possibilities for interesting employment in the textile industry. A wide variety of skilled and talented people is needed, including artists to create new designs, scientists to develop fibers and finishes, technicians to develop and work knitting and weaving processes, and marketing specialists to market fibers to mills and fabrics to manufacturers.

Fiber and Fabric Development

Research

Science and chemical engineering students may be interested in a career in the laboratories of the large chemical corporations that develop new fibers or at fabric companies or fiber associations that experiment with new treatments and finishes for fabrics.

Textile Design and Merchandising

Textile designers and stylists need a combination of specialized art and technical training. For print design, designers have to be able to apply their skills to two-dimensional design, yet with the understanding that the end use will be in a three-dimensional garment. Fabric stylists have to know the technical aspects of fiber and fabric production so that they are able to create interesting new blends of yarns, as well as new knit and woven constructions. Computer knowledge is also essential.

Production

The technical skills needed to work in a textile plant must be obtained in an engineering, textile, or vocational college. There are positions in the textile plant for project and process engineers, technicians, supervisors, and managers.

Marketing

For the extrovert, marketing provides a variety of interesting careers, including product development, public relations, advertising, and sales. Marketers work with both manufacturing and retail customers. Entry-level junior sales representatives can advance to sales, account, and marketing manager positions.

Training and Advancement

Since most textile firms are located in the South, location in that part of the country is necessary for most positions. Some marketing and styling positions are available in New York City and Los Angeles. Sales representatives may be located wherever there are manufacturing centers.

It is important to try to get some experience, perhaps selling in a fabric store, before graduation. Some textile producers offer training programs that offer new employees an opportunity to rotate jobs and get an overview of the company. Experienced and able people from both the technical and the marketing sides of the business may advance to management.

APPAREL MANUFACTURING

Career opportunities for young people entering the apparel industry vary widely. The most interesting aspect of manufacturing is its diversification. Each person within the company must know something about all areas so that the company operations run harmoniously. Each area of manufacturing—product development, production, and marketing—calls for different abilities.

Design and Merchandising

If you have creative abilities, consider becoming a fashion designer. The prospective fashion designer must be artistically creative, yet understand the technical and marketing aspects of the business as well. Besides being responsible for the original ideas for garments, designers must have a thorough knowledge of fabrics, must be able to make patterns, and must understand how a garment is put together. In some companies, designers are involved in every step of the production of the line, from concept to completed product.

Fashion designing is highly competitive. The better aspiring designers are prepared, the broader their opportunities will be. Graduation from a good design college is essential. Upon graduation, the budding designer might start as an assistant in the design or sample department. Any entry-level job will provide useful experience.

Merchandising offers the opportunity to mesh business acumen with a design sense. Retailing experience is very helpful as background training. The merchandiser works together with the designer in the planning stages so that the line of samples will be competitive. The merchandiser usually starts as an assistant merchandiser.

If you are interested in fashion design or merchandising, take every opportunity to observe and analyze new trends at fashion shows, visit manufacturers, and learn to objectively critique apparel and accessories that you see in stores. Also, designer Richard Tyler pointed out, sewing experience is very important for design students.[1]

Patternmaking

If you are technically oriented, you might enjoy a career as a patternmaker. Patternmakers have an important function in the production process: they translate the design idea into a pattern for the actual garment. A patternmaker must understand basic mathematics, have a good eye for proportion and line, and be able to achieve a perfect fit.

To prepare for a career as a patternmaker, you must learn how to drape a pattern on a dress form, how to draft perfect flat patterns, and know how to create patterns by computer. Your first job may be as an assistant or as a sample cutter or pattern grader.

Production

There are opportunities for both men and women as supervisors or managers in fashion production. Production managers must plan and monitor production to ensure that delivery dates are met. Therefore, a well-organized person is best suited for a career in fashion production. Besides technical knowledge, a production manager needs the ability to both manage and motivate people to get the job done.

An engineering or business education is an excellent background for a career in this area. Only a few large manufacturers have management training programs, so a graduate desiring a career in production should seek any entry-level position available, such as shipping or quality control, just to get a start in the field.

Marketing

If you are outgoing and enjoy working with people, you may like marketing, a career field that is involved with customers and clients. You might begin a career as a showroom assistant or junior sales representative in

New York or Los Angeles or traveling within a selling territory. A college education in fashion merchandising or marketing and retailing experience are recommended.

Training and Advancement

For the most part, fashion manufacturers are located in large cities. Students interested in design positions must be prepared in most cases to relocate to New York, Los Angeles, or wherever there is an opening.

As most manufacturers do not have training programs, you may try to arrange an internship with a manufacturer on your own. Your ingenuity will be appreciated. Initially, it is a good idea to get experience in a small company where you can observe the entire operation. Later, opportunities for advancement are better in large companies that promote from within.

RETAILING

Approximately one of every eight employed persons in the United States works in retailing in some capacity. It is absolutely necessary to get retail selling experience while getting a college education. Unless a person has dealt with customers and heard their comments, questions, and complaints, he or she cannot understand the basis of retailing. Working part-time as a salesperson at a store near your school or during the holidays, in the summer, on Saturdays, or after school may provide your initial opportunity and experience.

A few large stores offer summer internship programs for college students, which are excellent opportunities for experience. An internship gives the college student a better chance at employment after graduation. Since most stores do not offer this program, you may need to ask permission to work as an intern for no pay. Creating this kind of situation for yourself demonstrates your motivation and initiative. Use this time to ask questions and learn as much as you can about all aspects of running the store.

A college diploma is necessary for a retail management career. Retailers like the creative thinking of the merchandising majors as well as the business skills of the retailing majors. Many students are also getting MBA degrees to round out their education and give them an edge in the job market.

Training

After college graduation, a fortunate few are able to get into a retail management training program at large stores such as Macy's. A typical program consists of work experience in a variety of departments and formal classes conducted by senior executives and training department personnel. Training programs are followed by the opportunity to become a junior executive.

In large stores, there are usually two main tracks to management: one is through the buying line (merchandising), the other through the store line (operations). Most department stores' training programs combine both tracks, providing a well-rounded experience. Every store has its unique organization structure and job opportunities.

Buying Line or Merchandising Track

After a training program, the first junior executive position is that of assistant buyer. They spend much of their time maintaining sales and inventory records. In addition, they may act for buyers in their absence.

With experience, the assistant may become an associate or single-vendor buyer and, later, a buyer. A buyer might advance to the position of group buyer, divisional merchandise manager, or general merchandise manager. The general merchandise manager is part of senior management and sets merchandising policies for the entire store.

Store Line or Operations Track

The second career track in retailing is in store operations. The department manager is responsible for having the goods on the selling floor; keeping current records of stock; and, in a branch store, ordering replenishments of stock from the main store. This person needs a background in sales and management training. The department manager is the role model for sales staff and the liaison between sales associates, customers, and buyers.

The department manager may advance to section manager, floor manager, assistant store manager, operations manager, or manager of a branch store. The operations manager oversees building maintenance, overhead, receiving, and the movement of goods within the store. The store manager is responsible for merchandising, sales, employees, and the general success of the store.

Alternate Training

Most stores now offer flexible career paths from the merchandising track to the operations track and back again. For example, a trainee may begin work as a sales associate, then an assistant department manager, assistant buyer, department manager, associate buyer, and so on. Able performers from both merchandising and operations might successfully work their way up to senior management. Senior management is responsible for the administration and organization of the store, establishing store policies and controlling operations. Obviously, these managers need a solid background in the ranks of lower management as support.

PROMOTION

Fashion promotion is another creative career. Fashion promoters communicate a fashion message to the public to boost sales.

Copywriters Copywriters work on advertising and publicity for all levels of the industry. They may work directly for producers, manufacturers and retailers, or for agencies. Fashion writers and editors also work for trade and consumer fashion publications. The job requires a college journalism major and some experience, perhaps on a college newspaper.

Artists   Artists design advertising and catalog layouts and/or direct photo shoots. They might work for the in-house advertising department or for advertising agencies. Their artistic skills must be technically perfect. Naturally, adveritsing or graphic design training is necessary. Fluency with computer design programs is mandatory.

Visual merchandising designers   Visual merchandising styists work for the store, where they decorate store windows and arrange interior presentations of merchandise to attract customers. Advancement opportunities include positions as store design managers and corporate design directors. A college art or merchandising major is a prerequisite.

Special events director   Imagination and ingenuity are also needed to create special events. A fashion merchandising degree and experience in staging shows or running school publicity events is a good background.

CAREER RESEARCH

After determining how your interests and abilities fit into the fashion business, you should investigate the companies that could be prospective employers. There are many different types of companies, both large and small. The advantage of working for a large company is that there is usually opportunity for promotion. In a small company you can more easily learn every phase of the business.

Read about companies that interest you. Fashion and business libraries have directories, such as *The Fashion Guide, Standard & Poor's Register of Corporations*, or *Dun's Million Dollar Directory*, that list addresses and information on national and international companies. Local trade associations also have names and addresses of textile, fashion, and retail companies. You can write to these companies for annual reports or other available information.

Meet professionals at lectures, fashion shows, Fashion Group meetings, and career seminars. Interview them at their offices for class projects. Continually read trade periodicals to keep abreast of industry news so that you will be able to answer questions intelligently at an interview. You should know as much about the company as your interviewer!

THE INTERVIEW PROCESS

Preparations for an Interview

Graduating students often feel defeated before they start. However, it is necessary to be persistent and work at getting a job—prospective employers admire people with drive and enthusiasm. Tommy Hilfiger says, "Young people entering the business need both drive and persistence."[2]

Résumé

First, you need a *résumé* listing the appropriate highlights of your education, experience, and activities. List only the courses, experience, and activities that directly relate to your chosen career. Part-time or summer fashion retailing experience is very important.

Your résumé should be typed on a computer and printed. The professional look of your résumé should demonstrate your knowledge of visual presentation, as well as your familiarity with computers. Do not list a job objective; that should go in your cover letter.

Each résumé must be accompanied by a *letter of introduction* asking for an interview, stating where you can be reached by phone, your job objective, and the reason you want to work for that company.

You may need to send out as many as 100 résumés to land a job, but don't be discouraged, this is normal. If the company asks for *recommendation letters*, then you need to have a list of teachers and professionals who may be contacted.

Be sure to follow up the letter and résumé with phone calls or your letters may be ignored. Try to get interviews even if there are no positions open with the excuse that you want to ask them some questions about their company. Most often an applicant's enthusiasm and persistence can convince an employer that the applicant would be an asset to the company.

Portfolio

If you are seeking a creative position, you will need a portfolio in addition to a résumé. The portfolio should look professional, exhibiting only the best examples of your work. Include any projects that won awards or prizes. A design major might include sketches of new ideas (simple technical sketches on graph paper are fine) with fabric swatches and 8 by 10 inch photographs of completed garments worn by professional-looking models.

The Interview

Be sure to read a book on interview preparation! When you finally have obtained an interview, make the most of it. Each interview is good practice for the next one!

A professional appearance is absolutely essential for a job interview in the fashion field. You are making a visual statement of what you know about fashion and about your own self perception.

Your fashion and company research will be useful during the interview. Brush up on fashion terminology and read current trade periodicals and the *Wall Street Journal* beforehand.

The interviewer may ask questions such as "Why do you want to become a buyer (designer, etc.)?" and "Why do you want to work for this company?" Obviously, without proper research you could not specifically answer these questions. Also, beware of trick questions, such as "Tell me the worst experience you've had with a boss." You should also be prepared to ask interesting questions that show your interest in the job or the company. The fashion industry looks for sharp, focused minds.

No matter what your training or college major, companies will be looking for the following:

- ◆ Good skills learned in college and on the job
- ◆ A well-developed résumé
- ◆ A professional-looking portfolio (in design or communications)
- ◆ A fashionable, professional appearance
- ◆ The ability to express oneself clearly (except possibly for technical positions)
- ◆ A pleasant personality and a positive attitude to demonstrate that you will get along with your colleagues
- ◆ Enthusiasm, self-motivation, and a high energy level
- ◆ Awareness and an eagerness to learn
- ◆ A willingness to take responsibility

THE FIRST JOB

Your first job after school or college should be considered an *apprenticeship*, a period of learning on the job. If your employer has no training program, try to set up your own apprenticeship or internship so that you can move around and learn all aspects of the business. You may want to try to set up an unpaid internship during a summer vacation. Try to learn as much as possible. Think of your first job as a free education. Never stop learning and your career will always be rewarding. Odile Laugier, vice-president of design at Adrienne Vittadini told me, "I've been here thirteen years and I'm still learning."[3]

The important thing is to obtain experience. Then demonstrate how efficient and talented you are by doing a good job. Companies are always looking for responsible people to promote to better positions. If you are not promoted, at least you have gained experience for moving on to something else. Contacts that you make on the job will be valuable later. For example, fabric sales representatives often hear of job openings with apparel manufacturers and spread the word.

Be flexible and pleasant with your co-workers. A little humor and diplomacy go a long way toward promoting positive working relationships. Changes in fashion make the business exciting, but the creative people involved make it even more interesting.

Students often talk of opening their own businesses after graduation, and it seems that working for oneself would be easy. However, most small-company failures are due to lack of experience. Before opening your own business, get as much experience as possible, both in a large company and in a successful small one to see how they are run. Working for yourself is actually more difficult than working for someone else because you must be self-disciplined. There are rewards, of course, for those who have ambition and creativity and are willing to work long and hard.

If you want to move up in the fashion field, give your education, training, and work all the effort and enthusiasm you can. Make the most of each situation. You get out of life what you put into it. Best wishes for a successful and rewarding career.

PROJECTS TO PREPARE FOR A JOB INTERVIEW

1. Write your résumé. Include information on education, awards, experience, and interests that directly relate to your chosen field.

2. What fashion career do you think would bring you the greatest satisfaction? List the positive and negative aspects of this career in two columns on a sheet of paper. Analyze why you think you will do well and be happy in this career. What attributes do you have that you could bring to the job? How is your education preparing you? How will you enter the field, and what are your advancement expectations?

3. If you are a design or communication major, outline what you plan to include in your portfolio. Ask your teachers to help you select your best work. Develop an overall graphic theme for your portfolio.

4. Arrange to interview a professional in your chosen field (designer, retailer, sales representative, etc.). Ask about all aspects of the job. What does he or she like and not like about it? What makes it interesting? How did he or she start out and advance? What valuable advice can this professional give you? College interviews and contacts often lead to jobs.

5. Research a company that interests you. Write to them for an annual report or other information that might be available. Check out the *Guide to Periodical Literature* for articles about the company in publications. Read the material and make notes of important information that you need to remember for an interview.

NOTES

[1] *Vogue*, February 1995, p. 244.

[2] Interview, September 1994.

[3] Interview, April 30, 1992.

FASHION INDUSTRY TERMINOLOGY

Learning the terminology of the fashion industry is an important part of a fashion education. By using correct terminology, you show that you are familiar with the business. Many fashion terms are from the French language, since France has long been the capital of fashion innovation. For further clarification, check the index and refer to the text to see how the term was used.

accessories Articles worn or carried to complete a fashion look, such as jewelry, scarves, hats, handbags, or shoes.

acetate A man-made fiber of cellulose chains.

acrylic A man-made fiber made of long-chain synthetic polymer.

advertising Any paid message in the media used to increase sales.

advertising director The person in charge of the personnel and activities of the advertising department.

alta moda The Italian couture.

apparel Clothing, not necessarily fashionable.

apparel industry The manufacturers, jobbers, and contractors engaged in the manufacture of clothing (also called the garment business, the needle trades, the rag trade).

artisans People who do skilled work with their hands.

atelier (ah-tel-yay') French word for designer workshop. Ateliers are classified as *flou* (for soft dressmaking) or *tailleur* (for tailoring suits and coats).

balance Visual weight in design.

balance of trade Difference in value between a country's exports and imports.

base goods The solid fabric used as the basis for a group of sportswear.

bodies Garment silhouettes.

book inventory The dollar value of inventory, as stated in accounting records.

boutique (boo-teek') French word for a small shop with unusual clothing and atmosphere.

branch store Store owned and operated by a parent store; generally located in a suburban area under the name of the parent store.

brand name A trade name that identifies a certain product made by a particular producer.

bridge fashion The style and price range between designer and better.

buyer A merchandising executive responsible for planning, buying, and selling merchandise.

buying office An independent or store-owned office that is located at a market center and buys for one chain or for many stores.

buying plan A general description of the types and quantities of merchandise that a buyer expects to purchase for delivery within a specific period.

chain store organization A group of stores that sell essentially the same merchandise and are centrally owned, operated, and merchandised.

classic A fashion that is long-lasting.

classification An assortment of related merchandise grouped together within a department of a store.

collection A group of garments designed for a specific season.

commissionaire (ko-me-see-ohn-air') Store representative in foreign cities.

commodity merchandise Standard basic merchandise.

computer-aided design (CAD) An integrated computer system that aids in designing and patternmaking, used in both textile and apparel design.

computer-aided manufacturing (CAM) Computerized patternmaking, grading, marker making, cutting, and sewing machines.

computer-integrated manufacturing (CIM) Computer connection to integrate computer-aided design and manufacturing systems.

consumer Someone who buys merchandise.

consumer demand The effect consumers have on the marketplace.

consumer obsolescence The rejection of merchandise in favor of something newer, even though the "old" still has utility.

contemporary styling Sophisticated, updated styling; originally designed for the age group that grew out of juniors.

contractor An independent producer who does the sewing (sometimes the cutting) for manufacturers; an outside shop.

converter A textile producer that buys greige goods from mills and dyes, prints, and finishes it before selling it to a manufacturer.

cooperative advertising Advertising costs shared by a textile producer and/or a manufacturer and/or a retailer.

coordinated sportswear Sportswear designed to mix and match interchangeably.

corporate selling Selling management to management; without the use of sales representatives.

cotton A vegetable fiber from the boll of the cotton plant; the world's major textile fiber.

couture (koo-tour') French word for dressmaking; applied to fashion businesses that make clothes to order.

croquis Original paintings of textile designs.

custom made Apparel made to a customer's special order; cut and fitted to individual measurements; opposite of ready-to-wear.

cutter The person who cuts material during the manufacturing process.

cutting order Order of quantity to cut, how to cut, and what fabric to use.

cut to order Cut and produce only against orders.

cut to stock Cut and produce based on projected estimates of sales.

demographics Statistical studies of population characteristics such as birth rate, age distribution, or income.

department store General merchandise store, including apparel, household goods, and furniture.

designer A person employed to create ideas for garments or accessories in the fashion industry.

design resource Any resource from which a designer obtains ideas; can be trade newspapers, design reports, fashion magazines, museums, historic-costume books, nature, theater, films, fabrics, and so on.

design services Reports and ideas available by subscription to manufacturers and retailers; predictives.

direct-mail advertising Any printed advertising distributed directly to specific prospects by mail.

discount retailing Low-margin retailing; retailers able to offer inexpensive merchandise by buying in quantity and keeping operating costs low.

discretionary income Income left after basic necessities have been paid for.

display Visual presentation of merchandise or ideas.

disposable income Income minus taxes; a person's purchasing power.

divisional merchandise manager A person in the middle management of a retail store; executive responsible for merchandising activities of a related group of departments; supervises buyers and assistants.

dollar merchandise plan A budget or projection, expressed in dollars, of the sales goals of a merchandise classification, a department, or an entire store for a certain period, including the amount of stock required to achieve those sales.

doors Fashion industry jargon for the number of retail stores at which a particular product is sold.

draping A method of making a pattern by draping fabric on a dress form.

electronic data interchange (EDI) The exchange of business data between two parties by means of computer.

electronic retailing Shop-by-computer retailing.

elements of design Design ingredients: color, fabric, line, and shape.

ethnic or folk costume Traditional national or regional dress; often inspiration for fashion design.

fabrication Selection of the appropriate fabric for a garment.

factory outlet stores Stores that sell manufacturer's overruns directly to the consumer.

fad A short-lived fashion.

fashion The prevailing style of any given time; implies change in style.

fashion cycle Fashion change; refers to the introduction, acceptance, and decline of a fashion.

fashion director The fashion expert of an organization, who keeps it current with fashion developments and works with designers or buyers to form the fashion image of the company.

fashion editor The head fashion reporter at a magazine or newspaper, who analyzes the fashion scene and interprets it for readers.

fashion forecast A prediction of fashion trends.

Fashion Group An international association of professional women in the fashion business; founded in 1931.

fashion merchandising The planning required to have the right fashion merchandise available in the proper quantities and place at the right time and price to meet consumer demand.

fashion press Reporters of fashion news for magazines and newspapers.

fashion retailing The business of buying fashion merchandise from a variety of resources and reselling it to ultimate consumers at a convenient location.

fashion trend New directions in fashion styling.

Federation Française de la Couture French couture trade association composed of three main membership classifications (each called a Chambre Syndicale) and associated groups of manufacturers and artisans.

fibers Natural or synthetic strands from which yarns are made.

filament A continuous strand of fiber.

findings Trade term for the functional unseen trimmings needed to complete a garment, such as zippers and elastic.

finishing The last treatments given to fabrics; the final handwork or final touches done to a garment.

first pattern Trial pattern made in the design department for the sample garment.

flagship store Largest and most representative store in a chain organization.

flax A natural fiber made from the stem of the flax plant and used to make linen.

flexible manufacturing A combination of methods used to make manufacturing most effective.

franchising When a manufacturer sell the rights to retail its merchandise.

full-fashioned knits Knit garments with pieces shaped on the knitting machine.

furnishings Men's clothing category, including shirts, accessories, and item sportswear.

General Agreement on Tariffs and Trade (GATT) A former contract between goverments to provide a secure international trading environment, now replced by the World Trade Organization.

generic name Family name given to each type of fiber.

globalization The trend for manufacturers and retailers (and all businesses) to expand throughout the world.

grading Process of making a sample size pattern larger or smaller to make up a complete size range.

greige goods (gray goods) Unbleached, unfinished fabrics bought by converters.

gross margin The difference in dollars between net sales and the net cost of merchandise during a given period.

haute couture Those dressmaking houses in Paris that belong to the Chambre Syndicale of the Federation Française de la Couture and meet the criteria to be on its Couture-Creation list (see Chapter 8).

hot item A best-seller; also known as a runner or a ford.

Ideacomo Italian fabric producers' trade fair, held each November and May in Como, Italy, followed by presentations in New York.

ILGWU International Ladies' Garment Workers' Union.

imports Goods made in a foreign country.

inside shop When an apparel company has manufacturing facilities within its own factory.

Interstoff German term meaning "interfabric"; international fabric trade fair, held each November and May in Frankfurt, Germany.

issue plan Production schedule.

items Garments sold on an individual basis.

Jacquard loom (jah-kard') A loom invented by Joseph Jacquard in France in 1801 that weaves an elaborate pattern (such as damask, brocade, or tapestry) by controlling each warp thread separately.

jersey Basic construction of all weft knits.

jobber A middleman between the producer and the commercial consumer.

junior Size range of female apparel; in odd numbers, 3 to 15.

knockoff A copy of a higher-priced style.

leased department Within a store, a department run by an outside company.

licensing Giving a manufacturer permission to use a designer's name or designs in return for a fee or percentage of sales.

line An apparel manufacturer's collection of styles. Also, visual direction in a design caused by seams, details, or trimming.

line buying Buying lines from reliable manufacturers.

linen A vegetable fiber from the woody stalk of the flax plant.

loss leader An item sold at less than the regular wholesale price for the purpose of attracting retail buyers to other merchandise.

lyocell New type of solvent-spun cellulosic fiber.

MAGIC Men's Apparel Guild in California, the world's largest men's apparel trade show, held each February and August in Las Vegas.

man-made fibers Fibers made from cellulose in plants or from chemicals derived from petroleum, gas, and coal.

markdown The difference between the original retail price and a reduced price.

marker A pattern layout put on top of the fabric for the cutter to follow.

market A group of potential customers, or the place, area, or time at which buyers and sellers meet to transact business.

market driven Responding to market or consumer needs.

marketing The process of planning, promoting, and selling merchandise.

marketing chain The flow of product development, production, and distribution from concept to consumer.

markup Difference between cost price and selling price.

mass production The production of merchandise in quantity.

media Means of communication: newspapers, magazines, radio, TV, and direct mail.

merchandise representatives Consultants trained by manufacturers to train sales associates in the stores.

missy Size range in feminine apparel in even numbers, 6 to 16.

moda pronta Italian ready-to-wear.

mode Synonym for fashion; used mainly in Europe.

modular manufacturing A manufacturing method utilizing a small group of people who work together to produce a finished garment.

Multifiber Arrangement (MFA) A bilateral agreement among exporting and importing nations that provides the framework to prevent import surges.

national brands Manufacturers' brands that are available nationwide.

natural fibers Fibers that nature provides: cotton, wool, silk, flax, and ramie.

North American Free Trade Agreement (NAFTA) Trade agreement, implemented in 1994, creating a free market between the United States, Canada, and Mexico.

nylon A durable man-made fiber made of long-chain synthetic polymer.

off-price A price lower than the original wholesale price or below the normal wholesale price; usually special purchases, closeouts, or overruns.

offshore assembly Fabric purchased and cut in the United States but sent to Mexico or the Caribbean countries for sewing.

open-to-buy The amount of money a buyer can spend on merchandise to be delivered within a given period, minus the amount allocated to merchandise on order.

operations Steps in production; activities of running a business.

overhead The costs of operating the store or company.

overlock machine A machine with needle and loopers that creates an edge finish while sewing a seam.

physical inventory A physical count of stock on hand.

piece goods The trade term for fabrics.

piecework Rate by which many factory workers are paid.

polyester The most widely used man-made fiber, made of long-chain synthetic polymer.

Premier-Vision French term for "first look." International fabric trade fair held each March and October in Paris.

prestige or institutional advertising Advertising that promotes a store's image or goodwill rather than specific merchandise.

prêt-à-porter French for ready-to-wear; literally, "ready to carry."

preticketing Ticketing of merchandise by the manufacturer in order for the merchandise to be ready for prompt distribution at the retail store.

price line A specific price point at which an assortment of merchandise is offered for sale.

price range The range between the lowest and highest price lines carried.

private label A store's own brand.

production pattern The final pattern made to company size standards.

progressive bundle system A manufacturing system requiring one operator to repeat one assembly task and grouping operators to follow the order of production; section work.

promotion An activity designed to encourage the purchase of a product.

promotional stores Stores that stress special sales, bargains, and price reductions and claim to undersell competitors.

proportion The relation of one part of a design to another; an important principle of garment design.

psychographics The use of psychological, sociological, and anthropological factors to construct market segments.

publicity Nonpaid messages about a company and its policies, personnel, activities, or services.

Quick Response (QR) An attempt to speed ordering and distribution between all levels of the industry via electronic data interchange.

quotas A means of regulating exports and imports.

ramie A natural vegetable fiber from the stem of a nettlelike shrub.

rayon A man-made fiber made from rejuvenated cellulose.

ready-to-wear Apparel that is mass produced (opposite of custom made).

receiving The area of the store where packages are opened, checked, and marked.

repeat The repetition of a print in fabric design.

resource Term used by retailers for a manufacturer, wholesaler, vendor, or distributor. A company that sells goods in the market of finished apparel.

retailing The business of buying goods at wholesale markets and selling them at retail to the ultimate consumer.

retail price The wholesale price plus a markup covering the retailer's operating costs and a profit.

sales per square foot Amount sold per square foot of store floor space; measure of productivity.

sample The trial garment or prototype.

sample cut A 3- to 10-yard length of fabric used by the design department to make up a trial sample garment.

Savile Row Street in London famous for its men's tailors.

selected distribution Limiting the number of stores that may buy merchandise to maintain exclusivity.

sell-through The ability of a line to sell regularly and steadily at full price.

Seventh Avenue The main street of New York City's garment district; the term is used to represent the whole district.

showroom A place where sales representatives or management show a line of merchandise to potential buyers; called *salon de presentations* in France.

silhouette Outline of a garment.

silk The only natural fiber in filament form; obtained from the cocoons spun by silkworms.

soft goods Fashion and textile merchandise.

sourcing Worldwide search for the best available fabrics or garment production at the best price.

spandex A man-made fiber of long-chain synthetic polymer comprised of stretchable segmented polyurethane; known best by the DuPont brand name of Lycra.

special events Activities set up to attract customers to a selling place.

specialty store A retail establishment that handles narrow categories of goods, such as men's apparel, female apparel, or shoes.

spinning The process of extruding and hardening man-made fibers; the process of drawing and twisting staple fibers together into yarn or thread.

staple goods Goods for which there is a demand that continues over many seasons.

stock turnover The number of times a store's merchandise stock is sold and replaced in a given period.

store image The character or personality that a store presents to the public.

style Certain characteristics that distinguish a garment from other garments; a particular look in fashion.

style ranges Categories of styles that appeal to different consumers.

stylist A fashion expert; generally selects colors, prints, or styles for presentation or prepares fashion merchandise for photographic presentation in an advertisement or catalog.

tanning The process of transforming animal skins into leather.

target market The group of consumers to whom a producer, manufacturer, or retailer aims products, services, and advertising.

textile fabrics Cloth made from textile fibers by weaving, knitting, felting, crocheting, laminating, or bonding.

texture The surface interest in a fabric.

texturing The process of crimping or otherwise modifying continuous filament yarn to increase cover, abrasion resistance, warmth, resiliency, and moisture absorption or to provide a different surface texture.

toile (twahl) French word for a muslin sample garment.

trademark Company's individual registered mark and name for a product.

trend buying Buying from new resources to obtain fashion newness.

trendsetter A designer or fashion leader who sets a fashion direction that others follow.

trunk show Show of designer clothes that moves from store to store, often accompanied by a personal appearance by the designer.

unit control Systems for recording the number of units of merchandise bought, sold, in stock, or on order.

unit production systems (UPS) Computer-guided conveyors that move garments automatically from one work station to the next; automatic progressive-bundle system.

universal product codes (UPC) Standard codes that identify style, color, size, price, fabrication, and vendor on price tags and enable this information to be fed through an electronic data interchange system.

variants Modifications of basic generic fiber compositions for special applications.

vendor A seller, resource, manufacturer, or supplier.

vendor analysis Statistical analysis of the profits made on merchandise from individual vendors.

vertical integration The joining of companies at different levels of production and marketing, such as a fiber producer with a fabric mill.

visual merchandising Making merchandise visually attractive to customers.

warp knitting Knitting fabric in loops running vertically.

weaving The process of forming fabric by interlacing yarns on looms.

weft knitting Knitting fabric in loops horizontally or in a circle.

wholesale market Market where commercial consumers buy from producers.

wholesale price Price paid by commercial consumers for supplies and products.

Women's Wear Daily Trade publication of the women's fashion industry.

wool A natural fiber from animal fleece.

World Trade Organization (WTO) The governing body for international trade, which replaced GATT.

yarn A continuous thread produced by twisting or spinning fibers together.

Index